CIVIL WAR SITES

Help Us Keep This Guide Up to Date

Every effort has been made by the editors to make this guide as accurate and useful as possible. However, many changes can occur after a guide is published—establishments close, phone numbers change, hiking trails are rerouted, facilities come under new management, and so on.

We would love to hear from you concerning your experiences with this guide and how you feel it could be improved and be kept up to date. While we may not be able to respond to all comments and suggestions, we'll take them to heart, and we'll make certain to share them with the editors. Please send your comments and suggestions to the following address:

The Globe Pequot Press
Reader Response/Editorial Department
P.O. Box 480
Guilford, CT 06437

Or you may e-mail us at: editorial@GlobePequot.com

Thanks for your input, and happy travels!

CIVIL WAR SITES

*The Official Guide to
the Civil War Discovery Trail*

SECOND EDITION

CIVIL WAR PRESERVATION TRUST

James Campi, Editor
Mary Goundrey, Contributing Editor
Wendy Valentine, Contributing Editor

The Globe Pequot Press

GUILFORD, CONNECTICUT

Text design: Lesley Weissman-Cook; cannon art by Eileen Hine
Maps created by Trailhead Graphics © Morris Book Publishing, LLC

The Civil War Preservation Trust kindly thanks and acknowledges all those who provided photos. Photo credits appear with the photos.

ISBN 978-0-7627-4435-0

Manufactured in the United States of America
Second Edition/First Printing

The prices and rates listed in this guidebook were confirmed
at press time. We recommend, however, that you call
establishments to obtain current information before traveling.

CONTENTS

♦ NORTHEAST

♦ MIDDLE ATLANTIC

♦ COASTAL

◆ SOUTHERN HEARTLAND

◆ MIDWEST

◆ TRANS-MISSISSIPPI

◆ FAR WEST

◆ FOREIGN SITES

DIRECTORY OF MAPS

FOREWORD

By James Lighthizer

THE AMERICAN CIVIL WAR, which began with the bloodless bombardment of Fort Sumter in April 1861, was the most bloody and tragic conflict in our nation's history. For four long years the armies of the North and South roamed the countryside, clashing in more than 10,000 battles and skirmishes that sounded the death knell of slavery and defined us as a nation. When the smoke finally cleared in April and May 1865, more than 625,000 soldiers and 50,000 civilians had lost their lives.

Today, many of those very same battlefields and historic sites are perilously close to being lost forever. In many cases, such as at Chantilly in Virginia and Peachtree Creek in Georgia, only small remnants remain. Even at Gettysburg, certainly one of the most famous battlegrounds in world history, key terrain features in the once-rural Pennsylvania community have been swallowed up by development and sprawl.

It was the veterans themselves who first recognized the importance of protecting the battlegrounds where they and their comrades in arms sacrificed so much. One New York sergeant, engaged in seemingly endless combat before the Southern bastion of Atlanta, wrote home to his local paper: "If those works could be preserved by law, for the benefit of our curious posterity, they would last for many generations. Each battlefield would thus have its own monuments to celebrate the events that transpired there; each rifle-pit and battery speaking more to the heart of the spectator than would whole volumes of history."

We at the Civil War Preservation Trust are committed to protecting these last remaining links to the most tumultuous period in American history—for the benefit of posterity. With 70,000 members, the Civil War Preservation Trust is the largest nonprofit battlefield preservation organization in the United States. Our mission is to preserve America's remaining Civil War battlefields and to promote appreciation of these hallowed grounds through education and heritage tourism.

It is a labor of love. In partnership with sympathetic government officials, other nonprofit groups and the private sector, the Civil War Preservation Trust has rescued more than 24,500 acres of hallowed ground in 18 states. Among the sites rescued by the Trust are key parcels at Perryville in Kentucky; Antietam and Monocacy in Maryland; Champion Hill and Corinth in Mississippi; Gettysburg in Pennsylvania; Chattanooga and Franklin in Tennessee; Palmito Ranch in Texas; Brandy Station, Chancellorsville, and Fredericksburg in Virginia; and Harpers Ferry in West Virginia.

In addition to preserving historic land, the Civil War Preservation Trust conducts programs designed to inform the public about the events and consequences of the Civil War, to foster an understanding of the need for preservation, and to create a personal connection to the past. The Civil War Discovery Trail, a National Millennium Trail recognized by the White House for reawakening America's interest in its storied past, is just one of these programs.

I encourage you to use *Civil War Sites* to explore the more than 600 locales that comprise the Civil War Discovery Trail. Learn from them. Be inspired by them. Remember the sacrifices made on them. Then, help the Civil War Preservation Trust preserve them. Your commitment today will help ensure that present and future generations can follow in the footsteps of America's Civil War heroes.

James Lighthizer is President of the Civil War Preservation Trust (CWPT). Previously, he served as the Maryland Secretary of Transportation (1991–95), County Executive of Anne Arundel County, Maryland (1982–90), and as a Maryland State Legislator.

ACKNOWLEDGMENTS

THE CIVIL WAR PRESERVATION TRUST acknowledges with deep gratitude the assistance and support provided by its Board of Trustees and the National Advisory Board. A special thanks should be extended to The History Channel for its continued support of the Civil War Preservation Trust's preservation initiatives. The editor thanks the staff of the Civil War Preservation Trust for their enthusiasm and support of the guidebook and Civil War Discovery Trail program.

The Civil War Preservation Trust is not responsible for changes that occur after publication and regrets any errors and omissions in this book. We advise calling prior to visiting a site to confirm the information in this guide. We encourage you to share with us your comments and suggestions by mailing them to:

Civil War Preservation Trust
National Headquarters
1331 H Street, NW
Suite 1001
Washington, DC 20005

E-mail: cwpt@civilwar.org
Web site: www.civilwar.org

THE CIVIL WAR DISCOVERY TRAIL

THE CIVIL WAR DISCOVERY TRAIL links more than 600 sites in 31 states, the District of Columbia, and 3 foreign countries. The goal of the trail is to teach the story of the Civil War and its enduring impact on the America we know today. This guidebook is composed of sites along the trail.

Along the Trail visitors may explore destinations such as Ford's Theatre, where President Abraham Lincoln was shot; Antietam National Battlefield, the site of the bloodiest one-day battle in American history; antebellum plantations in Mississippi and Tennessee; and Port Hudson, Louisiana, where hundreds of African-American soldiers first proved their mettle in combat. The Trail includes battlefields, historic homes, railroad stations, cemeteries, and parks.

Civil War Discovery Trail sites are selected for their historic significance and educational opportunities. Each year several new and exciting sites are added. Since the first Globe Pequot Press edition of *Civil War Sites* was published in 2003, the Civil War Preservation Trust has added three foreign sites to the trail: in Wirral, England; Cherbourg, France; and St. George's, Bermuda.

For more information about the Civil War Discovery Trail, visit www.civilwardiscovery trail.com.

How to Use This Guidebook

FOR EASE OF USE, the sites in this guide to the Civil War Discovery Trail are organized by region. Within each region, states are listed alphabetically, as are cities and towns within each state. Directions for each listing lead visitors from the closest major interstate highway to the site. We suggest that you also use a state highway map in conjunction with the maps and directions in this guide. Sites are listed according to the closest town. Occasionally only the mailing address is listed under the site name. Whenever possible, each listing includes a phone number to call for further information. A Civil War Preservation Trust icon has been placed alongside those sites that the Trust has helped preserve.

In addition, some trail sites have indicated that they would be willing to provide a discount to Civil War Preservation Trust members; this is indicated in the "Visitor Services" information. Please have your membership card available to present at these sites.

THE AMERICAN CIVIL WAR

By James M. McPherson, Ph.D.

THE CIVIL WAR is the central event in America's historical consciousness. While the Revolution of 1776–83 created the United Sates, the Civil War of 1861–65 determined what kind of a nation it would be. The war resolved two fundamental questions left unresolved by the Revolution: whether the United States was to be a dissolvable confederation of sovereign states or an indivisible nation with a sovereign national government; and whether this nation, born of a declaration that all men were created with an equal right to liberty, would continue to exist as the largest slave-holding country in the world.

Northern victory in the war preserved the United States as one nation and ended the institution of slavery that had divided the country from its beginning. But these achievements came at the cost of 625,000 lives—nearly as many American soldiers as died in all the other wars in which this country had fought combined. The American Civil War was the longest and most destructive conflict in the Western world between the end of the Napoleonic Wars in 1815 and the onset of World War I in 1914.

The Civil War started because of uncompromising differences between the free and slave states over the power of the national government to prohibit slavery in the territories that had not yet become states. When Abraham Lincoln won election in 1860 as the first Republican president on a platform pledging to keep slavery out of the territories, seven slave states in the Deep South seceded and formed a new nation, the Confederate States of America. The incoming Lincoln administration and most of the Northern people refused to recognize the legitimacy of secession. They feared that it would discredit democracy and create a fatal precedent that would eventually fragment the no-longer United States into several small, squabbling countries.

The event that triggered war came at Fort Sumter in Charleston Harbor on April 12, 1861. Claiming this United States fort as its own, the Confederate army on that day opened fire on the Federal garrison and forced it to lower the American flag in surrender. Lincoln called out the militia to suppress this "insurrection." As a result, four more slave states seceded and joined the Confederacy. By the end of 1861, nearly a million armed men confronted one another along a line stretching 1,200 miles from Virginia to Missouri. Several battles had already taken place near Manassas Junction in Virginia; in the mountains of western Virginia, where Union victories paved the way for creating the new state of West Virginia; at Wilson's Creek in Missouri; at Cape Hatteras in North Carolina; and at Port Royal in South Carolina, where the Union navy established a base for a blockade to shut off the Confederacy's access to the outside world.

But the real fighting began in 1862. Huge battles like Shiloh in Tennessee; Gaines Mill, Second Manassas, and Fredericksburg in Virginia; and Antietam in Maryland foreshadowed even bigger campaigns and battles in later years, from Gettysburg in Pennsylvania to Vicksburg on the Mississippi to Chickamauga and Atlanta in Georgia. By 1864 the original Northern goal of a limited war to restore the Union had given way to a new strategy of "total war" to destroy the Old South and its basic institution of slavery and to give the restored Union a "new birth of freedom," as President Lincoln put it in his address at Gettysburg to dedicate a cemetery for Union soldiers killed in the battle there.

For three long years, from 1862 to 1865, Robert E. Lee's Army of Northern Virginia staved off invasions and attacks by the Union Army of the Potomac commanded by ineffective generals until Ulysses S. Grant came to Virginia from the western theater in 1864 to become general in chief of all Union armies. After bloody battles at places with names like The Wilderness, Spotsylvania, Cold Harbor, and Petersburg, Grant finally brought Lee to bay at Appomattox in April 1865. In the meantime Union armies and river fleets in the theater of war comprising the slave states west of the Appalachians won a long series of victories over Confederate armies commanded by hapless, unlucky Confederate generals. In 1864–65 Gen. William Tecumseh Sherman led his army deep into the Confederate heartland of Georgia and South Carolina, destroying the economic infrastructure, while Gen. George Thomas virtually destroyed the Confederacy's Army of the Tennessee at the Battle of Nashville.

By the spring of 1865, all the principal Confederate armies surrendered, and when Union cavalry captured the fleeing Confederate president Jefferson Davis in Georgia on May 10, 1865, resistance collapsed and the war ended. The final Confederate flag was lowered on November 6, 1865, when the CSS *Shenandoah* was surrendered to British authorities in Liverpool, England. Then the long, painful process of rebuilding a united nation free of slavery began.

James M. McPherson has taught at Princeton University since 1962, where he is George Henry Davis '86 Professor of American History. His book Battle Cry of Freedom *won the Pulitzer Prize for history in 1989, and* For Cause and Comrades *won the Lincoln Prize in 1998.*

NORTHEAST

Grant's Tomb, New York. CWPT files.

❖ CONNECTICUT ❖

MIDDLETOWN

 GENERAL MANSFIELD HOUSE

Middlesex County Historical Society, 151 Main Street, Middletown, CT 06457; (860) 346–0746; www.middlesexhistory .org; mchs@wesleyan.edu.

Description: Gen. Joseph King Feno Mansfield was a career soldier, graduating from West Point in 1822 and later serving in the Mexican War. General Mansfield served the Union during the Civil War. He was mortally wounded at the Battle of Antietam on September 17, 1862, and died the next day. His home has been preserved as a museum and includes an exhibit of Civil War artifacts, photographs, and documents relating to Mansfield and other local soldiers.

Admission Fees: Adults $5.00, children $1.00.

Open to Public: Wed., Thurs., and Fri. afternoons or by appointment.

Visitor Services: Museum, handicapped access, research archives.

Regularly Scheduled Events: None.

Directions: From I–91 take exit 22 south onto Route 9. Take exit 15, turn left on Main Street. Travel 2½ blocks, and the museum will be on the right-hand side.

❖ MAINE ❖

BRUNSWICK

 JOSHUA L. CHAMBERLAIN MUSEUM

(A Museum of the Pejepscot Historical Society)

226 Maine Street, Brunswick, ME 04011; (207) 729–6606; www.curtislibrary.com/ pejepscot.htm; pejepscot@suscom-maine.net.

Description: The Chamberlain Museum occupies the former home of Gen. Joshua Lawrence Chamberlain (1828–1914). Wounded six times in twenty-four engagements, Chamberlain, a former Bowdoin College professor, is best known for leading the heroic charge of the Twentieth Maine regiment down Little Round Top at Gettysburg. He was later selected by Grant to accept surrender of the Confederate infantry at Appomattox. Chamberlain returned to Maine, served four terms as governor, and more than a decade as president of Bowdoin College. Saved from demolition in 1983, the building continues to undergo extensive restoration.

Admission Fees: Adults $5.00, children $2.50. Combination tickets for the society's other museums are available at a discount, and society members receive free admission.

Open to Public: May–Oct., Tues.–Sat. 10:00 A.M.–5:00 P.M.; tours leave on the hour.

Visitor Services: Guided museum tours, public restrooms, gift shop, information on Chamberlain-related sites nearby, including his grave and Bowdoin College.

Regularly Scheduled Events: Chamberlain Days Symposium, scheduled for 2008 to honor 145th anniversary of Gettysburg. Call or visit Web site for details.

Directions: From I–295 take exit 28, following the signs for Bowdoin College. Proceed downtown on Pleasant Street, and turn right on Maine Street. Museum is at 226 Maine, opposite Bowdoin campus.

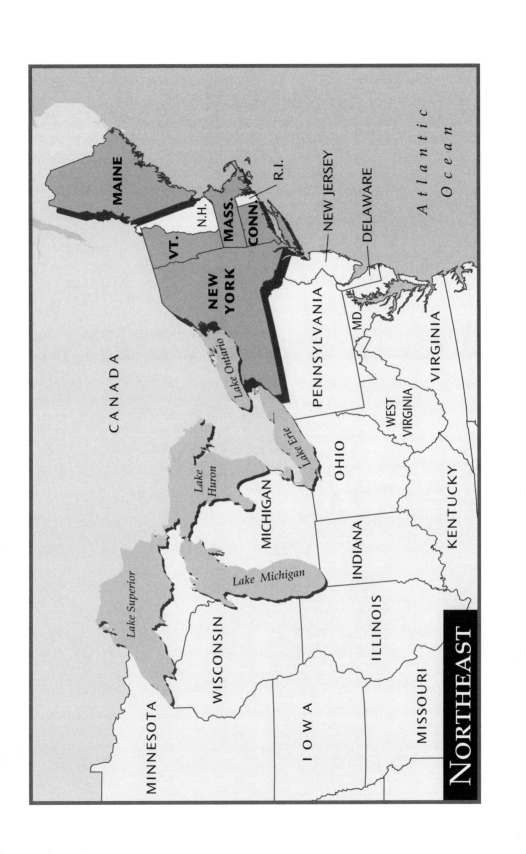

NORTHEAST

Connecticut, Maine, Massachusetts, New York, and Vermont Sites

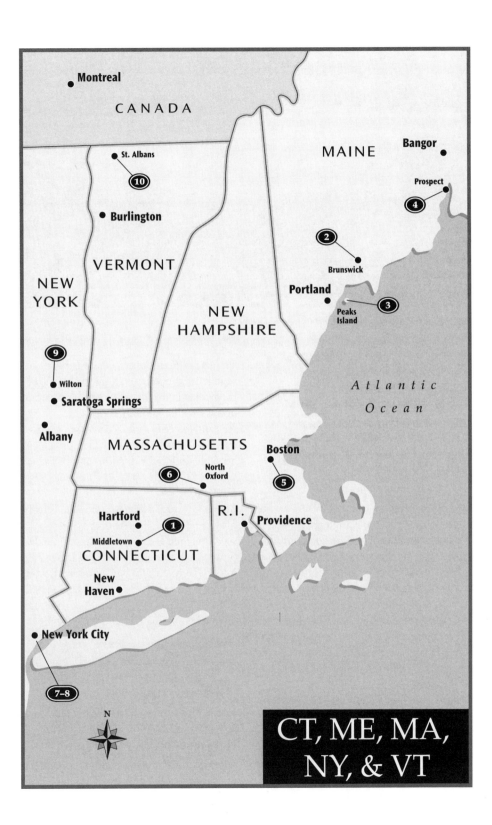

Burial site, Brunswick, Maine. Arnold Thibodeau–CWPT files.

PEAKS ISLAND

 FIFTH MAINE REGIMENTAL MUSEUM

45 Seashore Avenue, Peaks Island, ME 04108; (207) 766–3330; www.fifthmaine museum.org; director@fifthmaine museum.org.

Description: The Fifth Maine Regiment Memorial Hall was built in 1888 as the "Headquarters"of the Fifth Regiment Maine Volunteer Infantry 1861–64. For nearly sixty years the veterans and their families summered here, enjoying the cooling ocean breezes and magnificent view from the veranda of their beloved cottage. Under the stewardship of the Fifth Maine Regiment Community Association, the hall is maintained as a Civil War and local history museum and a cultural center for the island community.

Admission Fees: Free; suggested donation of $5.00 per person.

Open to Public: Memorial Day–Columbus Day, Sat.–Sun. 11:00 A.M.–5:00 P.M.; extended hours July–Labor Day, Mon.–Fri. 1:00 P.M.–4:00 P.M., Sat.–Sun. 11:00 A.M.–5:00 P.M.; other times by appointment.

Visitor Services: Public restrooms, information, handicapped access, gift shop (CWPT members eligible for a 10 percent discount at the gift shop), museum.

Regularly Scheduled Events: Annual events include lecture series, concert series, art show, and Civil War encampment; please call ahead for schedule.

*Directions:*Take exit 6A (Route 295) off the Maine Turnpike.Take exit 7 (Franklin Street) off Route 295. Follow Franklin Street past six stoplights; at the seventh light Franklin Street dead-ends into Casco Bay Lines. Pull into the terminal and purchase ferry tickets inside at the office, or order by calling (207) 774–7871. Peaks Island is a fifteen-minute ferry ride from the Portland waterfront.

PROSPECT

 FORT KNOX STATE HISTORIC SITE

Route 174, Prospect, ME 04981; (207) 469–6553 or (207) 469–7719; http://fort knox.maineguide.com; fofk1@aol.com.

Description: Fort Knox was built to protect the Penobscot River Valley from attack. The fort is a massive third-system defensive structure overlooking the Penobscot River. Fort Knox was used as a garrison for Union troops during the Civil War. The new Penobscot Narrows Bridge and Observatory features a 420-foot-tall observation tower overlooking the river, the only one of its kind in the Western Hemisphere.

Admission Fees: Adults $3.00, children $1.00, seniors and children under five free; observation tower, $2.00 additional fee per person.

Open to Public: Mon.–Sun. 9:00 A.M.–sunset.

Visitor Services: Public restrooms, information, handicapped access, gift shop, museum, trails.

Regularly Scheduled Events: Summer, interpretative tours; call or check Web site for events.

Directions: From I–95 in Bangor, travel south on Route 1A approximately 15 miles; turn left on Route 174 in Prospect. The fort will be several miles down Route 174 on the right.

❖ MASSACHUSETTS ❖

BOSTON

BOSTON AFRICAN AMERICAN NATIONAL HISTORIC SITE

14 Beacon Street, Suite 401, Boston, MA 02108; (617) 742–5415; www.nps.gov/ boaf; boaf@nps.gov.

Description: The Boston African American National Historic Site comprises historic buildings, which document the black community in Boston before the Civil War, including its role in the abolition of slavery in America and the Underground Railroad. The Robert Gould Shaw and Fifty-fourth Regiment Memorial is also interpreted. The memorial commemorates Col. Robert Gould Shaw and the Fifty-fourth Regiment Massachusetts Volunteer Infantry, the first African-American regiment to be recruited from the North to fight in the Civil War. The regiment was recruited, trained, and received political support from the Boston community.

Admission Fees: Free.

Open to Public: Mon.–Sat. 10:00 A.M.–4:00 P.M.; closed Sun.

Visitor Services: Public restrooms, information, handicapped access, gift shop, museum.

Regularly Scheduled Events: February, Black History Month program; call or check Web site for other events.

Directions: From the Massachusetts Turnpike (Route 90), take the Copley Square exit to Stuart Street, then turn left on Route 28 (Charles Street) to Boston Common. From Route 93, take Storrow Drive to the Copley Square exit, turn left on Beacon Street, right on Arlington Street, left on Boylston Street, and left on Charles Street (Route 28). Driving and parking are difficult on Beacon Hill. There are several parking garages in the vicinity within walking distance to the site.

NORTH OXFORD

CLARA BARTON BIRTHPLACE

68 Clara Barton Road, North Oxford, MA 01537; (508) 987–5375; www.clara bartonbirthplace.org.

Description: Clara Barton was born in this house on Christmas Day, 1821. Clara, the "Angel of the Battlefield," attended to the wounded of numerous Civil War battles, including Antietam and Fredericksburg. The Clara Barton birthplace contains artifacts from the Barton family as well as Civil War and American Red Cross artifacts.

CLARA BARTON

"Men have worshipped war till it has cost a million times more than the whole of the earth is worth. . . . Deck it as you will, war is Hell. . . . Only the desire to soften some of its hardships and allay some of its miseries ever induced me . . . to face its pestilent and unholy breath."

—Clara Barton

Clara Barton, founder of the American Red Cross, promoter of the right to vote for former slaves, and strong supporter of the early feminist movement, was born on Christmas Day, 1821, in North Oxford, Massachusetts. She began her career as a school teacher and opened one of the first free (public) schools in 1852 in Bordentown, New Jersey. However, she was not destined to remain a teacher.

During the Civil War, Barton dedicated herself to nursing and comforting the soldiers. She worked to ease the pain of the men and to lessen the unsanitary conditions that were considered normal during the war. At Antietam, Barton arrived with a wagon of much needed supplies and set up a hospital. Surgeons there had been using corn husks for bandages.

Though she worked alongside members of the U.S. Sanitary Commission and the U.S. Christian Commission, she never became closely allied with either group. She preferred to work alone, unhampered by organizations and outside interference. She was a true perfectionist and hated to delegate authority for fear that the job would not be well performed.

Because of this drive Barton often suffered from poor health. After the war she went to Europe for a rest tour. It was during this trip that she learned of the work of the International Red Cross, which had been operating in Europe since 1863. She worked with the Red Cross in Europe during the Franco-Prussian War and became so impressed that she vowed to bring its ideals to the United States, not an easy task. The public was apathetic, the government was uncooperative, and she was still in poor health. However, her efforts were rewarded in 1882, when the United States Senate ratified the Treaty of Geneva, creating the American Red Cross.

Barton spent the rest of her life working with the group and served as its president until 1904. On April 12, 1912, she died at her home in Glen Echo, Maryland.

NATIONAL PARK SERVICE

Admission Fees: Adults $7.50, children $5.00.

Open to Public: June 1–Columbus Day weekend, Wed.–Sun. 11:00 A.M.–5:00 P.M.; other times by appointment.

Visitor Services: Public restrooms, gift shop, museum.

Regularly Scheduled Events: May, Plant Sale and Open House; December, celebration of Clara Barton Week.

Directions: From the Massachusetts Turnpike take the Auburn exit (exit 10) and bear right after tollbooths onto Route 12 south. At the fourth traffic light, bear left to continue on Route 12 south for approximately 1.2 miles. Turn right onto Clara Barton Road. At the first stop sign, about 0.75 mile, turn right onto Ennis Road. Parking is available on your left, directly opposite the entrance to the museum.

NEW YORK

NEW YORK CITY

 GENERAL GRANT NATIONAL MEMORIAL

122nd Street at Riverside Drive, New York, NY 10027; (212) 666–1640; www .nps.gov/gegr.
Description: This grand memorial to Ulysses S. Grant commemorates the great Union commander and the nation's eighteenth president. The mausoleum is the final resting place of President Grant and his wife, Julia Dent Grant. Mosaics on the tomb depict Grant's victories during the Civil War.
Admission Fees: Free.
Open to Public: Daily 9:00 A.M.–5:00 P.M.; ranger-led programs, daily 10:00 A.M., noon, and 2:00 P.M.; closed Thanksgiving, Christmas, and New Year's Day.
Visitor Services: Tours, exhibits.
Regularly Scheduled Events: April 27, ceremony commemorating Ulysses S. Grant's birthday.
Directions: Subway: 1/9 train to 125th Street. Bus: M4, M5, M104 to 122nd Street; M100, M101 to Riverside Drive. Riverside Drive is also accessible from the Henry Hudson Parkway.

THE GREEN-WOOD CEMETERY

500 25th Street, Brooklyn, NY 11232-1755; (718) 788–7850; www.green-wood .com; grnwdtours@aol.com.
Description: Sixteen Union generals, including Henry Halleck, Henry Slocum, Abram Duryee, and Fitz-John Porter, and two Confederate generals are buried at the Green-Wood Cemetery. Several Civil War monuments, including the cast zinc Drummer Boy and the Soldiers' Monument, dot the cemetery's rolling hills. Approximately 3,000 grave sites of Civil War veterans have

been located, as detailed in a new book available at the cemetery.
Admission Fees: Free.
Open to Public: Daily 8:00 A.M.–4:00 P.M.; call for extended summer hours.
Visitor Services: Public restrooms, bookstore (CWPT members eligible for a 10 percent discount), tours.
Regularly Scheduled Events: May, Memorial Day concert; August, Battle of Brooklyn commemorative ceremony; call or check Web site for tours and other events.
Directions: From I–278 East cross the Verrazano Bridge, then continue straight off the bridge on I–278 East/Gowanus Expressway. Exit at 38th Street. At the bottom of the exit ramp, go straight 1 block to Fifth Avenue. Turn left on Fifth Avenue, proceed to 25th Street, and turn right into the Green-Wood Cemetery.

Grant's Tomb, New York. CWPT files.

WILTON

★ ULYSSES S. GRANT ⑨ COTTAGE STATE HISTORIC SITE

P.O. Box 229, Wilton, NY 12866; (518) 587–8277; www.grantcottage.org.

Description: Here at the summit of Mount McGregor, Ulysses S. Grant spent the last weeks of his life completing his memoirs. On July 23, 1885, Grant died, surrounded by his family, in the parlor of this Adirondack cottage. Visitors find the furnishings, decorations, and personal effects remain where they stood when Grant was here. The cottage first opened to the public in 1890.

Admission Fees: Adults $4.00, children and seniors $3.00; group rates available.

Open to Public: Memorial Day–Labor Day, Wed.–Sun. 10:00 A.M.–4:00 P.M.; Labor Day–Columbus Day, Sat.–Sun. 10:00 A.M.–4:00 P.M.; closed Columbus Day to Memorial Day weekend. Call for more information.

Visitor Services: Tours, gift shop, handicapped access; overlook with view of Hudson Valley.

Regularly Scheduled Events: July, Grant Remembrance Day; September, Civil War Weekend.

Directions: From I–87 take exit 16 and follow the signs. Grant Cottage is on the grounds of the Mount McGregor Correctional Facility, and all visitors must show ID.

❖ VERMONT ❖

ST. ALBANS

★ ST. ALBANS HISTORICAL ⑩ MUSEUM

9 Church Street, P.O. Box 722, St. Albans, VT 05478; (802) 527–7933; www.stamuseum.com; stamuseum .history@verizon.net.

Description: The museum building is the former Franklin County Grammar School, a three-story Renaissance Revival brick structure built in 1861 and used until 1969 for public education. On October 19, 1864, a group of twenty-two Confederate soldiers, escaped prisoners of war, entered St. Albans from Canada, robbed three banks of $208,000, shot several people, one of whom died, and escaped back to Canada. The incident greatly damaged relations between the Union and Canada. The St. Albans Raid is considered the northernmost engagement of the Civil War.

Admission Fees: Adults $5.00, children fourteen and under free.

Open to Public: Museum, June–Oct., Mon.–Fri. 1:00 P.M.–4:00 P.M.; research room, by appointment year-round.

Visitor Services: Information, handicapped access, research room, gift shop, trails.

Regularly Scheduled Events: None.

Directions: From U.S. 89 take exit 19. Go west 1 mile on highway access road, through intersection onto Main Street. Go north on Main Street 1 mile to Fairfield Street, then turn right. Turn left on Church Street. Museum is second building on the right, on the corner of Church and Bishop Streets. Parking is at the rear of the building.

ST. ALBANS

In order to preserve the Union and end slavery, Vermont contributed more than 34,000 soldiers who were involved in almost 150 different military engagements throughout the Civil War. Although the chances are good that you will find a battlefield monument dedicated to Vermont's soldiers on either side of the Mason-Dixon line, there is only one place historians point to in the Green Mountain State where the Confederacy made a show of force.

On October 19, 1864, as part of an intelligence operation, twenty-two Confederate soldiers conducted a raid on the town of St. Albans, robbing three banks of $208,000. They killed a local citizen and wounded several others before one of their own was shot and a posse chased them out of the state. In a matter of hours, the northernmost military engagement of the Civil War was over before it had hardly begun.

Canadian officials captured fourteen of the raiders a day later, tried them, and eventually released them after the Civil War ended. Only $80,000 in gold was returned to the St. Albans banks, and none of the raiders faced justice in a Vermont court.

Although much has changed in St. Albans since that time, I think the best place to get a good sense of what it must have been like that hectic day is to visit the St. Albans Historical Society before starting your walking tour of the town. When you are ready to begin your tour, you may want to visit the Franklin Lamoille Bank (then called the Franklin County Bank) on Main Street. Of the three banks the Confederates looted, this is the only one that remains in existence. You could also stroll into Taylor Park and survey the scene, just like those Vermont citizens who were unlucky enough to have encountered the raiders and be herded into the park like cattle.

Look toward the American House and imagine the leader of the raid, a young uniformed officer named Bennet H. Young, standing in front of the steps shouting, "I take possession of St. Albans, Vermont, in the name of the Confederate States of America!" Meanwhile, his cohorts would be filling their saddlebags with money and smashing bottles filled with flammable liquid onto nearby buildings in an unsuccessful attempt to set St. Albans on fire.

To complete the trip back in time, walk up the north end of Main Street where the road leads to Sheldon—the route the raiders took before crossing the Canadian border and into history.

—*Former senator Jim Jeffords, Vermont*

MIDDLE
ATLANTIC

Yorktown, Virginia. Karl Ringer–CWPT files.

❖ DELAWARE ❖

DELAWARE CITY

 FORT DELAWARE STATE PARK

P.O. Box 170, Delaware City, DE 19706; (302) 834-7941; www.destateparks.com.

Description: Fort Delaware was originally constructed as a mid-nineteenth-century coastal defense site. In 1861 the War Department determined that it would be an ideal site for Confederate prisoners. During the course of the war, 33,000 Confederates were imprisoned at the fort. Twenty-seven hundred died while in prison. It was reputed to be the "Andersonville of the North." The fort is located on Pea Patch Island in the Delaware River; visitors travel to the island aboard the *Delafort,* a ninety-passenger ferryboat.

Admission Fees: Ferry fare to Fort Delaware: Adults $6.00, children two–twelve $4.00, under 2 free.

Open to Public: 10:00 A.M.–6:00 P.M.; last weekend in Apr.–Sept. open weekends and holidays; Mid-June–Labor Day open Wed.–Sun., closed Mon.–Tues., except Monday holidays.

Visitor Services: Public restrooms, information, limited handicapped access, food, gift shop, museum, educational programs for groups, nature preserve, trails.

Regularly Scheduled Events: September, Cannon Fire Weekend.

Directions: From I–95 take Route 1; exit near Christiana Mall. Travel south on Route 1 to exit 152/Route 72. Turn left onto Route 72 east; proceed past Star Refinery and follow signs on Route 9 to Delaware City. Turn left at traffic light on Clinton Street and travel about 6 blocks. Look for State Park office and boat dock on the right.

❖ DISTRICT OF COLUMBIA ❖

 AFRICAN AMERICAN CIVIL WAR MEMORIAL AND MUSEUM

1200 U Street NW, Washington, DC 20009 (museum is located at 12th and U Streets NW); (202) 667-2667; www.afroamcivilwar.org; afroamcivilwar@yahoo.com.

Description: This national monument is the "first" national memorial to the 209,145 black soldiers and their 7,000 white officers who fought in the American Civil War from 1862 to 1865. The monument features sculptor Ed Hamilton's Spirit of Freedom Memorial. The names of the soldiers are engraved on plaques placed on curved walls behind the sculpture. The museum interprets the African-American experience in the Civil War.

Admission Fees: Free.

Open to Public: Monument open to the public daily twenty-four hours; museum hours, Mon.–Fri. 10:00 A.M.–5:00 P.M., Sat. 10:00 A.M.–2:00 P.M.

African American Civil War Memorial, Washington, D.C. CWPT files.

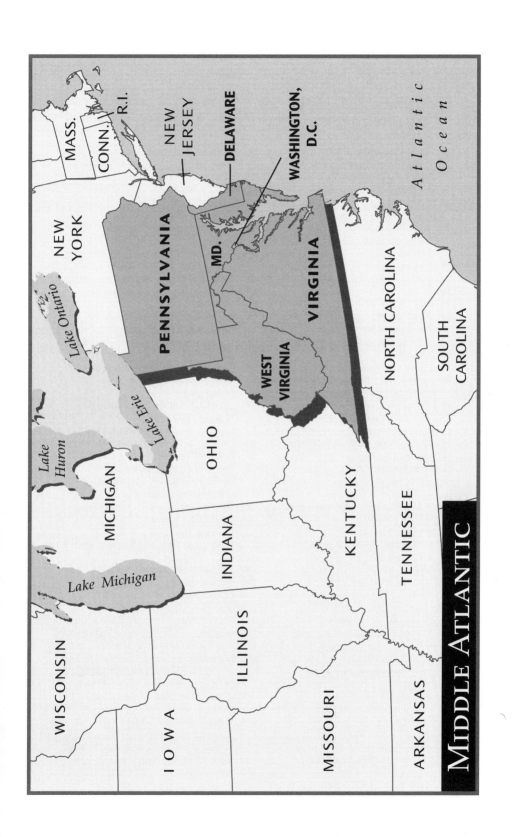

MIDDLE ATLANTIC

DELAWARE, DISTRICT OF COLUMBIA, MARYLAND, PENNSYLVANIA, AND WEST VIRGINIA SITES

1 Fort Delaware State Park
2 African American Civil War Memorial and Museum
3 Church of the Epiphany
4 Ford's Theatre National Historic Site
5 Fort Stevens/Fort Circle Parks
6 Frederick Douglass National Historic Site
7 Lincoln Cottage
8 Lincoln Memorial
9 National Building Museum
10 National Museum of Health and Medicine
11 The Navy Museum and the Washington Navy Yards
12 New York Avenue Presbyterian Church
13 Ulysses S. Grant Memorial
14 United States Soldiers' and Airmen's Home National Cemetery
15 Willard Intercontinental Hotel
16 Baltimore Civil War Museum
17 Camden Station
18 Fort McHenry National Monument and Historic Shrine
19 Maryland Historical Society
20 USS *Constellation* Museum
21 Fort Frederick State Park
22 South Mountain State Battlefield
23 Surratt House Museum
24 Thomas Viaduct
25 B & O Railroad Museum: Ellicott City Station
26 Fort Foote Park
27 Fort Washington Park
28 Barbara Fritchie House and Museum
29 Monocacy National Battlefield
30 Mount Olivet Cemetery
31 National Museum of Civil War Medicine
32 Clara Barton National Historic Site
33 Marietta Historic House Museum
34 Chesapeake and Ohio Canal National Historical Park
35 Montgomery County Historical Society
36 Point Lookout State Park and Civil War Museum
37 Antietam National Battlefield
38 Kennedy Farmhouse
39 Pry House Field Hospital Museum

40 Dr. Samuel A. Mudd Home and Museum
41 U.S. Army Military History Institute
42 Chambersburg/Franklin County Civil War Driving Tour
43 David Wills House
44 General Lee's Headquarters
45 Gettysburg Heritage Sites Self-Guided Walking Tour
46 Gettysburg National Military Park
47 Jennie Wade House Museum
48 The Shriver House Museum
49 The John Harris–Simon Cameron Mansion
50 The National Civil War Museum
51 Pennsylvania Civil War Flags Collection
52 The State Museum of Pennsylvania
53 Wheatland
54 Civil War and Underground Railroad Museum of Philadelphia
55 Clark Park
56 Grand Army of the Republic Civil War Museum and Library
57 Historical Society of Pennsylvania
58 The Johnson House Historic Site
59 Laurel Hill Cemetery
60 The Woodlands Cemetery
61 Soldiers and Sailors Memorial Hall and Military History Museum
62 The American House of Fritztown & Pappy G's Tavern
63 LeMoyne House
64-143 **Virginia Sites (See Virginia Sites Map)**
144 Camp Allegheny
145 Rich Mountain Battlefield Civil War Site
146 Bulltown Historic Area
147 Cheat Summit Fort
148 Grafton National Cemetery
149 Harpers Ferry National Historical Park
150 Droop Mountain Battlefield State Park
151 Jenkins Plantation Museum
152 Lewisburg National Register Historic District/Greenbrier County Visitor Center
153 Belle Boyd House/Civil War Museum of the Lower Shenandoah Valley
154 Philippi Covered Bridge
155 Philippi Historic District
156 Shepherdstown Historic District
157 Carnifex Ferry Battlefield State Park
158 Jackson's Mill Historic Area
159 West Virginia Independence Hall Museum

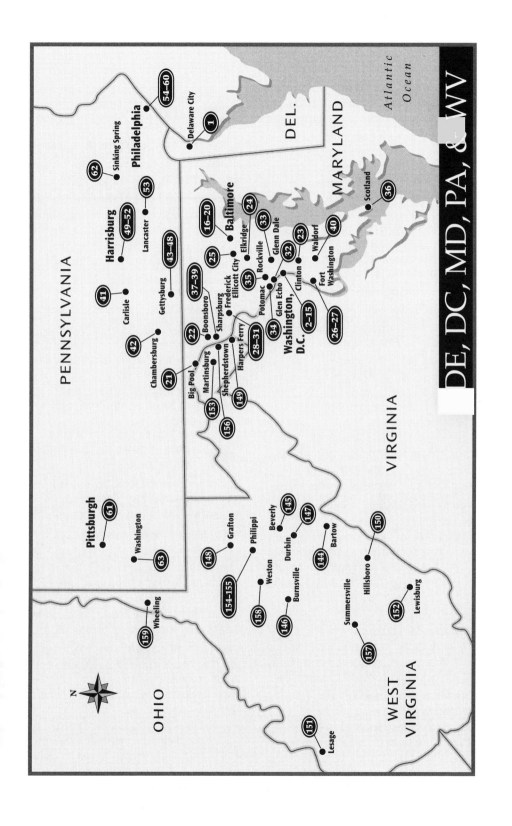

DE, DC, MD, PA, & WV

Visitor Services: Public restrooms, gift shop, guided tours.

Regularly Scheduled Events: May, Memorial Day ceremony; November, Veterans Day ceremony; descendent meetings monthly, first Saturday of every month.

Directions: Located at the U Street/Cardozo Metro station on the Green Line, at the intersection of U Street and Vermont Avenue NW.

 CHURCH OF THE EPIPHANY

1317 G Street NW, Washington, DC 20005; (202) 347–2635; www.epiphany dc.org; info@epiphanydc.org.

Description: Leading up to the Civil War, the Church of the Epiphany was the parish church of Jefferson Davis, who left Washington in 1861 to become president of the Confederate States of America. At least fifty Union generals were connected to the church in some way, including Gen. Frederick Lander, whose funeral as the first Union general killed during the war was held at the church. Epiphany's rector during the Civil War, the Rev. Dr. Charles H. Hall, was a strong Unionist who inspired Secretary of War Edwin Stanton to become an Epiphany parishioner for the rest of his life. Dr. Hall was also one of four Washington clergy to officiate at Lincoln's White House funeral. For six months in the latter half of 1862, Epiphany was taken over by the federal government for use as a hospital for Union troops.

Admission Fees: Free.

Open to Public: Church, Mon.–Fri. 10:00 A.M.–3:00 P.M., Sun. 12:30 P.M.–2:00 P.M.; parish house, Mon.–Fri. 9:00 A.M.–5:00 P.M.

Visitor Services: Handicapped access, information.

Regularly Scheduled Events: None.

Directions: From I–395 follow U.S. 1 north across the 14th Street Bridge into Washington. Continue north on 14th Street and turn right on G Street. The Church of the Epiphany is located on the corner of G and 13th Streets.

 FORD'S THEATRE NATIONAL HISTORIC SITE

511–516 10th Street NW, Washington, DC 20004; (202) 426–6841; www.nps .gov/foth; fords_theatre@nps.gov.

Description: President Abraham Lincoln was shot while attending a play at Ford's Theatre on April 14, 1865. Following the shooting, he was moved to the Petersen House, a neighboring boardinghouse, where he died nine hours later.

Admission Fees: Free.

Open to Public: Daily 9:00 A.M.–5:00 P.M., closed during matinees and rehearsals. Call to confirm hours.

Visitor Services: Museum, bookstore, limited handicapped access.

Regularly Scheduled Events: None.

Directions: Located on 10th Street NW between E and F Streets.

 FORT STEVENS/ FORT CIRCLE PARKS

Rock Creek Park, 5200 Glover Road NW, Washington, DC 20015; (202) 895–6070 (Rock Creek Nature Center); www.nps.gov/rocr.

Description: At the outset of the Civil War, a system of flanking forts and batteries was constructed around Washington. One such spot was Fort Massachusetts, built along the Seventh Street Pike, a thoroughfare leading to and from Washington. The fort was enlarged on two occasions. In 1863 its name was changed to Fort Stevens, in memory of Brig. Gen. Isaac Ingalls Stevens, who lost his life at Chantilly, Virginia. On July 11, 1864, Fort Stevens was the site of the only battle within the District of Columbia. Fort Stevens is one of the defenses that today form the Fort Circle Parks in Washington, D.C.; Maryland; and Virginia. Rock Creek Park administers Battery Kemble, Fort Bayard, Fort

FREDERICK DOUGLASS

"Human government is for the protection of rights, and when human government destroys human rights it ceases to be a government and becomes a foul and blasting conspiracy. If you look over your list of rights, you do not find among them any right to make a slave of your brother."
—Frederick Douglass

Frederick Douglass spent his early years in a home broken beyond most people's comprehension. His mother, a slave, was forced to leave him as an infant. He never knew the identity of his white father. He lived in poverty with grandparents and cousins. Beyond that, Douglass was a slave—listed on an inventory along with mules and bushels of wheat. But adversity did not break the spirit of young Douglass, for he possessed an intellectual curiosity undeterred by his circumstances. At age eight, he was sent to Baltimore as a house servant. He became fascinated by the "mystery of reading" and decided that education was "the pathway from slavery to freedom." Because it was illegal to educate slaves, Douglass learned to read and write by trading bread for reading lessons and tracing over words in discarded spelling books until his handwriting became smooth and graceful. By age thirteen, he was reading articles about the "abolition of slavery" to other slaves. When he escaped to freedom at age twenty, Douglass eagerly shared his hard-earned wisdom. His lifetime triumphs were many: abolitionist, women's rights activist, author, owner-editor of an antislavery newspaper, fluent speaker of many languages, minister to Haiti, and most respected African-American orator of the nineteenth century. In his closing years at Cedar Hill, he was deemed the "Sage of Anacostia," an accolade that celebrated the intellectual spirit within him that never grew old.

NATIONAL PARK SERVICE

Reno, Fort DeRussy, Fort Stevens, Fort Slocum, Fort Totten, and Fort Bunker Hill. For more information and the brochure "Civil War Defenses of Washington," contact the Rock Creek Nature Center at (202) 895–6070. (See also entries in this guide for Fort Foote in Fort Washington, Maryland, and Fort Ward in Alexandria, Virginia.)
Admission Fees: Free.
Open to Public: Daily from dawn to dusk; nature center, Wed.–Sun. 9:00 A.M.–5:00 P.M.
Visitor Services: Call about ranger-led tours and special ceremonies.
Regularly Scheduled Events: None.
Directions: Fort Stevens is located at 13th and Quackenbos Streets NW in Washington, D.C.

6 FREDERICK DOUGLASS NATIONAL HISTORIC SITE

1411 W Street SE, Washington, DC 20020; (202) 426–5961; www.nps.gov/frdo.
Description: The Frederick Douglass National Historic Site is the last home of Mr. Douglass, who is remembered as a nineteenth-century orator, abolitionist, and fighter for equality. He is also known for his contributions to the Civil War, serving as advisor under President Abraham Lincoln, who gave him the task of recruiting African-American regiments to fight for the Union.
Admission Fees: Admission to the visitor center is free. Call in advance for tour avail-

Frederick Douglass National Historic Site, Washington, D.C. CWPT files.

ability. Tours for groups of five or more need advance reservation (877–444–6777); tour fee ages two and up $1.50.

Open to Public: Daily 9:00 A.M.–4:00 P.M.; summer, daily 9:00 A.M.–5:00 P.M.

Visitor Services: Visitor center, museum.

Regularly Scheduled Events: February 14, wreath laying on Douglass's birthday.

Directions: From downtown cross the 11th Street (Anacostia) Bridge to Martin Luther King Jr. (MLK) Avenue. Turn left on W Street. The home is on top of the hill at 14th and W Streets SE. From I–295 north or south, take Pennsylvania Avenue east exit. Proceed east on Pennsylvania Avenue 2 blocks to Minnesota Avenue. Turn right onto Minnesota to Good Hope Road. Turn right on Good Hope Road, proceeding ½ block. Turn left on 14th Street, then turn left on W Street.

⑦ LINCOLN COTTAGE

c/o AFRH-W Box 1315, 3799 North Capitol Street NW, Washington, DC 20011-8400; (202) 829–0436; www .lincolncottage.org; lincoln_cottage @nthp.org.

Description: During the Civil War, Lincoln and his family resided seasonally in a cottage on the grounds of the federally owned Soldiers' Home, just over 3 miles north of the Capitol. During June–November 1862–64, the president commuted daily by horseback or carriage from the Soldiers' Home to the White House. At the Soldiers' Home, Lincoln met with cabinet members, political allies, adversaries, and unexpected visitors. Most importantly, he created his revolutionary policy of emancipation during his first season at the Soldiers' Home. In cooperation with the Armed Forces Retirement Home, the National Trust for Historic Preservation is preserving and restoring the Lincoln Cottage, which is anticipated to re-open in September 2007 as the premier historic site for public education about the Lincoln presidency.

Admission Fees: Call or check Web site for current rates.

Open to Public: Call or check Web site for hours.

Visitor Services: Public restrooms, handicapped access, gift shop, tours, exhibits.

Regularly Scheduled Events: Call or check Web site for events.

Directions: Lincoln Cottage is located at the intersection of Rock Creek Church Road at Upshur Street on the grounds of the Armed Forces Retirement Home (AFRH) in Northwest Washington, D.C.

 **LINCOLN MEMORIAL**

23rd Street NW, Washington, DC 20242; (202) 426–6841; www.nps.gov/linc.

Description: This classical structure contains Daniel Chester French's monumental sculpture of the sixteenth president of the United States. Lincoln's Gettysburg Address and Second Inaugural Address are carved on the marble walls.

Admission Fees: Free.

Open to Public: Daily 8:00 A.M.–midnight; rangers on duty 9:30 A.M.–11:30 P.M.; closed Christmas.

Visitor Services: Handicapped access, bookstore at "chamber level" of the monument.

Regularly Scheduled Events: None.

Directions: The memorial is located at the western end of the National Mall in downtown Washington between Constitution and Independence Avenues at 23rd Street NW. Due to limited parking, visitors are strongly encouraged to use the Metro.

 NATIONAL BUILDING MUSEUM

401 F Street NW, Washington, DC 20001; (202) 272–2448; www.nbm.com; mslaughter@nbm.org.

Description: Built between 1882 and 1887, the National Building Museum is housed in the former U.S. Pensions Bureau, which handled pensions for Civil War veterans. A 1,200-foot-long frieze around the building's exterior between the first and second stories depicts scenes of Civil War military units.

Admission Fees: Free.

Open to Public: Frieze visible on exterior of building at all times; museum, Mon.–Sat. 10:00 A.M.–5:00 P.M., Sun. 11:00 A.M.–5:00 P.M.; closed Thanksgiving, Christmas, and New Year's Day.

Visitor Services: Museum.

Regularly Scheduled Events: Call or check Web site for museum events.

Directions: From I–395 take either the 14th Street exit or the 12th Street exit (northbound) into the District of Columbia. Turn right onto Constitution Avenue. Follow Constitution Avenue east and turn left on Sixth Street. Continue north, turning right onto F Street. The museum is on the north side of F Street between Fourth and Fifth Streets; metered parking is available on all sides of the building.

 NATIONAL MUSEUM OF HEALTH AND MEDICINE

6900 Georgia Avenue NW, Washington, DC 20306; (202) 782–2200; www.nmhm .washingtondc.museum; nmhhminfo @afip.osd.mil.

Description: The National Museum of Health and Medicine was founded as the Army Medical Museum in 1862 to study and improve medical conditions during the American Civil War. The organizers of the museum hoped to centralize information gained through the experiences of Union

---

CIVIL WAR TO CIVIL RIGHTS HERITAGE TRAIL

Downtown Washington, D.C., is still rich with memories past and with the ideals bestowed upon our nation's capital by such figures as Abraham Lincoln, Clara Barton, Walt Whitman, Frederick Douglass, African Americans seeking freedom, and the hundreds of thousands of soldiers and citizens who flooded the city between 1860 and 1865. The Civil War was the crucial turning point in the development of the city from a minor Southern town into the grand capital it is today. The Civil War to Civil Rights Downtown Heritage Trail allows visitors to walk in the footsteps of great Americans whose lives were intertwined with the history of the nation and its capital city. See the 7th Street office of Clara Barton, the "Angel of the Battlefield." Visit the Church of the Epiphany, which was attended by Jefferson Davis before he became the president of the Confederate States of America and was used as a hospital during the war. See the pew where President Lincoln sat as he attended services at New York Avenue Presbyterian Church at Herald Square. Walk the escape route used by John Wilkes Booth after he assassinated President Lincoln at Ford's Theatre. The guidebook *Civil War to Civil Rights Downtown Heritage Trail* is available online or at bookstores across the country. For more information call the DC Heritage Tourism Coalition at (202) 661–7581 or visit www.culturaltourismdc.org.

---

doctors on the battlefield and share it with medical practitioners through exhibitions and publications. Among the most popular anatomical specimens and historical artifacts on display at the museum are those related to President Abraham Lincoln. These include the bullet that ended his life, the probe used to locate the bullet, a blood-stained shirt cuff from the museum surgeon who attended the autopsy, and bone fragments and hair from Lincoln's skull.

Admission Fees: Free; valid photo ID required.

Open to Public: Daily, 10:00 A.M.–5:30 P.M.; closed Christmas. Reservations required, call (202) 782–2200.

Visitor Services: Restrooms, telephones, group tours, ASL interpreters available with advance notice, wheelchair accessible, dining facilities nearby.

Regularly Scheduled Events: None.

Directions: Located 5 miles north of the White House between 16th Street and Georgia Avenue NW in Building 54 on the Walter Reed Army Medical Center Campus.

From downtown take 16th Street NW beyond Carter Baron Amphitheatre and the junction of Military Road. At the first gate after Aspen Street, turn right onto the medical center campus. At the circle turn right onto 14th Street. Proceed 1 block to stop sign. Museum is on the left. From I–495 take exit 31-B/Georgia Avenue–Silver Spring. Follow Georgia Avenue south beyond the junction with East-West Highway (Route 410), Alaska Avenue, and Fern Street to Elder Street NW. Turn right onto the medical center campus. Turn right at the stop sign and follow winding road past the hospital/garage complexes to the horseshoe-shaped drive at the museum's entrance.

THE NAVY MUSEUM AND THE WASHINGTON NAVY YARDS

Ninth and M Streets SE, Washington, DC 20374; (202) 433–4882 or (202) 433–6897; www.history.navy.mil.

Description: The Navy Museum exhibits numerous artifacts from Rear Adm. David

Farragut's flagship, the USS *Hartford,* plus many other Civil War objects in the exhibit *Securing the Seas for Union Victory.* The museum is on the Washington Navy Yard, where Rear Adm. John Dahlgren oversaw production of Civil War guns and frequently met with his friend President Abraham Lincoln.

Admission Fees: Free.

Open to Public: Mon.–Fri. 9:00 A.M.–5:00 P.M., Sat.–Sun. 10:00 A.M.–5:00 P.M. Due to increased security, all visitors must call (202) 433–6897 to make a reservation twenty-four hours in advance for weekday visits and by noon Friday for weekend visits. Photo ID required.

Visitor Services: Public restrooms, information, handicapped access, gift shop.

Regularly Scheduled Events: November, Seafaring Celebration.

Directions: From I–395N or I–295S, take the 6th Street SE exit. Proceed down the ramp and continue straight ahead to 8th Street SE. Turn right; go 2 blocks to M Street SE. On weekdays turn left and go to the second stop light at the intersection of 11th and M Streets. Make a right onto 11th Street and proceed 2 blocks to the 11th and O Street gate. On the weekend turn right and go to the first stop light at the intersection of 6th and M Streets. Make a left into the 6th and M Street gate.

 NEW YORK AVENUE PRESBYTERIAN CHURCH

1313 New York Avenue NW, Washington, DC 20005; (202) 393–3700; www .nyapc.org; office@nyapc.org.

Description: Located just 2 blocks from the White House, the present New York Avenue Presbyterian Church is a reproduction of the original church where President Lincoln and his family regularly attended services beginning in 1861. The church's pastor, Rev. Dr. Phineas Gurley, became a friend of the president and later led prayers at Lincoln's bedside when he was assassinated. Lincoln's pew is preserved in the center of the church.

Admission Fees: Free.

Open to Public: Daily 8:00 A.M.–5:00 P.M.

Visitor Services: Public restrooms.

Regularly Scheduled Events: None.

Directions: Follow I–395 to Massachusetts Avenue NW and then go west on New York Avenue. The church is located on the right between 13th and 14th Streets.

 ULYSSES S. GRANT MEMORIAL

U.S. Capitol Grounds West, Washington, DC.

Description: The Grant Memorial is one of the most important sculptural groups in Washington. It consists of a central equestrian statue of Grant, with two sculptured groups of military figures situated at either end of a large marble platform.

Admission Fees: Free.

Open to Public: Daily twenty-four hours.

Visitor Services: None.

Regularly Scheduled Events: None.

Directions: Located at Union Square at the

Grant Memorial, Washington, D.C. Mary Ann Rubis–CWPT files.

east end of the National Mall, directly below the west grounds of the Capitol. Due to limited parking, visitors are strongly encouraged to use Metro.

UNITED STATES SOLDIERS' AND AIRMEN'S HOME NATIONAL CEMETERY

21 Harewood Road NW, Washington, DC 20011-4902; (202) 829–1829; ussahnc superintendent@yahoo.com.

Description: One of the original national cemeteries established by Congress, the United States Soldiers' and Airmen's Home National Cemetery is located on land granted to Soldiers' Asylum in 1862. Abraham Lincoln is believed to have walked the grounds of the sixteen-acre site while staying at his cottage at the adjacent Soldiers' Home, today's Armed Forces Retirement Home. The cemetery received its first interment from the Battle of Second Manassas and filled with so many casualties in its first two years that it became evident more land would be required. This led to the establishment of Arlington National Cemetery, where all the Confederate interments from the Soldiers' Home were moved by an act of Congress in 1900. The cemetery now holds more than 5,000 casualties from the Civil War. Most notably, it is the final resting place of Maj. Gen. John Logan, Commander of the Grand Army of the Republic, who is credited with writing the general order that established the practice of decorating graves on what has become Memorial Day.

Admission Fees: Free.

Open to Public: Grounds, daily 8:00 A.M.–5:00 P.M.; office, by appointment.

Visitor Services: Public restrooms; superintendent available by appointment to provide information, pamphlets, and guided tours.

Regularly Scheduled Events: May, Memorial Day ceremony; Thursday morning preceding Memorial Day, Flags in Ceremony, Alpha Company, 3rd Infantry (The Old Guard).

Directions: From downtown Washington, D.C., follow North Capitol Street until it turns into Claremont Road. Turn left on Allison Street and left again on Rock Creek Church Road. Turn left on Harewood Road. The vehicle gate is approximately 100 feet on left.

WILLARD INTERCONTINENTAL HOTEL

1401 Pennsylvania Avenue NW, Washington, DC 20004-1010; (202) 628–9100 or (888) 567–8725; www.washington .interconti.com; washington@interconti .com.

Description: The Willard is a historic luxury hotel located 2 blocks from the White House. Since Henry Willard's purchase of the property in 1850, the hotel site has hosted every president from Franklin Pierce to George W. Bush as an overnight guest or at a social function. Following assassination threats, Abraham Lincoln stayed at the Willard the week prior to his inauguration. In February 1861 delegates met at the Willard for the Peace Convention in a final effort to circumvent the Civil War. Later that year, Julia Ward Howe wrote "The Battle Hymn of the Republic" while staying as a guest at the Willard.

Admission Fees: Lobby, free; call for room rates.

Open to Public: Daily twenty-four hours.

Visitor Services: Information, lodging, food.

Regularly Scheduled Events: None.

Directions: From I–395 take U.S. 1 north across the 14th Street Bridge into Washington. Stay on 14th Street past the Washington Monument. At Pennsylvania Avenue turn left; the hotel is on your immediate right.

❖ MARYLAND ❖

BALTIMORE

BALTIMORE CIVIL WAR MUSEUM

601 President Street, Baltimore, MD 21202; (410) 385–5188; www.mdhs.org.

Description: Built in 1849 as the terminus of the Philadelphia, Wilmington & Baltimore Railroad, President Street Station was an important junction for the Underground Railroad and the Civil War. It was the site of the first bloodshed of the war on April 19, 1861, when Southern sympathizers clashed with Massachusetts volunteers en route to Washington. The 1849 train station, one of the oldest in the country, houses a permanent collection that tells of Baltimore during the Civil War and also addresses Maryland's railroad history and the building's role in the Underground Railroad. *NOTE:* The museum was closed to the public for financial reasons on September 1, 2007. It is unclear when it will reopen.

Admission Fees: Adults $4.00, children three–seventeen, students with ID, and seniors $3.00, children twelve and under free.

Open to Public: Daily 10:00 A.M.–5:00 P.M.; closed Thanksgiving and Christmas.

Visitor Services: Museum, tours, gift shop, visitors center, restrooms, handicapped access.

Regularly Scheduled Events: April 19, commemoration of first bloodshed of the Civil War; call about other events.

Directions: From I–95 take exit 53 and follow signs to downtown. Turn right on Pratt Street and proceed approximately 0.75 mile to President Street; turn right. Museum is at corner of President and Fleet Streets. From I–83 follow 83 to its end where it becomes President Street. Follow President Street to Fleet Street.

CAMDEN STATION

Oriole Park at Camden Yards, 333 West Camden Street, Suite 500, Baltimore, MD 21201-2435; (410) 333–1560.

Description: On April 19, 1861, the first casualties of the Civil War occurred when the Sixth Massachusetts Infantry fought its way from President Street Station to Camden Station. Later in the war, President Lincoln went from Camden Station to Gettysburg, where he gave the Gettysburg Address, and then returned to the station on November 19, 1863. Lincoln's funeral train carrying his body to Springfield, Illinois, stopped at Camden Station in 1865. Camden Station has recently been restored, and the lobby now appears as it did in 1852. The first floor and basement house the Sports Legends Museum, with an area dedicated to railroad history.

Admission Fees: Station, free; call for museum and tour rates.

Open to Public: Daily 9:00 A.M.–5:00 P.M.

Visitor Services: Tours of Camden Yards and Historic Camden Station are available from the tour office (410–547–6234) at Camden Yards; historical information, handicapped access, restrooms, food.

Regularly Scheduled Events: None.

Directions: Take I–95 to downtown Baltimore. Follow signs to Oriole Park at Camden Yards.

FORT McHENRY NATIONAL MONUMENT AND HISTORIC SHRINE

2400 East Fort Avenue, Baltimore, MD 21230-5393; (410) 962–4290; www.nps .gov/fomc; fomc_superintendent@nps .gov.

Description: The fort was made famous

UNDERGROUND RAILROAD

"I's hoping and praying all the time I meets up with that Harriet Tubman woman. She the colored woman that takes slaves to Canada. She always travels the underground railroad, they calls it, travels at night and hides out in the day. She sure sneaks them out the South, I think she's a brave woman." —Thomas Cole, born a slave in Alabama in 1845

The Underground Railroad was perhaps the greatest protest against slavery in the United States. It was not really a railroad, with trains and stations, but rather a network of secret routes that slaves could use to escape to freedom in the northern states and Canada. Sometimes there was a guide, called a conductor, who led the escaped slaves to freedom. Other times, slaves just followed the North Star or used directions passed from person to person by word of mouth or through songs to freedom. The runaway slaves were in great danger, so they traveled at night and slept during the day to avoid being captured by "slave catchers." People of all races and religious backgrounds helped the slaves along the way, offering shelters to hide in during the day and providing food and water for the travelers.

Most of the escaped slaves were men between the ages of sixteen and thirty-five, though some women and children escaped too. Many of them had been field hands in the South, working under harsh conditions.

One famous conductor was known simply as "Moses," and the slave catchers spent years searching for him. Very few people knew that "Moses" was really a woman named Harriet Tubman, herself an escaped slave from Maryland. She led thousands of slaves to freedom in the North, and toward the end of the Civil War, she went South to tell the slaves that they had been freed by the Emancipation Proclamation, issued by President Lincoln on January 1, 1863.

NATIONAL PARK SERVICE

---

during the War of 1812 as the inspiration of Francis Scott Key's poem, "The Star Spangled Banner." The present-day fort reflects the Civil War period when Brig. Gen. William Morris commanded this heavily fortified (seventy-two guns) harbor fortification. With the suspension of habeas corpus, thirty-one members of the Maryland legislature were imprisoned here in 1861. During the Battles of Antietam and Gettysburg, the guns could be heard at Fort McHenry. Nearly 8,000 Confederate soldiers were detained here as prisoners of war after Gettysburg. The nation's largest display of 15-inch Rodman coastal guns may be seen at the fort.

Admission Fees: Adults $5.00, children under sixteen free.

Open to Public: Daily 8:00 A.M.–5:00 P.M.; call for extended summer hours.

Visitor Services: Exhibits and computer database of the 15,000 Confederate prisoners held here during the war, restrooms, handicapped access, gift shop, museum, tours.

Regularly Scheduled Events: Third weekend in April, Civil War Weekend; June 14, Flag Day festivities; second weekend in September, Star-Spangled Banner Weekend, commemorating the 1814 Battle of Baltimore and the writing of "The Star Spangled Banner."

Directions: From I–95 take exit 55 (Key Highway/McComas Street). Follow posted Fort McHenry signs on Key Highway to Lawrence Street; turn left on Lawrence Street and left on Fort Avenue. Proceed 1 mile to the park.

 MARYLAND HISTORICAL SOCIETY

201 West Monument Street, Baltimore, MD 21201; (410) 685–3750; www.mdhs .org; webcomments@mdhs.org.

Description: The Maryland Historical Society is the state's largest cultural institution. Including a museum, library, press, and extensive educational programs, the MHS collects, preserves, and interprets objects and materials reflecting Maryland's diverse heritage. Exhibitions include *Maryland in the Civil War,* which displays uniforms, documents, photographs, and ephemera illustrating Maryland's role in the Civil War. The MHS library also has numerous documents related to Civil War history.

Admission Fees: Adults $8.00, students thirteen–seventeen and seniors $6.00, children three–twelve $4.00.

Open to Public: Museum, Wed.–Sun. 10:00 A.M.–5:00 P.M.

Visitor Services: Handicapped access, gift shop, museum, library.

Regularly Scheduled Events: None.

Directions: From I–95 take exit 53 (I–395N); stay to the right and follow signs to Martin Luther King Jr. Boulevard; go north on King for 1.5 miles. Turn right on Druid Hill Avenue. Turn left on Park Avenue. Parking lot is on left.

 USS *CONSTELLATION* MUSEUM

Pier 1, 301 East Pratt Street, Baltimore, MD 21202-3134; (410) 539–1797; www .constellation.org; administration @constellation.org.

Description: The USS *Constellation* is the last Civil War–era naval vessel still afloat and the last tall-sail warship built by the U.S. Navy. Launched in 1854, the twenty-two-gun sloop-of-war USS *Constellation* served before the war as flagship of the U.S. Africa Squadron patrolling the waters off West Africa in search of ships engaging in the illegal slave trade. At the outbreak of the Civil War, she made the first Union navy capture at sea, overpowering *Triton,* a slaver brig sailing in coastal waters off Africa. She then spent two years on the Mediterranean station protecting Northern shipping from Confederate commerce raiders. In 1864 *Constellation* reported for duty with Rear Adm. David Farragut's West Gulf Blockading Squadron.

Since 1955 the ship has been preserved as a museum in Baltimore's Inner Harbor. A $9 million restoration project, completed in 1999, returned the ship's exterior to its 1860s configuration. Now, with all four decks open for exploration, visitors can enjoy a completely restored captain's cabin, sick bay, and wardroom in addition to engaging in hands-on demonstrations that take them back in time to a life at sea during the Civil War.

Admission Fees: Adults $8.75, seniors and active military $7.50, youths six–fourteen $4.75, children five and under free.

Open to Public: Nov.–Mar., daily 10:00 A.M.–4:30 P.M.; Apr.–Oct. 10:00 A.M.–5:30 P.M.; extended hours during the summer months.

Visitor Services: Public restrooms, handicapped access on top two decks, gift shop, audio guide, group tours, naval ceremonies, overnight adventures, onboard exhibits.

Regularly Scheduled Events: New Year's Eve Deck Party; spring and summer months, *Constellation's* Civil War Naval and Marine reenactment unit demonstrations; July 4 Blast! Celebration. Call or check Web site for full schedule of events.

Directions: From the north take I–95 south through the Fort McHenry Tunnel to I–395 north. From I–395 follow directions to Inner

---

MARYLAND CIVIL WAR TRAILS

This 90-mile, sixty-stop trail retraces the first Confederate invasion north of the Potomac River in 1862, which culminated in America's single bloodiest day at the Battle of Antietam. Travelers will discover well-preserved Civil War sites around Frederick, South Mountain, and Antietam National Battlefield Park. For information call 888–248–4597 or log on to www.mdisfun.org or www.civilwartrails.org.

Harbor. *Constellation* is located on Pier 1 between the Light Street and the Pratt Street Pavilions. From the south, take I–95 north to I–395 north and follow directions from I–395 north.

 BIG POOL

⭐21 FORT FREDERICK STATE PARK

11100 Fort Frederick Road, Big Pool, MD 21711; (301) 842–2155; www.dnr.state.md .us; park-ft-frederick@dnr.state.md.us

Description: This restored stone fort, built in 1756, was the cornerstone of Maryland's defenses during the French and Indian War. The site served as a Union garrison and was attacked by a Confederate detachment on Christmas Day 1861. The Union garrison repulsed the attack and was later withdrawn from the area. Exhibits interpret the history of the park from the English Colonial period through the Civilian Conservation Corps restoration in the 1930s.

Admission Fees: Fort, adults $2.00, children six–twelve $2.00, under six free. Park free, except small charge during special events.

Open to Public: Park, daily 8:00 A.M.–sunset; fort, Memorial Day–Labor Day, daily 9:00 A.M.–5:00 P.M.; Apr.–May and Sept.–Oct., open weekends only.

Visitor Services: Historic interpretation, visitor center and orientation film, exhibits, snacks and gifts, restrooms, handicapped access, camping, picnicking, hiking, boat rentals, fishing, C & O Canal towpath.

Regularly Scheduled Events: Call about military reenactments and other events throughout the year.

Directions: Located 18 miles west of Hagerstown, Maryland. From I–70 take exit 12 at Big Pool; proceed 1.5 miles east on Route 56; park is on the right-hand side of the road.

BOONSBORO

⭐22 SOUTH MOUNTAIN STATE BATTLEFIELD

Greenbrier State Park, 21843 National Pike, Boonsboro, MD 21713; (301) 791–4767; www.dnr.state.md.us.

Description: The Battle of South Mountain was fought on September 14, 1862, and is considered to be where Gen. Robert E. Lee's first invasion of the North was stopped. It was also the first battle of the war fought in Maryland. A seventeen-stop driving tour leads visitors through the battle that was a prelude to Antietam. The free driving tour brochure, "Battle of South Mountain," is available from the park address or at Gathland State Park. Also request a brochure of other Washington County Civil War sites called "Maryland Civil War Crossroads." Gathland State Park has a museum with Civil War exhibits.

Admission Fees: Free.

Open to Public: Apr. 1–Oct. 31, Wed.–Sun. 9:00 A.M.–5:30 P.M.; closed Nov. 1–Apr. 1.

Hours may vary; call ahead.

Visitor Services: Greenbrier State Park, restrooms, camping. Gathland Museum, exhibits, restrooms, living history, tours.

Regularly Scheduled Events: August, third Saturday, a candlelight tour of the battlefield at Crampton's Gap; September, first weekend after Labor Day, Civil War Living History program.

Directions: From I–70 take exit 35; follow Route 66 south to Boonsboro. Turn left onto Alternate Route 40 east; follow through town to the top of South Mountain and Turner's Gap. Turn left onto Monument Road to Washington Monument State Park.

Surratt House Museum, Maryland. Surratt House Museum.

CLINTON

 SURRATT HOUSE MUSEUM

9118 Brandywine Road, Clinton, MD 20735; (301) 868–1121; www.surratt.org.

Description: Built in 1852 for the Surratt family, this historic house served as a plantation home, tavern, and post office. During the Civil War it was a Confederate safe house and part of the intrigue surrounding John Wilkes Booth and the Lincoln assassination.

Admission Fees: Adults $3.00 ($1.00 off museum admission to CWPT members), children five–eighteen $1.00, seniors $2.00.

Open to Public: Mid-Jan.–Mid-Dec., Thurs.–Fri. 11:00 A.M.–3:00 P.M.; Sat.–Sun. noon–4:00 P.M.; open other days for special group tours.

Visitor Services: Library, gift shop, first floor handicapped accessible, tours, picnic area.

Regularly Scheduled Events: February, Antique Valentine exhibit; April and September, John Wilkes Booth escape route tour; spring and fall open house; December, Victorian Christmas.

Directions: From I–95 take exit 7A (Route 5) south; exit at Route 223/Woodyard Road west; take left onto Brandywine Road.

ELKRIDGE

 THOMAS VIADUCT

West of U.S. 1, Levering Avenue, Elkridge, MD 21227; (410) 313–1900.

Description: Built in 1835, this bridge was part of the main railroad between Baltimore and Washington, which allowed boat and rail transport to move troops and supplies during the Civil War. It is the oldest multi-arched curved bridge in the world and is still in use. For more information on the Thomas Viaduct, please visit the library at the Elkridge Heritage Society, 5825 Main Street, Elkridge, MD 21075; (410) 796–3282.

Admission Fees: Free.

Open to Public: Daily from dawn to dusk.

Visitor Services: None.

Regularly Scheduled Events: None.

Directions: From I–95 take exit 41 (Route 175); go east to Route 1 (1 block); go north on Route 1 to Elkridge (about 5 miles). Go past Harbor Tunnel Highway sign, turn at next left, and follow signs for Patapsco State Park (road goes under the viaduct).

ELLICOTT CITY

 B & O RAILROAD MUSEUM: ELLICOTT CITY STATION

2711 Maryland Avenue, Ellicott City, MD 21043; (410) 461–1944; www .ecborail.org; ellicottcity@borail.org.

Description: Completed by the Baltimore & Ohio Railroad in 1830, the Ellicott City Station is the oldest surviving railroad station in America. The station was a vital supply line to the west, and thousands of soldiers, prisoners of war, and casualties were moved through this building. The museum's award-winning Civil War living history program emphasizes the Maryland story. Historians portray soldiers, civilians, and musicians of the Civil War in an interactive setting.

Admission Fees: Adults $5.00, children two–twelve $3.00, children under two free, seniors $4.00.

Open to Public: Wed.–Sun. 11:00 A.M.–4:00 P.M.

Visitor Services: Museum, gift shop, restrooms.

Regularly Scheduled Events: Call or check Web site for schedule of events.

Directions: From I–95 take Route 32 west to Route 29 north. Take exit for Route 40 east and stay to right. Turn right at first traffic light on Rogers Avenue; follow signs to the Ellicott City Historic District.

FORT WASHINGTON

 FORT FOOTE PARK

13551 Fort Washington Road, Fort Washington, MD 20744; (301) 763–4600; www.nps.gov/fofo.

Description: Fort Foote is the only fort of the "Circle Fort" defenses around Washington, D.C., that remained active after the Civil War. It displays two mounted 15-inch Rodman cannons and is one of the best examples of undisturbed earthworks in the "circle" of forts built in the area.

Admission Fees: Free.

Open to Public: Daily 9:00 A.M.–sunset.

Visitor Services: Group tours by reservation.

Regularly Scheduled Events: None.

Directions: From I–495 take exit 3A (Maryland 210 south); proceed 3 miles to Old Fort Road; turn right, and travel 1 mile. At the second traffic light, turn left on Fort Foote Road. Travel approximately 2 miles; fort is on the left.

 FORT WASHINGTON PARK

13551 Fort Washington Road, Fort Washington, MD 20744; (301) 763–4600; www.nps.gov/fowa.

Description: This outstanding example of nineteenth-century seacoast fortifications was the only permanent fortification ever constructed to defend the nation's capital. During the first year of the Civil War, the fort controlled river access to Alexandria, Georgetown, and Washington, D.C., and maintained a training base for state militia troops from the North. The site was an active military post from 1808 through the end of World War II, but it never fired a shot in anger. Military and civilian living history presented from February to November.

Admission Fees: Cars $5.00, $3.00/person (walk, bike, bus).

Open to Public: Park, daily 8:00 A.M.–sunset; fort and visitor center, first Sun. in Apr.–last Sat. in Oct., daily 9:00 A.M.–5:00 P.M.; remainder of year buildings close at 4:30 P.M.

Visitor Services: Restrooms, information, limited handicapped access, gift shop, museum, trails.

Regularly Scheduled Events: First Sunday every month, artillery demonstrations; April–November, universal soldier program ("Military through the Ages"); Biannual Civil War Garrison Weekend.

Directions: From I–495 exit 3A (Indian Head Highway, Maryland 210) go 4 miles to

Fort Washington Road, turn right, and continue to park entrance.

FREDERICK

 BARBARA FRITCHIE HOUSE AND MUSEUM
154 West Patrick Street, Frederick, MD 21701; (301) 698–8992.

Description: On September 10, 1862, as Gen. "Stonewall" Jackson and his troops were leaving Frederick, ninety-five-year-old Barbara Fritchie earned her place as a legendary American heroine by defying those she believed to be wrong. This replica of the Barbara Fritchie House preserves many of her belongings.
Admission Fees: Adults $2.00, children under twelve and seniors $1.50.
Open to Public: Apr.–Sept., Mon., Thurs., Fri., and Sat. 10:00 A.M.–4:00 P.M., Sun. 1:00 P.M.–4:00 P.M.; Oct.–Nov., Sat. 10:00 A.M.–4:00 P.M., Sun. 1:00 P.M.–4:00 P.M. Call ahead to verify hours.
Visitor Services: Gift shop, tours.
Regularly Scheduled Events: None.
Directions: From I–70 take exit 54 toward Frederick. In Frederick turn left onto Patrick Street.

 MONOCACY NATIONAL BATTLEFIELD CWPT
4801 Urbana Pike, Frederick, MD 21704; (301) 662–3515; www.nps.gov/mono.

Description: This is the site of the July 9, 1864, battle where Lt. Gen. Jubal Early's Confederate forces, en route to Washington, D.C., were delayed for a day by Union forces under Maj. Gen. Lew Wallace. This battle allowed time for General Grant to deploy Union troops from the defenses of Petersburg, Virginia, to the Federal capital, saving it from Confederate invasion.
Admission Fees: Free.
Open to Public: Visitor center, Memorial Day–Labor Day, daily 8:00 A.M.–5:00 P.M.; rest of the year, Wed.–Sun. 8:00 A.M.–4:30 P.M.

Visitor Services: Visitor center, self-guided auto tour, restrooms, handicapped access, 0.5-mile loop trail.
Regularly Scheduled Events: None.
Directions: From I–270 take exit 26 (Route 80 north); travel 0.2 mile and turn left on Route 355 north; battlefield is 3.7 miles. From I–70 take exit 54 and proceed south on Route 355.

 MOUNT OLIVET CEMETERY

515 South Market Street, Frederick, MD 21701; (301) 662–1164 or (800) 662–1164; www.mountolivetcemetery inc.com; info@mountolivetcemetery inc.com.

Description: Mount Olivet Cemetery is the location of the Francis Scott Key Monument, as well as the graves of Gov. Thomas Johnson, Barbara Fritchie, and more than 800 Confederate Civil War soldiers, including 408 unknown soldiers from the Battle of Monocacy, and 300 soldiers in marked graves who died in local hospitals, most after the Battles of Antietam and Gettysburg.
Admission Fees: Free.
Open to Public: Daily from dawn to dusk.
Visitor Services: Handicapped-accessible public restrooms, visitor kiosk, and computer for locating people.
Regularly Scheduled Events: May, Memorial Day services; June, Confederate Memorial Day services.
Directions: From I–70 follow Route 85 north to the city of Frederick; Mount Olivet is located on Route 85.

 NATIONAL MUSEUM OF CIVIL WAR MEDICINE
48 East Patrick Street, Frederick, MD 21705; (301) 695–1864 or (800) 564–1864; www.civilwarmed.org; museum@ civilwarmed.org.

Description: This is the only museum in the world devoted exclusively to Civil War medicine. During the Civil War more than 625,000 soldiers died and countless others were maimed. Widespread disease, casualties, and bone-shattering wounds left a legacy of brutality and horror, but the resulting medical advances paved the way for modern medical practices. The museum features the only known surviving Civil War ambulances and surgeon's tent, a holding coffin, and Dr. E. R. Squibb's traveling medical chests, medical and dental instruments, uniforms, documents, photos, and books.

Admission Fees: Adults $6.50, seniors $6.00, children ten–sixteen $4.50, nine and under free; group rates available.

Open to Public: Mon.–Sat. 10:00 A.M.–5:00 P.M., Sun. 11:00 A.M.–5:00 P.M.

Visitor Services: Museum store, group tours (schedule two weeks in advance), Kid's Corner, restrooms, handicapped access.

Regularly Scheduled Events: Call or check Web site for schedule of living history and lecture events.

Directions: From I–270 and I–70 travel north on Market Street (Routes 355 and 85). Turn right on East South Street, left on South Carroll Street, left on east Patrick Street. Museum is 1½ blocks on left-hand side.

GLEN ECHO

CLARA BARTON NATIONAL HISTORIC SITE

5801 Oxford Road, Glen Echo, MD 20812; (301) 320–1410; www.nps.gov/clba.

Description: Built in 1891, this house was the final home of Clara Barton, founder of the American Red Cross. The house also served as the headquarters and warehouse space for the American Red Cross from 1897 to 1904. The museum houses a collection of furnishings used by Clara Barton in her Glen Echo home.

Admission Fees: Free.

Open to Public: Daily 10:00 A.M.–5:00 P.M.; tours hourly on the hour, house shown by guided tour only, last tour at 4:00 P.M.

Visitor Services: Handicapped access to first floor, tours, bookstore, exhibits.

Regularly Scheduled Events: April and September, Biannual Lamplight Open House; call or check Web site for additional events.

Directions: From I–495 take exit 40 on outer loop or exit 41 on the inner loop; follow signs for MacArthur Boulevard; turn left onto MacArthur Boulevard, then go east past Glen Echo Park on left. Take next left onto Oxford Road.

GLENN DALE

MARIETTA HISTORIC HOUSE MUSEUM

Prince George's County Historical Society, 5626 Bell Station Road, Glenn Dale, MD 20769; (301) 464–5291; www.pgparks.com.

Description: Marietta is an 1812 Federal-style brick house built by Supreme Court Justice Gabriel Duvall (1752–1844). The family was involved politically during the Civil War. Its furnishings are from 1812 to 1900, and the home is interpreted during the years of the Duvall family.

Admission Fees: Adults $3.00, students $1.00, seniors $2.00.

Open to Public: Library, Sat. noon–4:00 P.M.; museum, Fri. 11:00 A.M.–3:00 P.M., Sat. and Sun. noon–4 P.M., and by appointment. Call for expanded hours.

Visitor Services: Gift shop, restrooms, tours, handicapped access.

Regularly Scheduled Events: March, Civil War Encampment; April, Marching through Time; December, Holiday Candlelight Tours.

Directions: From I–95 take exit 20A (Annapolis Road/Route 450 east); proceed 4 miles; turn left on Route 193W; turn left on Bell Station Road.

POTOMAC

 CHESAPEAKE AND OHIO CANAL NATIONAL HISTORICAL PARK

Great Falls Tavern Visitor Center, 11710 MacArthur Boulevard, Potomac, MD 20854; (301) 739–4200; www.nps.gov/choh.

Description: The C & O Canal's location along the Potomac River, a dividing line between the Union and the Confederacy during the Civil War, made the canal strategically important to both sides. Several campaigns were fought on or near the canal, most notably the Battle of Falling Waters in Williamsport, Maryland, during the retreat from Gettysburg. Stretching 184.5 miles along the Potomac, the park includes six visitor centers in Maryland and Washington, D.C.

Admission Fees: Pedestrians and cyclists $3.00, vehicles $5.00.

Open to Public: Park, daily from dawn to dusk; Great Falls Tavern Visitor Center, daily 9:00 A.M.–4:45 P.M.; call for information on other visitor centers.

Visitor Services: Public restrooms, six visitor centers, exhibits, trails, tours, gift shop, canal boat rides.

Regularly Scheduled Events: Call or check Web site for schedule of events.

Directions: To reach Great Falls Tavern Visitor Center from I–495, take exit 41 (Carderock/Great Falls) and follow Clara Barton Parkway to the end. At the stop sign, turn left onto MacArthur Boulevard. Follow MacArthur approximately 3.5 miles into the park. MacArthur Boulevard ends at the park. Please call for directions to additional visitor centers in Georgetown, Brunswick, Williamsport, Hancock, and Cumberland.

ROCKVILLE

 MONTGOMERY COUNTY HISTORICAL SOCIETY

111 West Montgomery Avenue, Rockville, MD 20850; (301) 762–1492; www.montgomeryhistory.org; info @montgomeryhistory.org.

Description: The Beall-Dawson House was home to a slaveholding family. During the Civil War, Gen. George McClellan spent the night there as a guest of the Beall sisters, describing them as three women of "strong Union sentiment." Tours of the Stonestreet Museum of 19th Century Medicine focus on medical practices of the 1850s and 1860s.

Admission Fees: Admission to the Beall-Dawson House and the Stonestreet Museum, adults $5.00 ($1.00 off admission price for CWPT members), students and seniors $2.00, children under six free.

Open to Public: House and museum, Tues.–Sun. noon–4:00 P.M.; library, Tues.–Sat. 10:00 A.M.–4:00 P.M., Sun. 1:00 P.M.–4:00 P.M.

Visitor Services: Library, museum shop, restrooms, tours.

Regularly Scheduled Events: First Sunday after Labor Day, county birthday celebration; December, holiday tour; call or check Web site for lectures, tours, workshops.

Directions: From I–270 take Route 28 east. Turn left on West Montgomery Avenue. Turn left onto North Adams Street, and then make the next left onto Middle Lane. Historical Society complex is on left. Park in back.

SCOTLAND

 POINT LOOKOUT STATE PARK AND CIVIL WAR MUSEUM

11175 Point Lookout Road, Scotland, MD 20687; (301) 872–5688; www.dnr.state.md.us; park_pt_lookout@dnr.state.md.us.

Description: The museum documents local history during the Civil War era. The site originally functioned as a Union hospital, then became a prisoner-of-war camp. More than 52,000 prisoners passed through the facility.

Admission Fees: Vary seasonally; call for current fees.

Open to Public: Park, daily 6:00 A.M.–sunset; museum, varies seasonally, call for current hours.

Visitor Services: Handicapped access, visitor center, trails, boat rentals (seasonal), camping.

Regularly Scheduled Events: June, Blue and Gray Days; summer, monthly, Point Lookout Lighthouse Open House.

Directions: From I–95 take exit 7; follow Route 5 south for 65 miles.

SHARPSBURG

 ANTIETAM NATIONAL BATTLEFIELD CWPT

Sharpsburg Pike, Sharpsburg, MD 21782; (301) 432–5124; www.nps.gov/anti.

Description: The site of the bloodiest single-day battle in American history, Antietam witnessed twelve hours of combat on September 17, 1862, in which 23,000 soldiers were killed, wounded, or left missing. An 8.5-mile tour road leads through the battlefield filled with more than 300 markers, monuments, and Civil War cannons.

Admission Fees: Adults $4.00, family $6.00.

Open to Public: Daily 8:30 A.M.–5:00 P.M.; summer 8:30 A.M.–7:00 P.M.

Visitor Services: Civil War Explorer computer program, museum, restrooms, handicapped access, visitor center, trails.

Regularly Scheduled Events: First weekend in December, the Illumination; first Saturday in July, Maryland symphony and fireworks.

Directions: From I–70 take exit 29 to Route 65 south for approximately 10 miles.

Dunker Church, Antietam. Chris E. Heisey–CWPT files.

 KENNEDY FARMHOUSE

2406 Chestnut Grove Road, Sharpsburg, MD 21782; Captain South T. Lynn, (202) 537–8900; www.johnbrown.org; captain @johnbrown.org.

Description: In July 1859 abolitionist John Brown, a wanted man for his activities in the Kansas Territory, rented the home of the recently deceased Dr. Kennedy under the alias "Isaac Smith" for $35 in gold. Brown, his two sons, and Lt. Jeremiah Anderson used the farm as a staging area to prepare for their intended October raid on the Harpers Ferry arsenal. As the summer progressed, members of the Provisional Army of the United States arrived one or two at a time until twenty-one of them were hidden in the attic loft. The old farmhouse where Brown and his followers spent three and a half months has been completely restored with the use of federal, state, and philanthropic funds.

THE ANTIETAM CAMPAIGN

 The Battle of Antietam (or Sharpsburg) in Maryland on September 17, 1862, was the climax of the first of Confederate Gen. Robert E. Lee's two attempts to carry the war into the North. About 40,000 Southerners in the Army of Northern Virginia were pitted against the 87,000-man Federal Army of the Potomac under Union Gen. George B. McClellan. When the fighting ended, the course of the American Civil War had been irrevocably altered.

After his great victory at Manassas, Virginia, in August 1862, Lee had marched his Army of Northern Virginia into Maryland, hoping to find vitally needed men and supplies. McClellan followed, first to Frederick (where, through rare good fortune, a copy of the Confederate battle plan fell into his hands), then westward 12 miles to the passes of South Mountain. There, on September 14, at Turner's, Fox's, and Crampton's Gaps, Lee tried to block the Federals. But with his army divided and additional troops under Confederate Gen. Thomas J. "Stonewall" Jackson deployed to capture Harpers Ferry, Lee could only hope to delay the Northerners. McClellan forced his way through, and by the afternoon of September 15, both armies had established new battle lines west and east of Antietam Creek, near the town of Sharpsburg. When Jackson's troops reached Sharpsburg on September 16, fresh from the previous day's surrender of Harpers Ferry, Lee consolidated his position along the low ridge that runs north to south outside of town.

The battle opened at dawn on September 17, when Union Gen. Joseph Hooker's artillery began a murderous fire on Jackson's men in the Miller cornfield north of town. Hooker's troops advanced, driving the Confederates before them, and Jackson reported that his men were "exposed for near an hour to a terrific storm of shell, canister, and musketry."

About 7:00 A.M. Jackson was reinforced and succeeded in driving the Federals back. An hour later, Union troops under Gen. Joseph Mansfield counterattacked and, by 9:00 A.M., had regained some of the lost ground. Then, in an effort to extricate some of Mansfield's men from their isolated position near the Dunker Church, Union Gen. John Sedgwick's division of Edwin V. Sumner's corps advanced into the West Woods. There, Confederate troops struck Sedgwick's men on both flanks, inflicting appalling casualties.

Meanwhile, Union Gen. William H. French's division of Sumner's corps moved up to support Sedgwick, but veered south into Confederates under Gen. D. H. Hill posted along an old sunken road separating the Roulette and Piper farms. For nearly four hours, from 9:30 A.M. to 1:00 P.M., bitter fighting raged along this road (afterward known as Bloody Lane) as French, supported by Union Gen. Israel B. Richardson's division, also of Sumner's corps, sought to drive the Southerners back. Confusion and sheer exhaustion finally ended the battle here and in the northern part of the field generally.

Southeast of town, Union Gen. Ambrose E. Burnside's troops had been trying to cross a bridge over Antietam Creek since 9:30 A.M. Some 400 Georgians had driven them back each time. At 1:00 P.M. the Federals finally crossed the bridge (now known as Burnside Bridge) and, after a two-hour delay to reform their lines, advanced up the slope beyond. By late afternoon they had driven the Georgians back almost to Sharpsburg, threatening to cut off the line of retreat for Lee's

(continued)

decimated Confederates. Then, at about 4:00 P.M., Confederate Gen. A. P. Hill's division, left behind by Jackson at Harpers Ferry to salvage the captured Federal property, arrived on the field and immediately entered the fight. Burnside's troops were driven back to the heights near the bridge they had earlier taken. The Battle of Antietam was over. The next day, Lee began withdrawing his army across the Potomac River.

More men were killed or wounded at Antietam on September 17, 1862, than on any other single day of the Civil War. Federal losses were 12,410, and Confederate losses 10,700. Although neither side gained a decisive victory, Lee's failure to carry the war effort effectively into the North caused Great Britain to postpone recognition of the Confederate government. The battle also gave President Abraham Lincoln the opportunity to issue the Emancipation Proclamation, which, on January 1, 1863, declared free all slaves in states still in rebellion against the United States. Now the war had a dual purpose: to preserve the Union and end slavery.

Admission Fees: Free.

Open to Public: Grounds, daily from dawn to dusk; Kennedy Farmhouse, by appointment only.

Visitor Services: Tours.

Regularly Scheduled Events: None.

Directions: From Baltimore take I–70 West to U.S. 340 West. Continue on U.S. 340 West approximately 15 miles and turn left on Keep Tryst Road. Turn right on Sandy Hook Road and continue on Harpers Ferry Road. Make a slight right onto Chestnut Grove Road to the Kennedy Farmhouse.

 PRY HOUSE FIELD HOSPITAL MUSEUM

Antietam National Battlefield, 18906 Shepherdstown Pike, Sharpsburg, MD 21756; (301) 695–1864; www.civilwarmed .org; museum@civilwarmed.org.

Description: A complementary site to the National Museum of Civil War Medicine in Frederick, this museum focuses on field medicine as it was practiced at the Battle of Antietam. Located in the historic Philip Pry House, the exhibits include a re-creation of an operating theater, interpretive panels and objects relating to the care of the wounded and the effects on the civilian population in the area, and information on the Pry House.

Admission Fees: Suggested donation $2.00.

Open to Public: Pry House, Memorial Day– Oct. 31, daily 11:00 A.M.–5:00 P.M.; Nov. 1–first weekend Dec., Sat.–Sun. 11:00 A.M.–5:00 P.M.; closed second weekend Dec.–Memorial Day unless by group appointment. Grounds, daily 9:00 A.M.–dusk year-round.

Visitor Services: Public restrooms, gift shop, tours.

Regularly Scheduled Events: Call or check Web site for schedule of living history and lecture events.

Directions: From I–70 take exit 29A (MD-65/Sharpsburg). Go south on Sharpsburg Pike (SR-65) for 10.3 miles. In Sharpsburg at stop sign, turn right onto Shepherdstown Pike (SR-34). Go approximately 2.5 miles and follow the signs to the museum.

WALDORF

 DR. SAMUEL A. MUDD HOME AND MUSEUM

3725 Dr. Samuel A. Mudd Road, Waldorf, MD 20601; (301) 274–9358; www .somd.lib.md.us/museums/Mudd.htm.

Description: St. Catherine on the Zechia is the home and plantation of Dr. Samuel A. Mudd, who set the leg of John Wilkes Booth, assassin of President Lincoln, while Booth was fleeing Washington. For this deed Dr. Mudd was sent to Fort Jefferson Prison, Dry Tortugas Island, Florida, for life, but he was pardoned in 1869 by President Andrew Johnson. The museum houses a large number of items belonging to the Mudd family.

Admission Fees: Adults $5.00, children $1.00.

Open to Public: Apr.–Nov., Wed., Sat., and Sun., 11:00 A.M.–4:00 P.M.; last tour at 3:30 P.M.

Visitor Services: Handicapped access, restrooms.

Regularly Scheduled Events: December, Victorian Christmas.

Directions: From U.S. 301 at Waldorf, take Route 5. Bypass to Poplar Hill Road and travel approximately 3 miles. Turn right on Dr. Samuel Mudd Road; travel 0.4 mile to the house.

MIDDLE ATLANTIC

❖ PENNSYLVANIA ❖

CARLISLE

 U.S. ARMY MILITARY HISTORY INSTITUTE

950 Soldiers Drive, Carlisle Barracks, PA 17013-5021; (717) 245–3949 or (717) 245–3971; www.carlisle.army.mil/ahec; usamhi@carlisle.army.mil.

Description: The Institute is the U.S. Army's central historical repository, with vast holdings on many aspects of military history. These holdings include one of the greatest Civil War research collections in the world: 64,000 Civil War books, including 16,000 regimental histories; 85,000 Civil War photographs, drawings, and paintings; and unpublished letters, diaries, and memoirs of 6,000 Federal and Confederate soldiers. Some papers and pictures concern generals, but most cover U.S. and C.S. army junior officers and enlisted men: regular, volunteer, and militia; national, state, and territorial. A few are from other armed service branches or from civilians. All these Civil War holdings are available for study. The Institute is a public institution that welcomes and encourages public use of its holdings.

Admission Fees: Free.

Open to Public: Weekdays: 9:00 A.M.–4:45 P.M.; closed on weekends and federal holidays. Photo ID required.

Visitor Services: Library, archives, museum, information, indoor and outdoor exhibits, restrooms, handicapped access.

Regularly Scheduled Events: One evening per month September–May, guest lecturer speaks on a military history topic.

Directions: From I–81 take exit 48 (from the south) or exit 49 (from the north) and travel 2 miles southeast of the Pennsylvania Turnpike. The USAMHI is on the left-hand side of Army Heritage Drive, adjacent to the Carlisle Barracks Golf Course.

CHAMBERSBURG

 CHAMBERSBURG/ FRANKLIN COUNTY CIVIL WAR DRIVING TOUR

Chambersburg Heritage Center, 100 Lincoln Way East, Chambersburg, PA 17201; (717) 264–7101; www .chambersburg.org.

Description: The Chambersburg area saw more sustained military action during the war than any other place in Pennsylvania. In 1861 it was the staging point for Union Gen. Robert Patterson's unsuccessful Shenandoah Valley campaign. Following the Battle of Antietam in 1862, the town was an important supply and hospital center. Jeb Stuart raided Chambersburg on October 10,

1862, destroying warehouses and railroad yards. Approximately 65,000 Confederate troops camped around the town in June 1863 during the "Great Invasion." From there, Robert E. Lee made the decision to move toward Gettysburg. Chambersburg suffered its worst Confederate visitation on July 30, 1864, when cavalry under Gen. John McCausland burned the town because a ransom of $100,000 in gold or $500,000 in cash was not met. The fire destroyed more than 500 structures and gave Chambersburg the dubious distinction of being the only town in the North burned by the Confederates during the war. Serving as an interpretive center for Franklin County, the Heritage Center provides information on walking and driving tours of dozens of Civil War sites in the area.

Admission Fees: Free walking and driving tour brochures available by contacting or visiting the Heritage Center.

Open to Public: Heritage Center, Mon.–Fri. 8:00 A.M.–5:00 P.M., Sat. 10:00 A.M.–3:00 P.M.

Visitor Services: Heritage Center, information, handicapped access, museum, gift shop.
Regularly Scheduled Events: Civil War seminars four times per year.
Directions: From I–81 take exit 16 and follow U.S. 30 west downtown. The Heritage Center is located on the square in historic downtown Chambersburg.

GETTYSBURG

 DAVID WILLS HOUSE

12 Lincoln Square, Gettysburg, PA 17325; (717) 334–1124 or (877) 874–2478; www.nps.gov/gett.

Description: The "Lincoln Room" is located in the historic Wills House, where President Lincoln stayed the night before he gave his Gettysburg Address on November 19, 1863. The house was used as a hospital site after the Battle of Gettysburg. *NOTE:* Currently closed for renovations, the David Wills House is expected to reopen in spring 2008.

Little Round Top, Gettysburg National Military Park, Gettysburg, Pennsylvania. CWPT files.

GETTYSBURG NATIONAL MILITARY PARK

It is a great honor to be the United States Congressman for one of our nation's most hallowed sites, the Gettysburg National Military Park in Pennsylvania. I have vivid memories of my numerous visits to the Gettysburg Battlefield during my childhood and remain in awe of the courage and selflessness exhibited by Union and Confederate troops on those fateful days in July 1863.

Since first being elected to Congress in 2000, I have focused my efforts on enhancing the visitor's experience at Gettysburg for future generations. The National Park Service, in partnership with the Gettysburg National Battlefield Museum Foundation, is in the process of restoring the Gettysburg Battlefield to its 1863 appearance, while building a state-of-the-art museum and visitor center to better educate visitors and protect an extensive collection of artifacts and documents. We need to inspire our youth to study the causes and consequences of the events that took place on this hallowed ground.

The Battle of Gettysburg was a pivotal turning point in American history. It was the largest and bloodiest battle to ever take place in North America, and ultimately it helped preserve the United States of America. Four months later, it was the site of Abraham Lincoln's Gettysburg Address, where he extolled America's "new birth of freedom" amidst a battle-ravaged community and nation that were just beginning to come to terms with the price of that freedom.

In 1860 the total population of the United States was 31.4 million people. About 3.8 million men, 12.4 percent of the total population, enrolled in the military. And 620,000, 2 percent of the population, lost their lives during the Civil War.

The Civil War touched the lives of every American family and impacted the very fabric of American life. The American people have never yet again been so thoroughly engaged in such a struggle.

Today, an average of 1.8 million visitors come to Gettysburg to better appreciate the significance of the Gettysburg Campaign, the Civil War, and to pay tribute to the bravery of those soldiers who, in Lincoln's words, "gave the last full measure of devotion." Thanks to the dedicated efforts of the National Park Service, many nonprofit preservation organizations, and countless volunteers, those stories will be preserved and re-discovered for generations to come.

—Congressman Todd R. Platts, Pennsylvania

The new museum will focus on Abraham Lincoln and the Gettysburg Address.
Admission Fees: Call for fees.
Open to Public: Call for hours.
Visitor Services: Call for information.
Regularly Scheduled Events: None.
Directions: Follow Route 30 to the center of the Borough of Gettysburg. Located at the intersection of York and Baltimore Streets.

 GENERAL LEE'S HEADQUARTERS

401 Buford Avenue, Gettysburg, PA 17325; (717) 334–3141; www.civilwar headquarters.com; generallee@ civil warheadquarters.com.

Description: Gen. Robert E. Lee and his staff used this stone house, located on historic

JOURNEY THROUGH HALLOWED GROUND

The Journey Through Hallowed Ground's scenic and historically rich landscape encompasses four states, stretching from Gettysburg, Pennsylvania, in the north to Thomas Jefferson's Monticello in Virginia to the south. According to the late historian C. Vann Woodward, this region has "soaked up more of the blood, sweat, and tears of American history than any other part of the country and has bred more founding fathers, inspired more soaring hopes and ideals, and witnessed more triumphs, failures, victories, and lost causes than any other place in the country."

Some of the most notable battles of the Civil War were fought along this corridor. Visitors who tour the Journey have the opportunity to experience the historic landscapes of Antietam, Brandy Station, Chancellorsville, Gettysburg, Harpers Ferry, Manassas, Monocacy, and The Wilderness, among others. Numerous smaller sites related to the war also dot the region. Ball's Bluff Battlefield, the location of one of the nation's smallest military burial grounds and the site of a disastrous Union defeat in 1861, is just one of many Civil War treasures to be found on the Journey.

Incredibly rich in natural resources, the region offers hundreds of thousands of acres of land and Civil War battlefields that have been protected through federal and state ownership, as well as by private conservation easements that keep the land undeveloped in perpetuity. The Piedmont region is characterized by rolling hills, beautiful rivers, fields, forests, and historic Main Street communities. A network of scenic byways and backcountry roads crisscross the region, offering views of hills and distant mountains. There are rivers to enjoy, trails to hike, and open space on which to reflect upon the sacrifices and lessons of leadership that permeate this historic countryside.

The historic resources of the Journey Through Hallowed Ground represent a remarkable concentration of intact history in America. With one World Heritage Site, eight presidential homes, thirteen National Historic Landmarks, sixteen National Parks, and sixty National Register Historic Districts, the Journey Through Hallowed Ground is truly a remarkable region.

The Journey Through Hallowed Ground Partnership is a nonprofit organization dedicated to raising national awareness of the unparalleled history in the region. With its communities, farms, businesses, and heritage sites, we have an opportunity to celebrate and promote the very fabric of America, which stands today in the historic, scenic, and natural beauty of this region.

The Journey Through Hallowed Ground is dedicated to encouraging both Americans and world visitors to Take the Journey™ and appreciate, respect, and experience this uniquely American cultural landscape. For more information and to order the *Official Journey Through Hallowed Ground Guidebook*, visit www.hallowedground.org.

Seminary Ridge, as his personal headquarters on July 1, 1863, during the Battle of Gettysburg.

Admission Fees: Adults $3.00, children fifteen and under free.

Open to Public: Daily 9:00 A.M.–5:00 P.M.; closed Dec.–Feb.; call for extended summer hours.

Visitor Services: Museum, gift shop, restrooms.

Abraham Trostle Barn, Gettysburg Battlefield. Larry Underwood.

Regularly Scheduled Events: None.
Directions: Located 23 miles east of I–81 on U.S. 30. From Harrisburg take U.S. 15 south for 36 miles to U.S. 30 west.

 GETTYSBURG HERITAGE SITES SELF-GUIDED WALKING TOUR
Gettysburg, PA 17325; (717) 337–3491; www.mainstreetgettysburg.org; info @mainstreetgettysburg.org.

Description: Located in rural south-central Pennsylvania, the town of Gettysburg is surrounded by Gettysburg National Military Park. In July 1863, 2,400 residents found themselves in the midst of the Battle of Gettysburg and cared for 21,000 wounded in its aftermath. In November 1863 President Abraham Lincoln delivered the Gettysburg Address and dedicated the Soldiers' National Cemetery. The walking tour, which is available as a downloadable PDF file from www.mainstreetgettysburg.org or as a brochure, illustrates the impact that the Battle

of Gettysburg had on this small rural community during those fateful days in 1863, offering a sampling of Gettysburg-related battle sites.
Admission Fees: Free.
Open to Public: Twenty-four hours a day.
Visitor Services: Lodging, public restrooms, information, gas, handicapped access, food, gift shop, museum.
Regularly Scheduled Events: None.
Directions: Located on Route 30, 5 miles west of the Route 30 and Route 15 interchange.

 GETTYSBURG NATIONAL MILITARY PARK CWPT
97 Taneytown Road, Gettysburg, PA 17325; (717) 334–1124 or (877) 874–2478; www.nps.gov/gett.

Description: Gettysburg National Military Park preserves and protects the Gettysburg battlefield and the Soldiers' National Cemetery, site of Lincoln's Gettysburg Address. The three days of fighting on July 1,

Friend to Friend Monument, Gettysburg National Park, Gettysburg, Pennsylvania. Chris E. Heisey–CWPT files.

2, and 3, 1863, are considered a turning point in the war and marked the end of the second and final invasion of the North by the Confederate forces. *NOTE:* A new fully handicapped-accessible visitor center with the restored Cyclorama is scheduled to open in spring 2008. Plans include a shuttle bus between the new visitor center and Gettysburg historic sites.

Admission Fees: Park, free; electric map, adults $4.00, children six–sixteen and seniors $2.00.

FOR MORE INFORMATION

For Gettysburg visitor information, contact the Gettysburg Convention and Visitors Bureau, Department 702, 35 Carlisle Street, Gettysburg, PA 17325; (717) 334–6274.

Open to Public: Battlefield, Apr.–Oct. daily 6:00 A.M.–10:00 P.M., Nov.–Mar. 6:00 A.M.–7:00 P.M.; visitor center, daily 8:00 A.M.–5:00 P.M., summer 8:00 A.M.–6:00 P.M.

Visitor Services: Museum, bookstore, information, restrooms, licensed battlefield guides available by reservation, limited handicapped access.

Regularly Scheduled Events: March, battle seminar; weekends April–October, living history encampments; mid-June–mid-August, ranger-guided walks; July, battle anniversary events; November, Gettysburg Address anniversary ceremony and parade.

Directions: Located 78 miles north of Washington, D.C.; take I–270 north to Frederick, Maryland; take U.S. 15 north directly to the park. From Harrisburg, Pennsylvania, take U.S. 15 south for approximately 36 miles directly into the park.

JENNIE WADE HOUSE MUSEUM

548 Baltimore Street, Gettysburg, PA 17325; (717) 334–4100; www.gettysburg battlefieldtours.com.

Description: During the Battle of Gettysburg, twenty-year-old Mary Virginia "Jennie" Wade and her mother stayed at the home of her sister, Mrs. J. Lewis McClellen, who had just given birth to her first child. While baking bread for the Union troops, a stray bullet passed through two doors, striking and killing Jennie. Jennie Wade became Gettysburg's heroine. The 1863 home is now a museum that tells the story and life of Jennie Wade.

Admission Fees: Adults $7.25, children $3.50, seniors $6.53.

Open to Public: Mar.–May, daily 9:00 A.M.–5:00 P.M.; end of May–Aug., 9:00 A.M.–9:00 P.M.; Sept.–Oct., 9:00 A.M.–7:00 P.M.; Oct.–Nov., 9:00 A.M.–4.15 P.M.; closed Nov. 26–beginning of March.

Visitor Services: Gift shop, information, tours.

Regularly Scheduled Events: None.

Directions: From I–15 take Baltimore Street exit (Route 97) north to Gettysburg. Jennie Wade House is located on the right-hand side, adjacent to the Gettysburg Tour Center.

 ### THE SHRIVER HOUSE MUSEUM

309 Baltimore Street, Gettysburg, PA 17325; (717) 337–2800; www.shriver house.com; mail@shriverhouse.org.

Description: George and Hettie Shriver were born and raised on neighboring farms just outside of Gettysburg. In the spring of 1860, they moved into town and purchased a lot on Baltimore Street to build a new home for their growing family and with space to accommodate their new business, Shriver's Saloon & Ten-Pin Alley. Their plans were cut short, however, by the eruption of the Civil War. George mustered into Cole's cavalry, and Hettie was left alone to take care of their two children. During the Battle of Gettysburg, Confederate sharpshooters commandeered the Shriver House and for two days exchanged fire with their adversaries on Cemetery Hill. The half-hour tour offers a glimpse of what civilian life was like during the war.

Admission Fees: Adults $6.95, children $4.75, seniors $6.50; group rates available.

Open to Public: Apr.–Nov., daily 10:00 A.M.– 5:00 P.M.; Dec., Feb., and Mar., Sat.–Sun. noon–5:00 P.M.; closed Jan. and Feb., except by group reservation.

Visitor Services: Museum, gift shop, restrooms, tours.

Regularly Scheduled Events: Annual Christmas candlelight tour of house decorated for 1860s Christmas; annual reenactment of "Confederates Take the Shriver House" during July Fourth holiday.

Directions: Take Route 15 to Route 97 north into Gettysburg (Baltimore Street). Follow Baltimore Street for about 0.5 mile. The Shriver House is on the left before Breckenridge Street.

HARRISBURG

 ### THE JOHN HARRIS–SIMON CAMERON MANSION

219 South Front Street, Harrisburg, PA 17104; (717) 233–3462; www.dauphin countyhistory.org.

Description: From 1863 to 1889 this was the home of Simon Cameron, Lincoln's first secretary of war. Cameron was a controversial figure who had proposed arming African Americans early in the war effort and was forced to resign as a result. He also established Harrisburg as a central location for the movement of Union troops and material. Among the mansion tour highlights are the exhibition *Simon Cameron: In the Eye of the Civil War* and Gen. and Mrs. Cameron's 1863 drawing room.

Admission Fees: Adults $7.00, children $5.00, seniors $6.00; group rates available.

Open to Public: Mon.–Thu. 10:00 A.M.–4:00 P.M.; reservations requested.

Visitor Services: Museum, gift shop, restrooms, tours.

Regularly Scheduled Events: None.

Directions: From I–83 take the Second Street exit. Get in the left lane and turn left on Washington Street; turn right onto River Street at the sign reading MANSION TOURS; then turn left into the parking lot.

 ### THE NATIONAL CIVIL WAR MUSEUM

1 Lincoln Circle at Reservoir Park, Harrisburg, PA 17103; (717) 260–1861; www.nationalcivilwarmuseum.org.

Description: The National Civil War Museum presents a comprehensive and even-handed overview of America's greatest tragedy. Exhibits are factual, humanistic, educational, and entertaining. High-resolution video and sound-and-light shows complement the world-class collection of Civil War artifacts. Personal possessions of Lincoln, Davis, Lee, Grant, Jackson, McClellan, and

Johnny Reb and Billy Yank are included in the collection.

Admission Fees: Adults $8.00, seniors $7.00, children eight and up $6.00, no charge for children seven and under; family rate $30.00; groups of adults/seniors $5.50; school group rate with a five-to-one chaperone ratio $4.50.

Open to Public: Mon.–Sat. 10:00 A.M.–5:00 P.M.; Sun. noon–5:00 P.M.; Labor Day–March 31, closed Mon.–Tues.

Visitor Services: Public restrooms, information, food/full-service cafe, gift shop, handicapped access.

Regularly Scheduled Events: March, Annual Birthday Celebration; October, Annual Autumn Fest; November, Annual Victorian Holiday Gala; and more.

Directions: From Route 83 exit at 50B (Progress Street). Follow Route 22 west (Walnut Street) for 2.5 miles. Turn left at the Parkside Cafe, where Walnut Street continues, then left immediately again onto Reservoir Drive. Turn right onto Concert Drive and follow to museum.

 PENNSYLVANIA CIVIL WAR FLAGS COLLECTION

State Capitol of Pennsylvania, Room 630, North Third and State Streets, Harrisburg, PA 17120; (717) 783–6484; http://cpc.leg.state.pa.us.

Description: Gen. George Meade gave more than 400 Pennsylvania Civil War flags to the state in 1865. The flags were later stored in glass cases in the Main Capitol Building from 1914 until 1983, when they were removed and conserved. The flags and flagstaffs are now housed in a study and storage facility.

Admission Fees: Free.

Open to Public: Mon.–Fri. 9:00 A.M.–3:30 P.M.; visitors must call ahead to make an appointment to visit the collection.

Visitor Services: Public restrooms, information, handicapped access, research assistance.

Regularly Scheduled Events: None.

Directions: Route 81 or 83 to the state capitol building at Third and State Streets. Call to schedule tour beforehand.

 THE STATE MUSEUM OF PENNSYLVANIA

300 North Street, Harrisburg, PA 17120-0024; (717) 787–4980; www.state museumpa.org.

Description: Among the museum's holdings is a large and important collection of Civil War materials, including flags, uniforms, firearms, swords, accoutrements, and soldiers' personal gear. A new Civil War exhibit is under development. The temporary Civil War gallery is limited to a group of five paintings by Carl Rochling, including the famous *The Battle of Fredericksburg.*

Admission Fees: Free.

Open to Public: Tues.–Sat. 9:00 A.M.–5:00 P.M., Sun. noon–5:00 P.M.

Visitor Services: Gift shop, information, restrooms, handicapped access.

Regularly Scheduled Events: None.

Directions: From I–83 south take Second Street exit, then turn right on North Street. Proceed 2 blocks to Third and North; museum is on opposite corner. From I–81 take exit 66 (Front Street); turn left on North Street.

LANCASTER

 WHEATLAND

1120 Marietta Avenue, Lancaster, PA 17603; (717) 392–8721; www.wheatland .org; marketing@wheatland.org.

Description: Wheatland was the home of James Buchanan, fifteenth president of the United States (1857–61). He lived at Wheatland both prior to and following his administrations, from 1848 to 1868. The guided house tour discusses his extensive political career and daily life during the Civil War era.

Admission Fees: Adults $7.00, students $5.00, children $2.00, seniors $6.00, groups of fifteen or more by reservation $4.00/ person.

Open to Public: Apr.–Oct., daily 10:00 A.M.– 4:00 P.M.; Nov., Mon., Fri., and Sat. 10:00 A.M.–4:00 P.M., Sun. noon–4:00 P.M.; Dec., limited hours first week of the month and between Christmas and New Year's Day, call ahead for schedule. Closed Jan.–Mar.

Visitor Services: Museum, snacks, gift shop, information, restrooms, tours.

Regularly Scheduled Events: December, Victorian Christmas candlelight tours; call or check Web site for schedule of events.

Directions: From Harrisburg and I–83, take 283 east toward Lancaster, 27 miles. Exit onto Route 741 east; go straight at the end of the ramp and follow Route 741 east for 3.2 miles. Turn left onto Route 23 east (Marietta Road). Travel 1.7 miles to Wheatland, on the right with a white fence.

PHILADELPHIA

 ### CIVIL WAR AND UNDERGROUND RAILROAD MUSEUM OF PHILADELPHIA

1805 Pine Street, Philadelphia, PA 19103; (215) 735–8196; www.cwurmuseum.org.

Description: Founded in 1888, the Civil War and Underground Railroad Museum of Philadelphia is America's oldest Civil War institution, interpreting the struggle for freedom, equality, and national unity in the nineteenth century. With three floors of remarkable Civil War treasures donated by the very people who fought in the conflict, the museum holds perhaps the most significant cache of Union artifacts that remains in private hands. The research library of books and pamphlets on the Civil War era is one of the most comprehensive in the United States.

Admission Fees: Adults $5.00, students $3.00, seniors $4.00.

Open to Public: Thurs.–Sat. 11:00 A.M.–4:30 P.M.

Visitor Services: Gift shop, information, research library, restrooms, limited handicapped access.

Regularly Scheduled Events: Call or check Web site for events.

Directions: From I–76 east take South Street exit (left-hand exit). At the top of the ramp, turn left; follow South Street to 18th, then turn left. Follow 18th Street 2 blocks to the corner of 18th and Pine Streets. From I–95 north or south, take I–676 (Vine Street Expressway). Follow I–676 to merge with the Schuylkill Expressway, I–76; follow I–76 east, get into the left lane; take the South Street exit, as before.

 ### CLARK PARK

Downtown Philadelphia; www.clark park.info; friends@clarkpark.info.

Description: Clark Park is located on the former Satterlee Hospital site. A stone from the battlefield at Gettysburg was placed in the park in 1916 to commemorate the 10,000 Union soldiers treated at Satterlee Hospital; a plaque rests at the base of the stone.

Admission Fees: Free.

Open to Public: Daily during daylight hours.

Visitor Services: Handicapped access.

Regularly Scheduled Events: None.

Directions: From I–76 take exit on University Avenue. Proceed straight for about 3 blocks to the first large intersection. Turn left onto Baltimore Avenue and continue from 38th Street to 43rd Street. Clark Park and the Gettysburg stone are on the left between 43rd and 44th Streets.

 ### GRAND ARMY OF THE REPUBLIC CIVIL WAR MUSEUM AND LIBRARY

4278 Griscom Street, Philadelphia, PA 19124-3954; (215) 289–6484; www .garmuslib.org; garmuslib@verizon.net.

Description: The museum contains an extensive collection of Civil War artifacts, battle relics, personal memorabilia, paintings, documents, and photographs that were initially assembled by the veterans who formed Post 2 of the Grand Army of the Republic.

Admission Fees: Free, donations appreciated.

Open to Public: Tues.–Wed. 10:00 A.M.–3:00 P.M., first Sun. of every month, and by appointment.

Visitor Services: Public restrooms, information, handicapped access, gift shop.

Regularly Scheduled Events: First Sunday of the month, topical presentation.

Directions: From I–95 exit at Bridge Street; go west on either Bridge or Wakeling Street; follow to Griscom Street and turn left to museum.

HISTORICAL SOCIETY OF PENNSYLVANIA

1300 Locust Street, Philadelphia, PA 19107, (215) 732–6200; www.hsp.org.

Description: HSP is one of the nation's largest nongovernmental repositories of documentary materials, housing more than 600,000 books, 300,000 graphics, and 20 million manuscript items. The collection contains Union muster rolls, consolidated reports, returns, some correspondence, and reminiscences. Among the major groups of regimental papers are enlistment certificates. There is a wealth of diaries written by soldiers during their service. The James Buchanan and Salmon P. Chase collections comprise papers, correspondence, and other documents on political trends, economic conditions, and social history before, during, and after the Civil War. The Civil War collections are described in more depth on the society's Web site.

Admission Fees: Research library, adults $6.00/day, students $3.00. All researchers must present photo ID.

Open to Public: Tues. and Thurs. 12:30 P.M.–5:30 P.M., Wed. 12:30 P.M.–8:30 P.M., Fri.

10:00 A.M.–5:00 P.M.; entry ends forty-five minutes prior to closing.

Visitor Services: Research library, restrooms, handicapped access.

Regularly Scheduled Events: None.

Directions: From I–95 take I–676 (Vine Street Expressway) exit; take the Broad Street/Central Philadelphia exit and proceed south on 15th Street. After 5 blocks, turn left onto Locust Street; museum is located on 13th and Locust Streets.

THE JOHNSON HOUSE HISTORIC SITE

6306 Germantown Avenue, Philadelphia, PA 19144; (215) 438–1768; www .johnsonhouse.org; jhhistoricsite @verizon.net.

Description: The Johnson House is the only documented, accessible, and intact stop on the Underground Railroad open to the public in Philadelphia. Built in 1768, the Johnson House was home to generations of a Quaker family active in the abolitionist movement to end the enslavement of African Americans. The Johnsons transformed their home into a safe place for those escaping slavery. It became a stop where men, women, and children could rest and be refreshed as they journeyed north to freedom. The house was damaged during the Battle of Germantown in 1777.

Admission Fees: Adults $5.00, children twelve and under $3.00.

Open to Public: Thurs.–Fri. 10:00 A.M.–4:00 P.M., Sat. 1:00 P.M.–4:00 P.M.

Visitor Services: Public restrooms, gift shop, museum.

Regularly Scheduled Events: March, Women's History Month; June, Juneteenth Celebration in recognition of the passage and ratification of the Thirteenth Amendment; August, Jazz in the Garden.

Directions: From I–76 merge onto the Roosevelt Expressway/U.S. 1 north toward Roosevelt Boulevard. Take the West Roberts Avenue exit toward Germantown Avenue.

Make a slight right from West Roberts Avenue onto West Berkely Street and turn left onto Germantown Avenue. The house stands on the corner of Germantown Avenue and Washington Lane.

 59 LAUREL HILL CEMETERY

3822 Ridge Avenue, Philadelphia, PA 19132; (215) 228–8200; www.thelaurel hillcemetery.org; info@thelaurelhill cemetery.org.

Description: Laurel Hill is one of the first rural "garden" cemeteries in the country. It is a treasure trove of Victorian-style funeral monuments and one of the first true arboretums and municipal parks in America. Laurel Hill contains the graves of many distinguished Civil War–era personalities, including Gen. George G. Meade.

Admission Fees: Free.

Open to Public: Mon.–Fri. 8:00 A.M.–4:30 P.M., Sat.–Sun. 9:30 A.M.–5:00 P.M., closed major holidays.

Visitor Services: Public restrooms, information, archives, museum, trails.

Regularly Scheduled Events: New Year's Eve, General Meade Birthday Party; May, Memorial Day program; October, Halloween tours and Gravediggers' Ball.

Directions: From I–76 take the Ridge Avenue exit, go east on Ridge Avenue to the cemetery gatehouse.

 60 THE WOODLANDS CEMETERY

4000 Woodland Avenue, Philadelphia, PA 19104-4560; (215) 386–2181.

Description: The Woodlands Cemetery, incorporated in 1840 on the grounds of the historic Hamilton Mansion, built about 1788, is the grave site of many individuals associated with the Civil War. Among those veterans buried at the Woodlands are Maj. Gen. David Bill Birnay, Dr. John Hill Briton, Sidney George Fisher, Adm. Charles Stewart, Mary Grew, and Emily Bliss Souder.

Grand Army of the Republic markers mark the graves of other Civil War veterans. The cemetery grounds overlook the Schuylkill River, used to transport Union soldiers wounded at Gettysburg to nearby Satterlee Hospital, the largest U.S. Army hospital used during the Civil War. The hospital was located in nearby Clark Park.

Admission Fees: Free.

Open to Public: Grounds, daily 9:00 A.M.–5:00 P.M.; office, Mon.–Fri. 10:00 A.M.–4:30 P.M.

Visitor Services: A map of grave sites is available at the office.

Regularly Scheduled Events: None.

Directions: To the Woodlands from I–76, exit at University Avenue; turn left on Baltimore Avenue, then left on Woodland Avenue. Proceed left through gates at 40th Street and follow white arrows.

PITTSBURGH

 61 SOLDIERS AND SAILORS MEMORIAL HALL AND MILITARY HISTORY MUSEUM

4141 Fifth Avenue, Pittsburgh, PA 15213; (412) 621–4253; www.soldiersand sailorshall.org; frontdesk@soldiersand sailorshall.org.

Description: Soldiers and Sailors Memorial Hall opened in 1910 to commemorate Allegheny County veterans who served in the Civil War. The museum's Civil War holdings include flags, uniforms, weapons, battlefield memorabilia, photographs, artwork, and an extensive collection of GAR post records. There is also a fine Civil War library. Memorial Hall's military collection spans the period from the 1860s to the war in Iraq and also contains a Hall of Valor, honoring area residents who earned the Silver Star or higher decorations in American wars.

Admission Fees: Adults $5.00; veterans, seniors, and children six–twelve $3.00; group tours by appointment.

Open to Public: Mon.–Sat. 10:00 A.M.–4:00 P.M.

Visitor Services: Gift shop, information, restrooms, handicapped access.

Regularly Scheduled Events: Call or check Web site for events.

Directions: From Pennsylvania Turnpike take I–376 west to Oakland exit; continue in right lane up hill to second traffic light; turn left on South Bouquet Street, then turn right at next light onto Forbes Avenue. Turn left on Bigelow Boulevard. From I–79 take exit I–279 to I–376; take Forbes Avenue exit; turn left on Bigelow Boulevard.

SINKING SPRING

THE AMERICAN HOUSE OF FRITZTOWN & PAPPY G'S TAVERN

737 Fritztown Road, Sinking Spring, PA 19608; (610) 670–1100.

Description: John J. K. "Pappy" Gittelman, a decorated Civil War hero who was a corporal in the 17th Pennsylvania Volunteer Cavalry, was the popular proprietor of the American House Hotel of Fritztown, one of the best-known hostelries in the area, from 1876 to 1907. The present-day owners of the American House of Fritztown & Pappy G's Tavern have preserved the historic building as a casual fine dining establishment decorated with authentic Civil War–era antiques related to the history of the region and Pappy G's involvement in the Civil War. Guests are encouraged to take a staff-guided tour of the site, walk the original plank floors, admire the original stamped tin ceilings, and read the original handwritten newlywed prayer signed by "John J. K. Gittelman & Wife" in the Newlywed Room on the second floor.

Admission Fees: Historic building and grounds, no charge; call for dinner menu.

Open to Public: Wed.–Sat. 4:00 P.M.–10:00 P.M.

Visitor Services: Information, limited handicapped access, casual fine dining.

Regularly Scheduled Events: Civil War reenactments and living histories; special traditional menus for selected holidays, call for reservations.

Directions: From Philadelphia take the Pennsylvania Turnpike to exit 22 (Morgantown) and take I–176 north to Route 422 west. At the traffic light just past McDonalds in Sinking Spring, fork to the left and head west on Columbia Avenue, which turns into Fritztown Road. The American House is located 1.9 miles ahead on the right. From Harrisburg take the Pennsylvania Turnpike to exit 21 (Reading). After exiting, take Route 222 north toward Reading and turn left onto Route 724 west in Shillington. Turn left onto Old Fritztown Road and travel approximately 3 miles to the T intersection, making a left on Fritztown Road. The American House will be on the right shortly after the railroad tracks.

WASHINGTON

  LeMOYNE HOUSE

Civil War Room and Military Heritage Museum, 49 East Maiden Street, Washington, PA 15301; (724) 225–6740; www .wchspa.org; info@wchspa.org.

Description: The LeMoyne House is the 1812 home of Dr. F. Julius LeMoyne, a physician, abolitionist, and humanitarian. The house was a stop on the Underground Railroad and is designated a National Historic Landmark. Dr. LeMoyne was a candidate for governor of Pennsylvania on an antislavery platform. His son, Dr. Frank LeMoyne, was a surgeon for the Union during the Civil War. The military museum occupies one room in the LeMoyne House. The core collection contains Civil War artifacts, including military equipment and uniforms and a military history library.

Admission Fees: Adults $4.00, children $2.00.

Open to Public: Tues.–Fri. 11:00 A.M.–4:00 P.M., Sat. by appointment.
Visitor Services: Gift shop, information.
Regularly Scheduled Events: None.

Directions: Located 25 miles south of Pittsburgh, at the intersection of Interstates 70 and 79. From I–70/79 exit at Route 19 south. Turn right at Route 40 west. LeMoyne House is in the first block on the right.

❖ VIRGINIA ❖

ALEXANDRIA

 ALEXANDRIA NATIONAL CEMETERY

1450 Wilkes Street, Alexandria, VA 22314; (703) 221–2183; www.cem.va.gov.

Description: At the outbreak of the Civil War, Alexandria was one of the primary campsites for Union soldiers sent to defend Washington, D.C. As the war moved west, the Alexandria area continued to serve as a major Union supply and replacement center, and the soldiers who died there during training or from disease were the first burials in the cemetery. One of the fourteen original national cemeteries established in 1862, Alexandria National Cemetery was nearly filled to capacity by 1864. This eventually led to the planning, development, and construction of Arlington National Cemetery. One memorial of interest in the cemetery was dedicated in 1922 to four "Pursuers of President Lincoln's Assassin" who drowned in the Potomac River while in pursuit of John Wilkes Booth.
Admission Fees: Free.
Open to Public: Daily from dawn to dusk.
Visitor Services: Contact Quantico National Cemetery at (703) 221–2183 for grave location information.
Regularly Scheduled Events: None.
Directions: From I–95 take the U.S. 1 north exit to Old Town Alexandria. The cemetery is located 6 blocks west of U.S. 1 at the end of Wilkes Street.

 CHRIST CHURCH

118 North Washington Street, Alexandria, VA 22314; (703) 549–1450; www.historicchristchurch.org.

Description: Lovely English-style church built between 1767 and 1773 and attended by George Washington and Robert E. Lee. Washington's pew is marked, as is the communion rail where he was confirmed. Robert E. Lee married Washington's great-granddaughter, Mary Custis, and the couple attended Christ Church. Lee and his daughters were confirmed at the church on July 1, 1853. A silver plaque in the chancel marks the spot. The church graveyard at the corner of Cameron and Washington Streets is the burial spot for thirty Confederate soldiers.
Admission Fees: Free.
Open to Public: Mon.–Sat. 9:00 A.M.–4:00 P.M., Sun. 1:00 P.M.–4:00 P.M.
Visitor Services: Gift shop.
Regularly Scheduled Events: None.
Directions: From I–395 take exit 1B (Route 1 north) to Old Town Alexandria. Turn right onto King Street, then left onto Columbus. Church is on the right, at the corner of Cameron and North Washington Streets.

 FORT WARD MUSEUM AND HISTORIC SITE

4301 West Braddock Road, Alexandria, VA 22304; (703) 838–4848; www.fortward.org; fort.ward@ci.alexandria.va.us.

Description: A reconstruction of one of the sixty-eight major forts built to protect Wash-

Virginia

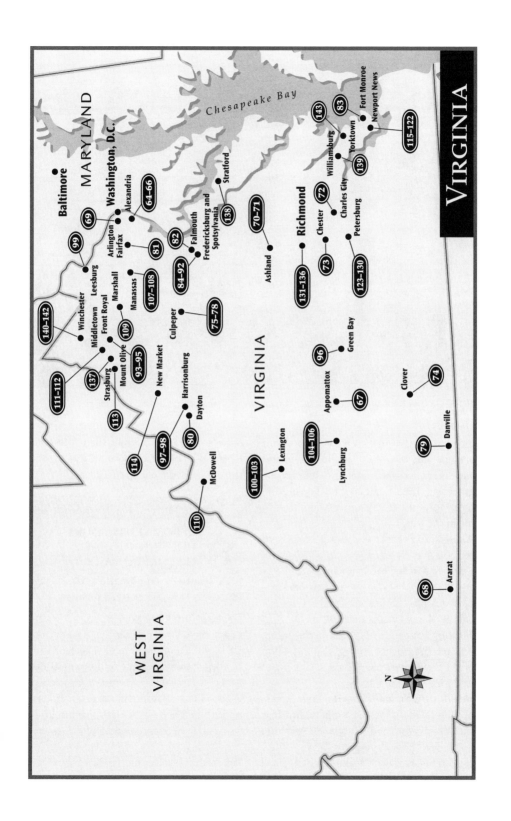

McLean House at Appomattox Courthouse, Appomattox, Virginia. Chris E. Heisey—CWPT files.

ington, D.C., during the Civil War, Fort Ward was the fifth-largest fort in the system and was considered to be a model of military engineering. It was named after James Harmon Ward, the first Union naval officer to die in the war.

Admission Fees: Free; small fee for group tours with reservation.

Open to Public: Museum and fort, Tues.– Sat. 9:00 A.M.–5:00 P.M., Sun. noon–5:00 P.M., closed Mon.; park open daily 9:00 A.M.– sunset; library by appointment.

Visitor Services: Public restrooms, information, handicapped access, gift shop (CWPT members eligible for a 10 percent discount), museum, trails.

Regularly Scheduled Events: June, Annual Living History Day; December, Christmas in Camp; spring and fall bus tours; lecture and video series throughout the year.

Directions: From I–395 take Seminary Road exit east to North Howard Street. Turn left

onto North Howard Street, then right onto West Braddock Road. Museum and historic site are immediately on the left.

APPOMATTOX

APPOMATTOX COURT HOUSE NATIONAL HISTORICAL PARK CWPT

State Route 24, Appomattox, VA 24522; (804) 352–8987; www.nps.gov/apco.

Description: Gen. Robert E. Lee surrendered the Army of Northern Virginia to Gen. Ulysses S. Grant here on April 9, 1865. The historic meeting of Lee and Grant at the McLean House is captured in the picturesque village of Appomattox Court House, which still reflects its 1865 appearance. This site marks the formal ending of the American Civil War.

Admission Fees: Memorial Day–Labor Day, $10.00 per car, adults $4.00, children sixteen

and under free; remainder of year, $5.00 per car, adults $3.00, children sixteen and under free; students, fee waivers possible.
Open to Public: Daily 8:30 A.M.–5:00 P.M.; closed Thanksgiving, Christmas, and New Year's Day.
Visitor Services: Public restrooms, information, handicapped access, gift shop, museum, trails.
Regularly Scheduled Events: Memorial Day–Labor Day, living history programs; April, Anniversary of the Surrender; December, Christmas Open House.
Directions: From I–81 at Lexington, travel east on Virginia Route 60 approximately one and a half hours to Virginia Route 24 south. Located on Virginia Route 24, 3 miles northeast of Appomattox.

ARARAT

 LAUREL HILL, BIRTHPLACE OF J. E. B. STUART CWPT
1091 Ararat Highway, Ararat, VA 24053; (276) 251–1833; www.jebstuart.org; laurelhill@jebstuart.org.

Description: Laurel Hill was the birthplace and boyhood home of Confederate Maj. Gen. J. E. B. Stuart. He was one of the most celebrated cavalrymen of the Confederacy. His units served as the eyes and ears of Robert E. Lee's Army of Northern Virginia.
Admission Fees: Free.
Open to Public: Daily from dawn to dusk.
Visitor Services: Gift shop; trails.
Regularly Scheduled Events: First weekend in October, annual Civil War encampment and reenactment; first weekend in May, Revolutionary War reenactment.
Directions: From Stuart, Virginia, take Route 8 (Salem Highway) south to Route 103 west (Dry Pond/Claudville Highway). Turn right and proceed to Route 773 (Ararat Highway); turn right. Laurel Hill will be on the right several miles down the road. From Mount Airy, North Carolina, take Riverside

Drive (Route 104) north out of town. Cross the state line into Virginia. Route 104 will change to Ararat Highway (Route 773). Laurel Hill is about a mile ahead, on the left.

ARLINGTON

 THE ARLINGTON HOUSE/ ROBERT E. LEE MEMORIAL
Arlington Cemetery, Arlington, VA 22211; (703) 235–1530; www.nps.gov/ arho.

Description: Home of Gen. Robert E. Lee and Mary Custis Lee, a great-granddaughter of George Washington. The Union seized the estate, converting it into a training center and later a cemetery.
Admission Fees: Free; hourly parking fee for cemetery.
Open to Public: Daily 9:30 A.M.–4:30 P.M.; closed Christmas and New Year's Day.
Visitor Services: Public restrooms, visitor center.
Regularly Scheduled Events: None.
Directions: Located in Arlington National Cemetery. From the Blue Line Metro, exit at the Arlington Cemetery stop. Arlington House can be reached by a ten-minute walk or by shuttle bus from the visitor center.

ASHLAND

 COLD HARBOR BATTLEFIELD PARK
c/o Hanover County Parks and Recreation, 13017 Taylor Complex Lane, Ashland, VA 23005; (804) 365–4695; www.co .hanover.va.us/parksrec/default.htm; parksandrec@co.hanover.va.us.

Description: A county park with interpretive trails that commemorates and interprets the battle fought there from May 31 to June 12, 1864. The fifty-acre park surrounds the historic Garthright House. Included on the property are numerous Civil War trenches and rifle pits.

PRESERVING VIRGINIA'S CIVIL WAR HISTORY

There is no state more rich in Civil War history than Virginia. From Manassas to Appomattox, more battles were fought in Virginia than in any other state. Here, names like Fredericksburg, Chancellorsville, Spotsylvania, The Wilderness, and Cold Harbor were indelibly etched in history books.

As we remember Virginia's importance in the history of the Civil War, we must be mindful of the myriad of perspectives on its legacy. That legacy, which is found on the names of so many buildings and statues in the capital city of Richmond and throughout the Commonwealth not only honors our place in that history, but also reminds us of the responsibility and opportunity we have to share the whole story of the Civil War.

It is not only a story of the Union army of Lincoln against the Confederacy of Jefferson Davis. It is also the story of a fight for freedoms and ideals that our constitution promised but that were denied to so many.

As stewards of these precious historic sites and the painful realities that they embody for many Virginians and Americans, it is our responsibility to preserve and protect them. The Civil War Preservation Trust is at the forefront of the efforts to preserve historic sites throughout Virginia and other states where Civil War battles were fought, and I am proud that so many Virginians have aided in that cause.

With preservation comes the opportunity to interpret and educate. Our Virginia Civil War Trails program is a model of how that can be accomplished. Through cooperative efforts at the state and local levels, the program maintains interpretive waysides at hundreds of sites throughout the Commonwealth. Today the Virginia Civil War Trails program provides a framework that enables people to visit these historic places and engage in the compelling history that shaped America.

There is much to be learned from our history. By working together to preserve and interpret our Civil War battlefields we give ourselves and the generations to come a priceless gift.

—*Gov. Tim Kaine, Virginia*

Admission Fees: Free.

Open to Public: Daily during daylight hours.

Visitor Services: Walking trails with interpretive signs; persons who would have difficulty on a gravel trail may call ahead for vehicle access; restrooms and other services available at Richmond National Battlefield Park, approximately 0.5 mile away.

Regularly Scheduled Events: None.

Directions: Located on Cold Harbor Road (Route 156), 4 miles south of the Mechanicsville business district.

 NORTH ANNA BATTLEFIELD PARK

c/o Hanover County Parks and Recreation, 13017 Taylor Complex Lane, Ashland, VA 23005; (804) 365–4695; www.co .hanover.va.us/parksrec/default.htm.; parksandrec@co.hanover.va.us.

Description: Here at the Ox Ford portion of the North Anna battlefield, Confederates turned back the Union attacks of May 24– 25, 1864. A 2.4-mile walking trail features interpretive signs that detail the events of the battle. Trench works and rifle pits from the battle are located on the seventy-five-acre property and are considered some of the most pristine examples of earthworks in existence. Interpretive brochures are available by contacting the site.

Admission Fees: Free.

Open to Public: Daily during daylight hours.

Visitor Services: Interpretive trails and signs, picnic tables.

Regularly Scheduled Events: None.

Directions: Located on Verdon Road (Route 684), adjacent to the Martin Marietta Aggregates Stone Quarry, in Doswell (near King's Dominion).

CHARLES CITY

 BERKELEY PLANTATION AT HARRISON'S LANDING

12602 Harrison Landing Road, Charles City, VA 23030; (804) 829–6018 or (888) 466–6018; www.berkeleyplantation.com.

Description: During the Civil War the plantation was occupied by Gen. George McClellan's Union army. Following the Seven Days' Battles, 140,000 soldiers camped here in July and August 1862. President Lincoln visited Berkeley on two occasions during McClellan's encampment. Gen. Daniel Butterfield composed the familiar tune "Taps" here, first played by his bugler, O. W. Norton.

Admission Fees: Adults $11.00, children thirteen–sixteen $7.50, children six–twelve $6.00; group rates available.

Open to Public: Daily 9:00 A.M.–5:00 P.M.

Visitor Services: Public restrooms, food, gift shop, museum, guided tours, trails.

Regularly Scheduled Events: August, General McClellan's headquarters tour; first Sunday in November, First Thanksgiving Festival; December, Christmas at Berkeley Plantation; call or check Web site for full schedule of events.

Directions: From I–295 take exit 22A, Route 5E Charles City; travel 15 miles along Route 5E to Berkeley entrance.

CHESTER

 BERMUDA HUNDRED CAMPAIGN TOUR

c/o 4303 Pinewood Court, Prince George, VA 23875; (804) 751–4664; www.chesterfieldtourism.com.

Description: Follow the Army of the James from May 5 through June 15, 1864, in the Bermuda Hundred Campaign. A self-guided tour brochure is available at Richmond National Battlefield and Petersburg National Battlefield Visitors Center or by mail from the above address.

Admission Fees: Free.

Open to Public: Daily during daylight hours.

Visitor Services: None.

Regularly Scheduled Events: None.

Directions: Begin tour at Fort Darling at Richmond National Battlefield Park, off I–95, exit 64. Tour brochure provides driving directions.

CLOVER

 STAUNTON RIVER BATTLEFIELD STATE PARK

1035 Fort Hill Trail, Randolph, VA 23962; (434) 454–4312 or (804) 786–1712; www.dcr.virginia.gov/state_parks/stb.shtml.

Description: On June 25, 1864, a ragtag band of Confederate soldiers, boys, and old men commanded by Capt. Benjamin L. Farinholt repelled a Union force sent to burn the Southern Railroad Bridge over the Staunton River. Brig. Gen. James H. Wilson and Brig. Gen. August V. Kautz led the Union cavalry. Today, the remains of Farinholt's fortification stands on the high bluff overlooking the river and bridge site on the south side of the river.

Admission Fees: Free.

Open to Public: Park, daily 8:00 A.M.–dusk; visitor center, Oct.–Apr. Wed.–Sat. 9:00 A.M.–4:00 P.M., Sun. 11:00 A.M.–4:00 P.M.;

May–Sept., Mon.–Sat. 9:00 A.M.–4:30 P.M., Sun. 11:00 A.M.–4:30 P.M.

Visitor Services: Public restrooms, information, handicapped access, gift shop, museum, trails.

Regularly Scheduled Events: Call for events, dates, and times.

Directions: Take Route 360 to Route 92. One mile north of Clover, turn right onto Route 600. Proceed about 2.5 miles to entrance. Turn right on Route 855 and follow signs.

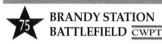

CULPEPER

★ 75 BRANDY STATION BATTLEFIELD CWPT

c/o Civil War Preservation Trust, 1331 H Street NW, Suite 1001, Washington, DC 20005; (800) 298–7878.

Description: On June 9, 1863, the Gettysburg campaign began when U.S. Maj. Gen. Pleasonton's cavalry surprised Gen. J. E. B. Stuart's troopers in what was to be the largest cavalry battle ever fought on the North American continent. Although more than 1,500 men fell that day, the fight proved inconclusive. However, it did reveal Confederate forces slipping into the Shenandoah Valley and made clear to both armies that Southern horsemen had finally met their match.

Admission Fees: Free.

Open to Public: Daily from dawn to dusk.

Visitor Services: Driving tour, walking trails, interpretive signage.

Regularly Scheduled Events: None.

Directions: From U.S. 29 going south, turn right on Route 276 (Beverly Ford Road). Pass the airport, and turn left when you see the Brandy Station sign.

★ 76 CEDAR MOUNTAIN BATTLEFIELD CWPT

c/o Civil War Preservation Trust, 1331 H Street NW, Suite 1001, Washington, DC 20005; (800) 298–7878.

Description: On August 9, 1862, numeri-

cally superior Confederates under Gen. "Stonewall" Jackson nearly suffered defeat at the hands of a small Union force commanded by Maj. Gen. Nathaniel P. Banks until a counterattack by Maj. Gen. A. P. Hill's division led the Southerners to victory. Success here, at what is considered the first battle of the Second Manassas campaign, gave the Army of Northern Virginia the initiative and pushed the war north from Richmond.

Admission Fees: Free.

Open to Public: Daily from dawn to dusk.

Visitor Services: Walking trails, interpretive signage.

Regularly Scheduled Events: None.

Directions: From Washington, D.C., take U.S. 15/29 south in Warrentown. Near Culpeper, take the bypass to Route 15 south. After a few miles turn right on General Winder Road (Route 657) to site.

★ 77 GRAFFITI HOUSE AT BRANDY STATION

19484 Brandy Road, Brandy Station, VA 22714; (540) 727–7718; www.brandy stationfoundation.com; director@ brandystationfoundation.com.

Description: A two-story frame structure located directly beside the railroad tracks, the Graffiti House is believed to have been constructed in 1858. According to local tradition, the building was used as a hospital site for both Union and Confederate causalities following the First Battle of Manassas, the Battle of Brandy Station, and other local battles. The Graffiti House is named for the signatures, inscriptions, and drawings of the Civil War soldiers who recuperated on the second floor. Much of the graffiti that still survives is on exhibit in the house. Other exhibits depict the Civil War history of Brandy Station and Culpeper County.

Admission Fees: Individuals $3.00; group rates available.

Open to Public: Apr.–Nov., Wed. and Fri.– Sun.11:00 A.M.- 4:00 P.M.; Dec.–Mar., Wed. and Sat. 11:00 A.M.–4:00 P.M.

Visitor Services: Information, exhibits, gift shop.

Regularly Scheduled Events: April–October, battlefield tours every other Saturday. Call for schedule of lecture events.

Directions: The Graffiti House is located just off Route 15/29, between Warrenton and Culpeper, about 5 miles west of the Rappahannock River. Upon reaching Brandy Station on Route 15/29, turn south on Alanthus Road. Go approximately 200 yards to the intersection with Brandy Road and turn left. Proceed straight on Brandy Road to the Graffiti House, located next to the old church on the right side of the road.

 **MUSEUM OF CULPEPER HISTORY**

803 South Main Street, Culpeper, VA 22701; (540) 829–1749; www.culpeper museum.com; contact@culpeper museum.com.

Description: The museum's campus includes a 4,000-square-foot Colonial Williamsburg–designed brick facility that houses the primary exhibit galleries, museum, gift shop, and offices. In addition, visitors can enjoy the Burgandine House, a fully restored eighteenth-century log cabin, and a working American Indian village. The grounds are complemented by ample green space for picnicking and outdoor programs and a spacious parking area with a highly visible location on Main Street.

Admission Fees: Adults $3.00 (suggested donation), children free.

Open to Public: Mon.–Sat. 10:00 A.M.–5:00 P.M., May–Oct., Sun. 12:30 P.M.–4:00 P.M.; closed Jan.

Visitor Services: Public restrooms, gift shop, information, handicapped access.

Regularly Scheduled Events: July, Annual American Heritage Riverfest; September, Annual Dinosaur Ball.

Directions: From I–66 take Route 29 south to Culpeper. Take Route 3 exit (Fredericksburg, Culpeper), turning right onto Route 3.

Continue to second stoplight (Business 29/Main Street) and turn right at intersection. Continue for 0.3 mile, turning right onto Mason Street. Museum is on your right. From I–64 take Route 29 north to fourth Culpeper exit (Route 3/Fredericksburg, Culpeper), turn left onto Route 3 and follow directions above. From I–95 take Route 3 west to Culpeper. Turn right on Business 29/Main Street. Continue for 0.3 mile, turning right onto Mason Street. Museum is on your right.

DANVILLE

 SUTHERLIN MANSION, DANVILLE MUSEUM OF FINE ARTS AND HISTORY

975 Main Street, Danville, VA 24541; (434) 793–5644; www.danvillemuseum .org; artandhistory@danvillemuseum .org.

Description: Built in 1859 for Danville's leading citizen, the Sutherlin Mansion is known as the temporary residence of Confederate president Jefferson Davis for the week of April 3–10, 1865. In this house Davis authored his last official proclamation as president of the Confederacy. The government remained in Danville until April 10, when it received news of Lee's surrender at Appomattox. A permanent exhibit, *Between the Lines: Danville 1861–1865,* interprets Danville's role in the Civil War as a supply depot and the mansion as the "Last Capitol of the Confederacy."

Admission Fees: Free; suggested donation $5.00.

Open to Public: Mon.–Fri. 10:00 A.M.–5:00 P.M., Sat.–Sun. 2:00 P.M.–5:00 P.M.

Visitor Services: Public restrooms, information, handicapped access, gift shop, museum, guided tours.

Regularly Scheduled Events: April, History on the Lawn.

Directions: From I–29 continue to Virginia 86. Take the U.S. 29/West Main Street ramp, turning left onto West Main Street (which becomes Main Street). The museum will be 0.25 mile on the right.

DAYTON

 HARRISONBURG-ROCKINGHAM HISTORICAL SOCIETY

382 High Street, Dayton, VA 22821; (540) 879–2616; www.heritagecenter .com; heritag1@heritagecenter.com.

Description: The museum has many Civil War exhibits relating to the Shenandoah Valley. One of the highlights of the museum is a 12-foot electronic relief map and narrative program whose 300 lights follow the movements of the contending armies in Stonewall Jackson's 1862 Valley Campaign.

Admission Fees: Adults $5.00, children $1.00; local students and Harrisonburg/ Rockingham Historical Society members free.

Open to Public: Mon.–Sat 10:00 A.M.–4:00 P.M.; closed Sun.

Visitor Services: Public restrooms, information, handicapped access, museum, gift shop, picnic area.

Regularly Scheduled Events: None.

Directions: From I–81 take exit 245 at Harrisonburg. Turn west onto Port Republic Road. Proceed straight through intersection with South Main Street (or Route 11), at which point the road you are traveling on becomes Maryland Avenue. At the next intersection (with South High Street/Route 42), turn left onto Route 42. Travel several miles leaving Harrisonburg and passing the Wal-Mart shopping center. Turn right onto Route 732. (Be alert to horses and buggies traveling in this area.) A quarter mile along 732, stop at a three-way intersection, turn left over the one-lane bridge onto College Street, then immediately turn right onto Bowman Road. Make a quick left onto High

Street. The Historical Society is on your left with ample parking.

FAIRFAX

 FAIRFAX MUSEUM AND VISITOR CENTER

10209 Main Street, Fairfax, VA 22030; (703) 385–8414; www.fairfaxva.gov/ museumvc/mvc.asp.

Description: This regional history museum and Virginia visitor center is located in 1873 school building. Museum features exhibits and information on Fairfax during the Civil War. Walking tours of Historic Fairfax are available during the fall and spring and include the following Civil War–related sites: Dr. William Gunnell House (ca. 1835), Fairfax County Courthouse (1800), Ratcliffe-Allison House (1812), Ford House (ca. 1835), as well as many other historic buildings.

Admission Fees: Museum, free; walking tours, adults $4.00, children $2.00.

Open to Public: Museum, daily 9:00 A.M.–5:00 P.M.; walking tours, fall and spring, call for more information.

Visitor Services: Public restrooms, handicapped access, gift shop, tours.

Regularly Scheduled Events: Spring and fall, walking tours; June, Biennial Blenheim Civil War Weekend; call for additional information.

Directions: From I–66 exit onto Route 50 east. Follow until Route 50 becomes Main Street (Route 236). Proceed 4 miles, and museum is on the right. From I–495 exit onto Route 236 west (Little River Turnpike); continue for approximately 6 miles and turn left into the museum parking lot (the turning lane is just west of the Route 236 intersection with Locust Street).

FALMOUTH

 82 **WHITE OAK CIVIL WAR MUSEUM**

985 White Oak Road, Falmouth, VA 22405; (540) 371–4234; www.whiteoak museum.com; whiteoakcivilwar museum@msn.com.

Description: The White Oak Civil War Museum has four rooms displaying an extensive collection of Union and Confederate artifacts recovered from encampments and battlefields in Strafford County and the Fredericksburg area.

Admission Fees: Adults $4.00, seniors and children thirteen–seventeen $2.00, children seven–twelve $1.00.

Open to Public: Wed.–Sat. 10:00 A.M.–5:00 P.M.

Visitor Services: Public restrooms, handicapped access, information, museum.

Regularly Scheduled Events: None.

Directions: Take I–95 to Route 3 east. In downtown Fredericksburg, continue on Route 3 Business (William Street). Turn left on Ferry Road and right on White Oak Road (Virginia 218).

FORT MONROE

 83 **THE CASEMATE MUSEUM/ FORT MONROE**

20 Bernard Road, Fort Monroe, VA 23651; (757) 788–3391, www.monroe .army.mil/Monroe/sites/installation/ museum/Casemate_Museum.aspx.

Description: The Casemate Museum is located within the moat area of Fort Monroe, America's largest stone fort. The fort remained a major Union stronghold throughout the war, denying the Confederacy access to Norfolk and Richmond from the ocean. It was also the regional headquarters of the Freedman's Bureau. Exhibits include many Civil War artifacts and the cell of Confederate president Jefferson Davis, who was imprisoned here after the Civil War (1865–1867).

Admission Fees: Free.

Open to Public: Daily 10:30 A.M.–4:30 P.M.

Visitor Services: Public restrooms, information, handicapped access, gift shop, museum, trails.

Regularly Scheduled Events: October, Halloween lantern tour; mid-December, Christmas lantern tour.

Directions: From I–64 take exit 268 (Fort Monroe); turn left onto Mallory Street, then turn right onto Mellen Street and follow it into the fort; follow road signs to the museum.

FREDERICKSBURG AND SPOTSYLVANIA

 84 **CIVIL WAR LIFE—THE SOLDIER'S MUSEUM**

4712 Southpoint Parkway, Fredericksburg, VA 22407; (540) 834–1859; www .civilwar-life.com; civilwarlife@yahoo .com.

Description: The museum houses the Fredericksburg and Spotsylvania County area's most extensive on-display collection of original Civil War artifacts, with emphasis on the common soldier. In partnership with the Center for Civil War Photography, the museum has a new gallery, The Classic Photographs of Civil War Virginia, and the only three-dimensional Civil War theater anywhere.

Admission Fees: Adults $5.00 (10 percent discount for CWPT members), children seven–sixteen $2.00, seniors $4.50.

Open to Public: Daily 10:00 A.M.–5:00 P.M.; June–Aug., daily 9:00 A.M.–5:00 P.M.; closed Thanksgiving, Christmas, and weekdays in Jan.

Visitor Services: Handicapped access, information, area's largest Civil War store, 3-D theater.

Regularly Scheduled Events: None.

FREDERICKSBURG AND SPOTSYLVANIA NATIONAL MILITARY PARK

The Fredericksburg and Spotsylvania National Military Park is home to some of America's most significant and historic Civil War battlefields, and it lays claim to one of Robert E. Lee's greatest victories.

This park, situated off the Rappahannock River in the serene Fredericksburg area, played host to four major battles during the war. The battles of Fredericksburg (December 13, 1862), Chancellorsville (May 1–May 6, 1863), The Wilderness (May 5–7, 1863), and Spotsylvania Court House (May 8–21, 1864) saw more than 100,000 brave soldiers fall. These battlefields have the grave distinction of being some of the bloodiest and most hollowed ground in America.

History can be felt and seen throughout Virginia's First Congressional District, especially as one enters the grounds of our many preserved battlefields—the setting of epic battles that wrote an enduring chapter in the history of our nation. So many men died on this soil, in the cause of preservation, emancipation, and defense of homeland. These men fought on opposing sides, yet they all fought with a passion for what they believed in.

The May 1863 clash between Confederate Gen. Robert E. Lee's troops and Union Gen. Joseph Hooker's men fills the history books and national lore. Despite being forced to leave his defenses and fight in open ground, Lee was successful in defeating a Union army twice his size and driving it back toward the Rappahannock River. Yet this victory proved bittersweet for General Lee, as one of the Confederate's most spirited leaders, Thomas "Stonewall" Jackson, fell victim to friendly fire and perished. A visit to the house at Guiney Station where Jackson died is a must-see when you are visiting the Fredericksburg and Spotsylvania National Military Park.

All of this history and much more await you at the Fredericksburg and Spotsylvania National Military Park. One of the most cherished Civil War sites in America, these battlefields will not disappoint.

—*U.S. Congresswoman Jo Ann Davis, Virginia*

Directions: From I–95 take exit 126 (Massaponax). Proceed south on Route 1 to Southpoint 1. Turn left on Southpoint Parkway and proceed to the museum on the left, located next to the Spotsylvania Visitor's Center.

FIRST DAY AT CHANCELLORSVILLE BATTLEFIELD CWPT

85

c/o Civil War Preservation Trust, 1331 H Street NW, Suite 1001, Washington, DC 20005; (800) 298–7878.

Description: The First Day at Chancellors-ville Battlefield is the site of the opening clash of this famous battle, fought on May 1, 1863. The battle pitted the leading elements of Confederate Gen. Robert E. Lee's Army of Northern Virginia and Union Gen. Joseph Hooker's Army of the Potomac. After several hours of fighting in the clearings along the Orange Turnpike, Hooker withdrew his forces, leaving the battlefield—and the initiative—in the hands of the Gray Fox, Lee. Lee's army would not relinquish the initiative until two months later, in a small Pennsylvania town known as Gettysburg.

Admission Fees: Free.

Open to Public: Daily from sunrise to sunset.

Visitor Services: Walking trails and interpretive signs to be installed by 2008.

Regularly Scheduled Events: None.

Directions: From I–95 take exit 130B, Route 3 west. Continue on Route 3 (Plank Road) approximately 5 miles. Immediately after passing Chancellor Elementary School and Corter Road, the battlefield will be on your right. The parking area is approximately 0.5 mile ahead.

 FREDERICKSBURG AREA MUSEUM

907 Princess Anne Street, Fredericksburg, VA 22401; (540) 371–3037; www.famcc.org; famoffice@earthlink.net.

Description: This 1816 Town Hall/Market House was used as a hospital during the Civil War. Today, a portion of the permanent exhibit examines the civilian experiences during the war. The museum owns a large Civil War weapons collection as well as numerous letters and diaries from the period.

Admission Fees: Adults $5.00, students under eighteen 80 cents, groups $4.00, 80 cents for student groups, students in Planning District 17 free, seniors $4.00.

Open to Public: Mar.–Nov., Mon.–Sat. 10:00 A.M.–5:00 P.M., Sun. 1:00 P.M.–5:00 P.M.; Dec.–Feb., Mon.–Sat. 10:00 A.M.–4:00 P.M., Sun. 1:00 P.M.–4:00 P.M.

Visitor Services: Public restrooms, information, handicapped access, gift shop.

Regularly Scheduled Events: Children's programs held throughout the year, except for the months of November and December.

Directions: From I–95 take exit 130A and follow Route 3 east into downtown. Museum is at the corner of Route 3 (William Street) and Princess Anne Street.

 FREDERICKSBURG AND SPOTSYLVANIA NATIONAL MILITARY PARK CWPT

120 Chatham Lane, Fredericksburg, VA 22405; (540) 371–0802; www.nps.gov/frsp.

Description: Portions of four major Civil War battlefields (Fredericksburg, Chancellorsville, The Wilderness, and Spotsylvania

Fredericksburg National Cemetery, Fredericksburg, Virginia. Michael Melford–CWPT files.

Court House) and several other smaller historic sites (Chatham, Salem Church, and Guinia Station) comprise the park. The four battlefields witnessed the death or wounding of more than 100,000 men over two years. It is the bloodiest ground in North America. The battles here reflect a continuum of war—the ebb and flow of a nation at war with itself—and the changing nature of the human experience (both civilian and military) during the four years of combat. The battles offer important insights into the minds and methods of great leaders, men like Lee, Jackson, and Grant. The battlefields reflect the changing nature of battlefield tactics as they evolved from open field fighting to trench warfare. These changes had major implications for the soldiers' experience in battle, which changed dramatically between 1862 and 1864.

Admission Fees: Free; nominal fee to view films.

Open to Public: Park and visitor center open daily 9:00 A.M.–5:00 P.M.; call for extended summer hours. The Jackson Shrine is closed Tues.–Fri. in winter, and Wed. and Thurs. in spring and summer.

Visitor Services: Public restrooms, information, handicapped access, gift shop, museum, summer tours, trails.

Regularly Scheduled Events: Memorial Day, commemorative program; Sunday closest to December 13, Fredericksburg Battle Commemoration.

Directions: From I–95 take exit 130A east on Route 3 for 2 miles; turn left on Lafayette Boulevard and continue 0.4 mile to the visitor center on the left.

HARRIS FARM BATTLEFIELD CWPT

c/o Central Virginia Battlefields Trust, P.O. Box 3417, Fredericksburg, VA 22402; (540) 374–0900.

Description: The last major action of the Battle of Spotsylvania Court House occurred on May 19, 1864, at the Harris Farm. On discovering that U. S. Grant had pulled his forces away from the Muleshoe sector, Robert E. Lee sent 6,000 men under Richard Ewell to locate the Union right flank. The fighting that ensued against heavy artillery manned by troops fresh out of the defenses of Washington saw repeated Confederate assaults beaten back until Ewell's corps withdrew having suffered 15 percent casualties.

Admission Fees: Free.

Open to Public: Daily from sunrise to sunset.

Visitor Services: Interpretive signage.

Regularly Scheduled Events: None.

Directions: From Four Mile Fork (the junction of Routes 1, 1A, and 208) take Route 208 south toward Spotsylvania Court House. After a few miles you will cross Route 628. The original farm driveway is now blocked. The monument is accessed by subdivision roads, as is Mrs. McGee's farmhouse. About 600 yards down, enter Bloomsbury Lane. Turn onto Agnes Lane and proceed to Pond View Drive on the left. The parking area is at the intersection of Pond View Drive and Harris Farm Road.

HISTORIC KENMORE

1201 Washington Avenue, Fredericksburg, VA 22401; (540) 373–3381; www .ferryfarm.org; mailroom@gwf foundation.org.

Description: Kenmore was built in 1775 by Fielding Lewis and his wife, Betty Washington Lewis, George Washington's sister. Located in downtown Fredericksburg, Historic Kenmore witnessed the Battle of Fredericksburg in December 1862 as Union forces crossing the Rappahannock River en route to Richmond were blocked by the Confederates. Patches in the roof and walls bear witness to the shells that struck Kenmore during the battle. Following the 1864 Battle of the Wilderness, some of the thousands of wounded soldiers brought to Fredericksburg were hospitalized at Kenmore.

Admission Fees: Adults $5.00, students $3.00, children six and under free, seniors $4.00; group rates and combination ticket to Washington's Ferry Farm available.

Open to Public: Daily 10:00 A.M.–5:00 P.M.; closed Thanksgiving Day and most of the week between Christmas and New Year's Day.

Visitor Services: Restrooms, limited handicapped access, signs, guided tours.

Regularly Scheduled Events: Call or check Web site for schedule of events.

Directions: Take I–95 to Route 3 east. In downtown Fredericksburg, continue on Route 3 Business (William Street) to Washington Avenue. Turn left on Washington, right on Lewis Street, and left back onto Washington to reach Kenmore.

 SPOTSYLVANIA COUNTY MUSEUM

8956 Courthouse Road, Spotsylvania, VA 22553; (540) 582–7167; www .spotsylvania.va.us.

Description: Built in 1856 under the supervision of prominent builder Samuel Alsop, the Old Berea Christian Church was scarred by shots and shells during the 1864 Battle of Spotsylvania Court House. Housed in the well-preserved church, the Spotsylvania County Museum's Civil War exhibit includes weaponry, reproduction uniforms, and information on soldier life.

Admission Fees: Free; donations accepted.

Open to Public: Mon.–Sat. 9:00 A.M.–5:00 P.M.

Visitor Services: Public restroom, museum, genealogical library.

Regularly Scheduled Events: None.

Directions: Take I–95 to Fredericksburg/ Massaponax exit 126. Take Route 1 north to Courthouse Road (Route 208). Make a left on Courthouse Road and take it west to Spotsylvania Court House. Turn left at the

traffic light. The Spotsylvania County Museum will be on the right.

 SPOTSYLVANIA COURT HOUSE HISTORIC DISTRICT

Spotsylvania County Visitors Center– Courthouse, 9102 Courthouse Road, Spotsylvania, VA 22553; Spotsylvania, (540) 507–7996; Fredericksburg, (540) 891–8687; (877) 515–6197; www .spotsylvania.va.us.

Description: Strategically important on the route to Richmond, Spotsylvania Court House was the scene of one of the bloodiest engagements of the war. The Battle of Spotsylvania Court House, one of four Civil War battles that occurred in Spotsylvania County, marked the beginning of the fall of the Confederacy. The county's two visitor centers, in Spotsylvania and Fredericksburg, offer a ten-minute orientation video to the area's history and information on attractions in the Fredericksburg, Spotsylvania, and Stafford areas.

Admission Fees: Free.

Open to Public: Daily 9:00 A.M.–5:00 P.M.; extended summer hours.

Visitor Services: Public restrooms, handicapped access, information, gift shop, tickets, maps, and brochures.

Regularly Scheduled Events: None.

Directions: To reach the Spotsylvania County Visitors Center–Courthouse (in Spotsylvania), take I–95 to Fredericksburg/ Massaponax exit 126. Take Route 1 north to Courthouse Road (Route 208). Make a left on Courthouse Road. After 7 miles the divided highway becomes a two-lane country road. The visitor center will be on your right, just before the stop light at the T junction (in front of the Holbert Building). To reach the Spotsylvania County Visitors Center– Massaponax (in Fredericksburg), take I–95 to Fredericksburg/Massaponax exit 126. Take Route 1 south to Southpoint Parkway on your left. The visitor center will be on your left.

WASHINGTON'S FERRY FARM

268 King's Highway, Fredericksburg, VA 22405; (540) 373–3381; www.ferryfarm .org; mailroom@gwffoundation.org.

Description: The boyhood home of George Washington, Ferry Farm hosted on its property a ferry that crossed the Rappahannock River. During the Civil War, Ferry Farm served as a staging ground for the Union offensive against the Confederate-held city of Fredericksburg. After the bloody battle, the farm served as part of the Union army's winter camp.

Admission Fees: Adults $5.00, students $3.00, children six and under free, seniors $4.00; group rates and combination ticket to Historic Kenmore available.

Open to Public: Daily 10:00 A.M.–5:00 P.M.; closed Thanksgiving Day and most of the week between Christmas and New Year's Day.

Visitor Services: Public restrooms, limited handicapped access, information, interpreters, self-guided tour, trails.

Regularly Scheduled Events: Call or check Web site for schedule of events.

Directions: Take I–95 to Route 3 east. In downtown Fredericksburg, continue on Route 3 Business (William Street) to the Ferry Road intersection, staying in the right lane. Passing through the traffic light, Ferry Farm will be visible on the right. The entrance is about 0.1 mile past Ferry Road.

FRONT ROYAL

 BATTLE OF FRONT ROYAL DRIVING TOUR

Mailing Address: Front Royal Visitors Center, 414 East Main Street, Front Royal, VA 22630; (540) 635–5788 or (800) 338–2576; www.ci.front-royal.va.us; tourism@ci.front–royal.va.us.

Description: The Battle of Front Royal occurred on May 23, 1862, as Gen. Stonewall Jackson, with 16,000 Confederate troops, liberated Front Royal from Union forces. The Confederate First Maryland engaged the Union First Maryland in a decisive battle that completely surprised and baffled Union Gen. Nathaniel Banks, whose forces were camped just 10 miles to the west in Strasburg. The battle so startled President Lincoln and the Union military that they withdrew a large contingent of troops headed for McClellan's planned attack on Richmond and sent them to defend the Shenandoah Valley.

Admission Fees: A free brochure is available from the visitor center; the tour is also offered in book, CD, and cassette tape formats.

Open to Public: Visitor center, daily 9:00 A.M.–5:00 P.M.

Visitor Services: Lodging, public restrooms, information, gas, handicapped access, food, gift shop, museum, trails, camping.

Regularly Scheduled Events: May, Virginia Wine and Craft Festival; October, Festival of Leaves.

Directions: From I–66 exit 13, follow Route 55 west to the visitor center. From I–66 exit 6, take Route 340 south and follow the signs to the visitor center.

 BELLE BOYD COTTAGE

101 Chester Street, Front Royal, VA 22630; (540) 636–1446; www.warrenhs .org.

Description: This 1860 interpretation of a middle-class house emphasizes the life of famed Confederate spy Belle Boyd. The information she gathered helped Gen. Jackson win the Battle of Front Royal.

Admission Fees: Individuals age ten and over $3.00.

Open to Public: Wed.–Fri. 10:00 A.M.–3:30 P.M., Sat. and Sun. by appointment.

Visitor Services: Gift shop, guided tours.

Regularly Scheduled Events: Saturday nearest May 23, Battle of Front Royal Tour;

second Saturday in October, Festival of Leaves.

Directions: From Washington, D.C., take I–66 west. Take exit 13 (Linden/Front Royal), then go 5 miles on Route 55 west to Route 522. Follow Route 522 (Commerce Street) into Front Royal; turn left onto Main Street and right onto Chester Street.

 WARREN RIFLES CONFEDERATE MUSEUM

95 Chester Street, Front Royal, VA 22630; (540) 636–6982 or (540) 635–2219.

Description: Exhibits include memorabilia of Belle Boyd, Mosby's Rangers, Stonewall Jackson, Robert E. Lee, Jefferson Davis, and others, together with arms, uniforms, and historic documents.

Admission Fees: Adults $2.00, children under twelve free.

Open to Public: Apr. 15–Nov. 1, Mon.–Sat. 9:00 A.M.–4:00 P.M., Sun. noon–4:00 P.M.; remainder of year, open by appointment.

Visitor Services: None.

Regularly Scheduled Events: None.

Directions: From I–66 take Front Royal exit; follow Main Street to Chester Street.

GREEN BAY

 SAILOR'S CREEK BATTLEFIELD HISTORICAL STATE PARK CWPT

c/o Twin Lakes State Park, 788 Twin Lakes Road, Green Bay, VA 23942; (434) 392–3435; www.dcr.virginia.gov/state_parks/twi.shtml.

Description: Gen. Robert E. Lee's ragged, hungry army fled Petersburg and Richmond, planning to converge and meet a supply train at Amelia. The expected supplies did not arrive. Then disaster struck. Lee's column bogged down along Sailor's Creek near Rice, and Federals overtook them on April 6, 1865, and decimated the stalled Confederates. Total Confederate losses have been estimated at approximately 8,000.

Admission Fees: Free.

Open to Public: Daily from dawn to dusk.

Visitor Services: Interpretive driving tour.

Regularly Scheduled Events: June–August, Overton-Hillsman House tours; call or check Web site for full schedule of events.

Directions: From Route 360 take Route 307; turn right onto Route 617, which goes through the park. From Route 460 take Route 307; turn left onto Route 617, which goes through the park.

HARRISONBURG

 CROSS KEYS BATTLEFIELD CWPT

c/o Civil War Preservation Trust, 1331 H Street NW, Suite 1001, Washington, DC 20005; (800) 298–7878.

Description: While in pursuit of Stonewall Jackson's army, U.S. Gen. John Frémont encountered the division of Maj. Gen. Richard Ewell on June 8, 1862. Ewell had been charged by Jackson with blocking Frémont's advance. After an artillery duel and infantry attacks made in vain, Frémont pulled back, allowing Ewell to slip across the Shenandoah River, burning the bridge behind him and aiding the balance of Jackson's command in defeating Federal forces at nearby Port Republic.

Admission Fees: Free.

Open to Public: Daily from dawn to dusk.

Visitor Services: None.

Regularly Scheduled Events: None.

Directions: From Harrisburg take Port Republic Road 5 miles. Site will be on the left. Property begins at the crest of the hill by the UDC marker.

 PORT REPUBLIC BATTLEFIELD CWPT

c/o Civil War Preservation Trust, 1331 H Street NW, Suite 1001, Washington, DC 20005; (800) 298–7878.

Description: On June 9, 1862, in the last battle of Stonewall Jackson's Valley Campaign, the Stonewall Brigade was repulsed after an unsupported attack against Union positions held at Port Republic by Gen. James Shields. After Confederate reinforcements arrived, thwarting a Federal counterattack, Gen. Richards Taylor's "Louisiana Tigers" relentlessly assaulted the formidable artillery position, forcing Shields to retreat and leaving Jackson in control of the Upper Valley.

Admission Fees: Free.

Open to Public: Daily from dawn to dusk.

Visitor Services: Walking trails and interpretive signage.

Regularly Scheduled Events: None.

Directions: From Harrisonburg take Port Republic Road through Port Republic; turn left on Route 340. Follow 340 for 1.5 miles and turn right on Route 708. Park at the markers in front of the church.

LEESBURG

 BALL'S BLUFF BATTLEFIELD REGIONAL PARK

Balls Bluff Road, Leesburg, VA 20176; (703) 779–9372; www.nvrpa.org; temple hallfarm@nvrpa.org.

Description: Surrounding the national cemetery, this regional park preserves the site of the Battle of Ball's Bluff, on October 21, 1861, the largest Civil War engagement to take place in Loudoun County. Hiking trails and interpretive signs aid in the understanding of this important and tragic part of American history.

Admission Fees: Free.

Open to Public: Sunrise to sunset every day.

Visitor Services: Information, trails, fishing.

Regularly Scheduled Events: Weekends May–October, free battlefield tours; call for schedule.

Directions: From Route 7 west toward Leesburg, take the Route 15 bypass north. Turn right on Battlefield Parkway. Take the first left onto Ball's Bluff Road. The park is located at the end of the road.

LEXINGTON

 LEE CHAPEL AND MUSEUM

Washington and Lee University, 11 University Place, Lexington, VA 24450-0303; (540) 463–8768; leechapel.wlu.edu; leechapel@wlu.edu.

Description: Built in 1867 during Lee's term as president of Washington College, the chapel contains his office, a museum with items belonging to Lee and his family, the Washington-Custis-Lee portrait collection, his tomb, and the famous recumbent statue of General Lee by Valentine. Lee's horse Traveller is buried nearby.

Admission Fees: Free, donations encouraged.

Open to Public: Apr. 1–Oct. 31, Mon.–Sat. 9:00 A.M.–5:00 P.M., Sun. 1:00 P.M.–5:00 P.M.; Nov. 1–Mar. 31, Mon.–Sat. 9:00 A.M.–4:00 P.M., Sun. 1:00 P.M.–4:00 P.M. Call ahead to verify hours; university needs take priority.

Visitor Services: Public restrooms, handicapped access, gift shop.

Regularly Scheduled Events: October 12, annual Lee memorial service and the program *Remembering Lee.*

Directions: Take I–81 or I–64 to Lexington. Follow Virginia Route 11 Business to Jefferson Street. The Lee Chapel parking lot is at the intersection of Jefferson and Henry Streets.

 STONEWALL JACKSON'S GRAVE

Stonewall Jackson Memorial Cemetery, 312½ South Main Street, Lexington, VA 24450; (540) 463–2931.

Description: Stonewall Jackson's grave is marked by Valentine's bronze statue of the general.

Admission Fees: Free.

Open to Public: Daily from dawn to dusk.

Visitor Services: None.

Regularly Scheduled Events: None.

Directions: From I–64 take exit 55 to Route

11 south, which becomes Jefferson Street. Follow Jefferson Street until it ends. Turn left onto South Main Street, where the cemetery is located.

 ## STONEWALL JACKSON HOUSE

8 East Washington Street, Lexington, VA 24450; (540) 463–2552; www .stonewalljackson.org; sjhl@ rockbridge.net.

Description: This is the only home that Thomas Jonathan "Stonewall" Jackson ever owned, and it is where he lived while a professor of natural philosophy at the Virginia Military Institute. Visitors may stroll in the restored garden and enjoy a guided tour of mid-nineteenth-century rooms where the famous Confederate general lived immediately before the Civil War. Many of his personal possessions are on display.

Admission Fees: Adults $6.00, children under age eighteen $3.00, children under six free, groups with advance reservations $5.00.

Open to Public: Mon.–Sat. 9:00 A.M.–5:00 P.M., Sun. 1:00 P.M.–5:00 P.M. The last tour begins thirty minutes before closing.

Visitor Services: Public restrooms, limited handicapped access, museum shop, museum, gardens.

Regularly Scheduled Events: January 21, Stonewall Jackson's birthday; April (during even years), Biennial Stonewall Jackson Symposium.

Directions: From I–81 take 188N or from I–64 take exit 55. Follow the Historic Lexington Visitor Center signs to Washington Street in downtown Lexington. The Jackson House is located 1 block west of the visitor center.

 ## VIRGINIA MILITARY INSTITUTE MUSEUM

Jackson Memorial Hall, Lexington, VA 24450; (540) 464–7334; www.vmi.edu/ museum.

Description: This museum, rich in Civil War

Stonewall Jackson's grave, Virginia. Roger L. Belton–CWPT files.

history, displays some of Stonewall Jackson's uniforms, including the one he was wearing when he was mortally wounded by his own men, and the mounted hide of his horse, Little Sorrel. The museum is in Jackson Memorial Hall, which features a mural of the heroic cadet charge in the Battle of New Market, May 15, 1864. The graves of six cadets killed in the battle are on the grounds. VMI was shelled and burned by the Union army in June 1864.

Admission Fees: Free.

Open to Public: Sun.–Sat. 9:00 A.M.–5:00 P.M. Museum is closed from mid-December until the beginning of January; please call ahead to confirm schedule.

Visitor Services: Public restrooms, information, handicapped access, gift shop (with a 10 percent discount for CWPT members).

Regularly Scheduled Events: None.

Directions: Located on the Virginia Military Institute Campus. From I–81 take Lexington exit (Route 11) 2 miles to VMI campus.

LYNCHBURG

★ AUTO DRIVING TOUR
104 OF CIVIL WAR LYNCHBURG

757 Sandusky Drive, Lynchburg, VA 24502; (434) 832–0162; www.historic sandusky.org; civilwar@historic sandusky.org.

Description: The driving tour consists of audiocassette or CD and map of the Civil War sites associated with the Battle of Lynchburg, June 17–18, 1864, and Civil War Lynchburg. Stops include battlefield areas, headquarters building, cemeteries, and hospital buildings. Most stops include Civil War Trails signs.

Admission Fees: Nominal charge for audiocassette or CD and map available by mail, or in bookstores throughout central Virginia.

Open to Public: Daily.

Visitor Services: Marked trails.

Regularly Scheduled Events: None.

Directions: I–64 to Route 29 south into Lynchburg. I–81 to I–581 in Roanoke. Take exit 4, onto Route 460 east. Follow Route 460 east into Lynchburg.

★ OLD CITY CEMETERY AND
105 PEST HOUSE MEDICAL MUSEUM

Fourth and Taylor Streets, Lynchburg, VA 24501; (434) 847–1465; www.grave garden.org; occ@gravegarden.org.

Description: The Confederate section of the historic Old City Cemetery contains the individually marked graves of more than 2,200 Confederate soldiers from fourteen states. Excellent records on these burials are available at Cemetery Center. Close by are three small museums that interpret the Civil War period: Pest House Medical Museum, Station House Railroad Museum, and the nineteenth-century Mourning Museum.

Admission Fees: Cemetery, grounds, and Mourning Museum, free; other museums open by tour reservation only, adults $5.00, children $2.00.

Open to Public: Cemetery and grounds of the Pest House, daily from dawn to dusk; tours by appointment.

Visitor Services: Public restrooms, information, handicapped access, gift shop.

Regularly Scheduled Events: Monthly educational programs emphasizing various aspects of cemetery history and horticulture. Please call for additional information.

Directions: From I–64 take Route 29 south to Business Route 29 south at Lynchburg and follow the signs to the cemetery. From I–81 take Route 501 east at Lexington into Lynchburg and follow the signs to the visitor center; or from Route 81 take Route 460 east at Roanoke into Lynchburg and follow the signs to the visitor center.

★ SANDUSKY HISTORIC SITE
106 AND CIVIL WAR MUSEUM

757 Sandusky Drive, Lynchburg, VA 24502; (434) 832–0162; www.historic sandusky.org; civilwar@historic sandusky.org.

Description: The museum is housed in a Federal-style house (ca. 1808) that served as headquarters for Union Gen. David Hunter during the Battle of Lynchburg, June 17–18, 1864. During the war Lynchburg was a vital Confederate rail depot and had a large hospital. Hunter advanced against Lynchburg in June 1864. Gen. John Breckinridge's troops arrived by rail, and, after a brief skirmish on June 18, Hunter, short on supplies, retreated into West Virginia. His retreat opened up the Shenandoah Valley for Confederate Gen. Jubal Early's advance into Maryland, threatening Washington, D.C. A modern visitor center featuring a fifteen-minute orientation film on the Battle of Lynchburg and exhibits on Civil War medicine was scheduled to open spring 2007.

Admission Fees: Nominal charge.

Open to Public: Please call ahead.

Visitor Services: Public restrooms, gift shop.

Regularly Scheduled Events: Third week-

Stone House at Manassas National Military Park, Manassas, Virginia. CWPT files.

end in June, Lynchburg Civil War Days; December, Christmas Open House.

Directions: Located in Lynchburg on Sandusky Drive just off of Business Route 460.

MANASSAS

 THE MANASSAS MUSEUM SYSTEM

9101 Prince William Street, Manassas, VA 20110; (703) 368–1873; www .manassasmuseum.org.

Description: The museum interprets the history and material culture of Manassas and the northern Virginia Piedmont region. Exhibits depict early settlement and plantation life, the building of the railroad junction, the Battles of First and Second Manassas, and the region's post–Civil War reconstruction. The museum system also includes a restored earthwork fortification built by General Beauregard as part of his defense of Manassas Junction.

Admission Fees: Adults $3.00, seniors and children $2.00, groups $2.00/person.

Open to Public: Tues.–Sun. 10:00 A.M.–5:00 P.M.; closed Mon.

Visitor Services: Public restrooms, information, handicapped access, gift shop (a 10 percent discount for CWPT members), museum, walking and driving tours.

Directions: From I–66 east take exit 47 to Virginia 234 south. Proceed south about 3 miles; bear right, following Route 234. Enter Old Town area, travel under the railroad overpass, then turn left at the stoplight (Prince William Street). Proceed to the top of the hill. Museum is on the right. From I–66 west from Washington, D.C., take exit 53; then travel 7.5 miles on Route 28 south. Then follow signs.

 MANASSAS NATIONAL BATTLEFIELD PARK CWPT

6511 Sudley Road, Manassas, VA 20109; (703) 361–1339; www.nps.gov/mana.

Description: Gen. Thomas J. "Stonewall" Jackson figured prominently in two Confederate victories here. Also known as "Bull Run," the First Battle of Manassas on July 21, 1861, ended any illusion of a short war. The Second Battle of Manassas, August 28–30, 1862, brought Southern forces to the height of their military power. The two battles are commemorated on this 5,000-acre battle-field park.

Admission Fees: Adults $3.00, children under seventeen free, seniors free with a Golden Age Pass.

Open to Public: Park, daily dawn to dusk; visitor center, daily 8:30 A.M.–5:00 P.M.

Visitor Services: Public restrooms, handi-capped access, gift shop, museum, picnic area, trails.

Regularly Scheduled Events: May, Memorial Day services in the Confederate cemetery; anniversary programs commemorating the two battles.

Directions: The park is 26 miles southwest of Washington, D.C. The visitor center is on Virginia Route 234 (Sudley Road), 0.75 mile north of I–66 interchange (exit 47B).

MARSHALL

 JOHN MOSBY HERITAGE AREA, RECTOR HOUSE

1461 Atoka Road, Marshall, VA 20115; (540) 687–6681; www.mosbyheritage area.org; info@mosbyheritagearea.org.

Description: Once the stage for Civil War activity in northern Virginia, the Mosby Heritage Area geographically encompasses what was commonly known as "Mosby's Confederacy." Here Col. John Singleton Mosby led his Rangers in dramatic raids and fought many cavalry battles. Brochures, maps, and audio tours outlining a variety of driving tours in the heritage area's seven Virginia and West Virginia counties are available by contacting the Mosby Heritage Area Association, headquartered in the Rector House.

Admission Fees: Rector House and driving tour, free; individual sites vary in admission fees.

Open to Public: Rector House, Mon.–Fri. 9:00 A.M.–5:00 P.M.; closed most major holidays. Individual sites vary in hours.

Visitor Services: Information, free driving tour brochures, audio tours available for purchase, gift shop.

Regularly Scheduled Events: February, Winter Lecture Series (four in the series); October, second weekend, Civil War conference.

Directions: From I–495 take Route 66 west to Route 50, then take 50 west to Middleburg.

MCDOWELL

 McDOWELL BATTLEFIELD CWPT

c/o Civil War Preservation Trust, 1331 H Street NW, Suite 1001, Washington, DC 20005; (800) 298–7878.

Description: The first of Gen. Stonewall Jackson's victories in his 1862 Valley Campaign was the result of Jackson's attempt to stop the Federal brigades of Generals Robert Milroy and Robert Schenck from infiltrating the Shenandoah Valley from western Virginia. On May 8, Milroy attacked Confederate positions on Sitlington Hill and was repulsed after four hours of desperate combat. The Federal retreat into western Virginia allowed Jackson's columns to concentrate on other Union threats in the valley.

Admission Fees: Free.

Open to Public: Daily from sunrise to sunset.

Visitor Services: Pull-off area with interpretive signage, walking trail.

Regularly Scheduled Events: None.

Directions: From I–81 exit at Staunton. Take Route 250 west for about 30 miles. On crossing the crest of Bull Pasture Mountain, you will see a marker noting SITLINGTON HILL— the parking area is shortly after on the left.

MIDDLETOWN

 BELLE GROVE PLANTATION

336 Belle Grove Road, Middletown, VA 22645; (540) 869–2028; www.bellegrove .org; info@bellegrove.org.

Description: The site of the 1864 Battle of Cedar Creek, Belle Grove Plantation was built between 1794 and 1797. Boasting sweeping battlefield views, Belle Grove offers tours of the parlor Gen. Phil Sheridan used as headquarters and the nursery in which General Ramseur died. A fine collection of sketches drawn at Belle Grove during the battle illustrates the tour.

Admission Fees: Adults $8.00, children six–twelve $4.00, seniors $7.00; group rates available.

Open to Public: Apr.–Oct., Mon.–Sat. 10:00 A.M.–4:00 P.M., last tour at 3:15 P.M.; Sun. 1:00 P.M.–5:00 P.M., last tour at 4:15 P.M. Nov.–Dec., only open during special events; closed Jan.–Mar.

Visitor Services: Public restrooms, information, handicapped access, gift shop, museum.

Regularly Scheduled Events: December, Christmas tours.

Directions: From I–66 west take I–81 north. Take exit 302, turn right (west) for 0.5 mile to Route 11. Turn left (south) on Route 11 and go through the town of Middletown; turn right at Belle Grove Road 1 mile south of Middletown.

⭐ 112 CEDAR CREEK BATTLEFIELD VISITORS CENTER CWPT

8437 Valley Pike, Middletown, VA 22645; (540) 869–2064 or (888) 628–1864; www.cedarcreekbattlefield.org; cedarcrk@visuallink.com.

Description: Cedar Creek Battlefield is the site of the last major battle in the Shenandoah Valley, which occurred on October 19, 1864. This dramatic conflict between Jubal Early and Phil Sheridan was the only Civil War battle during which both sides experienced victory and defeat on the same day. The morning rout by Confederate troops was short-lived, as Federal troops counterattacked and captured their camp by nightfall.

Admission Fees: Free.

Open to Public: April–Oct., Mon.–Sat. 10:00 A.M.–4:00 P.M., Sun. 1:00 P.M.–4:00 P.M.; Nov.–Mar., by appointment only.

Visitor Services: Public restrooms, information, gift shop, museum.

Regularly Scheduled Events: Third weekend in October, Cedar Creek living history and reenactment on the actual battlefield.

MIDDLE ATLANTIC

Belle Grove Plantation, Virginia. Chris E. Heisey–CWPT files.

Directions: From I–66 take I–81 north to Middletown, exit 302 (Route 627). Go west on Route 627 to Route 11; go 1 mile south to Cedar Creek.

MOUNT OLIVE

 FISHER'S HILL BATTLEFIELD <u>CWPT</u>

c/o Civil War Preservation Trust, 1331 H Street NW, Suite 1001, Washington, DC 20005; (800) 298–7878.

Description: A key action in the 1864 Shenandoah Valley campaign, this September 22 engagement came on the heels of the Confederate retreat from Third Winchester. Despite holding a formidable defensive position at what was called the "Gibraltar of the Valley," Gen. Phil Sheridan's forces overwhelmed Gen. Jubal Early's line, sending them retreating toward Waynesboro and opening the way for Sheridan to carry out the Federal scorched-earth policy in the valley that came to be known as "The Burning."

Admission Fees: Free.

Open to Public: Daily from dawn to dusk.

Visitor Services: Walking trails with interpretive signage.

Regularly Scheduled Events: None.

Directions: Take exit 298 (Route 11 south) off I–81. Follow the signs for Route 11 through Strasburg. South of Strasburg turn right onto Route 601. Follow this road through the village of Fisher's Hill. (This will involve a turn to the right and then to the left as you cross Tumbling Run.) Continue on 601 until you pass under I–81. The sign for Fisher's Hill and the parking area are on the left.

NEW MARKET

 NEW MARKET BATTLEFIELD STATE HISTORICAL PARK AND HALL OF VALOR MUSEUM <u>CWPT</u>

8895 George Collins Parkway, New Market, VA 22844; (540) 740–3101; www .vmi.edu/newmarket; harrissh@vmi.edu.

Description: At New Market in 1864, about 6,000 Federals under Gen. Franz Sigel clashed with 4,500 Confederates led by Gen. John Breckinridge. The Hall of Valor, focal

Field of Lost Shoes, New Market Battlefield, New Market, Virginia. Chris E. Heisey–CWPT files.

point of the 280-acre battlefield park, presents a survey of the entire Civil War through its exhibits.

Admission Fees: Adults $9.00, children six–seventeen $5.00, seniors $8.00; group rates available.

Open to Public: Daily 9:00 A.M.–5:00 P.M.; closed most major holidays.

Visitor Services: Public restrooms, information, handicapped access, gift shop, museum, picnic areas, trails.

Regularly Scheduled Events: May, reenactment of the Battle of New Market; October, Spirits of New Market Lantern Tour; December, Christmas on the Farm.

Directions: From I–81 take exit 264 at New Market; turn onto Route 211 west and immediately turn right onto Route 305 (George Collins Parkway) and stop at the Visitor Center Contact Station on your left to purchase tickets. The New Market Battlefield State Historical Park is located at the end of George Collins Parkway.

NEWPORT NEWS

 **115 DAM NUMBER 1**

Newport News Park, 13560 Jefferson Avenue, Route 143, Newport News, VA 23603; (757) 886–7912; ww.nnparks.com.

Description: To halt Gen. George McClellan's march up the peninsula toward Richmond, Gen. John B. Magruder built three dams to create impassable lakes on the Warwick River and fortified the dams to prevent frontal assaults by Union forces.

Admission Fees: Free.

Open to Public: Park, daily from dawn to dusk; interpretive center, Memorial Day–Labor Day, Wed.–Sun. 9:00 A.M.–5:00 P.M.; remainder of year, Sat.–Sun. 9:00 A.M.–5:00 P.M.

Visitor Services: Interpretive center.

Regularly Scheduled Events: None.

Directions: From I–64 east take exit 250B, Fort Eustis Boulevard. Turn left at junction

of Fort Eustis Boulevard and Route 143 (Jefferson Avenue). Park is on the right.

 **116 ENDVIEW PLANTATION**

362 Yorktown Road, Newport News, VA 23603; (757) 887–1862; www.endview.org; endview@nngov.com.

Description: Endview was built by Col. William Harwood around 1760. It was the pre–Civil War home of Capt. Humphrey Harwood Curtis, M.D., commander of the Warwick Beauregards (Company H, Thirty-second Virginia Regiment). The house served as a Confederate and a Union hospital during the Peninsula Campaign. The house now serves as a living history museum interpreting the Peninsula Campaign of 1862.

Admission Fees: Adults $6.00, seniors $5.00, children $4.00, group rates available.

Open to Public: Mon. and Wed.–Sat. 10:00 A.M.–4:00 P.M., Sun. 1:00 P.M.–5:00 P.M.; Jan.–Mar., closed Tues.–Wed.

Visitor Services: Information, handicapped access, gift shop, museum, trails.

Regularly Scheduled Events: March, Civil War reenactment; living history programs throughout the year.

Directions: From I–64 east take exit 247, turn left on Route 143 (Jefferson Avenue), then turn left at traffic light at Yorktown Road (Route 238). Endview is 0.25 mile on the right. From I–64 west take exit 247, turn right on Yorktown Road (Route 238), and proceed straight through traffic light. Endview is on the right.

117 LEE HALL MANSION

163 Yorktown Road, Newport News, VA 23603; (757) 888–3371; www.leehall.org.

Description: This Italianate plantation house was built circa 1859 by affluent planter Richard Decatur Lee. Confederate Maj. Gen. John Bankhead McGruder and Gen. Joseph Johnston used the mansion as a headquarters during the 1862 Peninsula

Campaign. A small redoubt on the lawn, built during the campaign, was the site of a Confederate hot-air observation balloon launching.

Admission Fees: Adults $6.00, children seven–eighteen $4.00, seniors $5.00, groups $5.00.

Open to Public: Mon. and Wed.–Sat. 10:00 A.M.–4:00 P.M., Sun. 1:00 P.M.–5:00 P.M. Guided tours are offered every half hour, with the last tour a half hour before closing. Closed on major holidays.

Visitor Services: Public restrooms, information, handicapped access, gift shop, museum, guided tours.

Regularly Scheduled Events: October, An Evening with Edgar Allan Poe; December, A Lee Family Christmas, Antebellum Holidays; various living history programs throughout the year. Call or visit the Web site for more information.

Directions: From I–64 east take exit 247. Turn left on Route 143 (Jefferson Avenue), then right at traffic light at Route 238 (Yorktown Road). Lee Hall is 0.25 mile on the right. From I–64 west take exit 247. Turn left on Route 238 (Yorktown Road). Lee Hall is 0.25 mile on the right.

LEE'S MILL, RIVERSRIDGE CIRCLE

Mailing address: 9285 Warwick Boulevard, Newport News, VA 23607; (757) 247–8523; www.warmuseum.org.

Description: These fortifications overlooking the Warwick River formed part of Confederate Maj. Gen. John Bankhead Magruder's Second Peninsula defensive line. On April 5, 1862, Lee's Mill was the scene of a brief skirmish that stopped Union Maj. Gen. George B. McClellan's march toward Richmond. The Lee's Mill fortifications prompted McClellan to besiege the Confederate defenses during the first phase of the Peninsula Campaign.

Admission Fees: Free.

Open to Public: Daily during daylight hours.

Visitor Services: Interpretive trail, guided tours by appointment.

Regularly Scheduled Events: None.

Directions: From I–64 east take exit 250 onto Route 105 south toward Fort Eustis (second exit). Turn right on Route 60 east. At first traffic light turn right into Lee's Mill subdivision, then turn left on Riversridge Road. Entrance is on the left past town houses. From I–64 west take exit 250 onto Route 105 south toward Fort Eustis (first exit) and follow directions above.

THE MARINERS' MUSEUM

100 Museum Drive, Newport News, VA 23606; (757) 596–2222; ww.mariner.org; marketing@mariner.org.

Description: The Mariners' Museum, which opened in March 2007, is home to the USS *Monitor* Center. The *Monitor* Center is the definitive authority and repository for the original salvaged artifacts, as well as other materials, research, and programming related to the history of the famous Civil War ironclad ship that revolutionized naval warfare. The center also tells the story of the Confederate ironclad CSS *Virginia*, which *Monitor* engaged in an epic battle off Hampton Roads, Virginia, on March 9, 1862.

Admission Fees: Adults $8.00, children six–seventeen $6.00, children five and under free.

Open to Public: Mon.–Sat. 10:00 A.M.–5:00 P.M., Sun. noon–5:00 P.M.; closed Thanksgiving and Christmas.

Visitor Services: Handicapped access, 550-acre park and lake, museum, food.

Regularly Scheduled Events: Call or check Web site for events.

Directions: From I–64 in Newport News, take exit 255 (Jefferson Avenue). Merge onto Jefferson Avenue/Virginia Route 143 east and turn right on J. Clyde Morris Boulevard/Route 312 south. Continue on the Avenue of the Arts and turn left at Museum Drive.

SKIFFES CREEK REDOUBT

9285 Warwick Boulevard, Newport News, VA 23607; (757) 247–8523; www.warmuseum.org.

Description: The Skiffes Creek Redoubt formed part of Confederate Gen. John Bankhead Magruder's Second Peninsula defensive line. The redoubt was constructed in early April 1862 during the Peninsula campaign's Warwick-Yorktown Line siege. The fortification helped defend the right flank of the Confederate defensive line until abandoned during the evening of May 3, 1862.

Admission Fees: Free.

Open to Public: Daily, from sunrise to sunset.

Visitor Services: Information, handicapped access.

Regularly Scheduled Events: None.

Directions: From I–64/Fort Eustis Boulevard interchange, follow Fort Eustis Boulevard west to interchange with Route 60. Take Route 60 west to the first stoplight at Enterprise Drive. Take a left on Enterprise Drive. The redoubt will be on your left.

 VIRGINIA WAR MUSEUM

9285 Warwick Boulevard, Newport News, VA 23607; (757) 247–8523; www.warmuseum.org; info@warmuseum.org.

Description: The museum offers a comprehensive review of U.S. military history since 1775 and, within this context, provides its visitors with a detailed survey of the Civil War.

Admission Fees: Adults $6.00, children seven–eighteen $4.00, seniors sixty-two and older $5.00, active military (with military personnel ID) $1.00.

Open to Public: Mon.–Sat. 9:00 A.M.–5:00 P.M., Sun. 1:00 P.M.–5:00 P.M.

Visitor Services: Public restrooms, handicapped access, gift shop, picnic area.

Regularly Scheduled Events: Call or check Web site for events.

Directions: From I–64 take the Mercury Boulevard/James River Bridge exit (263A from east/263 from west); follow south on Mercury Boulevard to last traffic light before bridge. At the traffic light turn right into Huntington Park; follow signs to the museum.

 YOUNG'S MILL

9285 Warwick Boulevard, Newport News, VA 23607; (757) 247–8523; www.warmuseum.org.

Description: Young's Mill, a circa 1820 tide mill, was situated on Deep Creek. The mill dam provided a crossing for the Hampton (Great Warwick) Road. Confederate Gen. John Bankhead Magruder selected Young's Mill as the right flank of his First Peninsula defensive line in May 1861. When Union Gen. George B. McClellan began his march toward Richmond during the Peninsula campaign, elements of the IV Corps skirmished with Confederate soldiers defending the fortifications surrounding the mill on April 4, 1862.

Admission Fees: Free.

Open to Public: Daily from sunrise to sunset.

Visitor Services: Information, handicapped access.

Regularly Scheduled Events: None.

Directions: From I–64/Oyster Point Road interchange, follow Oyster Point Road to Warwick Boulevard (Route 60). The mill will be on the left side of the road.

PETERSBURG

 BLANDFORD CHURCH AND CEMETERY

111 Rochelle Lane, Petersburg, VA 23803; (804) 733–2396; www.petersburg-va.org; blandfordchurch@mindspring.com.

Description: The church features fifteen stained-glass windows, thirteen of which

PETERSBURG

You can buy a ticket for Blandford Church and Cemetery, the Siege Museum, and Centre Hill Mansion at the Petersburg Visitors Center, 425 Cockade Alley, Petersburg, VA 23803; (800) 368–3595; the prices are adults $11.00, children seven–twelve, seniors, and active military $9.00.

were donated by states in memory of the 30,000 Confederate soldiers buried in the cemetery. The church was used as a field hospital during the war.

Admission Fees: Adults $5.00, children seven–twelve and seniors, and active military $4.00.

Open to Public: Daily 10:00 A.M.–5:00 P.M.; tours every half hour.

Visitor Services: Public restrooms, gift shop, guided tours, picnic area.

Regularly Scheduled Events: June, Confederate Memorial Day ceremony; October, Halloween Cemetery Tour.

Directions: From I–95 north take the Wythe Street exit; turn right on Crater Road; turn left on Rochelle Lane. From I–95 south take Crater Road exit; turn right on Rochelle Lane.

 **CENTRE HILL MANSION**

1 Centre Hill Avenue, Petersburg, VA 23803; (804) 733–2401; www.petersburg-va.org.

Description: The mansion was built in 1823 by Robert Bolling and is a combination of Federal, Greek Revival, and Colonial architectural styles. Two United States presidents, Abraham Lincoln and William Howard Taft, visited the home. After the fall of Petersburg, the mansion was used as a headquarters for the Union army.

Admission Fees: Adults $5.00; children seven–twelve, seniors, and active military $4.00.

Open to Public: Daily 10:00 A.M.–5:00 P.M.; tours every half hour.

Visitor Services: Public restrooms, gift shop, tours.

Regularly Scheduled Events: January, Ghost Watch Night.

Directions: From I–95 south take the Petersburg/Washington Street exit. Go one stoplight, then turn right onto Jefferson Street. Take first left onto Franklin Street; take immediate right to Centre Hill Avenue.

 **HATCHER'S RUN BATTLEFIELD CWPT**

c/o Civil War Preservation Trust, 1331 H Street NW, Suite 1001, Washington, DC 20005; (800) 298–7878.

Description: February 5–7, 1864, saw about 14,000 Southerners hold off a force of more than 34,000 Union troops in what had been an attempt to intercept Confederate supply trains. Although the Federals did not achieve their goal, they were now able to extend their line of entrenchments to the Vaughan Road Crossing of Hatcher's Run. This would put them 3 miles closer to the Southside Railroad and would tighten the vice around the Army of Northern Virginia.

Admission Fees: Free.

Open to Public: Daily from dawn to dusk.

Visitor Services: Interpretive signage.

Regularly Scheduled Events: None.

Directions: From I–85 southwest of Petersburg, get off at the Route 1 south exit just past the Squirrel Level Road exit. Drive approximately 5 miles until you come to Dabney Mill Road (Route 613) on the left (you pass Route 613 on the right earlier, called White Oak Road), turn. Proceed about 2.5 miles, watching for the state historical marker on the right side of the road.

PAMPLIN HISTORICAL PARK AND THE NATIONAL MUSEUM OF THE CIVIL WAR SOLDIER

6125 Boydton Plank Road, Petersburg, VA 23803; (800) 726–7546; www.pamplin park.org; pamplinpark@mindspring .com.

Description: Located on the grounds of the battle of April 2, 1865, which ended the nine-month siege of Petersburg and led to the evacuation of the Confederate capitol at Richmond, Pamplin Historical Park features four award-winning museums, restored antebellum plantation homes, battlefield trails, costumed living history presentations, and guided tours. The park is also the home of Civil War Adventure Camp, where citizens of the twenty-first century can experience life as a Civil War soldier.

Admission Fees: Adults $13.50, children six–eleven $7.50, seniors $12.00; group rates available.

Open to Public: Daily 9:00 A.M.–5:00 P.M.

Visitor Services: Public restrooms, information, handicapped access, food, gift shop, museum, picnic area, interpretive trails, guided walks, living history.

Regularly Scheduled Events: April, Civil War Weekend; July, Old Time Fair; August, Kids Days; October, Plantation Harvest Days.

Directions: From I–85 take exit 63A (U.S. 1 south), Pamplin Park is 1.5 miles down, on left-hand side of the road.

 PETERSBURG NATIONAL BATTLEFIELD CWPT

1539 Hickory Hill Road, Petersburg, VA 23803; (804) 732–3531; www.nps.gov/ pete; pete_superintendent@nps.gov.

Description: The Union army waged a ten-month campaign here in 1864–65 to seize Petersburg, the center of railroads supplying Richmond and the Confederate Army of Northern Virginia. Petersburg National Battlefield consists of several different units, including the following:

Grant's Headquarters at City Point: Between June 1864 and April 1865, City Point was transformed from a sleepy village of fewer than 300 inhabitants into a bustling supply center for the 100,000 Federal soldiers on the siege lines in front of Petersburg and Richmond.

Five Forks Unit: On April 1, 1865, Union forces were able to capture this important crossroads that protected a nearby railroad supply line. The next evening, Petersburg was evacuated, and Lee began his retreat that ended at Appomattox Court House.

Admission Fees: Vehicle $5.00.

Open to Public: Battlefield, dawn to dusk; visitor center, daily 8:00 A.M.–5:00 P.M.

Regularly Scheduled Events: Late March or early April, Annual Battle of Five Forks Living History Program; summer, ranger-guided tours.

Visitor Services: Public restrooms, handicapped access, bookstore, picnic area, trails.

Directions: From I–95 take exit 52; take Wythe Street (Route 36) east to park. The park is located 2.5 miles east of the center of Petersburg on Route 36.

 POPLAR GROVE NATIONAL CEMETERY

1539 Hickory Hill Road, Petersburg, VA 23803; (804) 732–3531; www.nps.gov/ pogr.

Description: The cemetery was established in 1868 for Union soldiers who died during the Petersburg and Appomattox campaigns. Of the 6,178 interments, 4,110 are unknown. Others are buried in the City Point National Cemetery in Hopewell. Most Confederate soldiers who died during the siege are buried in Blandford Cemetery in Petersburg.

Admission Fees: Free.

Open to Public: Daily during daylight hours.

Visitor Services: Public restrooms.

Directions: From I–85 take Squirrel Level Road exit south to Wells Road and follow to

Halifax Road. Turn right. Proceed to Vaughan Road; turn right. Travel approximately 2 miles to cemetery; there is a sign on the left.

 **SIEGE MUSEUM**

15 West Bank Street, Petersburg, VA 23803; (800) 368–3595 or (804) 733–2404; www.petersburg-va.org.

Description: The human side of the ten-month siege of Petersburg is portrayed in exhibits and in a film narrated by Petersburg native Joseph Cotton.

Admission Fees: Adults $5.00, children and seniors $4.00, groups $4.00/person.

Open to Public: Daily 10:00 A.M.–5:00 P.M.

Visitor Services: Public restrooms, handicapped access, gift shop.

Regularly Scheduled Events: Special tours.

Directions: From I–95 take exit 52 (Washington Street). At third traffic light turn right onto Sycamore Street and go to Petersburg Visitors Center at the end of the street for directions.

 **WHITE OAK ROAD BATTLEFIELD** CWPT

c/o Civil War Preservation Trust, 1331 H Street NW, Suite 1001, Washington, DC 20005; (800) 298–7878.

Description: As the Appomattox campaign, and the war, drew to a close, Gen. Gouverneur Warren was determined to cut communications between the commands of Lee and Pickett. On March 31, 1864, Warren's V Corps, in cooperating with Gen. Phil Sheridan's advances through Dinwiddie Court House, assaulted entrenched Confederates on White Oak Road. Gen. Bushrod Johnson's counterattack stemmed the Union tide temporarily, but when the smoke cleared, Warren had secured the crossroads.

Admission Fees: Free.

Open to Public: Daily from sunrise to sunset.

Visitor Services: Walking trail with interpretive signage.

Regularly Scheduled Events: None.

Directions: From Petersburg take I–85 south off I–95. After about 6 miles, exit at Route 1 south. Follow Route 1 for about 8 miles. After crossing Hatcher's Run, turn right onto White Oak Road (Route 613). Go approximately 2.75 miles, then turn right onto Claiborne Road (Route 631). Immediately turn right into the grassy area and park.

RICHMOND

 HOLLYWOOD CEMETERY

412 South Cherry Street, Richmond, VA 23220; (804) 648–8501; www.hollywood cemetery.org; info@hollywoodcemetery .org.

Description: This impressive and gorgeously landscaped cemetery contains the graves of Confederate president Jefferson Davis, Gen. J. E. B. Stuart, Gen. George E. Pickett, and other Confederate notables, as well as 18,000 Confederate soldiers. Presidents James Monroe and John Tyler are also buried at this site. Magnificent holly trees give the cemetery its name.

Admission Fees: Free.

Open to Public: Grounds, daily 8:00 A.M.–5:00 P.M.; office, Mon.–Fri. 8:30 A.M.–4:30 P.M.

Visitor Services: Public restrooms, information, gift shop: tour maps $1.00, generals guide $5.00, Confederate dead listing $10.00.

Regularly Scheduled Events: February, J. E. B. Stuart ceremony; June, Jefferson Davis ceremony.

Directions: From I–95 south take the Belvedere Street exit. At the stoplight turn right and at the next stoplight, turn right. Follow Belvedere to Spring Street. Turn right; go to the end of Spring Street and turn right onto Cherry Street. Travel on Cherry for 1 block; make a U-turn into Hollywood Cemetery.

THE MUSEUM AND WHITE HOUSE OF THE CONFEDERACY

1201 East Clay Street, Richmond, VA 23219; (804) 649–1861; www.moc.org; info@moc.org.

Description: The Museum of the Confederacy, the leading center for the study of the Confederacy, houses the world's largest Confederate Civil War artifact collection, including flags, photos, documents, and other personal effects of legendary generals and common soldiers. The White House of the Confederacy served as Jefferson Davis's executive mansion during the war.

Admission Fees: Museum and White House combination, adults $10.00, students $5.00, seniors $9.00; group rates available.

Open to Public: Mon.–Sat. 10:00 A.M.–5:00 P.M., Sun. noon–5:00 P.M.; closed Wed. and most major holidays.

Visitor Services: Public restrooms, information, handicapped access, gift shop.

Regularly Scheduled Events: Spring, evening lecture series, Annual Fund-raising Weekend: Celebrate South; fall, Roller-Bottimore Lecture Series; summer, day camp opportunities for children, teachers' institute.

Directions: From I–95 take exit 74C (Broad Street) to 11th Street; turn right onto 11th, then right onto Clay Street. The museum is 2 blocks down on Clay Street, on the right. Parking is straight ahead in the hospital parking deck adjacent to the museum.

RICHMOND NATIONAL BATTLEFIELD PARK <u>CWPT</u>

470 Tredegar Street, Richmond, VA 23219; (804) 771–2145; www.nps.gov/rich; rich_interpretation@nps.gov.

Description: Commemorates several battles to capture Richmond, which was the Confederate capital during the Civil War. From the beginning of the war, "On to Richmond" was the rallying cry of Union troops, and the city was their primary objective for four years. Extensive remains of Union and Confederate earthworks are preserved. Included battlefields are Gaines Mill, Malvern Hill, Glendale, and Cold Harbor. Featuring three floors of exhibits, the main visitor center occupies one of the surviving buildings that made up the Tredegar Ironworks.

Admission Fees: Free; parking fee applies.

Open to Public: Park, daily dawn to dusk; visitor center, daily 9:00 A.M.–5:00 P.M.

Visitor Services: Public restrooms, information, handicapped access, food, gift shop, museum, trails.

Regularly Scheduled Events: April, Civil War Day; summer, battlefield talks and tours. Please call or visit the Web site for more information.

Directions: From I–95 north take exit 74C west; from I–95 south take exit 75; from I–64 west take the Fifth Street exit (Downtown).

133A GAINES MILL BATTLEFIELD

Description: On June 27, 1862, Confederate forces under Gen. A. P. Hill and Gen. James Longstreet attacked Gen. Fitz John Porter's forces at Gaines Mill, during the Peninsula campaign. Due to poor coordination of Southern commanders, Porter was able to hold his line long enough for Gen. George McClellan to reposition his forces on the James River, while exacting severe casualties on Confederacy forces.

Admission Fees: Free.

Open to Public: Daily from dawn to dusk.

Visitor Services: None.

Regularly Scheduled Events: None.

Directions: From I–95 to I–295 exit onto Route 156 north (Cold Harbor Road). Make a right-hand turn at the stoplight in order to remain on Route 156. Follow the Gaines Mill Battlefield signs.

133B MALVERN HILL BATTLEFIELD

Description: Last of the Seven Days' Battles of the Peninsula Campaign, July 1, 1862.

Gen. George McClellan's II and V Corps, retreating along the James River, defended the strong natural position of Malvern Hill against Gen. Robert E. Lee's assault. While the Army of the Potomac continued its retreat, it inflicted great losses on the disorganized Confederate forces.

Admission Fees: Free.

Open to Public: Daily from dawn to dusk.

Visitor Services: None.

Regularly Scheduled Events: None.

Directions: From I–295 take exit 22A and go east on Route 5, New Market Road. Turn northeast on Long Bridge Road, turn south on Carter's Mill Road, and turn northeast on Willis Church Road to CWPT signage. There are also other interpretive markers in the area.

133C GLENDALE BATTLEFIELD AND VISITORS CENTER

Description: On June 30, 1862, the sixth day of the Seven Days' Battles, the disorganized attack of the Army of Northern Virginia across White Oak Swamp was repulsed by the Army of the Potomac. Gen. Robert E. Lee was once again unsuccessful in cutting off Gen. George McClellan's escape from the peninsula.

Admission Fees: Free.

Open to Public: Daily from dawn to dusk; visitor center, June–Aug. daily 9:00 A.M.–5:00 P.M.

Visitor Services: Visitor center.

Regularly Scheduled Events: None.

Directions: From I–295 take exit 22A and go east on Route 5 (New Market Road). Turn north on Long Bridge Road, east on Darbytown Road, and south on Charles City Road. Turn west on Western Run Road to CWPT signage. There are also other interpretive markers in the area.

133D COLD HARBOR BATTLEFIELD AND VISITORS CENTER

Description: On the night of May 31, 1864, both Union and Confederate forces converged on Old Cold Harbor, along the flat lowlands of the Chickahominy River. The following twelve days saw Gen. Ulysses Grant's Army of the Potomac attacking the heavily entrenched line of the Army of Northern Virginia in what was one of the bloodiest battles in history. Although it was a great Confederate victory, they were never able to replace their losses in the field.

Admission Fees: Free.

Open to Public: Daily from dawn to dusk; visitor center, daily 9:00 A.M.–5:00 P.M.

Visitor Services: Information, public restrooms, exhibits, gift shop.

Regularly Scheduled Events: None.

Directions: From I–95 to I–295 exit onto Route 156 north (Cold Harbor Road). Make a right-hand turn at the stoplight in order to remain on Route 156. Continue past Gaines Mill Battlefield. The Cold Harbor Battlefield is 0.5 mile farther.

 ### THE VALENTINE RICHMOND HISTORY CENTER

1015 East Clay Street, Richmond, VA 23219; (804) 649–0711; www.richmond historycenter.com; info@richmond historycenter.com.

Description: The Valentine collects, preserves, and interprets the materials of the life and history of Richmond, including the Civil War. The studio contains the bust statues of Robert E. Lee, Stonewall Jackson, Albert Sidney Johnston, Jefferson Davis, G. E. Pickett, and other Confederate Civil War figures, as well as the plaster cast of *Recumbent Lee.* The 1812 Wickham House, a National Historic Landmark, illustrates the social and architectural history of that time period. The Valentine maintains the South's largest costume and textile collection and extensive holdings in photographs, documents, industrial artifacts, and decorative arts. Lunch is served year-round in the garden.

Admission Fees: Museum, adults $7.00, children seven–twelve $4.00, three–six $1.00, students and seniors $6.00.

Open to Public: Museum, Tues.–Sat. 10:00 A.M.–5:00 P.M., Sun. noon–5:00 P.M.; closed Mon.

Visitor Services: Public restrooms, food.

Regularly Scheduled Events: None.

Directions: From I–95, take exit 74C (Broad Street). Turn right onto Broad Street, then right onto 11th. Turn left at Clay Street, then left on 10th. The museum parking lot is on the left.

 THE VIRGINIA CAPITOL

Capitol Square, Richmond, VA 23219; (804) 698–1788; legis.state.va.us; vacap tours@leg.state.va.us.

Description: Designed by Thomas Jefferson, this officially became the capitol of the Confederacy on May 21, 1861. The Congress of the Confederacy shared the building with the Virginia State Legislature from July 1861 to March 1865. In February 1862 Confederate president Jefferson Davis was inaugurated on the grounds of Capitol Square. A statue of Robert E. Lee and busts of Confederate heroes Stonewall Jackson, J. E. B. Stuart, Joseph E. Johnson, and Fitzhugh Lee, among others, are located here.

Admission Fees: Free.

Open to Public: Mon.–Sat. 9:00 A.M.–5:00 P.M.

Visitor Services: Guided tours, handicapped access, gift shop.

Regularly Scheduled Events: None.

Directions: From I–95 take Third Street exit (Coliseum) and continue straight. Turn left onto Franklin Street, then left onto Ninth Street. Capitol Square is the first right.

 VIRGINIA HISTORICAL SOCIETY

428 North Boulevard, Richmond, VA 23220; (804) 358–4901; www.vahistorical .org.

Description: The Virginia Historical Society offers the most comprehensive collection of Virginia history in existence and features the largest display of Virginia artifacts on permanent view. At its center is *The Story of Virginia: An American Experience.* The exhibition's Civil War section features the work of Union soldier Pvt. Robert Knox Sneden, who spent thirteen months in Confederate captivity, including some time at Andersonville. Sneden produced nearly 1,000 Civil War watercolors, considered the largest collection of Civil War soldier art produced, and a 5,000-page memoir. The Mural Gallery features *Four Seasons of the Confederacy,* Civil War murals by French artist Charles Hoffbauer, and a display of the largest collection of Confederate-made weaponry in the world. The Battle Abbey, part of the VHS complex, is a memorial to the Confederate soldier, and the Civil War horse statue stands as a memorial to all horses and mules that were war casualties. The research library offers access to countless Civil War documents.

Admission Fees: Adults $5.00, seniors $4.00 ($2.00 on Tuesdays), students and children $3.00. Free on Sun. and for Historical Society members.

Open to Public: Mon.–Sat. 10:00 A.M.–5:00 P.M., Sun. (galleries only) 1:00 P.M.–5:00 P.M.; library closed Sun.; VHS closed most major holidays.

Visitor Services: Public restrooms, information, handicapped access, gift shop, museum, research library.

Regularly Scheduled Events: Call for information on lectures and special events held year-round.

Directions: From I–95 take exit 78; turn onto Boulevard heading south, then take a left on Kensington Avenue and enter the parking lot.

STRASBURG

 HUPP'S HILL BATTLEFIELD PARK: STONEWALL JACKSON MUSEUM AND CRYSTAL CAVERNS AT HUPP'S HILL

33229 Old Valley Pike, Strasburg, VA 22657; (540) 465–5884; www.wayside ofva.com; wayside@shentel.net.

Description: Hupp's Hill Battlefield Park, site of an 1864 battle, has interpreted walking trails along original trenches. Stonewall Jackson Museum interprets Jackson's 1862 Valley Campaign and selected battles of the 1864 Valley Campaign with many hands-on exhibits. Crystal Caverns was used as a hiding place for escaped slaves in the Underground Railroad network and as a field hospital and a prison camp during the war.
Admission Fees: Museum, adults $5.00; children, seniors, and military $4.00. Caverns, adults $10.00, children $8.00, seniors and military $4.00.
Open to Public: Daily 10:00 A.M. to 5:00 P.M.
Visitor Services: Public restrooms, information, handicapped access (museum), gift shop, museum, vending machines, trails.
Regularly Scheduled Events: October, Battlefield Lantern Tour.
Directions: From I–81 take exit 298 and travel south on U.S. 11 for 0.5 mile; turn right at the signs.

STRATFORD

 STRATFORD HALL PLANTATION

483 Great House Road, Stratford, VA 22558; (804) 493–8038; www.stratford hall.org.

Description: Built by Thomas Lee in the 1730s, Stratford Hall Plantation is the birthplace of Robert E. Lee and was home to four generations of the Lee family, including the only brothers to sign the Declaration of Independence: Richard Henry Lee and Francis Lightfoot Lee. Stratford was also home to Henry "Light Horse Harry" Lee, Revolutionary War hero. The 1,700-acre working plantation includes the Great House; newly renovated visitor center; formal flower, vegetable, and boxwood gardens; log cabin dining room; and gift shop.
Admission Fees: Adults $10.00, children six–eleven $5.00, seniors and military $9.00; group rates available.
Open to Public: Daily 9:30 A.M.–4:00 P.M.; tours begin on the hour; closed most major holidays.
Visitor Services: Gift shop, tours.
Regularly Scheduled Events: None.
Directions: From Richmond take Virginia Route 360 through Rappahannock to Warsaw; take Route 3 west to Route 214 to Stratford Hall. From I–95 at Fredericksburg take Route 3 east to Route 214; go 2 miles. The gate is on the left.

WILLIAMSBURG

 COLONIAL WILLIAMSBURG

P.O. Box 1776, Williamsburg, VA 23187; (757) 229–1000 or (800) HISTORY; www .colonialwilliamsburg.org; info@cwf.org.

Description: Known worldwide as the nation's largest living history museum, Colonial Williamsburg operates the restored eighteenth-century capital of colonial Virginia. Although the primary focus of the 173-acre property is the Colonial period, there are a number of Civil War–related sites to be explored in the town. In addition to being the site of the Battle of Williamsburg (May 5, 1862), the town was a central mustering point for Confederates in 1861. Several Confederate hospitals were located here. Beginning in mid-1862, the town was occupied by Federal forces for three years. Much of the battlefield, several Confederate redoubts, and

many Civil War–specific buildings survive.
Admission Fees: Capitol Day Pass (single-day admission to selected sites), adults $34, children six–seventeen $15; passes to additional sites and annual passes available.
Open to Public: Daily 9:00 A.M.–5:00 P.M., with seasonal variations. Evening programs are also available. Please call for additional information.
Visitor Services: Lodging, public restrooms, gas, handicapped access, food, gift shops, museum, tours, visitor center.
Regularly Scheduled Events: July Fourth celebrations, including fireworks and entertainment; second Sunday after Thanksgiving, Grand Illumination held, including fireworks and entertainment; Colonial Williamsburg holiday celebrations held from Thanksgiving to New Year's Day.
Directions: From I–64 east take exit 238. Turn right onto Virginia 143 east, then turn right onto Route 132 south and go through the traffic light and bear to the left, following the signs to the visitor center.

WINCHESTER

 STONEWALL CONFEDERATE CEMETERY
Mount Hebron Cemetery, 305 East Boscawen Street, Winchester, VA 22601; (540) 662–4868; www.mthebroncemetery.org.

Description: Part of the Third Battle of Winchester, this cemetery contains the remains of more than 3,000 Confederate soldiers killed in nearby battles. Some of the Civil War notables buried here are the Ashby brothers (Gen. Turner Ashby and Capt. Richard Ashby) and the Patton brothers (George and Tazewell Patton, grandfather and granduncle of World War II's Gen. George Patton). Stonewall Confederate Cemetery is part of Mount Hebron Cemetery.
Admission Fees: Free.
Open to Public: Grounds, daily 7:00 A.M.–5:00 P.M.; office, Mon.–Fri. 8:00 A.M.–5:00 P.M.

Visitor Services: A roster listing the Confederate burials is available from the office ($5.00).
Regularly Scheduled Events: June, Confederate Memorial Day.
Directions: From I–81 take Route 7, which turns into Berryville Avenue. Turn left on Pleasant Valley Road and proceed 1 block. Follow the iron fence to the gatehouse entrance.

 STONEWALL JACKSON'S HEADQUARTERS MUSEUM
415 North Braddock Street, Winchester, VA 22601; (540) 667–3242; www.winchesterhistory.org; cshull@winchesterhistory.org.

Description: This house served as the headquarters of Confederate Gen. Thomas J. "Stonewall" Jackson from November 1861 to March 1862. From here Jackson familiarized himself with the terrain that would later play a vital role in his famous Shenandoah Valley Campaign.
Admission Fees: Adults $5.00, children seven–eighteen $2.50, seniors (60+) $4.50, groups of twenty or more $4.00.
Open to Public: Apr.–Oct., Mon.–Sat. 10:00 A.M.–4:00 P.M., Sun. noon–4:00 P.M.; Nov., Dec., and Mar., Fri. and Sat. 10:00 A.M.–4:00 P.M., Sun. noon–4:00 P.M.; closed Jan. and Feb.
Visitor Services: Public restrooms, information, gift shop, museum.
Regularly Scheduled Events: None.
Directions: From I–81 take exit 313. Follow Millwood Pike to Pleasant Valley Road, then turn left onto Cork, right onto Cameron, left onto Piccadilly, right onto Loudon Street, left onto North Avenue, and finally left onto Braddock Street. Follow the signs.

 THIRD WINCHESTER BATTLEFIELD CWPT
c/o Civil War Preservation Trust, 1331 H Street NW, Suite 1001, Washington, DC 20005; (800) 298–7878.

Description: The largest of all battles fought

in the Shenandoah Valley saw Gen. Jubal Early's command outnumbered three to one against Gen. Phil Sheridan's 35,000-man force. Though manning a stubborn resistance and despite a stunning counterattack by the divisions of Generals Gordon and Rodes, Early's army was eventually overwhelmed and sent reeling through the streets of Winchester, effectively sealing the Confederacy's fate in the valley.

Admission Fees: Free.

Open to Public: Daily from dawn to dusk.

Visitor Services: Walking and biking trails and interpretive signs have been installed.

Regularly Scheduled Events: None.

Directions: From I–80 south take the Route 11 exit. Take a left off the exit ramp onto Route 11. Turn right at the first road that you see, Redbud Road, and follow it for about 1 mile. The site will be on the right-hand side.

YORKTOWN

 COLONIAL NATIONAL HISTORICAL PARK

Mailing Address: P.O. Box 210, Yorktown, VA 23690; (757) 898–3400; www.nps.gov/colo.

Description: Though established to commemorate the Colonial era, this park also possesses extensive vestiges of the Civil War. In spring 1862 Union Gen. George B. McClellan began his Peninsula Campaign to capture Richmond. Confederate Gen. John B. Magruder fortified Yorktown and southward, blocking McClellan's advance. McClellan began siege operations. On the night of May 3–4, 1862, two days before McClellan's grand bombardment was to begin, the Confederates withdrew. Yorktown became a Union garrison and served as headquarters for the Federally held district of Eastern Virginia until mid-1864.

Admission Fees: Adults $5.00, children sixteen and under free.

Open to Public: Visitor center, daily 9:00 A.M.–5:00 P.M.; closed on Christmas.

Visitor Services: Public restrooms, information, visitor center.

Regularly Scheduled Events: Memorial Day weekend, Civil War weekend.

Directions: From I–64 west take exit 242B, Route 199; take Route 199 east to the Colonial Parkway and follow the signs to Yorktown. From I–64 east take exit 250B and follow Route 105 to Route 17; take Route 17 north to the exit for Yorktown via the Colonial Parkway. From the north or south, follow Route 17 and take the exit for Yorktown, via the Colonial Parkway.

❖ WEST VIRGINIA ❖

BARTOW

 CAMP ALLEGHENY

c/o Monongahela National Forest, 200 Sycamore Street, Elkins, WV 26241; (304) 636–1800; www.fs.fed.us/r9/mnf.

Description: Established by Confederate forces in the summer of 1861 to control the Staunton-Parkersburg Turnpike, this camp, at 4,400 feet above sea level, was one of the highest of the Civil War. Although Confederate Gen. Edward Johnson's troops won the battle against Union forces under the command of Gen. R. H. Milroy, the loss of men because of the harsh winter climate and the logistical nightmare of keeping the camp supplied contributed to the decision to abandon it in April 1862.

Admission Fees: Free.

Open to Public: Daily from dawn to dusk.

Visitor Services: Interpretive signs.

Regularly Scheduled Events: None.

Directions: From I–81 at Staunton, take U.S. 250 west to just beyond the Virginia–West Virginia line; turn left at County Road

3, and take a right at the T. Go 2 more miles. *NOTE:* Road is sometimes closed due to snow; call (304) 636–1800 for road information.

BEVERLY

RICH MOUNTAIN BATTLEFIELD CIVIL WAR SITE CWPT

P.O. Box 227, Beverly, WV 26253; (304) 637–RICH (7424); www.richmountain .org; richmt@richmountain.org.

Description: Rich Mountain Battlefield Civil War Site includes the battle site, Confederate Camp Garnett, and the connecting section of the old Staunton–Parkersburg Turnpike. On July 11, 1861, Union troops under Gen. George B. McClellan routed Confederates holding the pass over Rich Mountain. This victory led to General McClellan's appointment to command the Army of the Potomac. It also gave the Union control of northwestern Virginia, allowing the formation of the state of West Virginia two years later. Visitors are strongly encouraged to go to the visitor center at Millstone Road, Napier, for directions and information before proceeding to the battle site at the top of the mountain.

Admission Fees: Free.

Open to Public: Daily from dawn to dusk; Beverly Visitors Center, Mon.–Fri. 9:00 A.M.–4:00 P.M. Also open from May–Oct. on Sat. 9:00 A.M.–4:00 P.M., Sun. noon–4:00 P.M.; call ahead to verify seasonal hours.

Visitor Services: Battle site: trails, lookouts, visitor center: brochures, display, gift shop.

Regularly Scheduled Events: July (odd-numbered years), biennial reenactment/living history.

Directions: From I–79 take exit 99 at Weston. Take U.S. 33 east to Elkins, then U.S. 219/250 south to Beverly. Turn west in Beverly onto Rich Mountain Road and follow road 5 miles up the mountain to battlefield. Camp Garnett is 1.5 miles farther. *NOTE:*

Road is sometimes closed due to snow. Call ahead and check local weather information.

BURNSVILLE

BULLTOWN HISTORIC AREA

c/o Burnsville Lake, Corps of Engineers, HC 10, Box 24, Burnsville, WV 26335; (304) 452–8170 (visitor center, May–Sept.), (304) 853–2371 (office); www.lrh .usace.army.mil/projects/lakes/bus/ bulltown.

Description: The Battle of Bulltown occurred at the site of fortifications on a knoll overlooking a key covered bridge that once crossed the Little Kanawha River along the Weston–Gauley Turnpike. The highway was the artery for transportation in central West Virginia, connecting the northern and southern portions of the state. Had Confederate commander (and Stonewall Jackson's cousin) Col. William L. "Mudwall" Jackson's assault on Bulltown been successful, he would have cut communications between troops in northern West Virginia and the Kanawha Valley, creating an opportunity to march on Wheeling, the center of Union support in West Virginia.

At the site are fortifications dug to protect the fort, the burial site of seven unknown Confederate soldiers, intact sections of the turnpike, and the Cunningham House. The Cunningham House housed supporters of the Confederacy at the time of the Civil War. Today it serves as the center for Historic Bulltown Village, including farm buildings, two relocated log homes, and the log St. Michael's Church that date from before the Civil War.

Admission Fees: Free.

Open to Public: Interpretive center, May–Sept. 10:00 A.M.–6:00 P.M.

Visitor Services: Interpretive center, information, restrooms, handicapped access (some trails are paved; unpaved trails may require someone to assist those in wheelchairs), camping, trails; seasonal tours of battlefield and historic village or by appointment.

Regularly Scheduled Events: None.

Directions: From I–79 exit at Flatwoods or Roanoke and follow signs for Bulltown, Burnsville Lake (approximately 10 miles from Flatwoods and 20 miles from the Roanoke exit on U.S. 19 and Route 4). Look for a sign that reads BULLTOWN CAMPGROUND/HISTORICAL AREA (Millstone Road). Travel 1 mile and take the first left to find parking area.

DURBIN

 CHEAT SUMMIT FORT

c/o Monongahela National Forest, 200 Sycamore Street, Elkins, WV 26241; (304) 636–1800; www.fs.fed.us/r9/mnf.

Description: Gen. George B. McClellan ordered this pit-and-parapet fort to be built in 1861 under the command of Gen. R. H. Milroy to secure the Staunton–Parkersburg Turnpike and protect the Baltimore and Ohio Railroad. The Confederate failure to take the fort in September 1861 was central to the failure of Robert E. Lee's western Virginia campaign.

Admission Fees: Free.

Open to Public: Daily from dawn to dusk.

Visitor Services: Brochure, interpretive signs, viewing platform, trails.

Regularly Scheduled Events: April or early May, semiannual living history and reenactment.

Directions: From I–79 near Weston, take U.S. 33 east to Elkins, then U.S. 250 south to just before Cheat Bridge. Turn right at the sign and right again at the T. Go about 1 mile to the top. *NOTE:* Road is sometimes closed due to snow; call (304) 636–1800 for road information.

GRAFTON

 GRAFTON NATIONAL CEMETERY

431 Walnut Street, Grafton, WV 26354; (304) 265–2044; www.cem.va.gov.

Description: Grafton was established in 1867 by congressional legislation to offer a final resting place for the men who died during the Civil War. Burials were removed from other cemeteries to make Grafton the final resting place for 2,133 soldiers, including 664 unknown soldiers. Grafton is notably the site of the grave of the first casualty of land engagement of the Civil War, Pvt. T. Bailey Brown.

Admission Fees: Free.

Open to Public: Daily from dawn to dusk.

Visitor Services: Information, restrooms.

Regularly Scheduled Events: May, Memorial Day parade and service—continuous since 1879; November, Veterans Day service.

Directions: From I–79 take exit 124 (Jerry Drive/Route 279E) then take Route 50 east for 14 miles.

HARPERS FERRY

 HARPERS FERRY NATIONAL HISTORICAL PARK CWPT

P.O. Box 65, Harpers Ferry, WV 25425; (304) 535–6029; www.nps.gov/hafe.

Description: Site of abolitionist John Brown's 1859 raid on the First Federal Arsenal. Harpers Ferry changed hands eight times during the war. It became the base of operations for Union invasions into the Shenandoah Valley. Gen. Stonewall Jackson achieved his most brilliant victory here in September 1862 when he captured 12,500 Union soldiers.

Admission Fees: Bicycles, motorcycles, and walk-ins $4.00, cars $6.00.

Open to Public: Daily 8:00 A.M.–5:00 P.M.

Visitor Services: Museum, gift shop, information, restrooms, handicapped access, trails.

Regularly Scheduled Events: September, Battle of Harpers Ferry living history weekend; call or check the Web site for full schedule of events.

Directions: From Washington take I–270 north to I–70 to Route 340 west. From Gettysburg take Maryland Route 15 south to Route 340 west. From Shenandoah Valley take I–81 north to West Virginia 51 east. From Baltimore take I–70 west to Route 340 west.

HILLSBORO

 DROOP MOUNTAIN BATTLEFIELD STATE PARK

HC 64 Box 189, Hillsboro, WV 24946; (304) 653–4254 or (800) CALL–WVA; www.droopmountainbattlefield.com; droomountain@wvdnr.gov.

Description: Droop Mountain Battlefield is the site of one of West Virginia's largest and last important Civil War battles. The battle was fought on November 6, 1863, between the Union army of Gen. William Averell and the Confederate army of Gen. John Echols. Echols's army was pushed south into Virginia and never regained control of southeastern West Virginia.

Admission Fees: Free.

Open to Public: Daily 6:00 A.M.–10:00 P.M. The park is open year-round but is often unattended in winter. Please call (304) 653–4254 for tour information.

Visitor Services: Museum, information, restrooms, trails, lookout tower.

Regularly Scheduled Events: Second weekend of October (in even-numbered years), biennial battle reenactment.

Directions: Take I–64 to Lewisburg; travel north on U.S. 219 for 27 miles.

LESAGE

 JENKINS PLANTATION MUSEUM

8814 Ohio River Road, Lesage, WV 25537; (304) 762–1059; www.wvculture .org/sites/jenkins.html; jenkins plantation@wvculture.org.

Description: Jenkins Plantation was the home of Confederate Brig. Gen. Albert Gallatin Jenkins. Jenkins led the Eighth Virginia and served in the CSA Congress. Jenkins was wounded at Gettysburg but recovered and continued to serve the Confederacy. He was mortally wounded at the Battle of

Jenkins Plantation Museum, Lesage, West Virginia. CWPT files.

BELLE BOYD

Isabelle "Belle" Boyd was one of the Confederacy's most famous spies. She grew up in Martinsburg, Virginia (now West Virginia), in a family with strong Southern ties. During the Civil War her father was a soldier in the Stonewall Brigade, and at least three other members of her family were convicted of being Confederate spies. On July 4, 1861, she shot and killed a Union soldier who was accosting her mother in her home. According to her autobiography, *In Camp and Prison*, Boyd also passed military information to Gen. Stonewall Jackson a number of times during his 1862 Valley campaign and in particular at the battle of Front Royal on May 23, 1862.

According to the story, Boyd was visiting her aunt in Front Royal when her aunt's house was seized by Union soldiers. Boyd eavesdropped on the soldiers as they planned their next move. She then crossed the battle lines just before the battle began, in order to get the information to Jackson. She was fired on by Union troops but arrived safely with valuable information about troop strength, disposition, and intentions.

Boyd was well known to the Union army and the press, who dubbed her "La Belle Rebelle," "the Siren of the Shenandoah," and the "Secesh Cleopatra."

Boyd was arrested six or seven times and imprisoned in Washington, D.C. Not a model inmate, Boyd waved Confederate flags from her window, sang "Dixie," and devised a unique way of communicating with the outside world. Her contact would throw a rubber ball into her cell, and Boyd would sew messages inside the ball and toss it back through the bars in the window.

BERKELEY COUNTY HISTORICAL SOCIETY

Cloyd's Mountain in May 1864. His family home, on what was once a 4,400-acre slave plantation, is restored to mid-nineteenth-century appearance.

Admission Fees: Free.

Open to Public: Tues.–Sat. 10:00 A.M.–4:00 P.M.

Visitor Services: Public restrooms, information.

Regularly Scheduled Events: February, African-American History Month; May, Civil War Camp; September, Annual Homestead Gathering; December, Holiday Party.

Directions: From I–64 take the Barboursville exit 18. Take Merritts Creek Road north, following signs toward West Virginia 2. Turn right on West Virginia 2, travel north 10.4 miles. Jenkins Plantation Museum is on the left.

LEWISBURG

LEWISBURG NATIONAL REGISTER HISTORIC DISTRICT/GREENBRIER COUNTY VISITOR CENTER

540 North Jefferson Street, Lewisburg, WV 24901; (800) 833–2068; www.green brierwv.com; info@greenbrierwv.org.

Description: Lewisburg was the site of a Civil War battle on May 23, 1862, when Union forces attempted to sever railroad communications between Virginia and Tennessee. There is a Confederate cemetery in town, a library used as a hospital with Confederate graffiti on the walls, a church with a cannonball hole, another church that served as a Confederate morgue, and a monument to the Confederate dead.

Admission Fees: Free, except for the North House ($4.00). A detailed walking tour guide is free at the visitor center.

Open to Public: Visitor center, Mon.–Fri. 10:00 A.M.–5:00 P.M.; Memorial Day–Thanksgiving, also open Sat. 10:00 A.M.–4:00 P.M., Sun. noon–4:00 P.M.; North House Museum, Mon.–Sat. 10:00 A.M.–4:00 P.M.

Visitor Services: Lodging, gas, food, museum, gift shop, information, restrooms, camping, trails.

Regularly Scheduled Events: None.

Directions: From I–64 take exit 169. Travel south on U.S. 219 for 1.5 miles; the visitor center will be on your right.

MARTINSBURG

 ### BELLE BOYD HOUSE/ CIVIL WAR MUSEUM OF THE LOWER SHENANDOAH VALLEY

126 East Race Street, Martinsburg, WV 25401; (304) 267–4713; www.bchs.org; bchs15@earthlink.net.

Description: Belle Boyd, West Virginia's best-known Civil War spy, lived in this house. Belle endorsed the Confederate cause, even shooting a Yankee soldier. She supplied information to Stonewall Jackson about enemy activities and was imprisoned twice. Also on-site is the Civil War Museum of the Lower Shenandoah Valley and the Berkeley County Museum. The Archives and Research Center offers facilities to research the local Berkeley, Jefferson, and Morgan areas.

Admission Fees: Free.

Open to Public: Mon.–Sat. 10:00 A.M.–4:00 P.M.; closed Wed., Sun., and major holidays. Belle Boyd House is closed Christmas–April 15; tours available by appointment.

Visitor Services: Gift shop, information, restrooms, museum, research archives, handicapped access.

Regularly Scheduled Events: Second Saturday in May, Heritage Day; first weekend in September following Labor Day, fall his-

toric house tour; three weekends following Thanksgiving, Christmas open house.

Directions: From I–81 take Route 9 east into Martinsburg (Route 9 turns into Queen Street). Go under the railroad bridge and make the first left onto Commerce about 2 blocks, and you will be facing the Belle Boyd House.

PHILIPPI

 ### PHILIPPI COVERED BRIDGE

108 North Main Street, Philippi, WV 26416; (304) 457–3700; www.philippi .org/bridge.

Description: The bridge was on the site of the first land battle of the Civil War on June 3, 1861. During this battle Union troops took command of the bridge and used it as a barracks.

Admission Fees: Free.

Open to Public: Daily from dawn to dusk.

Visitor Services: Lodging, gas, gift shop, information, restrooms, handicapped access, camping, trails.

Regularly Scheduled Events: None.

Directions: From I–79 take exit 115; follow Route 20 south to Route 57 east and take U.S. 119 north to Philippi (22 miles from exit 115).

 ### PHILIPPI HISTORIC DISTRICT

108 North Main Street, Philippi, WV 26416; (304) 457–3700; www.philippi.org.

Description: The city of Philippi was the site of the first land battle of the Civil War on June 3, 1861. It was also the site of the first amputation of the Civil War, on James Hanger. Philippi is home to many historic sites, as well as a historical museum containing Civil War–era artifacts.

Admission Fees: Free.

Open to Public: Daily.

Visitor Services: Lodging, gas, food, museum, gift shop, information, restrooms, handicapped access, camping, trails.

PHILIPPI

It is my belief that no Civil War pilgrimage is truly complete without a visit to Philippi, a picturesque community in the heart of north-central West Virginia.

A casual visitor might think that Philippi has always been the quiet college town it is today. But locals and historians know the full story. They know how the peace was shattered at 4:30 A.M. on June 3, 1861, by the blast of a Union cannon perched high on a hill overlooking the city. Philippi, with its proximity to key transportation corridors in strategic western Virginia, had just witnessed the start of the first land battle in the bloodiest struggle ever waged on American soil. Soldiers in both blue and gray would march through the town for months to come, seeking control of the region's travel routes.

Like so many Americans, I am drawn to the historic sites of the Civil War. Walking the streets of towns such as Gettysburg, Sharpsburg, or Philippi—where a covered wooden bridge, still in use today, was once hastily converted into a Union barracks—is a humbling experience. One gains a deeper understanding of how the war intruded on so-called ordinary lives. This leads to a profound appreciation for the courage of soldiers and civilians, and sympathy for the sacrifices they made.

Unfortunately, many of their stories are not widely known. That is why I am pleased that the people of Philippi are eager to share their unique moment in Civil War history—an occasion when, according to one published history, the town was "the liveliest spot in the Old Dominion." The site where Confederate and Union forces first engaged in ground battle is a true piece of our heritage. It is a heritage that we, as Americans, must study, cherish, and preserve.

—*U.S. Congressman Alan B. Mollohan, West Virginia*

Regularly Scheduled Events: First weekend of June, Blue and Gray Reunion (including reenactment of the Battle of Philippi).

Directions: From I–79 take exit 115. Follow Route 20 south to Route 57 east and take U.S. 119 north to Philippi (22 miles from exit 115).

SHEPHERDSTOWN

 156 SHEPHERDSTOWN HISTORIC DISTRICT

German Street, Shepherdstown, WV 25443; (304) 876–2786; www.shepherds townvisitorscenter.com; info@shepherds townvisitorscenter.com.

Description: In the wake of the Battle of Antietam, Shepherdstown became one vast Confederate hospital, with public and private buildings in town serving as military hospitals for the wounded. On September 20, 1862, the last significant battle of the Maryland campaign occurred at Boteler's Ford, about a mile down the Potomac River from Shepherdstown. Elmwood Cemetery, on the outskirts of town, has a Confederate section; most of those buried there were casualties of the 1862 Maryland campaign. Henry Kyd Douglas, a staff officer for Stonewall Jackson, is among them.

Admission Fees: Free.

Open to Public: Daily from dawn to dusk.

Visitor Services: Lodging, gas, food, gift shops, information.

Regularly Scheduled Events: None.

Henry Patterson House, Carnifax Ferry Battlefield, Summersville, West Virginia. Chris E. Heisey–CWPT files.

Directions: From I–81 south take exit 16E. Take Route 9 east to Route 45 east, 8 miles to Shepherdstown. From I–81 north take exit 12. Take Route 45 east to Route 9 east, 7 miles to Kerneysville. Go left on Route 480 (at Kerneysville), 4 miles to Shepherdstown.

SUMMERSVILLE

CARNIFEX FERRY BATTLEFIELD STATE PARK

Carnifex Ferry Road, Summersville, WV 26651; (304) 872–0825; www .carnifexferrybattlefieldstatepark.com.

Description: Nestled on the rim of the Gauley River Canyon near Summersville, Carnifax Ferry Battlefield State Park is an important Civil War battle site. On September 10, 1861, Union troops led by Brig. Gen. William S. Rosecrans engaged the Confederates and forced them to evacuate an entrenched position on the Henry Patterson farm, which overlooked Carnifax Ferry. The Confederate commander, Brig. Gen. John B. Floyd, retreated across the ferry to the south side of the Gauley River and on eastward to Meadow Bluff near Lewisburg. This Civil War battle represented the failure of a Confederate drive to regain control of the Kanawha Valley. As a result, the movement for West Virginia statehood proceeded without serious threat from the Confederates.

Admission Fees: Free.

Open to Public: Park, daily from dawn to dusk; museum, Memorial Day weekend–Labor Day weekend, Sat., Sun., holidays 10:00 A.M.–5:00 P.M.

Visitor Services: Museum, information, restrooms, picnic facilities, trails.

Regularly Scheduled Events: Odd-numbered years in September, battle reenactment.

Directions: Located off Route 129 approximately 5 miles west of U.S. 19 near Summersville. U.S. 19 is a north–south connection between I–77 and I–79.

WESTON

 JACKSON'S MILL HISTORIC AREA

160 WVU Jackson Mill, Weston, WV 26452; (304) 269–5100; www.jacksonmill.wvu.edu; jmill@wvu.edu.

Description: The Jackson's Mill Museum is the midpoint of a historic area representing the life of Gen. Thomas "Stonewall" Jackson. Greatly influenced by his Uncle Cummins, who raised him after the death of his parents, young Tom developed much of his character by building and working in this mill. Also featured are an operating gristmill, general store, blacksmith shop, barn, and a one-room cabin.

Admission Fees: Adults $5.00, children $2.00; groups, students $3.00, adults $6.00/person.

Open to Public: Apr., May, Sept., and Oct., Thurs.–Sun., 10:00 A.M.–5:00 P.M.; Memorial Day–Labor Day, Tues.–Sun., 10:00 A.M.–5:00 P.M.; Nov.–Mar., call for appointment.

Visitor Services: Museum, gift shop, information, restrooms, limited handicapped access, trails, guided tours.

Regularly Scheduled Events: April, Civil War artillery school; December, winter lights celebration; call or visit the Web site for other events.

Directions: From I–79 take exit 99. Turn west on U.S. 33 toward Weston, go 4 miles to the fourth stoplight and turn right on U.S. 19 north. After 5 miles turn left onto Jackson's Mill Road, and Jackson's Mill will be 2.5 miles ahead on the right.

WHEELING

 WEST VIRGINIA INDEPENDENCE HALL MUSEUM

1528 Market Street, Wheeling, WV 26003; (304) 238–1300; www.wvculture.org.

Description: Journey back in time to 1862, when Wheeling was in Virginia, a state ripped apart by the Civil War. The state of West Virginia was born in this building, now a National Historic Landmark, during that conflict. The museum, a West Virginia Division of Culture and History site, focuses on the creation of the state, with changing exhibits on West Virginia's culture and history.

Admission Fees: Adults $3.00, students $2.00, groups $3.00.

Open to Public: Mon.–Sat. 10:00 A.M.–4:00 P.M.; closed state holidays.

Visitor Services: Interpretive film, audio tour, restrooms, handicapped access.

Regularly Scheduled Events: June 20, West Virginia Day anniversary celebration, the re-creation of the original event with period music, lectures, Civil War reenactors, and light refreshments.

Directions: From I–70 take the downtown Wheeling exit (Main Street). Proceed south on Main Street to 16th Street, then turn left and go 1 block to Market Street. The building is across Market Street on the left. Proceed through the light and turn left into the parking lot behind the building.

COASTAL

Fort Sumter, South Carolina. Michael Squire–CWPT files.

❖ FLORIDA ❖

ELLENTON

 GAMBLE PLANTATION HISTORIC STATE PARK

The Judah P. Benjamin Confederate Memorial, 3708 Patten Avenue, Ellenton, FL 34222; (941) 723–4536; www.floridastateparksorg/gambleplantation.

Description: The mansion was the home of Maj. Robert Gamble and served as the center of a large sugar plantation in the antebellum period. Confederate secretary of state Judah P. Benjamin took refuge in the house as he fled the country after the fall of the Confederacy.

Admission Fees: Park, free; tours, adults $5.00, children $3.00.

Open to Public (by tour only): Thurs.–Mon. 9:30 A.M., 10:30 A.M., 1:00 P.M., 2:00 P.M., 3:00 P.M., 4:00 P.M.; park, 8:00 A.M.–dusk.

Visitor Services: Handicapped access, gift shop, visitor center, tours, picnic facilities.

Regularly Scheduled Events: None.

Directions: From I–75 take exit 224; go 1 mile west on U.S. 301.

FERNANDINA BEACH

 FORT CLINCH STATE PARK

2601 Atlantic Avenue, Fernandina Beach, FL 32034; (904) 277–7274; www.floridastateparks.org/fortclinch.

Description: The construction of Fort Clinch was begun in 1847, but the fort was never fully completed. It was occupied by Confederate troops from early 1861 until it was evacuated under threat of a large Union naval expedition in March 1862. Union troops occupied the fort for the remainder of the war.

Admission Fees: Park, cars $5.00; fort, adults $2.00, children under six free.

Open to Public: Fort, daily 9:00 A.M.–5:00 P.M.; park, daily 8:00 A.M.–dusk.

Visitor Services: Visitor center, guided tours, handicapped access, trails.

Regularly Scheduled Events: First weekend of each month, reenactors join park rangers in performing sentry duty and drills; April–October, candlelight tours Friday and Saturday ($3.00); first weekend in May, special Union garrison reenactment; second week in October, Confederate garrison reenactment.

Directions: From I–95 take exit 373 onto State Road A1A. Travel 16 miles east on A1A to Fernandina; turn right onto Atlantic; go 2 miles and look for the sign on Atlantic Avenue for Fort Clinch. The fort is on the left.

GULF BREEZE

 FORT BARRANCAS, GULF ISLANDS NATIONAL SEASHORE

1801 Gulf Breeze Parkway, Gulf Breeze, FL 32563; (850) 455–5167; www.nps.gov/guis.

Description: Confederate forces occupied this fort from early 1861 until they withdrew in May 1862. Artillery fire was exchanged in late 1861 and early 1862 with Union-held Fort Pickens in the harbor.

Admission Fees: Free.

Open to Public: Mar.–Oct., daily 9:30 A.M.–4:45 P.M.; Nov.–Feb., daily 8:30 A.M.–3:45 P.M.

Visitor Services: Self-guided tours, guided tours on weekends.

Regularly Scheduled Events: None.

Directions: Take State Road 292 to U.S. Naval Air Station. Located on the base of Pensacola U.S. Naval Air Station at the south end of Navy Boulevard.

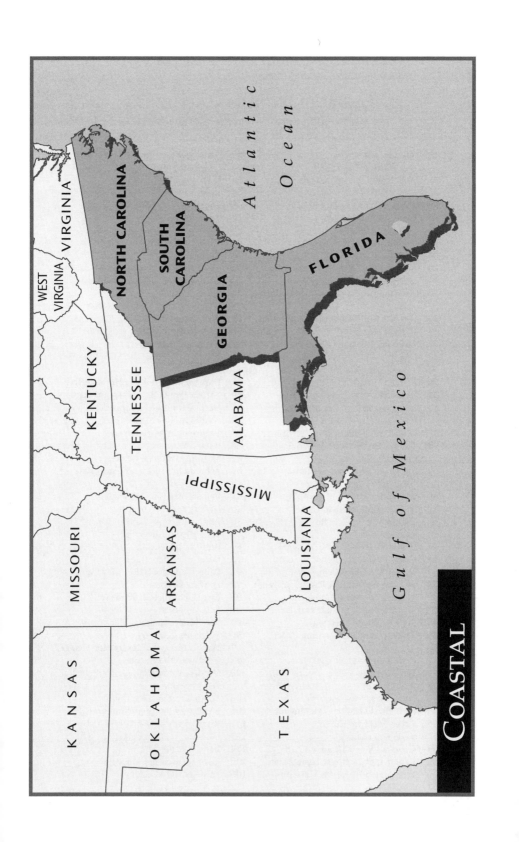

COASTAL

GEORGIA, NORTH CAROLINA, AND SOUTH CAROLINA SITES

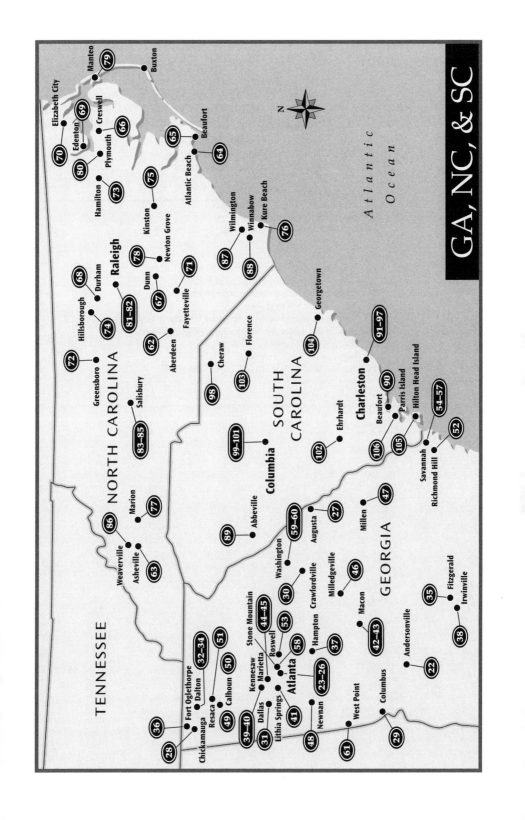

Florida Sites

1 Gamble Plantation Historic State Park
2 Fort Clinch State Park
3 Fort Barrancas, Gulf Islands National Seashore
4 Fort Pickens, Gulf Islands National Seashore
5 Yulee Sugar Mill Ruins Historic State Park
6 Camp Milton Historic Preserve
7 Museum of Science and History
8 Museum of Southern History
9 Jupiter Inlet Lighthouse
10 Fort East Martello Museum and Gardens
11 Fort Jefferson, Dry Tortugas National Park
12 Fort Zachary Taylor Historic State Park
13 Wardlaw-Smith-Goza Conference Center
14 Olustee Battlefield Historic State Park
15 Castillo de San Marcos National Monument
16 Seguí-Kirby Smith House
17 Fort Ward, San Marcos de Apalache Historic State Park
18 St. Marks Lighthouse, St. Marks National Wildlife Refuge
19 Knott House Museum
20 Museum of Florida History
21 Natural Bridge Battlefield Historic State Park

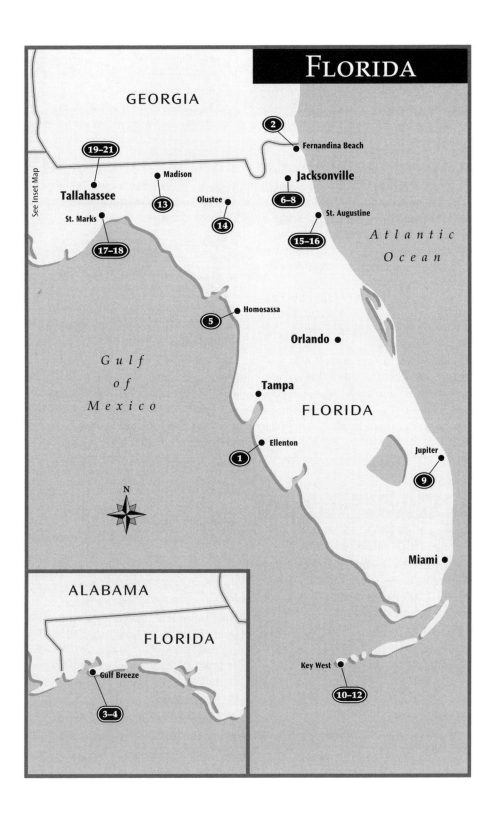

FLORIDA

GEORGIA

19–21

2
● Fernandina Beach

● Madison

Tallahassee

St. Marks ●

13

Olustee ●

14

● **Jacksonville**

6–8

● St. Augustine

15–16

17–18

Atlantic

Ocean

● Homosassa

5

Orlando ●

Gulf

of

Mexico

Tampa
●

FLORIDA

● Ellenton

1

Jupiter
●

9

N

Miami ●

See Inset Map

ALABAMA

FLORIDA

● Gulf Breeze

3–4

Key West ●

10–12

FORT PICKENS, GULF ISLANDS NATIONAL SEASHORE

1801 Gulf Breeze Parkway, Gulf Breeze, FL 32563; (850) 934–2600; www.nps.gov/guis.

Description: Originally built 1829–34, Fort Pickens was held by Union troops throughout the Civil War. The fort's commander refused demands that the fort surrender to state forces at the beginning of the war.
Admission Fees: Cars, $8.00 for seven days; persons over age sixty-two free; pedestrians, bicycles, motorcycles $3.00.
Open to Public: Apr.–Oct., daily 9:30 A.M.–5:00 P.M.; Nov.–Mar., daily 8:30 A.M.–4:00 P.M.
Visitor Services: Visitor center, handicapped accessible pathways.
Regularly Scheduled Events: None.
Directions: Take U.S. 98 east across Pensacola Bay to Gulf Breeze. Take State Road 399 to Pensacola Beach; then travel 9 miles west on Fort Pickens Road. *NOTE:* Due to hurricane damage to the road, the fort is only accessible by boat or a 14-mile hike. The road was expected to reopen in 2007.

HOMOSASSA

 YULEE SUGAR MILL RUINS HISTORIC STATE PARK

c/o Crystal River State Park, 3400 North Museum Pointe, Crystal River, FL 34428; (352) 795–3817; www.floridastateparks.org/yuleesugarmill.

Description: The Yulee Sugar Mill Ruins were originally part of the sugar plantation of Confederate Sen. David Levy Yulee of Florida. The mill operated for thirteen years and supplied sugar products for the Confederate war effort. Union forces burned Yulee's plantation during the war, but the mill was spared. Today the mill has been partially restored. Interpretive signs guide visitors through the complex.
Admission Fees: Free.

Open to Public: Daily 8:00 A.M.–sunset.
Visitor Services: Public restrooms, picnic tables, mill structures.
Regularly Scheduled Events: None.
Directions: Located on State Road 490, west of U.S. 19 in Homosassa. From I–75 take Wildwood exit; go west on State Road 44 to U.S. 19; then travel south about 10 miles on U.S. 19 to Homosassa Springs. Turn right on State Road 490 and proceed about 2.5 miles to the site.

JACKSONVILLE

 CAMP MILTON HISTORIC PRESERVE

851 North Market Street, Jacksonville, FL 32202; (904) 630–0142; www.campmilton.com.

Description: Camp Milton was the site of several encounters between Confederate and Union soldiers during the Civil War. It was also the largest encampment of Confederate forces in Florida, with 8,000 troops having assembled near its log and earth barricades. This important military outpost on the vital corridor between Jacksonville and the panhandle was named for Florida's Civil War governor, John Milton.
Admission Fees: Free.
Open to Public: Daily, 9:00 A.M.–5:00 P.M.
Visitor Services: Public restrooms, handicapped access, trails.
Regularly Scheduled Events: February, Prelude to Olustee Battle Reenactment.
Directions: From downtown Jacksonville take I–10 west to Chaffee Road exit. Turn left at the signal heading north; Chaffee Road ends at Old Plank Road. Turn left heading west. The next stop sign is Halsema Road; turn right heading north. Camp Milton is 0.25 mile from the intersection.

COASTAL

Museum of Science and History, Jacksonville, Florida. CWPT files.

★ MUSEUM OF SCIENCE AND HISTORY
7

1025 Museum Circle, Jacksonville, FL 32207; (904) 396–MOSH (6674); www .themosh.org.

Description: This general museum includes an exhibit on the Union transport ship *Maple Leaf,* which struck a Confederate mine in St. Johns River and sank in 1864. Recently discovered and partially excavated, the shipwreck has yielded well-preserved examples of military and civilian equipment.

Admission Fees: Adults $8.00, seniors and active military $6.50, children three–twelve $6.00.

Open to Public: Mon.–Fri. 10:00 A.M.–5:00 P.M., Sat. 10:00 A.M.–6:00 P.M., Sun. 1:00 P.M.–6:00 P.M.

Visitor Services: Handicapped accessible, gift shop.

Regularly Scheduled Events: None.

Directions: From I–95 north take San Marco Boulevard, exit 108. Travel on San Marco 3 blocks until San Marco ends at a T intersection with Museum Circle. MOSH is straight ahead. From I–95 south take Riverside/Mary Street/Main Street/Prudential Drive, exit 107. Follow signs for the Mary Street exit; take the Mary Street exit, remaining in the left lane of the exit ramp. At the bottom of the exit ramp at the light, turn left (north) onto San Marco; proceed straight ahead on San Marco 1 block until San Marco ends at a T intersection with Museum Circle. MOSH is straight ahead.

★ MUSEUM OF SOUTHERN HISTORY
8

4304 Herschel Street, Jacksonville, FL 32210; (904) 388–3574.

Description: This museum displays artifacts and memorabilia from the antebellum and Civil War periods. Exhibits include those on camp life, military equipment, and civilian personal items. The museum has an adjoining historical research library, with genealogical research assistance available.

Admission Fees: Adults $3.00, children under sixteen free with an adult. Group tours available by appointment.

Open to Public: Tues.–Sat. 10:00 A.M.–4:00 P.M.

Visitor Services: Information, handicapped accessible.

Regularly Scheduled Events: None.

Directions: From I–95 go west on I–10; then take U.S. 17 south to San Juan Avenue. Turn left, then go to first light (Herschel Street), turn left, and go 1 block.

JUPITER

 JUPITER INLET LIGHTHOUSE

500 Captain Armours Way, Jupiter, FL 33469; (561) 747–6639; www.jupiter lighthouse.org; visit@lrhs.org.

Description: The lighthouse was designed by then Lt. George G. Meade, later Federal commander at Gettysburg. Construction was completed in 1860. Early in the Civil War, Confederate sympathizers removed the illuminating apparatus and buried it in Jupiter Creek. At the end of the war, the newly appointed lighthouse keeper recovered the lighting mechanism, and the lamp was relit in 1866.

Admission Fees: $6.00 (applies to lighthouse climbers).

Open to Public: Lighthouse, Sat.–Wed. 10:00 A.M.–4:00 P.M.

Visitor Services: Information, gift shop, museum.

Regularly Scheduled Events: None.

Directions: From I–95 take exit for Indiantown Road east. Turn left/north at U.S. 1, then turn right/east at Beach Road. Turn right into Lighthouse Park.

KEY WEST

 FORT EAST MARTELLO MUSEUM AND GARDENS

3501 South Roosevelt Boulevard, Key West, FL 33040; (305) 296–3913; www .kwahs.com.

Description: The Fort East Martello Museum and Gardens in Key West, once a military battery for the U.S. Army, is now home to Civil War artifacts, Stanley Papio sculptures, and Mario Sanchez art. The museum sponsors a variety of temporary art and history exhibitions, educational programs, and art classes, as well as permanent displays of Florida Keys history. The battery was built in 1862 to defend Fort Taylor from the possible threat of a land attack during the Civil War. No attack ever occurred, and neither the East nor West Martello Towers were finished. Today the East Martello Tower houses a general art gallery and Key West museum.

Admission Fees: Adults $6.00, children $3.00, seniors $5.00, Monroe County students and military free; call for group discounts and reservations.

Open to Public: Daily 9:30 A.M.–4:30 P.M.; last admission is at 4:00 P.M.; closed during hurricane season (Aug.–Oct.).

Visitor Services: Public restrooms, information, handicapped access, gift shop.

Regularly Scheduled Events: None.

Directions: From State Road A1A turn left on South Roosevelt Boulevard. Located next to the Key West Airport.

FORT JEFFERSON, DRY TORTUGAS NATIONAL PARK

P.O. Box 6208, Key West, FL 33041; (305) 242–7700; www.nps.gov/drto.

Description: Once known as the "Gibraltar of the Gulf," Fort Jefferson is the largest all-masonry fort in the Western Hemisphere. It was garrisoned by Union troops throughout the Civil War and also served as a military prison. Dr. Samuel Mudd and three Lincoln conspirators were imprisoned at the fort.

Admission Fees: Adults, children seventeen and older $5.00.

Open to Public: Daily during daylight hours.

Visitor Services: Gift shop, visitor center; camping, snorkeling, fishing, swimming, bird-watching. Guided tours of Fort Jeffer-

son are offered daily.
Regularly Scheduled Events: None.
Directions: Fort Jefferson is located on Garden Key, Dry Tortugas, 70 miles west of Key West. Passenger ferries and seaplane depart daily from Key West, weather permitting.

FORT ZACHARY TAYLOR HISTORIC STATE PARK

P.O. Box 6560, Key West, FL 33041; (305) 292–6713; www.forttaylor.org.

Description: When Florida seceded from the Union, Federal troops in Key West quickly moved to secure Fort Taylor and prevent it from falling into Confederate hands. The cannons that have been found buried inside the fort constitute one of the largest groups of Civil War heavy artillery in existence.

Admission Fees: Cars with two occupants $6.00, plus 50 cents per person; adults $1.50, children six and under free.

Open to Public: Park, daily 8:00 A.M.–sunset; fort, daily 8:00 A.M.–5:00 P.M.

Visitor Services: Tours (daily noon and 2:00 P.M.).

Regularly Scheduled Events: Second weekend in February, Civil War Heritage Days reenactment.

Directions: Located at the southwest end of Key West at Southard Street on Truman Annex.

MADISON

WARDLAW-SMITH-GOZA CONFERENCE CENTER

121 Northwest Marion Street, Madison, FL 32340; (850) 973–2288 ext. 132/107; www.nfcc.edu/alumfdn.

Description: This circa 1860 antebellum mansion was briefly used as a hospital for casualties following the Battle of Olustee in 1864. The next year, Confederate secretary of war John C. Breckinridge reportedly spent the night here, while making his escape after the fall of the Confederacy.

Admission Fees: Free.

Open to Public: By appointment only.

Visitor Services: Tours, conference center.

Regularly Scheduled Events: December, Christmas Open House.

COASTAL

Fort Zachary Taylor, Key West, Florida. Phillip Pollock–CWPT.

Directions: From I–10 take the Madison/Perry exit; follow State Road 14 north to Madison. Turn left on U.S. 90 at the courthouse and proceed 2 blocks. House is on the right.

 OLUSTEE BATTLEFIELD HISTORIC STATE PARK

5828 Battlefield Trail Road, Olustee, FL 32072; (386) 397–7005; www.floridastate parks.org/olustee.

Description: The largest Civil War battle in Florida occurred on February 20, 1864, when Union troops marched west from Jacksonville hoping to disrupt the flow of beef and other supplies from central Florida to the Confederacy. Confederate skirmishers lured them into a forest at Olustee. The battle ended with 2,807 casualties, a Confederate victory, and the containment of Union troops at Jacksonville until the war ended.

Admission Fees: Free.

Open to Public: State park, daily 8:00 A.M.–sunset; interpretive center, Thurs.–Mon. 9:00 A.M.–5:00 P.M.

Visitor Services: Interpretive center, public restrooms, information, trails.

Regularly Scheduled Events: February, reenactment of the Battle of Olustee; September, Civil War Expo.

Directions: From I–10 take exit 45 onto U.S. 90; follow signs to Olustee Battlefield.

 CASTILLO DE SAN MARCOS NATIONAL MONUMENT

1 South Castillo Drive, St. Augustine, FL 32084; (904) 829–6506; www.nps.gov/casa.

Description: Built in 1672–95 as a colonial Spanish fortress, it was renamed Fort Marion in 1821 (and reverted to its original Spanish name in 1942). Confederate forces

Seguí-Kirby Smith House, St. Augustine, Florida. CWPT files.

occupied this fort from early 1861 until they withdrew the next year.

Admission Fees: Adults $6.00, children under fifteen free.

Open to Public: Daily 8:45 A.M.–4:45 P.M.

Visitor Services: Self-guided tours, exhibits.

Regularly Scheduled Events: None.

Directions: From I–95 exit at State Road 16 east into St. Augustine; turn right for 2 miles on San Marcos Street.

 16 SEGUÍ-KIRBY SMITH HOUSE

6 Artillery Lane, St. Augustine, FL 32084; (904) 825–2333; www.staugustine historicalsociety.org/sahslibrary@bell south.net.

Description: This house was the birthplace of Gen. Edmund Kirby Smith, the last Confederate general to surrender. His mother, Frances Kirby Smith, lived in this house during the early part of the Union occupation of St. Augustine until she was exiled from the city for spying. The house is now the St. Augustine Historical Society research library. The collection is open to the public for research and is composed of files and books on Florida history, including those on the Civil War period and the Kirby Smith family. There are two bronze statues in the garden, and a plaque inside the building commemorating its famous former resident.

Admission Fees: Free.

Open to Public: Tues.–Fri. 9:00 A.M.–4:30 P.M., third Saturday of the month 9:00 A.M.– 12:30 P.M.; closed the last two weeks of July.

Visitor Services: Research library.

Regularly Scheduled Events: None.

Directions: From I–95 north exit at State Road 207; turn left at U.S. 1, then right at King Street (next light). Turn right on Aviles Street and proceed south 1 block. House is at the corner of Aviles Street and Artillery Lane.

 ## ST. MARKS

 17 FORT WARD, SAN MARCOS De APALACHE HISTORIC STATE PARK

1022 Desoto Park Drive, Tallahassee, FL 32301; (850) 925–6216 or (850) 922–6007; www.floridastateparks.org/sanmarcos.

Description: These ruins are located at the confluence of the St. Marks and Wakulla Rivers. The site has been occupied by Spanish, British, American, and Confederate troops. During the Civil War, Confederate soldiers built earthworks and placed artillery at the fort, which was threatened but not attacked in March 1865.

Admission Fees: Adults $1.00, children six and under free.

Open to Public: Thurs.–Mon. 9:00 A.M.–5:00 P.M.

Visitor Services: Museum, visitor center, information.

Regularly Scheduled Events: None.

Directions: Off State Road 363, turn right to Old Fort Road, then turn left to site, located south of Tallahassee.

18 ST. MARKS LIGHTHOUSE, ST. MARKS NATIONAL WILDLIFE REFUGE

1255 Lighthouse Road, St. Marks, FL 32355; (850) 925–6121; www.fws.gov/ saintmarks@fws.gov.

Description: The lighthouse was the site of several military operations during the Civil War. In June 1862 the Union navy shelled the area, destroying a small Confederate fortification nearby. A year later the navy returned and burned the lighthouse's interior steps, trying to prevent its use as a Confederate lookout tower.

Admission Fees: Cars $5.00.

Open to Public: Refuge, daily from dawn to dusk; lighthouse, only open on special occasions, call ahead.

COASTAL

Visitor Services: Trails, public restrooms.
Regularly Scheduled Events: None.
Directions: Located in the St. Marks National Wildlife Refuge, south of Tallahassee off County Road 59, south of Newport.

TALLAHASSEE

 KNOTT HOUSE MUSEUM

301 East Park Avenue, Tallahassee, FL 32301; (850) 922–2459; www.flheritage .com.

Description: Brig. Gen. Edward Moody McCook arrived in Tallahassee on May 10, 1865, riding from Macon, Georgia, with two regiments of Union cavalry. He set up headquarters at the present-day Knott House and announced President Lincoln's Emancipation Proclamation on May 20.
Admission Fees: Free.
Open to Public: Wed.–Fri., tours at 1:00, 2:00, and 3:00 P.M.; Sat., tours on the hour starting at 10:00 A.M.; last tour at 3:00 P.M.
Visitor Services: Information, handicapped access, gift shop, museum.
Regularly Scheduled Events: May, Emancipation Celebration.
Directions: Take exit 29 east from I–10. Travel south on North Monroe Street to downtown Tallahassee; take a left onto Park Avenue.

 MUSEUM OF FLORIDA HISTORY

500 South Bronough Street, Tallahassee, FL 32399-0250; (850) 245–6400; www .flheritage.com/museum.

Description: The state history museum includes a Civil War exhibit that displays selected firearms, soldiers' personal effects, and battle flags carried by Florida's military units. Also included is information dealing with the Civil War's impact on civilians on the home front. The museum also administers the state's Old Capitol, which houses exhibits on the antebellum, Civil War, and Reconstruction periods in Florida's history.
Admission Fees: Free.
Open to Public: Mon.–Fri. 9:00 A.M.–4:30 P.M., Sat. 10:00 A.M.–4:30 P.M., Sun. and holidays noon–4:30 P.M.
Visitor Services: Information, handicapped access, gift shop.
Regularly Scheduled Events: None.
Directions: From I–10 take Havana/Tallahassee exit. Proceed south on Monroe Street for 7 miles; turn right on Jefferson Street, then travel past three stoplights to museum. Located on the ground floor of the R. A. Gray Building, 500 South Bronough Street, 1 block west of the Capitol Building.

 NATURAL BRIDGE BATTLEFIELD HISTORIC STATE PARK

7502 Natural Bridge Road, Tallahassee, FL 32305; (850) 922–6007; www.florida stateparks.org/naturalbridge.

Description: On March 6, 1865, a small battle was fought south of Tallahassee at Natural Bridge, where the St. Marks River goes underground. Confederate troops, supported by cadets and home guards, defeated a Union attempt to cross the river and forced the Union troops to retreat to the coast.
Admission Fees: Free.
Open to Public: Daily 8:00 A.M.–sunset.
Visitor Services: Information, picnic area, public restrooms, handicapped access.
Regularly Scheduled Events: Early March, reenactment of the Battle of Natural Bridge.
Directions: Travel south from Tallahassee on State Road 363 to Woodville; then proceed 6 miles east of Woodville on Natural Bridge Road.

ANDERSONVILLE

During the Civil War both Union and Confederate armies had to deal with thousands of prisoners and find ways to care for them. Neither side expected a long conflict or the eventual need that arose to care for large numbers of prisoners. As the numbers of prisoners increased, special prison camps were built, many similar to the one at Andersonville in Georgia.

Of the more than 211,400 Union soldiers captured by Confederate forces, 30,208 died in prison camps. Union forces captured 462,000 Confederates, including those who surrendered at the war's close. Of these, 25,976 died in prison camps.

The most common problems confronting prisoners in the North and South were overcrowding, poor sanitation, and an improper diet. The confined soldiers suffered terribly. Mismanagement by prison officials as well as by the prisoners themselves brought on additional hardships.

Andersonville, or Camp Sumter as it was known officially, was the largest of many Confederate military prisons established during the Civil War. It was built in early 1864 after Confederate officials decided to move the large number of Federal prisoners in and around Richmond to a place of greater security and more abundant food. During the fourteen months it existed, more than 45,000 Union soldiers were confined here. Of these, almost 13,000 died of disease, poor sanitation, malnutrition, overcrowding, or exposure to the elements.

Andersonville prison had ceased to exist by May 1865. During July and August 1865, Clara Barton, together with a detachment of laborers, soldiers, and a former prisoner named Dorence Atwater, went to Andersonville to identify and mark the graves of the Union dead. Atwater, a member of the Second New York Cavalry, was nineteen years old when he was sent to Andersonville and became keeper of the books in which prisoners' deaths were recorded. His lists proved invaluable to Barton.

Clara Barton's efforts to get medical supplies, aid, and care for the troops led President Lincoln to ask her to try to ascertain the whereabouts of missing soldiers, so relatives could be informed. This mission was what brought her to Andersonville.

Today, Andersonville National Historic Site is unique in the National Park System as the only park to serve as a memorial to all Americans ever held as prisoners of any war.

NATIONAL PARK SERVICE

COASTAL

❖ GEORGIA ❖

ANDERSONVILLE

 ANDERSONVILLE NATIONAL HISTORIC SITE

496 Cemetery Road, Andersonville, GA 31711; (912) 924–0343.

Description: Andersonville was the location of Camp Sumter, a Confederate prisoner-of-war camp. During its fourteen months of operation, 45,000 Union prisoners were held here, and nearly 13,000 died and are buried in its national cemetery. Andersonville is also the memorial to all prisoners of war in American history. The National Prisoner of War Museum tells the story of POW experiences from the American Revolution to the present.

Admission Fees: Free.

Prison at Andersonville National Historic Site, Andersonville, Georgia. CWPT files.

Open to Public: Park, daily 8:00 A.M.–5:00 P.M.; museum, daily 8:30 A.M.–5:00 P.M.

Visitor Services: Public restrooms, handicapped access, gift shop, museum.

Regularly Scheduled Events: Second weekend of March, Annual Living History weekend.

Directions: Traveling south on I–75, take exit 127 (Georgia State Route 26W). Go through Montezuma to the intersection of Georgia 49. Turn left and go 6 miles. Park entrance is on the left. Traveling north on I–75, use exit 101 to Americus, then north on Georgia 49 to Andersonville. Park entrance is on the right.

ATLANTA

 THE ATLANTA CYCLORAMA

800-C Cherokee Avenue SE, Atlanta, GA 30315; (404) 624–1071.

Description: This cyclorama is a painting in the round that depicts the Battle of Atlanta. The painting is 42 feet in height, 358 feet in circumference, weighs more than 9,000 pounds, and covers a canvas area of more than 16,000 square feet. A three-

dimensional panorama with music and narration awaits the visitor. There is also a film narrated by James Earl Jones on the Atlanta campaign.

Admission Fees: Adults $7.00, seniors $6.00, children six–twelve $5.00, groups of adults $4.00, groups of children $2.00.

Open to Public: Daily 8:50 A.M.–4:30 P.M.

Visitor Services: Public restrooms, information, handicapped access, gift shop, museum.

Regularly Scheduled Events: None.

Directions: Take I–20 to Boulevard Avenue, exit 59a, and follow the signs.

 ATLANTA HISTORY CENTER

130 West Paces Ferry Road NW, Atlanta, GA 30305; (404) 814–4000; www.atlhist .org.

Description: Learn how Atlanta grew into the South's leading city, about African-American history, the Civil War, *Gone With the Wind,* and a whole lot more. The Atlanta History Center's exhibition, *Turning Point: The American Civil War,* interprets the key turning points in the Civil War, including the Atlanta campaign of 1864. The museum has the largest collection of Civil War artifacts in Georgia and one of the five largest Civil War collections in the country, housing approximately 7,500 objects of all types: guns, uniforms, military equipment, and memorabilia. Also visit the 1840s Tullie Smith Farm and the Swan House, an elegant 1928 mansion. McElreath Hall contains the center's research library and archives.

Admission Fees: Adults $15.00, seniors sixty-five plus and students thirteen and up with ID $12.00, youths four–twelve $10.00, children three and under free. Group rates available with a reservation.

Open to Public: Mon.–Sat. 10:00 A.M.–5:30 P.M., Sun. noon–5:30 P.M.

Visitor Services: Public restrooms, handicapped access, food, gift shop, museum, library and archives, trails, historic homes, picnic area.

Regularly Scheduled Events: April, Sheep to Shawl; November–December, candlelight tours.

Directions: From I–75 take the West Paces Ferry Road exit. Go east 2.6 miles on West Paces Ferry Road, and the Atlanta History Center is on the right. By MARTA: From the Lenox station, take bus 23 to the intersection of Peachtree and West Paces Ferry Roads; walk west on West Paces Ferry Road past the second traffic light (Slaton Drive) to pedestrian entrance.

 25 GEORGIA STATE CAPITOL

431 State Capitol, Atlanta, GA 30334; (404) 651–6996; www.sos.state.ga.us/museum.

Description: In 1864 Federal troops encamped on the grounds of Atlanta City Hall. Today Georgia's capitol stands on this site. The dome of the classical Renaissance-style building is topped with native gold. Statues of Civil War governors and other historic figures, as well as United Daughters of the Confederacy (UDC) historic markers, are located on the grounds. Capitol museum

---

FOR MORE INFORMATION

Look for "The Presence of the Past—Tracking Georgia's Civil War Heritage." This brochure identifies forty-one selected sites, including museums, buildings, and battlefields, that represent Georgia's Civil War history. "The Presence of the Past" is available at Georgia Welcome Centers or by calling (404) 657–7294.

COASTAL

collections include Confederate-era flags, portraits, and statuary.

Admission Fees: Free.

Open to Public: Mon.–Fri. 8:00 A.M.–5:30 P.M.; tours, 10:00 A.M., 11:00 A.M., 1:00 P.M., 2:00 P.M.

Visitor Services: Public restrooms, information, handicapped access, museum.

Regularly Scheduled Events: None.

Directions: From the south take I–75/I–85 north; take exit 245 (Capitol Avenue). Continue through stop sign. At first light turn left onto Capitol Avenue. Capitol is 1 mile on the left. From the north take I–75/I–85 south; take exit 248A (Martin Luther King Jr. Drive). Capitol is on the left.

 26 HISTORIC OAKLAND CEMETERY

248 Oakland Avenue SE, Atlanta, GA 30312; (404) 688–2107; www.oaklandcemetery.com.

Description: Oakland Cemetery is a repository for approximately 6,800 soldiers, known and unknown. It has been the site of Memorial Day services since 1866 and boasts two beautiful monuments to the Confederate dead. It is also the final resting place for five generals.

Admission Fees: Free; guided walking tours, adults $10.00, seniors $3.00, children $5.00.

Open to Public: Daily from dawn to dusk; business office, Mon.–Fri. 9:00 A.M.–5:00 P.M.

Visitor Services: Public restrooms, handicapped access, records research.

Regularly Scheduled Events: Fall, Sunday in the Park (Victorian afternoon at the cemetery).

Directions: From I–75 south take I–20 east to Boulevard East. From I–75 north take exit 248A onto Butler Street; make first right onto Decatur Street. Go three lights to Grant Street and turn right; at stop sign turn left. The gate will be in front of you.

AUGUSTA

 AUGUSTA MUSEUM OF HISTORY

560 Reynolds Street, Augusta, GA 30901; (706) 722–8454; www.augusta museum.org; amh@csra.net.

Description: Augusta was a major manufacturing center for the Confederacy, with the Augusta Arsenal and the Confederate Powder Works Factory. Artifacts from both Confederate munitions centers are exhibited in the museum. In addition, the museum features Confederate uniforms, accoutrements, flags, firearms, and swords.

Admission Fees: Adults $4.00 ($1.00 off the admission price for CWPT members), seniors $3.00, children six–eighteen $2.00, under five free.

Open to Public: Tues.–Sat. 10:00 A.M.–5:00 P.M., Sun. 1:00 P.M.–5:00 P.M.

Visitor Services: Public restrooms, information, handicapped access, museum shop; Augusta Riverwalk.

Regularly Scheduled Events: None.

Directions: From I–20 take exit 200, Riverwatch Parkway. Follow signs to Augusta, staying on Riverwatch as it enters Augusta and becomes Jones Street. Continue on Jones Street until it ends at a T intersection. Turn left on 10th Street, then turn right on Reynolds Street. Follow Reynolds Street to Sixth Street. Museum is on Sixth Street between Reynolds and Broad Streets. Parking is available off either street.

CHICKAMAUGA

 GORDON-LEE MANSION

217 Cove Road, Chickamauga, GA 30707; (706) 375–4728; www.gordon-lee mansion.com; glmbbi@aol.com.

Description: Prior to the Battle of Chickamauga, the Gordon-Lee Mansion served as headquarters to the Union Army of the Cumberland's Gen. William Rosecrans. Seven division hospitals were set up on-site during the battle until the mansion was captured by the Confederate Army of Tennessee's Gen. Joseph Wheeler on the second day of the battle and used as a hospital for the Confederate army. When 14,000 veterans returned to the site for the Blue-Gray Barbecue in 1889, they formed the oldest and largest Civil War battlefield park in the United States, the Chickamauga-Chattanooga National Military Park.

Admission Fees: Call for current rates.

Open to Public: By appointment only.

Visitor Services: Public restrooms, gift shop, information, guided tours.

Regularly Scheduled Events: September, War Between the States Day; December, candlelight tour.

Directions: From I–75 take exit 350 (Georgia 2) to U.S. 27 south. Follow signs to the site from downtown Chickamauga.

COLUMBUS

 NATIONAL CIVIL WAR NAVAL MUSEUM AT PORT COLUMBUS

1002 Victory Drive, Columbus, GA 31901; (706) 327–9798; www.port columbus.org; cwnavy@portcolumbus .org.

Description: The nation's only museum dedicated solely to the story of the Civil War at sea offers 40,000 square feet of cutting-edge exhibits, including original Civil War ships, many artifacts, flags, weapons, and uniforms. The museum also features rebuilt portions of the USS *Hartford* and *Monitor* and CSS *Albemarle,* which includes a dramatic battle theater.

Admission Fees: Adults $6.50, seniors $5.50, students, children six and under free.

Open to Public: Mon.–Sun. 9:00 A.M.–5:00 P.M.

Visitor Services: Public restrooms, information, gift shop.

Regularly Scheduled Events: March, living history event; April, Civil War army encampment; first weekends in June and July, Civil War naval history re-creations; December, Victorian holiday open house.

Directions: I–185 South from I–85, take exit 1B, Victory Drive. Proceed 5 miles and turn left into South Commons, then left into museum parking lot.

CRAWFORDVILLE

 ALEXANDER H. STEPHENS STATE HISTORIC PARK

456 Alexander Street, Crawfordville, GA 30631; (706) 456–2602; www.gastate parks.org.

Description: This historic park consists of the 1875 house and outbuildings belonging to Alexander Stephens, vice president of the Confederacy. Located beside Stephens's home is a Confederate museum that houses one of Georgia's finest collections of Civil War artifacts.

Admission Fees: Adults $3.00, children five–eighteen $1.50; call for group rates.

Open to Public: Tues.–Sat. 9:00 A.M.–5:00 P.M., Sun. 2:00 P.M.–5:00 P.M.; last tour at 4:00 P.M.

Visitor Services: Public restrooms, information, gift shop, museum, trails, camping.

Regularly Scheduled Events: December, Victorian Christmas.

Directions: From I–20 take exit 148 and follow signs to the park (approximately 2 miles).

DALLAS

 PICKETT'S MILL BATTLEFIELD STATE HISTORIC SITE

4432 Mount Tabor Road, Dallas, GA 30157; (770) 443–7850; www.pickettsmill park.org; park@pickettsmillpark.org.

Description: The Battle of Pickett's Mill involved 24,000 troops and resulted in a Confederate victory. The Union forces under Gen. Oliver O. Howard suffered 1,600 casualties, while the Confederates under Gen. Patrick R. Cleburne suffered only 500. The battlefield is in an excellent state of preservation.

Admission Fees: Adults $3.00, seniors $2.50, children $1.75; call for group rates.

Open to Public: Tues.–Sat. 9:00 A.M.–5:00 P.M., Sun. noon–5:00 P.M.; closed Mon. (except federal holidays).

Visitor Services: Public restrooms, information, gift shop, museum, trails.

Regularly Scheduled Events: First weekend in June, annual living history encampment; Autumn, reenactment of the Confederate night attack; all year, weekend interpretive programs.

Directions: From I–75 take exit 277 and follow Georgia 92 south to Dallas-Acworth Road. Take Dallas-Acworth Road to Mount Tabor Road and turn left; after 1 mile you will see the entrance on the left.

DALTON

 DALTON CONFEDERATE CEMETERY

West Hill Cemetery, Ridge Street, Dalton, GA 30720; (706) 270–9960.

Description: Four hundred twenty-one Confederate soldiers, whose names were only learned recently, and four unknown Union soldiers are buried here. A memorial wall has been erected listing the names of the Confederates. Dalton was a home to several important Confederate hospitals during the war.

COASTAL

Admission Fees: Free.
Open to Public: Daily from dawn to dusk.
Visitor Services: None.
Regularly Scheduled Events: April, Confederate Memorial Day.
Directions: From 1–75 take exit 333 Walnut Avenue/Highway 52 east. Go 1.6 miles and turn left on Thornton Avenue. Go 1 mile, then turn left on Cuyler Street. The cemetery entrance is straight ahead.

OLD WESTERN AND ATLANTIC RAILROAD TUNNEL AND CLISBY AUSTIN HOUSE

215 Austin Road, Dalton, GA 30720; (706) 876–1571 or (800) 331–3258; www .tunnelhillheritagecenter.com; heritage @whitfieldcountyga.com.

Description: Completed in 1850, the tunnel is the oldest railroad tunnel in the Southeast. Throughout the war the tunnel was a major link in the supply line of the Confederate armies until 1863. In April 1862 the tunnel played a role in the "Great Locomotive Chase," when Union soldiers attempted to cut the important rail line by stealing the train locomotive, the General, and heading north toward Chattanooga. The engine's fuel supply dwindled, and the raid failed. In 1864 Sherman occupied Tunnel Hill and set up his headquarters in the nearby Clisby Austin House.
Admission Fees: Adults $3.00, children twelve and under $2.00; call for group rates.
Open to Public: Mon.–Sat. 9:00 A.M.–5:00 P.M.
Visitor Services: Public restrooms, information, handicapped access, gift shop, museum.
Regularly Scheduled Events: September, Battle of Tunnel Hill reenactment.
Directions: From 1–75 take exit 336, U.S. 41, at Rocky Face. Go north on U.S. 41 approximately 5 miles to Tunnel Hill. Just before crossing the bridge over the railroad tracks, turn right onto Oak Street. Go approx-

imately 0.5 mile; when the road curves, continue straight on Clisby Austin Road.

PRATER'S MILL

500 Prater's Mill Road, Dalton, GA 30721; (706) 694–6455; www.pratersmill .org.

Description: Prater's Mill is a water-powered gristmill on the banks of the Coahulla Creek, built in 1855. During the Civil War both armies camped at the site. While occupied by the Union army, the mill was considered a valuable resource for food and was not destroyed.
Admission Fees: Free.
Open to Public: Grounds open daily; buildings open twice annually during the fair.
Visitor Services: Interpretive markers.
Regularly Scheduled Events: May, Mother's Day weekend; October, Columbus Day weekend; Prater's Mill Country Fair is held during both weekends.
Directions: Located on Georgia 2, 10 miles northeast of Dalton. From I–75 take exit 341, Tunnel Hill-Varnell; travel north on Georgia 201 for 4.5 miles. Turn right on Georgia 2 and continue 2.6 miles to the site.

FITZGERALD

BLUE AND GRAY MUSEUM

116 North Johnston Street, P.O. Box 1285, Fitzgerald, GA 31750; (229) 426–5069; www.fitzgeraldga.org; bgmuseum@mchsl.com.

Description: Fitzgerald's Blue and Gray Museum tells a story unique in the nation: how a colony of Union veterans cleared a forest and built this town in Georgia among former enemies, replaced hatred and division with understanding and brotherhood, and organized Battalion 1, Blue and Gray. A true reuniting of America!
Admission Fees: Adults $3.00, children $1.00.

Open to Public: Tues.–Sat. 10:00 A.M.–4:00 P.M., Sun. 1:00 P.M.–5:00 P.M.

Visitor Services: Public restrooms.

Regularly Scheduled Events: Check with museum for events.

Directions: From I–75 take exit 82 in Ashburn. Go east under overpass for 5 miles. Turn right on Georgia 107; travel 20 miles straight until dead end on Merrimac Drive, then turn right on Merrimac. Go to traffic light and take a left onto Central Avenue. Watch for museum signs.

FORT OGLETHORPE

 CHICKAMAUGA AND CHATTANOOGA NATIONAL MILITARY PARK

P.O. Box 2128, Fort Oglethorpe, GA 30742; (706) 866–9241; www.nps.gov/ chch.

Description: This national military park commemorates the Battle of Chickamauga and the battle for Chattanooga. The objective was the Chattanooga, Tennessee, region, the gateway to the Deep South. Without a fight the Union army maneuvered the Confederates out of Chattanooga, and despite being defeated at Chickamauga on September 19–20, 1863, the Union army was able to hold on to the city. The Confederates, failing to properly exploit their Chickamauga victory, lay siege to the town, and two months later were defeated in the battles for Chattanooga on November 23–25, 1865. Fighting on Lookout Mountain and Missionary Ridge was most decisive.

Admission Fees: Free; orientation film, adults $3.00, seniors and children six–sixteen $1.50, under six free.

Open to Public: Visitor center, daily 8:30 A.M.–5:30 P.M.; call for summer hours; battlefield grounds, 8:00 A.M.–dusk.

Visitor Services: Public restrooms, information, handicapped access, gift shop, museum, trails.

Regularly Scheduled Events: September

Chickamauga and Chattanooga National Military Park, Fort Oglethorpe, Georgia. CWPT files.

and November on weekend closest to battle dates, anniversary commemorations.

Directions: From I–75 in Georgia take exit 141; go west on Georgia 2, 6 miles to U.S. 27. Turn left onto U.S. 27 to battlefield. From I–24 in Tennessee take exit 180B; go south on U.S. 27 to battlefield.

HAMPTON

 NASH FARM BATTLEFIELD

4361 Jonesboro Road, Hampton, GA 30228; (770) 954–2031 or (678) 479–0932; www.henrycountybattlefield.com.

Description: On August 20, 1864, U.S. Gen. Judson Kilpatrick's cavalry raid escalated at the Nash Farm when 4,700 Federal cavalry charged and broke through the Texans. This was the largest cavalry breakthrough sabre charge in Georgia's history. Nash Farm was also the site of Confederate Gen. Stephen D. Lee's campsite in September 1864.

COASTAL

Admission Fees: Free.
Open to Public: By appointment only; historian available for tours Mon.–Fri. after 2:00 P.M.
Visitor Services: Public restrooms, handicapped access.
Regularly Scheduled Events: April, Southern Heritage Festival; July, Georgia Independence Festival; November, Civil War Reenactment.
Directions: From Atlanta take I–75 south to exit 221, Jonesboro Road (the second Jonesboro Road located in Henry County). Turn off the highway and go west approximately 6 miles. Nash Farm will be on the left.

IRWINVILLE

THE JEFFERSON DAVIS MEMORIAL STATE HISTORIC SITE

338 Jeff Davis Park Road, Fitzgerald, GA 31750; (229) 831–2335; www.gastate parks.org.

Description: On May 10, 1865, after a flight which lasted nearly a month and saw the breakdown of the remnant Confederate government, forces of the First Wisconsin and the Fourth Michigan cavalries captured Confederate president Jefferson Davis here. In the rush to apprehend Davis and collect a piece of the $100,000 reward for his capture, two Michigan soldiers, John Rupert and John Hines, were mistakenly shot and killed by friendly Wisconsin troopers. It was also at this site where the untrue story that Davis tried to escape in his wife's clothing started. Most important, it was here that the Confederacy breathed its last breath, and with the fall of the executive branch, ceased to exist.
Admission Fees: Adults $3.00, children six–eighteen $1.75, seniors $2.50.
Open to Public: Wed.–Sat. 9:00 A.M.–5:00 P.M., Sun. 2:00 P.M.–5:30 P.M.

Visitor Services: Public restrooms, information, handicapped access, gift shop, museum, trails.
Regularly Scheduled Events: April, Confederate Memorial Day; June, Jefferson Davis Birthday Commemoration; December, 1860s Christmas. Call for schedule.
Directions: From I–75 take exit 78; go east 14 miles to Irwinville on Georgia 32. Follow the signs once you are in town. The park is 1 mile north of Irwinville.

KENNESAW

KENNESAW MOUNTAIN NATIONAL BATTLEFIELD PARK CWPT

905 Kennesaw Mountain Drive, Kennesaw, GA 30152; (770) 427–4686; www.nps.gov/kemo.

Description: In June 1864 Confederate Gen. Joseph E. Johnston delayed Gen. William T. Sherman's advance toward Atlanta for two weeks at Kennesaw Mountain. The 2,884-acre national park preserves the battleground where Johnston's army temporarily stopped the Union advance southward.
Admission Fees: Free.
Open to Public: Visitor center, Mon.–Fri. 8:30 A.M.–5:00 P.M., Sat.–Sun. 8:30 A.M.–6:00 P.M.; park, daylight hours.
Visitor Services: Public restrooms, information, handicapped access, gift shop, museum, trails. Gift shop offers a discount to CWPT members.
Regularly Scheduled Events: June, anniversary commemoration.
Directions: From I–75 take exit 269 onto Barrett Parkway; take Barrett Parkway across U.S. 41 to old U.S. 41 and turn left. Take Old U.S. 41 to the intersection with Stilesboro Road; turn right on Stilesboro and immediately into the park gate.

Kennesaw Mountain National Battlefield, Kennesaw, Georgia. CWPT files.

 SOUTHERN MUSEUM OF OF CIVIL WAR AND LOCOMOTIVE HISTORY

2829 Cherokee Street, Kennesaw, GA 30144; (770) 427–2117; www.southern museum.org.

Description: The Southern Museum of Civil War and Locomotive History, a Smithsonian Institution affiliate, allows visitors to glimpse the daily lives of soldiers during the Civil War; relive the excitement of the "Great Locomotive Chase" and see the stolen locomotive, the General; and examine the role railroads played during the war. The museum also houses a replica postwar locomotive factory.

Admission Fees: Adults $7.50, children four and up $5.00, seniors $6;50; group rates available.

Open to Public: Mon.–Sat. 9:30 A.M.–5:00 P.M., Sun. noon–5:00 P.M.; closed New Year's Day, Easter, Thanksgiving, and Christmas.

Visitor Services: Handicapped access, gift shop.

Regularly Scheduled Events: April, Big Shanty Festival; May, All Aboard Days; December, Civil War Christmas.

Directions: From I–75 take exit 273 (Wade Green Road). Turn west, and it is 2.5 miles to Kennesaw site. The museum is approximately 30 miles north of Atlanta.

LITHIA SPRINGS

 SWEETWATER CREEK STATE CONSERVATION PARK

P.O. Box 816, Lithia Springs, GA 30122; (770) 732–5871; www.georgiastatepark .org.

Description: The park features a variety of natural and cultural resources, including the ruins of the New Manchester Manufacturing Company, a Civil War–era textile mill.

COASTAL

Sweetwater Creek, Lithia Springs, Georgia. CWPT files.

Gen. William T. Sherman's forces burned the mill and the surrounding town during their campaign for Atlanta in 1864, and the factory's female factory workers were deported to the North.

Admission Fees: Parking, $3.00; free guided tours are available to groups with reservations.

Open to Public: Park, daily 7:00 A.M.–9:45 P.M.; trails close at dusk.

Visitor Services: Public restrooms, information, handicapped access, food, gift shop, boat rentals, trails.

Regularly Scheduled Events: September, New Manchester Day; June, arts and crafts festival.

Directions: From I–20 west take exit 44 (Thornton Road) and turn left onto Camp Creek Parkway. Go 0.25 mile and across bridge to Blairs Bridge Road; go about 2 miles to a four-way stop. Turn left on Mount Vernon Road, which leads into the park. The park office is the first left after you cross the bridge.

MACON

 CANNONBALL HOUSE AND MUSEUM

856 Mulberry Street, Macon, GA 31201; (478) 745–5982; www.cannonballhouse .org.

Description: This Greek Revival home, circa 1853, was struck during the Battle of Dunlap Hill on July 30, 1864, by a cannonball fired from one of Union Gen. George Stoneman's guns, positioned on a bluff overlooking the river at what is now Ocmulgee National Monument. Union forces were thought to have been firing on the Johnston-Hay House on the next corner, which was known to have stored the Confederate treasury. The original brick structure, formerly the kitchen, is located on the property and houses a collection of artifacts from the Civil War.

Admission Fees: Adults $5.00, children six and under free, seniors and military $4.00.

Open to Public: Mon.–Sat. 10:00 A.M.–5:00 P.M.

Visitor Services: Gift shop, garden; located on trolley tour with other points of interest.
Regularly Scheduled Events: March, Cherry Blossom Festival; October, Historic Ghost Tours; December, Victorian Tea Parties around the Christmas Tree.
Directions: Take I–75 to I–16, exit at Spring Street, turn right, and cross bridge and proceed through two traffic lights. Turn left on Mulberry Street; museum is fourth house on the right.

 **GRISWOLDVILLE BATTLEFIELD** CWPT

c/o Georgia State Parks, 205 Butler Street, Suite 1352, Atlanta, GA 30334; (404) 656–2770.

Description: The town of Griswoldville was developed around a mill and armament factory that produced Griswold pistols and other equipment. On November 22, 1864, Maj. Gen. William T. Sherman's columns, on their March to the Sea, engaged and all but destroyed the Georgia militia and the town of Griswoldville. A seventeen-acre tract that was the site of the battle has been purchased and preserved; it is managed by Georgia State Parks as an unmanned site.
Admission Fees: Free.
Open to Public: Daily during daylight hours.
Visitor Services: Interpretive signage, parking.
Regularly Scheduled Events: None.
Directions: From Macon take U.S. 80 east to Georgia 57; take Georgia 57 toward Gordon to Henderson Road, turn left, and proceed approximately 1.25 miles. Turn right on Griswoldville Road and proceed approximately 1.5 miles to Baker Cemetery Road. Battle site and parking are on the left.

MARIETTA

 MARIETTA NATIONAL CEMETERY

500 Washington Avenue, Marietta, GA 30060; (770) 428–3258; www.cem.va.gov.

Description: The national cemetery is the burial site of more than 13,000 Union soldiers who were casualties from battles in the area, including New Hope Church, Pickett's Mill, and Kennesaw Mountain.
Admission Fees: Free.
Open to Public: Grounds, daily from dawn to dusk; office, Mon.–Fri. 8:00 A.M.–4:30 P.M.
Visitor Services: Restrooms.
Regularly Scheduled Events: Services held on Memorial Day and Veterans Day; first week in February, Four Chaplains Day; second week in September, Special POW/MIA Day; December, anniversary week of Pearl Harbor Day.
Directions: From I–75 north take exit 265; turn left onto North Marietta Parkway (120 Loop). Turn left onto Cole Street. The cemetery is straight ahead. There is access to the cemetery from Cole Street or Washington Street.

 WESTERN AND ATLANTIC PASSENGER DEPOT

Marietta Welcome Center and Visitors Bureau, No. 4 Depot Street, Marietta, GA 30060; (770) 429–1115; www.marietta square.com.

Description: This Victorian brick structure was built in 1898 on the site of the original 1840s passenger depot that was burned by Gen. William T. Sherman's troops in 1864. The depot in Marietta is where Andrews's Raiders boarded the General in 1862 and began their fateful journey—"The Great Locomotive Chase" (Andrews's Raid). The depot is also the site from which female workers from the Roswell mills were deported to the North as prisoners of war.

COASTAL

Admission Fees: Free.

Open to Public: Mon.–Fri. 9:00 A.M.–5:00 P.M., Sat. 11:00 A.M.–4:00 P.M., Sun. 1:00 P.M.–4:00 P.M.

Visitor Services: Public restrooms, information, handicapped access, gift shop.

Regularly Scheduled Events: April, Taste of Marietta; December, A Heritage Hometown, Marietta pilgrimage Christmas home tour.

Directions: From I–75 take exit 265. Heading west toward Marietta, proceed 2.5 miles to Mill Street; turn left onto Mill Street. A parking lot is immediately on the right. The Welcome Center is across railroad tracks from parking lot.

MILLEDGEVILLE

 THE OLD GOVERNOR'S MANSION

120 South Clarke Street, Milledgeville, GA 31061; (478) 445–4545; www.gcsu .edu/mansion.

Description: The mansion served as the executive residence of Georgia's governors from its completion in 1839 until 1868. Gov. Joseph E. Brown and his family resided in the mansion during the Civil War. Gen. William T. Sherman spent one night at the mansion during his March to the Sea.

Admission Fees: Adults $10.00, seniors and students $6.00, children $2.00.

Open to Public: Tues.–Sat. 10:00 A.M.–4:00 P.M., Sun. 2:00 P.M.–4:00 P.M.; closed Christmas Eve–New Year's Day.

Visitor Services: Public restrooms, handicapped access, gift shop, museum.

Regularly Scheduled Events: Thanksgiving–Christmas, Victorian Christmas at the mansion.

Directions: From I–20 take U.S. 441 south to Milledgeville. From I–16 take the Spring Street exit to Georgia 49 to Milledgeville. The mansion is on the corner of Hancock (Georgia 49) and Clarke Streets, directly across from Georgia College and State University.

MILLEN

 MAGNOLIA SPRINGS STATE PARK

1053 Magnolia Springs Drive, Millen, GA 30442; (478) 982–1660; www.gastate parks.org; magsps@brke.net.

Description: Three sites were chosen to relieve the overcrowding from Andersonville Prison. During the Civil War this site was called Camp Lawton and was used as a prison camp because of its natural springs, plentiful timber for building stockades, and nearness to the railroad. Almost twice the size of Andersonville, it was designed to hold 40,000 prisoners. Sherman's March to the Sea forced its evacuation after only six weeks. In that short span of time, more than 500 prisoners died at Camp Lawton. The earthwork fort that guarded the prison stands over the present-day park.

Admission Fees: Parking, $3.00/car, $50.00/bus.

Open to Public: Park, daily 8:00 A.M.–10:00 P.M.; park office, daily 8:00 A.M.–5:00 P.M.

Visitor Services: Lodging, public restrooms, information, food, gift shop, aquarium, camping.

Regularly Scheduled Events: Last weekend of March, Arts & Crafts Festival, with Civil War artillery demonstration.

Directions: From I–16 at Metter, take Georgia 121 to Millen, then take a left onto U.S. 25. The park is 5 miles north of Millen on U.S. 25. From I–20 exit onto Bobby Jones Expressway (I–520) and go approximately 7 miles to U.S. 25 exit. The park is 47 miles on U.S. 25.

NEWNAN

 MALE ACADEMY MUSEUM

30 Temple Avenue, Newnan, GA 30263; (770) 251–0207; www.nchistoricalsociety .org/mam.htm.

Description: Newnan, a hospital town, was the site of the Battle of Brown's Hill. Part of Sherman's Atlanta Campaign, the battle started at the train depot. Medical items and the battle are currently interpreted at the museum.

Admission Fees: Adults $2.00, children under twelve free.

Open to Public: Tues.–Thurs. 10:00 A.M.– noon and 1:00 P.M.–3:00 P.M., Sat. and Sun. 2:00 P.M.–5:00 P.M.

Visitor Services: Information, handicapped access, gift shop.

Regularly Scheduled Events: None.

Directions: From I–85 take exit 47 (Georgia 34/Bullsboro Drive). Head west approximately 3.5 miles to College Street, turn left and go 1 block to Temple Avenue. Male Academy Museum is on the southeast corner of the intersection.

NORTHWEST GEORGIA

 ATLANTA CAMPAIGN PAVILION PARKS

Description: These five roadside parks were constructed in the 1930s by the WPA to graphically describe the Atlanta Campaign, which occurred May 7–September 2, 1864. The parks are located on U.S. 41 in Ringold, Dalton, Resaca, Cassville, and Dallas.

Admission Fees: Free.

Open to Public: Daily during daylight hours.

Visitor Services: Memorial plaques.

Regularly Scheduled Events: None.

Directions: Located along U.S. 41, which parallels I–75 in northwest Georgia. The "Blue and Gray Trail" brochure includes a map and directions. A brochure and map

are available free from Georgia's Historic High Country Travel Association, P.O. Box 6177, Dalton, GA 30722; (800) 331–3258; or on the Internet at www.georgiahighcountry .org.

 BLUE AND GRAY TRAIL

Georgia's Historic High Country Travel Association, P.O. Box 6177, Dalton, GA 30722; (800) 331–3258; www.georgiahigh country.org.

Description: Northwest Georgia was the setting for some of the Civil War's most dramatic events. The trail features sixty-one sites that are accessible to visitors, including battlefields, museums, cemeteries, forts, and railroad depots.

Admission Fees: The "Blue and Gray Trail" brochure and map are available free from Georgia's Historic High Country Travel Association or on the Internet at www .georgiahighcountry.org.

Open to Public: Consult the brochure for hours of individual sites.

Visitor Services: Varies by site.

Regularly Scheduled Events: None.

Directions: The "Blue and Gray Trail" brochure includes a map and directions.

RESACA

 RESACA CONFEDERATE CEMETERY

c/o Calhoun-Gordon Counties Chamber of Commerce, 300 South Wall Street, Calhoun, GA 30701; (800) 887–3811.

Description: The Resaca Confederate Cemetery is the final resting place for approximately 400 Confederate soldiers who fell in the bloody two-day Battle of Resaca on May 14 and 15, 1864, between the forces of Generals Johnston and Sherman. The daughters of Maj. John Green, the superintendent of the Georgia Railroad, collected and reinterred the bodies from shallow graves to this plot known as the Confederate Cemetery, the first of its kind in Georgia.

Admission Fees: Free.

Open to Public: Daily during daylight hours.

Visitor Services: Brochure available.

Regularly Scheduled Events: Third weekend in May, memorial service during the reenactment of the Battle of Resaca.

Directions: From I–75 take exit 133; travel east on Georgia 136. Turn left (north) on U.S. 41, proceeding 1.7 miles. Turn right into the cemetery.

RICHMOND HILL

 52 FORT McALLISTER STATE HISTORIC PARK

3894 Fort McAllister Road, Richmond Hill, GA 31324; (912) 727–2339; www .fortmcallister.org.

Description: Located on the south bank of the Great Ogeechee River, this park is the home of the best-preserved earthwork fortification of the Confederacy. The sand-and-mud earthworks were attacked seven times by Union ironclads but did not fall until captured in 1864 by Gen. William T. Sherman. This coastal park, nestled among giant live oaks and a beautiful salt marsh, offers a museum containing Civil War artifacts as well as camping and picnic facilities.

Admission Fees: Adults $4.00, children $2.50, seniors $3.50; group prices vary.

Open to Public: Daily 8:00 A.M.–5:00 P.M.; closed Christmas.

Visitor Services: Public restrooms, information, handicapped access, gift shop, museum, camping.

Regularly Scheduled Events: Saturday before Memorial Day, Memorial Day celebration; first weekend in December, Winter Civil War Muster.

Directions: From I–95 take exit 90. Go east on Georgia 144 and turn left on Spur 144 to park.

ROSWELL

 53 BULLOCH HALL

180 Bulloch Avenue, P.O. Box 1309, Roswell, GA 30077; (770) 992–1731; www.bullochhall.org; info@bulloch hall.org.

Description: This 1840 home was built by Maj. James Bulloch and was the site of the December 1853 marriage between Martha Bulloch and Theodore Roosevelt of New York (they later became the parents of President Theodore Roosevelt and grandparents of Eleanor Roosevelt, wife of President Franklin D. Roosevelt). The house is now a museum, featuring period rooms, a research library, and a Civil War artifact room. The surrounding historic district features many structures of the Civil War period. The Roswell Presbyterian Church was a Union hospital in 1864. The former locations of several mills that were burned by Gen. William Sherman are marked.

Admission Fees: Adults $8.00, children $6.00.

Open to Public: Mon.–Sat. 10:00 A.M.–3:00 P.M. (last tour at 3:00 P.M.), Sun. 1:00 P.M.–3:00 P.M. (last tour at 3:00 P.M.).

Visitor Services: Public restrooms, information, handicapped access, gift shop, museum, tours.

Regularly Scheduled Events: Mid-March, Great American Coverup quilt show; December, reenactment of 1853 wedding, Christmas at Bulloch Hall.

Directions: From I–85 or I–285, travel north on Georgia 400. Take Northridge exit and turn right. Take the next right onto Roswell Road. Turn right on Roswell Road to Historic Roswell Square, then turn left at light onto Georgia 120. The parking lot is 200 yards ahead on the right.

SAVANNAH

 FORT JAMES JACKSON

1 Old Fort Jackson Road, Savannah, GA 31404; (912) 232–3945; www.chsgeorgia .org; fortjackson@chsgeorgia.org.

Description: The original brick fort, now the oldest standing brick fortification in Georgia, was begun in 1808 and was manned during the War of 1812. Fort Jackson was enlarged and strengthened between 1845 and 1860. It saw its greatest wartime activity serving as the headquarters for the Confederate defenses on the Savannah River during the Civil War. The fort was part of a system of nine fortifications that protected the river with a total firepower of nearly one hundred heavy guns. Today visitors to Fort Jackson can see a variety of military hardware, including projectiles and cannons from the CSS *Georgia,* a Confederate ironclad that lies at the bottom of the Savannah River.

Admission Fees: Adults $3.50; students, military, and seniors $2.50; children under five free.

Open to Public: Daily 9:00 A.M.–5:00 P.M.

Visitor Services: Public restrooms, information, handicapped access, gift shop, museum.

Regularly Scheduled Events: None.

Directions: From I–95 take exit for I–16 east toward Historic Downtown Savannah; take Montgomery Street exit. Turn right on Liberty Street, left on East Broad Street, right onto President Street. Follow approximately 2 miles, turn left on Woodcock Road, and follow road to Savannah River.

 FORT PULASKI NATIONAL MONUMENT

P.O. Box 30757, Savannah, GA 31410-0757; (912) 786–5787; www.nps.gov/fopu.

Description: On April 11, 1862, Union forces overtook the fort in only thirty hours. The fall of Fort Pulaski secured Union control over Southern ports and kept Savannah from exporting cotton and importing vital military and civilian goods. This remarkably intact example of nineteenth-century military architecture is preserved for future generations.

COASTAL

Damage from Union artillery, Fort Pulaski, Savannah, Georgia. James Campi.

Admission Fees: Adults $3.00, children under sixteen free, seniors free with Golden Age Passport; maximum charge of $4.00 per car.

Open to Public: Park, daily 8:30 A.M.–5:15 P.M.; visitor center, daily 8:30 A.M.–5:00 P.M.; call for extended summer hours.

Visitor Services: Public restrooms, information, handicapped access, gift shop, museum, trails.

Regularly Scheduled Events: None.

Directions: From I–95 follow I–16 or U.S. 80 to Savannah. Head east on U.S. 80 toward Tybee Island. Fort Pulaski is approximately 15 miles east of Savannah.

 56 GREEN-MELDRIM HOUSE

St. John's Church, 1 West Macon Street, Savannah, GA 31401; (912) 233–3845.

Description: This restored and furnished mid-nineteenth-century Gothic Revival–style home of Charles Green served as the headquarters for Union Gen. William Sherman during the winter of 1864–65. While staying at the Green-Meldrim House, Sherman sent a telegram to President Lincoln presenting the city of Savannah to him as a Christmas present. The house is currently owned and operated by St. John's Episcopal Church.

Admission Fees: Adults $7.00, children $2.00, groups call for special rates.

Open to Public: Tues., Thurs., Fri., and Sat. 10:00 A.M.–3:30 P.M.; closed Mon., Wed., and Sun.; closed two weeks before Easter, Dec. 15–Jan. 15, and the week of Nov. 11.

Visitor Services: Guided tours.

Regularly Scheduled Events: None.

Directions: At the end of I–16 east is Montgomery Street. At first traffic signal turn right on Liberty Street. Go 5 blocks and turn right on Bull Street. Go 1 block to Madison Square. The house fronts Madison Square between Charlton and Harris Streets.

 57 SAVANNAH HISTORY MUSEUM

303 Martin Luther King Jr. Boulevard, Savannah, GA 31401; (912) 651–6825; www.chsgeorgia.org; shm@chsgeorgia.org.

Description: The museum is located in the passenger station of the Central Georgia Railroad. There are many exhibits pertaining to the history of Savannah, including the Civil War. Exhibits include uniforms, weaponry, and the battle flag of the Savannah Volunteer Guard, which fought at Sailor's Creek, Virginia. Other artifacts include weaponry from the CSS *Georgia* and one of the rarest keg torpedoes in the world.

Admission Fees: Museum, adults $4.25, seniors $3.75, children six–twelve $3.00.

Open to Public: Mon.–Fri. 8:30 A.M.–5:00 P.M., Sat.–Sun. 9:00 A.M.–5:00 P.M.

Visitor Services: Public restrooms, information, handicapped access, food, gift shop.

Regularly Scheduled Events: None.

Directions: Take I–16 east until it merges into Montgomery Street; turn right onto Martin Luther King Jr. Boulevard; take first left into visitor center parking lot.

STONE MOUNTAIN

 58 GEORGIA'S STONE MOUNTAIN PARK

P.O. Box 778, Stone Mountain, GA 30086; (770) 498–5690; www.stone mountainpark.com.

Description: Located 16 miles east of Atlanta, Stone Mountain Park is a 3,200-acre world of recreation and family fun. The centerpiece of the park is Stone Mountain itself, the world's largest exposed mass of granite. The memorial carving on the face of the mountain is about the size of a football field. The carving commemorates the Confederate states, with the figures of Jefferson Davis, Robert E. Lee, and Stonewall Jackson. The park also features a restored antebellum plantation and the Discovering Stone Mountain Museum, containing a large Civil War collection.

Admission Fees: Park entry, free. Vehicle parking permit, cars, $8.00/day or $35.00 annual pass available. Separate attractions (skylift, train, riverboat, antebellum plantation, Antique Car and Treasure Museum, Discovering Stone Mountain Museum, Crossroads 1870's Southern Town), adults $4.50–$7.00, children three–eleven $4.00–$7.00; call for group rates.

Open to Public: Park, daily all year 6:00 A.M.–midnight. Attractions open daily; call for seasonal hours.

Visitor Services: Lodging, public restrooms, information, handicapped access, food, gift shop, conference center; trails, golf, tennis, camping.

Regularly Scheduled Events: Last weekend of each month, Civil War living history demonstrations; March, Taste of the South; mid-April, Civil War encampment; first weekend after Labor Day, Yellow Daisy Festival; October, Highland Games, Tour of Southern Ghosts; December, Deck the Halls at the Antebellum Plantation.

Directions: From I–285 east take exit 39B (U.S. 78); go 7 miles east to Stone Mountain Park exit.

WASHINGTON

ROBERT TOOMBS HOUSE HISTORIC SITE

216 East Robert Toombs Avenue, Washington, GA 30673; (706) 678–2226; www.gastateparks.org.

Description: Home of Gen. Robert Augustus Toombs, a successful planter, lawyer, and outspoken Georgia politician, who used his influence to persuade the state to secede from the Union. As secretary of state of the Confederacy, general, and seasoned battle leader, he never took the postwar oath of allegiance to the United States and died as an unreconstructed Rebel.

Admission Fees: Adults $3.00, seniors $2.50, children six–eighteen $1.75, under six free; call for group rates.

Open to Public: Tues.–Sat. 9:00 A.M.–5:00 P.M.

Visitor Services: Public restrooms, information, handicapped access to first floor.

Regularly Scheduled Events: First Saturday in April, spring home tour and living history demonstration; second Sunday in December, Christmas at the Toombs House.

Directions: Washington is 45 miles east of Athens on U.S. 78 and 50 miles west of Augusta. From I–20 take exit 59 (Thomson/Washington). Follow U.S. 78 east into downtown Washington. Turn left on Robert Toombs Avenue.

WASHINGTON HISTORICAL MUSEUM

308 East Robert Toombs Avenue, Washington, GA 30673; (706) 678–2105; www.washingtongeorgia.net.

Description: Exhibits in this Federal-style house (ca. 1835) highlight the Confederacy and the Reconstruction era as well as domestic art and local history. A guided tour is available to interpret memorabilia from the last Confederate cabinet meeting as Jefferson Davis fled south. The display includes Jefferson Davis's camp chest, original photos, signed documents, and Gen. Robert Toombs's uniform.

Admission Fees: Adults age thirteen and older $3.00, children five–twelve $2.00, under five free; call for special rates for groups of fifteen or more.

Open to Public: Tues.–Sat. 10:00 A.M.–5:00 P.M., Sun. 12:30 P.M.–3:30 P.M.

Visitor Services: Public restrooms, information, gift shop, tour.

Regularly Scheduled Events: None.

Directions: From I–20 take exit 148 (Crawfordville). Take Georgia 22 and follow the signs.

COASTAL

WEST POINT

 FORT TYLER

1111 West Sixth Avenue, West Point, GA 31833-0715; (706) 773–8378; www.forttyler.com.

Description: This earthen fort was built to defend the strategic Chattahoochee River bridges and military depot in West Point. It was the site of one of the last engagements of the Civil War, fought on April 16, 1865, between Union cavalry under command of Col. Oscar LaGrange and Confederates under Gen. Robert Tyler. The Confederates, numbering fewer than 300 men, managed to withstand advances by 3,500 Union soldiers for eight hours before the fort was finally captured.

Admission Fees: Free.

Open to Public: Daily during daylight hours.

Visitor Services: Handicapped access; trails.

Regularly Scheduled Events: None.

Directions: From I–85 take exit 1 to West Point. Cross over the Chattahoochee River and turn right on Third Avenue in downtown. Turn left on 10th Street, then turn right at the historical marker on West Sixth Avenue. Monument marks trail to fort.

❖ NORTH CAROLINA ❖

ABERDEEN

 MALCOLM BLUE FARM

P.O. Box 603, Aberdeen, NC 28315; (910) 944–7558; malcolmbluefarm.org.

Description: On March 9, 1865, a wing of Gen. William Sherman's army, commanded by Gen. Thomas J. Jordan, commandeered the farmstead, with officers taking over half of the house. The Confederates camped in the back of the farmstead and at nearby Bethesda Church. At dawn on March 10, the Battle of Monroe's Crossroads took place on what is now Fort Bragg.

Admission Fees: Adults $2.00.

Open to Public: Wed.–Sat. 11:00 A.M.–2:00 P.M.; closed Sun.–Tues.

Visitor Services: Public restrooms, handicapped access, gift shop, museum.

Regularly Scheduled Events: June, Bluegrass Festival; September, Malcolm Blue Historical Crafts and Farmskills Festival; December, Christmas Open House.

Directions: From I–95 in Fayetteville, take U.S. 401, Cape Fear Valley Hospital exit, to Raeford. Turn west on Highway 211 into the town of Aberdeen. Within the city limits, turn right on PeeDee Road, and then right on Bethesda Road. Malcolm Blue Farmstead is approximately 1 mile down the road on the left.

ASHEVILLE

 SMITH-McDOWELL HOUSE

283 Victoria Road, Asheville, NC 28801; (828) 253–9231; www.wnchistory.org; smh@wnchistory.org.

Description: This 1840 brick mansion was the home of William Wallace McDowell. McDowell organized the Buncombe Rifleman North Carolina Volunteers Company E, the first Confederate troops in western North Carolina. The house is restored with period rooms and special history exhibits. Also on the grounds is the Buncombe County Civil War Memorial, which lists the names of the 553 Union and Confederate soldiers from Buncombe County who died during the war.

Admission Fees: Adults $7.00, students with ID $6.00, children five–eighteen $3.00; call for group rates.

Open to Public: Thurs.–Sat. 10:00 A.M.–

4:00 P.M., Sun. noon–4:00 P.M.

Visitor Services: Information, handicapped access, gift shop, museum.

Regularly Scheduled Events: May, Heritage Alive Fair; mid-November–mid-January, Victorian Christmas Celebration.

Directions: From 1–40 take exit 50 toward downtown Asheville. Proceed 0.5 mile and stay right as road forks. Proceed 1 mile. Turn left on Victoria Road. The museum is 0.5 mile down Victoria Road on the right-hand side.

ATLANTIC BEACH

 FORT MACON STATE PARK

2300 East Fort Macon Road, P.O. Box 127, Atlantic Beach, NC 28512; (252) 726–3775; www.clis.com/friends; fort .macon@ncmail.net.

Description: Construction of this "Third System" brick fort began in 1826 to guard Beaufort Inlet and Beaufort Harbor, North Carolina's only major deepwater ocean port. The fort was garrisoned in 1834 and named after U.S. Sen. Nathaniel Macon. On April 14, 1861, local militia seized the fort for the state of North Carolina and the Confedera-cy. Union forces under Maj. Gen. Ambrose E. Burnside recaptured the fort in 1862. For the duration of the war, the fort protected ships recoaling in Beaufort.

Admission Fees: Free.

Open to Public: Fort, daily 9:00 A.M.–5:30 P.M.; Closed Christmas. Guided tours Memorial Day–Labor Day.

Visitor Services: Public restrooms, information, gift shop, museum, trails.

Regularly Scheduled Events: April, July, September, Civil War reenactment.

Directions: From I–40 or I–95 take U.S. 70 east to Morehead City. Turn off U.S. 70 onto the Atlantic Beach Bridge; follow road to stoplight at Route 58 and turn left onto 58 South. Park is at the end of the road.

BEAUFORT

 BEAUFORT HISTORIC SITE

100 Block Turner Street, Beaufort, NC 28516; (252) 728–5225; www.historic beaufort.com; beauforthistoricsite @earthlink.net.

Description: Tours of the site include the Josiah Bell House, home of Rebel spy Josiah

COASTAL

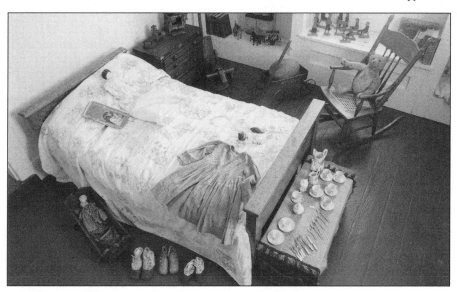

Child's room in Josiah Bell House, Beaufort Historic Site, North Carolina. Diane Hardy.

Fisher Bell. Records show that 40 percent of Beaufort residents sympathized with the Union. Beaufort also boasts a historic cemetery that has been consecrated by both Northern and Southern clergy.

Admission Fees: Adults $8.00, children $4.00.

Open to Public: Mar.–Nov., Mon.–Sat. 9:30 A.M.–5:00 P.M., closed Sun. (June–Aug., open Sun. 1:00 P.M.–4:00 P.M.); Dec.–Feb., Mon.–Sat. 10:00 A.M.–4:00 P.M.

Visitor Services: Public restrooms, information, gift shop, museum.

Regularly Scheduled Events: April, "Publick Day"; June, Beaufort Old Homes and Garden Tour/Antiques Show and Sale; December, Carolina Christmas Walk.

Directions: From I–95 take U.S 70 east to the town of Beaufort. Turn right on Turner Street. Site is located 3 blocks down on the left.

CRESWELL

★ SOMERSET PLACE STATE
66 HISTORIC SITE
2572 Lake Shore Road, Creswell, NC 27928; (252) 797–4560; www.somerset place.nchistoricsites.org; somerset @ncmail.net.

Description: At the dawn of the Civil War, Somerset Place was a wealthy planter's estate and home to more than 300 enslaved men, women, and children. As a result of the war, it was transformed into a shadowy remnant that proved home to no one. The stories surrounding that transformation provide a microscopic view of social, emotional, economic, and legal impacts of the war on individual Southerners of different races and genders.

Admission Fees: Free.

Open to Public: Apr.–Oct., Mon.–Sat. 9:00 A.M.–5:00 P.M., Sun. 1:00 P.M.–5:00 P.M.; Nov.–Mar., Mon.–Sat. 10:00 A.M.–4:00 P.M., Sun. 1:00 P.M.–4:00 P.M.

Visitor Services: Information, gift shop, public restrooms.

Regularly Scheduled Events: December, Annual Christmas Open House.

Directions: From I–95 take North Carolina 64 east to Creswell; follow highway signage 7 miles south to site.

DUNN

★ AVERASBORO
67 BATTLEFIELD
P.O. Box 1811, Dunn, NC 28335; (910) 891–5019; www.averasboro.com; info @averasboro.com.

Description: This is the site of the 1865 Battle of Averasboro, where the outnumbered and outgunned Confederates of Gen. William Hardee's corps delayed the left wing of Gen. William Sherman's army advance north from Fayetteville. The Battle of Averasboro was fought on the 8,000-acre Smithville Plantation along the Cape Fear River, March 15–16, 1865. The delay enabled the relocation of additional Confederates for Gen. Joseph E. Johnston's final offensive of the war at the Battle of Bentonville, fought 25 miles to the north on March 19–21, 1865.

Admission Fees: Free.

Open to Public: Battlefield site, daily from dawn to dusk; museum, Tues.–Sat. 10:00 A.M.–4:00 P.M., Sun. 1:00 P.M.–4:00 P.M.

Visitor Services: Information, handicapped access, gift shop, public restrooms, museum.

Regularly Scheduled Events: March, annual anniversary reenactment or living history and periodic demonstrations; call for more information.

Directions: From I–95 take exit 71. Continue west for 3 miles to intersection with North Carolina Highway 82. Take Highway 82 east for 2 miles. The Averasboro Battlefield Museum is on the right, just past the Lebanon Plantation House.

DURHAM

BENNETT PLACE STATE HISTORIC SITE

4409 Bennett Memorial Road, Durham, NC 27705; (919) 383–4345; www.bennett place.nchistoricsites.org; bennett @ncmail.net.

Description: It was at Bennett Farmhouse that Gens. Joseph E. Johnston and William T. Sherman met in April 1865 and signed an agreement for the surrender of all of the Confederate troops in North Carolina, South Carolina, Georgia, and Florida, almost 90,000 men. This surrender on April 26, 1865, followed Gen. Robert E. Lee's surrender at Appomattox by seventeen days and was the largest troop surrender of the Civil War.
Admission Fees: Free.
Open to Public: Tues.–Sat. 10:00 A.M.–5:00 P.M.; closed Sun., Mon, and most major holidays.
Visitor Services: Public restrooms, information, handicapped access, gift shop, museum.
Regularly Scheduled Events: April, living history event, with surrender reenactment on five-year cycle; fall, living history event; early December, Annual Christmas Open House.
Directions: From I–85 north take exit 170; follow the signs. From I–85 south take exit 173; follow the signs.

EDENTON

EDENTON BELL BATTERY CANNON

"St. Paul," 505 South Broad Street, Edenton, NC 27932; (252) 482–7800; www.visitedenton.com.

Description: This site displays the bronze twelve-pounder field howitzer "St. Paul" of the Edenton Bell Battery. The battery's field pieces were all cast from the town's bells. The battery fought with the Army of North-

Bennett Place State Historical Site, Durham, North Carolina. Chris E. Heisey–CWPT files.

ern Virginia in several major battles and returned to fight with the Department of North Carolina in the eastern section of the state.
Admission Fees: Guided tour, adults $7.00, students $3.50, family $15.00.
Open to Public: Daily during daylight hours.
Visitor Services: Lodging, public restrooms, information, gas, handicapped access, food, gift shop, museum, camping, trails.
Regularly Scheduled Events: None.
Directions: From I–64 in Norfolk, Virginia, take U.S. 17 south 70 miles to Edenton. From I–95 in Rocky Mount, North Carolina, take U.S. 64 east 35 miles to Williamston; take U.S. 17 north 34 miles to Edenton.

ELIZABETH CITY

MUSEUM OF THE ALBEMARLE

501 South Water Street, Elizabeth City, NC 27909; (252) 335–1453; www.museum ofthealbemarle.com.

Description: The museum tells the story of the people who have lived in the Albemarle

COASTAL

region from prehistory to the present. The Albemarle region is the northeastern corner of North Carolina and was the earliest part of the state to be settled. During the Civil War many battles were fought here. At the museum you can see remnants of the CSS *Black Warrior,* part of the Confederate Mosquito Fleet destroyed on the Pasquotank River during the Battle of Elizabeth City in 1862.

Admission Fees: Free.

Open to Public: Tues.–Sat. 9:00 A.M.–5:00 P.M., Sun. 2:00 P.M.–5:00 P.M.

Visitor Services: Public restrooms, information, handicapped access, gift shop, museum.

Regularly Scheduled Events: September, A Day on the River.

Directions: From Norfolk, Virginia, take U.S. 17 south to Elizabeth City. The highway will become U.S. 17/158. Turn right on U.S. 158 east/Elizabeth Street. Turn right on Water Street; the museum is on the corner of Water and Ehringhaus.

FAYETTEVILLE

 MUSEUM OF THE CAPE FEAR/ARSENAL PARK

P.O. Box 53693, 801 Arsenal Avenue, Fayetteville, NC 28305; (910) 486–1330; www.ncmuseumofhistory.org; mcf @ncmail.net.

Description: The Federal government built the arsenal in Fayetteville to produce a variety of ordinance. In April 1861 local militia accepted a peaceful surrender of the arsenal, and shortly thereafter it became a significant producer of arms and ammunition for the Confederacy. Gen. William Sherman's army destroyed the arsenal in March 1865. Today extant tower and building foundations, as well as a 35-foot-high steel facsimile of an original tower, represent the focal points of the public presentation.

Admission Fees: Free.

Open to Public: Tues.–Sat. 10:00 A.M.–5:00 P.M., Sun. 1:00 P.M.–5:00 P.M.

Visitor Services: Public restrooms, information, handicapped access, gift shop.

Regularly Scheduled Events: Military demonstrations throughout the year; call ahead for schedule.

Directions: From I–95 take exit 56 (U.S. 301) south to Grove Street, turn right onto Grove Street, then follow Grove to Bragg Boulevard. Turn left on Bragg Boulevard, follow it to Hay Street, turn right onto Hay Street, and take second left onto Bradford. The site is on the first street on the right.

GREENSBORO

 GREENSBORO HISTORICAL MUSEUM

130 Summit Avenue, Greensboro, NC 27401-3016, (336) 373–2043; www .greensborohistory.org.

Description: The Greensboro Historical Museum serves as the local history museum, with an extensive military history exhibit and Civil War–related items. The collection includes a rare Tarpley carbine, made in Greensboro during the Civil War; haversack contents; weapons; a display featuring the Guilford Grays, a local volunteer militia unit; a Confederate school text; contemporary artwork by Don Troiani; and excerpts from a local resident's Civil War diary about life in Greensboro. The museum property was the site of a Confederate hospital after the Battle of Bentonville; several Civil War veterans are buried in the First Presbyterian Church cemetery, which is now a part of the museum complex.

Admission Fees: Free.

Open to Public: Tues.–Sat. 10:00 A.M.–5:00 P.M., Sun. 2:00 P.M.–5:00 P.M.; closed city holidays.

Visitor Services: Public restrooms, information, handicapped access, gift shop, guided group tours with reservation.

Regularly Scheduled Events: None.

Directions: From I–85/I–40, take the Elm/ Eugene Street exit. Turn north on Elm/

Eugene, and follow several miles into the Greensboro downtown area. Turn right onto Bellemeade Street, follow it to Lindsay Street, and turn right. There is free parking on both Lindsay and Church Streets. A map is available on the museum's Web site.

HAMILTON

 FORT BRANCH

2883 Fort Branch Road, Hamilton, NC 27857; (252) 792–4902 or (800) 776–8566; www.fortbranchcivilwarsite.com; adjutant@fortbranchcivilwarsite.com.

Description: Located on Rainbow Bluff overlooking the Roanoke River, Fort Branch protected Roanoke River Valley farms and the Weldon Railroad bridge from destruction by Federal gunboats. Fort Branch also served as protection for the construction site of the CSS *Albemarle* at Edward's Ferry, a key in the Confederacy's effort in regaining control of the Atlantic coast. The Weldon Railroad bridge was critical to the Army of Northern Virginia in receiving supplies from the port of Wilmington via the Wilmington and Weldon Railroad. The fort features seven of the eleven original cannons on-site as well as well-preserved earthworks.

Admission Fees: Free, except on reenactment weekend, $5.00/car, $10.00/bus or fifteen-passenger van.

Open to Public: Apr.–Nov., Sat.–Sun. 1:30 P.M.–5:30 P.M.; extended hours for reenactment weekend and other times by appointment. Closed second weekend in November through last weekend in March.

Visitor Services: Public restrooms, information, handicapped access, gift shop, museum.

Regularly Scheduled Events: First full weekend in November, annual battle reenactment weekend; first Saturday in December, Fort Branch opens only for Christmas program.

Directions: From I–95 take exit 138 at Rocky Mount; follow U.S. 64 east to Robersonville and take North Carolina 903 north; 0.5 mile south of Hamilton, turn right on the Fort Branch Road and go 2 miles. The site is on your left.

HILLSBOROUGH

 ORANGE COUNTY HISTORICAL MUSEUM

201 North Churton Street; Hillsborough, NC 27278; (919) 732–2201; www.orange countymuseum.org; info@orangecounty museum.org.

Description: The museum contains Civil War weapons, muster rolls, and other artifacts to help interpret Orange County's role during the war.

Admission Fees: Free.

Open to Public: Apr.–Dec., Tues.–Sat. 11:00 A.M.–4:00 P.M.; Jan.–Mar., Tues.–Sat. noon–3:00 P.M., Sun. 1:00 P.M.–4:00 P.M.

Visitor Services: Public restrooms, information, gift shop, museum; trails.

Regularly Scheduled Events: December, candlelight tours.

Directions: Exit off I–40 or I–85 directly into Historic Hillsborough.

KINSTON

 CSS *NEUSE* STATE HISTORIC SITE

2612 West Vernon Avenue, Kinston, NC 28504; (252) 522–2091; www.cssneuse .net; cssneuse@ncmail.net.

Description: The CSS *Neuse* State Historic Site houses and interprets the archaeological remains of the Confederate ironclad *Neuse,* one of only three Civil War ironclads on display in the United States. The CSS *Neuse* was an integral factor in preventing Union forces from moving from New Bern to Goldsboro. When Union troops occupied Kinston in March 1865, the *Neuse* was burned by her crew and sank to the bottom of the Neuse River. The *Neuse* was raised in

COASTAL

THE CIVIL WAR AT SEA

One of the most neglected aspects of the Civil War is the role of the Union and Confederate navies in the conflict. The North's overwhelming naval superiority at the beginning of the war, coupled with the Union's enormous shipbuilding potential, were the keys to Federal victory on both land and sea.

The first shot of the naval war was fired four months before the war officially began with the Confederate bombardment of Fort Sumter, South Carolina. On January 9, 1861, a group of Citadel cadets fired on the *Star of the West*, a civilian vessel hired by the Federal government to provision the beleaguered garrison at Fort Sumter. The vessel fled back to New York after suffering minor damage.

Without a doubt, the most momentous innovation of the naval war was the introduction of ironclad vessels as armed combatants. Prior to the Civil War, a few experimental iron-plated ships were built in Europe. However, it wasn't until the CSS *Virginia* (formerly the USS *Merrimac*) wrought havoc on the Union fleet at Hampton Roads, Virginia, on March 8, 1862, that ironclad warships first performed in combat. One day later, on March 9, the USS *Monitor* fought the *Virginia* to a stalemate, ending the era of the wooden warship and changing naval warfare forever.

Despite being the first to introduce an ironclad into combat, the Confederacy simply could not compete with the North in either the quality or quantity of its ironclad warships. The standard Rebel "casemate" ironclad was no match for the Union's turreted gunships, patterned after the original *Monitor*. Most Confederate ironclads were destined to be scuttled by their own crews to avoid capture by the enemy. Only a few, like the CSS *Tennessee* at Mobile Bay and the CSS *Albemarle* on the Roanoke River, were defeated in combat.

On the western waterways, the industrious Northern navy built a fleet from scratch, constructing casemate ironclads for use on the Cumberland, Mississippi, and Tennessee Rivers. The ugly, low-profile ships, known as "Pook Turtles," were named after their designer, Samuel M. Pook. These ironclads were key to the Union successes at Fort Henry, Fort Donelson, and Island Number Ten. They also played a crucial role in Gen. Ulysses S. Grant's decisive 1863 campaign against Vicksburg. Later in the war, several of these ironclads would be nearly lost during Gen. Nathaniel Banks's bungled Red River campaign.

Although naval battles at Fort Donelson, New Orleans, and Mobile Bay provided the naval war with much of its drama, it was the mundane task of blockading Southern ports that led the Union to victory in the Civil War. These silent sentinels in blue slowly strangled the Confederate war effort, cutting off the South's lifeline to the manufacturing centers of Europe. The work of the blockaders was characterized by long periods of boredom interrupted by occasional running fights with fleeing blockade runners. For decades after the war, the Southern seacoast was strewn with the bleached and rotting timbers of blockade runners unable to escape the guns of the Federal fleet.

In retaliation for the blockade, the South refitted or built several fast, oceangoing warships to destroy Union commercial vessels at sea. These "commerce raiders" were considered nothing more than pirates by the Federal government, and large bounties were offered for their capture or destruction. The most famous raider was Capt. (later Adm.) Raphael Semmes, who commanded both the CSS *Sumter* and the CSS *Alabama*, two of the Confederacy's most notorious commerce raiders. Under Semmes's command, the *Alabama* would capture sixty-five Union merchantmen before she was sunk by the USS *Kearsarge* off the coast of France.

The last major battle of the naval war was the Union assault on Fort Fisher in January 1865. Fort Fisher, an imposing earthwork fort manned by 1,500 men, guarded the entry to Wilmington, North Carolina—the South's only remaining seaport by the end of 1864. After a spirited duel between the Union fleet and Confederate land-based batteries, the fort fell in a combined army-navy operation. The assault cost the Union more than 1,300 casualties and resulted in death or capture of the entire Rebel garrison.

With the fall of Fort Fisher, nearly all the waterways of the South were under Federal control. The Confederacy no longer had enough of a navy to resist the overwhelming might of the Union fleet. Most of what little did remain of the Confederate flotilla was bottled up on the James River, and those vessels were scuttled on April 3, 1865—the same morning Richmond fell to Grant's army.

However, even after the surrender of the Confederacy's remaining armies in April and May 1865, one Southern flag continued to wave defiantly at sea. The raider CSS *Shenandoah* continued to fight on in the Pacific until August 1865, when her commander learned that the war had ended. The curtain of the naval war finally drew to a close on November 6, 1865, when the *Shenandoah* surrendered herself to the Royal Navy at Liverpool, England.

1963; almost 15,000 artifacts were recovered as part of the excavation.

Admission Fees: Free.

Open to Public: Call ahead for hours of operation, as they change depending on the season.

Visitor Services: Public restrooms, information, handicapped access, gift shop, museum.

Regularly Scheduled Events: Third weekend in November, annual living history weekend.

Directions: From I–95 take Smithfield/Selma, North Carolina, exit; take U.S. 70 east to Kinston approximately 45 miles. In Kinston take Business U.S. 70; site is 0.5 mile on right.

KURE BEACH

 FORT FISHER STATE HISTORIC SITE

1610 Fort Fisher Boulevard South, P.O. Box 164, Kure Beach, NC 28449; (910) 458–5538; www.fortfisher.nchistoric sites.org; fisher@ncmail.net.

Description: Before its fall in January 1865, Fort Fisher protected blockade runners en route to Wilmington with supplies vital to the Confederate army. It was the largest of the earthen seacoast fortifications defending the last major open port to the Confederacy. The fall of Fort Fisher, on January 15, 1865, helped seal the fate of the Confederacy. The site boasts scenic easements of the Cape Fear River and the Atlantic Ocean.

Admission Fees: Free.

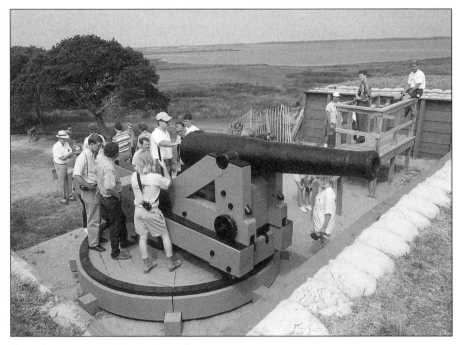

Shepards Battery, Fort Fisher, North Carolina. CWPT files.

Open to Public: Apr.–Sept., Mon.–Sat. 9:00 A.M.–5:00 P.M., Sun. 1:00 P.M.–5:00 P.M.; Oct.–Mar., Tues.–Sat. 10:00 A.M.–4:00 P.M., Sun. 1:00 P.M.–4:00 P.M.

Visitor Services: Public restrooms, information, handicapped access, gift shop, museum, guided tours.

Regularly Scheduled Events: January, annual commemorative anniversary program; summer, interpretive program.

Directions: Take I–40 to Wilmington; take U.S. 421 south approximately 20 miles to Kure Beach. Fort Fisher is on the right side of U.S. 421, 1 mile past Kure Beach.

MARION

 HISTORIC CARSON HOUSE

1805 U.S. Highway 70 West, Marion, NC 28752; (828) 724–4948; www.mcdowellnc.org; info@mcdowellnc.org.

Description: One of the sites of Gen. George Stoneman's raid in 1865, the Historic Carson House was commandeered as Union headquarters, and troops camped on the property for several days. A small skirmish between Stoneman's Raiders and the Confederate home guard took place on the property on April 19, 1865, in one of the last skirmishes of the war.

Admission Fees: Adults $3.00, children six–eighteen $1.50; group rates available.

Open to Public: May–Oct., Wed.–Sat. 10:00 A.M.–4:00 P.M.; remainder of year, by appointment only.

Visitor Services: Public restrooms, handicapped access, tours, research library.

Regularly Scheduled Events: September, Over Mountain Victory Train Celebration; December, Appalachian Authors' Fair.

Directions: From I–40 take the Marion exit to U.S. 70. Continue on U.S. 70 approximately 4 miles west of Marion and follow the signs to Carson House.

NEWTON GROVE

BENTONVILLE
78 BATTLEFIELD STATE
HISTORIC SITE CWPT

5466 Harper House Road, Four Oaks, NC 27524; (910) 594–0789; www.bentonvillebattlefield.nchistoricsites.org; bentonville@ncmail.net.

Description: Bentonville was the site of the last major battle of the Civil War, fought March 19–21, 1865, just three weeks before Lee's surrender to Grant at Appomattox. The battle is also significant as the largest battle ever fought on North Carolina soil, the last Confederate offensive operation of the war, and the only significant attempt to stop the march of Sherman's army after the fall of Atlanta.

Admission Fees: Free.

Open to Public: Apr.–Oct., Mon.–Sat. 9:00 A.M.–5:00 P.M.; Nov.–Mar., Tues.–Sat. 10:00 A.M.–4:00 P.M.; Sun. 1:00 P.M.–4:00 P.M.

Visitor Services: Public restrooms, information, gift shop, tours of Harper House Field Hospital, trails.

Regularly Scheduled Events: March, anniversary living history program; July–September, summer seasonal living history program; December, Christmas open house; every fifth year, anniversary commemoration reenactments.

Directions: From I–95 take exit 90; travel 15 miles south on U.S. 701, then left onto Route 1008. Travel 3 miles east to site. From I–40 take exit 343; travel 6 miles north on U.S. 701 to Route 1008. Travel 3 miles east to site.

OUTER BANKS

DARE COUNTY CIVIL WAR
79 HERITAGE TRAIL

Outer Banks Visitors Bureau, One Visitors Center Circle, Manteo, NC 27954; (252) 473–2138; www.outerbanks.org.

Description: The Dare County Civil War Heritage Trail covers 15 miles and has fifteen markers and wayside exhibits depicting the first combined military operation of the Civil War at Hatteras Inlet, the first amphibious landing of the Civil War, the cap-

COASTAL

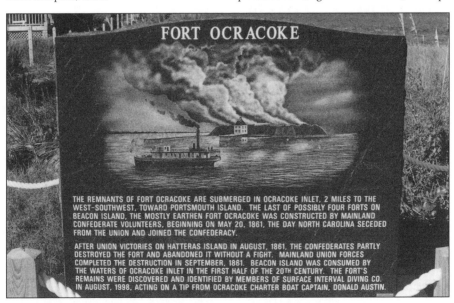

Fort Ocracoke, Dare County, North Carolina. Ocracoke Preservation Society Museum.

turing of Forts Hatteras and Clark, the naval engagement between the USS *Albatross* and the CSS *Beaufort,* and the Freedmen's colony located on Roanoke Island.

Admission Fees: Free.

Open to Public: Daily from dawn until dusk.

Visitor Services: Lodging, public restrooms, information, gas, handicapped access, food, gift shop, trails, camping.

Directions: From Norfolk, Virginia, take Highway 168 to Highway 12 on Hatteras Island.

PLYMOUTH

PORT-O-PLYMOUTH CIVIL WAR MUSEUM

302 Water Street, P.O. Box 296, Plymouth, NC 27962; (252) 793–1377; www.livinghistoryweekend.com; porto@plymouthnc.com.

Description: In 1862 Union troops stationed a garrison in the town of Plymouth to control the mouth of the Roanoke River. With the aid of Northern sympathizers, free African Americans, and slave runaways, they built four forts. The second-largest Civil War battle in North Carolina, the Battle of Plymouth, on April 17–20, 1864, involving 20,000 soldiers, six naval ships, and the ironclad CSS *Abermarle,* ended in a Confederate victory, after two years of Union occupation. The museum is currently restoring Fort Compher, the last remaining battle site left in Plymouth.

Admission Fees: Adults $3.00, children $1.00.

Open to Public: Mon.–Sat. 8:00 A.M.–5:00 P.M.

Visitor Services: Public restrooms, information, handicapped access, gift shop.

Regularly Scheduled Events: Fourth weekend in April, Living History Weekend.

Directions: From I–95 take U.S. 64 east for 50 miles to Plymouth; in Plymouth proceed to Washington Street and turn left. This street ends at the river; turn right on Water Street to the museum.

RALEIGH

NORTH CAROLINA MUSEUM OF HISTORY

5 East Edenton Street, Raleigh, NC 27601; (919) 807–7900; www.ncmuseum ofhistory.org.

Description: The North Carolina Museum of History encourages visitors to explore state, regional, and local North Carolina history. Exhibits change, so call for current offerings. Recent exhibits can be viewed online, including *North Carolina and the Civil War*, the story of North Carolinians who lived, served, and sacrificed during the bloody conflict.

Admission Fees: Free.

Open to Public: Tues.–Sat. 9:00 A.M.–5:00 P.M., Sun. noon–5:00 P.M.

Visitor Services: Public restrooms, information, handicapped access, gift shop.

Regularly Scheduled Events: Special activities for families during the weekends; call ahead for schedule.

Directions: From Chapel Hill and Durham, take I–40 east to exit 289 (Wade Avenue) to Capitol Boulevard south. Follow to Jones Street, turn left. After crossing Salisbury Street, the museum will be on the right-hand side.

NORTH CAROLINA STATE CAPITOL

1 East Edenton Street, Raleigh, NC 27601; (919) 733–4994; www.ncstate capitol.org; state.capitol@ncmail.net.

Description: The building is virtually unaltered from its Civil War–era appearance. Completed in 1840, the capitol's house chamber was the site of the 1861 Secession Convention, and the building served several sessions of the Confederate legislature. The capitol was occupied by staff officers of Gen.

William Sherman's army from April to May 1865, when it was peacefully surrendered. The capitol's dome was the site of one of the last U.S. Army wartime signal stations. The legislative chambers contain the original 1840 desks and chairs.

Admission Fees: Free.

Open to Public: Mon.–Fri. 8:00 A.M.–5:00 P.M., Sat. 10:00 A.M.–4:00 P.M., Sun. 1:00 P.M.–4:00 P.M.; closed New Year's Day, Thanksgiving Day, and Dec. 24–26.

Visitor Services: Public restrooms, information, handicapped access, gift shop, tours.

Regularly Scheduled Events: Last weekend in April, Civil War living history event; July, Traditional July 4 celebration; September, Civil War Heritage Festival.

Directions: From I–40, on the 440 Beltline, take the South Saunders Street/Wilmington Street exit. Edenton, Wilmington, Morgan, and Salisbury Streets border the Capitol.

SALISBURY

 83 DR. JOSEPHUS W. HALL HOUSE

226 South Jackson Street, Salisbury, NC 28144; (704) 636–0103.

Description: A symbol of Old Salisbury, this beautiful house was built in 1820. In 1859 Dr. Hall moved his family into the house. Dr. Hall served as chief surgeon at the Salisbury Confederate Prison during the Civil War. The house was used as headquarters for Union commander Gen. George Stoneman during his raid in North Carolina in 1865.

Admission Fees: Adults $3.00, children $1.00.

Open to Public: Sat.–Sun. 1:00 P.M.–4:00 P.M.

Visitor Services: Public restrooms, gift shop, museum.

Regularly Scheduled Events: Second weekend in October, annual tour; two weekends before Christmas and on Christmas Eve, annual Victorian Christmas at the Hall House.

Directions: From I–85 take exit 76B; travel on Innes Street for about 1 mile, then turn left at the Confederate Monument onto Church Street. Proceed 2 blocks and turn right onto West Bank Street. The house is on the second block.

 84 ROWAN MUSEUM

202 North Main Street, Salisbury, NC 28144; (704) 633–5946; www.rowan museum.org; rowanmuseum@vnet.net.

Description: The Rowan Museum is housed in an 1854 courthouse building considered to be one of the finest examples of pre–Civil War architecture in the state of North Carolina. The museum houses general history collections, including artifacts from the Confederate Prison in Salisbury and the munitions foundry that Union Gen. George Stoneman burned during his raid in the spring of 1865.

Admission Fees: Adults $3.00, students $1.50.

Open to Public: Thurs.–Sun. 1:00 P.M.–4:00 P.M.

Visitor Services: Public restrooms, information, handicapped access, gift shop.

Regularly Scheduled Events: None.

Directions: From I–85 take exit 76B into downtown Salisbury and follow East Innes Street downtown, crossing the railroad tracks, and turn right onto North Lee Street. Take the first left onto Council Street. The museum will be on the right-hand side immediately after crossing North Main Street, on the corner of West Council and North Main Streets.

 85 SALISBURY NATIONAL CEMETERY

202 Government Road, Salisbury, NC 28144; (704) 636–2661; www.cem.va.gov.

Description: This is the final resting place for the remains of 11,700 Union soldiers who died in the Confederate prison in Sal-

COASTAL

isbury during 1864–65. The cemetery contains the largest number of unknown burials of any of the national cemeteries.

Admission Fees: Free.

Open to Public: Grounds, daily from dawn to dusk; office and museum, Mon.–Fri. 7:30 A.M.–4:30 P.M.

Visitor Services: Museum, information, restrooms.

Regularly Scheduled Events: May, Memorial Day event; November, Veterans Day event.

Directions: From I-85 take exit 76B; travel west on Innes Street to Long Street. Proceed south on Long Street to Monroe Street, turn west on Monroe to Railroad Street, and turn south on Railroad Street. The cemetery is on the left.

WEAVERVILLE

ZEBULON B. VANCE BIRTHPLACE STATE HISTORIC SITE

911 Reems Creek Road, Weaverville, NC 28787; (828) 645–6706; www .nchistoricsites.org/vance/vance.html.

Description: This reconstructed log house with six log outbuildings depicts the 1830 farmstead where Civil War governor of North Carolina, Zebulon B. Vance, and his brother, Confederate Brig. Gen. Robert B. Vance, were born. Exhibits in the visitor center trace both brothers' careers.

Admission Fees: Free.

Open to Public: Apr.–Oct., Tues.–Sat. 9:00 A.M.–5:00 P.M.; Nov.–Mar., Tues.–Sat. 10:00 A.M.–4:00 P.M.

Visitor Services: Public restrooms, information, gift shop, museum.

Regularly Scheduled Events: Spring, Pioneer Day; autumn, Pioneer Days and Militia Encampment; December, Christmas Open House.

Directions: From I-240 take Weaverville exit onto U.S. 19/23 north; take New Stock Road exit and follow signs to site.

WILMINGTON

BELLAMY MANSION MUSEUM OF HISTORY AND DESIGN ARTS

503 Market Street, Wilmington, NC 28401; (910) 251–3700; www.bellamy mansion.org; info@bellamymansion .org.

Description: Built as the city residence of prominent planter John D. Bellamy, the Bellamy Mansion is a premier architectural and historical treasure in North Carolina. The mansion was completed in 1861, but the Bellamys were soon displaced from their new home due to fear of raging yellow fever and the threat of invasion by Union forces. The mansion was later commandeered as a Union headquarters. The Bellamys were able to return to their home in the fall of 1865.

Admission Fees: Adults $8.00, children $4.00, under six free.

Open to Public: Tues.–Sat. 10:00 A.M.–5:00 P.M., Sun. 1:00 P.M.–5:00 P.M.

Visitor Services: Gift shop, tours.

Regularly Scheduled Events: May, Confederate history month event; October, Halloween History-Mystery Tour; December, candlelight tour.

Directions: From the north take I-40 to U.S. 17 south to downtown Wilmington. From the south take U.S. 17 north to downtown Wilmington. Mansion is on the corner of Fifth and Market Streets.

WINNABOW

BRUNSWICK TOWN/ FORT ANDERSON STATE HISTORIC SITE

8884 St. Philips Road SE, Winnabow, NC 28479; (910) 371–6613; www .brunswick.nchistoricsites.org; brunswick@ncmail.net.

Description: Fort Anderson, an earthen fortification, was constructed in March 1862 as part of the overall Cape Fear defense system. This system was to protect the Cape Fear River channel to the port of Wilmington, which was a major supply line to Confederate forces. On February 19, 1865, a month after Fort Fisher's fall, a severe bombardment by the Union navy and an encircling movement by Union land forces caused the abandonment of Fort Anderson by Confederates, who fled northward to Wilmington.

Admission Fees: Free.

Open to Public: Tues.–Sat. 10:00 A.M.–4:00 P.M.

Visitor Services: Museum, gift shop, information, restrooms, handicapped access, trails.

Regularly Scheduled Events: February, Civil War encampment; late fall, Heritage Days.

Directions: Take I–40 south to Wilmington; follow signs for U.S. 74/76. Travel 3 miles outside Wilmington; take North Carolina 133 16 miles south to park.

❖ SOUTH CAROLINA ❖

ABBEVILLE

 BURT-STARK MANSION

400 North Main Street, Abbeville, SC 29620; (864) 366–0166; www.burt-stark .com; info@burt-stark.com.

Description: This house was the site of the last "council of war" held by Confederate president Jefferson Davis on May 2, 1865. Davis, along with a few members of his cabinet and several Confederate generals, was on his way south after the fall of Richmond and hoped to rally support. Although Davis still clung to the hope of military success, he was persuaded by subordinates that further resistance was futile and that the war was over.

Admission Fees: $4.00.

Open to Public: Fri.–Sat. 1:00 P.M.–5:00 P.M., or any day by appointment.

Visitor Services: Tours.

Regularly Scheduled Events: None.

Directions: From I–26 east or west, take exit 54; take Highway 72, 3 miles west to Clinton, 24 miles southwest to Greenwood, and 14 miles west to Abbeville. Turn right onto South Main Street, travel around square, and follow signs on North Main Street to house. From I–85 take exit 27; then take Highway 81 south to Anderson; Highway 28, 30 miles to Abbeville. South Carolina Highway 28 becomes North Main Street in Abbeville; follow signs on North Main Street to house.

BEAUFORT

 BEAUFORT NATIONAL CEMETERY

1601 Boundary Street, Beaufort, SC 29902; (843) 524–3925; www.cem.va.gov.

Description: This national cemetery was established in 1863 for the burial of Union soldiers who died during the Federal occupation of Beaufort and for the reinterment of Union soldiers' remains from various locations in South Carolina, Georgia, and Florida. More than 9,000 Union soldiers or veterans are buried here; 4,400 of them are unknown, including 2,800 prisoners of war from the prisoner of war camp at Millen, Georgia. Seventeen hundred African-American Union soldiers are also buried at Beaufort National Cemetery. There are 117 Confederate soldiers buried here.

Admission Fees: Free.

Open to Public: Office, Mon.–Fri. 8:00 A.M.–4:30 P.M.; grounds, daily from dawn to dusk.

Visitor Services: None.

Regularly Scheduled Events: None.

Directions: From I–95 take exit 33 to Beaufort; take U.S. 21 south through Pocotaligo,

Sheldon, and Garden's Corner; proceed past the U.S. Marine Corps Air Station on left. Beaufort National Cemetery is on the left-hand side of the road 2 miles after the air station.

CHARLESTON

 BATTERY 5, JAMES ISLAND NEW LINES

South Carolina Battleground Preservation Trust, P.O. Box 12441, James Island, SC 29422; (843) 689–3223; www.scbattlegrounds.org.

Description: Battery 5, a Confederate earthwork constructed in 1863 under the direction of Gen. P. G. T. Beauregard, commander of the Departments of South Carolina, Georgia, and Florida, was the eastern terminus of the James Island Siege Line. Intended to anchor the Confederate defenses of James Island and overlooking Seaside Creek and the Secessionville Peninsula, this battery is an excellent intact example of a Civil War earthwork.

Admission Fees: Free.

Open to Public: Daily from dawn to dusk.

Visitor Services: None.

Regularly Scheduled Events: None.

Directions: From I–26 take exit for U.S. 17 south toward Savannah; cross over Ashley River, take Highway 171 for 5 miles, and turn left onto Burclair Drive. Cross Secessionville Road to Seaside Plantation, then take second road on the right.

 DRAYTON HALL

(A National Trust Historic Site)
3380 Ashley River Road, Charleston, SC 29414; (843) 769–2600; www.drayton hall.org; dh@draytonhall.org.

Description: Begun in 1738, Drayton Hall is an authentic plantation house that tells the story of the rise, fall, and recovery of the South after the Civil War. The museum offers guided tours that describe the lifestyles of the Draytons, who supported the Confederacy, and of African Americans before and after freedom. Drayton Hall is the only antebellum plantation in the Charleston area that is open to the public.

Admission Fees: Adults $14.00, children twelve–eighteen $8.00, children six–eleven

Drayton Hall, Charleston, South Carolina. CWPT files.

$6.00, five and under free; call for group rates.

Open to Public: Mar.–Oct., daily 10:00 A.M.–4:00 P.M.; Nov.–Feb., daily 10:00 A.M.–3:00 P.M.; closed Thanksgiving, Christmas, and New Year's Day.

Visitor Services: Gift shop, handicapped access, free parking, guided house tour, self-guided walks of the marsh and the river, picnic area.

Regularly Scheduled Events: Spring, oyster roasts, candlelight concert; spring and fall weekends, nature walks; December, spirituals concert.

Directions: From I–526 take Highway 61 north (Ashley River Road); Drayton Hall is located on Highway 61, 9 miles northwest of Charleston.

 **FORT LAMAR HISTORIC PRESERVE**
DNR Heritage Trust Program, P.O. Box 167, Columbia, SC 29202; (803) 734–3886; www.dnr.sc.gov.

Description: Initially called the Tower Battery because of its 75-foot observation tower, Fort Lamar was renamed for Col. Thomas G. Lamar, who commanded Confederate troops at the fort during the Battle of Secessionville on June 16, 1862. In this fierce battle that saved Charleston, Lamar's men repulsed a Union army that outnumbered the defenders three-to-one.

Admission Fees: Free.

Open to Public: Daily from dawn to dusk.

Visitor Services: Self-guided trail.

Regularly Scheduled Events: June, commemoration of the Battle of Secessionville.

Directions: Take U.S. 17 to James Island, then head south on Highway 171 (Folly Road). Turn left onto Grimball Road and follow to Secessionville Road. Turn left onto Old Military Road, then turn left onto Fort Lamar Road. The entrance to the site is 0.8 mile on left.

 **FORT MOULTRIE** CWPT

(A unit of Fort Sumter National Monument)
1214 Middle Street, Sullivan's Island, SC 29482; (843) 883–3123; www.nps.gov/fomo.

Description: Fort Moultrie is administered by the Fort Sumter National Monument. Fort Moultrie's history covers more than 220 years of seacoast defense, from the first decisive victory in the American Revolution to protecting the coast from U-boats in World War II. Maj. Robert Anderson and eighty-five Federal soldiers occupied the fort, built in 1809, before they moved to Fort Sumter in December 1860. During the first battle of the Civil War (April 12–13, 1861), Confederates at Fort Moultrie fired on Union troops in Fort Sumter. Confederate forces successfully used both forts to protect Charleston from a combined Union navy and army siege from 1863 to 1865.

Admission Fees: Adults $3.00, children sixteen and under free, seniors $1.00, family $5.00, annual pass $50.00; no fee for school groups.

Open to Public: Daily 9:00 A.M.–5:00 P.M.; closed Christmas.

Visitor Services: Orientation film, museum, restrooms, bookstore, information, handicapped access.

Regularly Scheduled Events: None.

Directions: From Charleston take U.S. 17 north toward Mount Pleasant. Just over the Cooper River Bridge, turn right onto U.S. 703. Stay on this road to Sullivan's Island. At the stop sign turn right onto Middle Street; the fort is 1.5 miles from this intersection.

 **FORT SUMTER NATIONAL MONUMENT**
1214 Middle Street, Sullivan's Island, SC 29482; (843) 883–3123; www.nps.gov/fosu.

COASTAL

Fort Sumter, South Carolina. Michael Squire–CWPT files.

Description: Fort Sumter National Monument includes Fort Sumter, a coastal fortification that was begun in 1829 but was still not completed by the time the Civil War started here in April 1861. Confederate and South Carolina troops under the direction of Gen. P. G. T. Beauregard bombarded the Union garrison commanded by Maj. Robert Anderson beginning April 12, 1861, signalling the start of the American Civil War. Fort Sumter was occupied by a Confederate garrison for most of the war. During the siege of Charleston, 1863–65, Fort Sumter was reduced to one-third of its original size. After the war Fort Sumter was repaired but never rebuilt to its original height.

Admission Fees: Free; tour boat fees, adults $14.00, children six–eleven $8.00, seniors $12.50.

Open to Public: Daily, Mar. 10:00 A.M.–4:00 P.M.; Apr.–Labor Day 10:00 A.M.–5:30 A.M.; day after Labor Day–Nov. 10:00 A.M.–4:00 P.M.; Dec.–Feb. 11:30 A.M.–4:00 P.M.; closed Christmas.

Visitor Services: Museum, museum shop, restrooms, information, handicapped access. Accessible by private boat or by ferry; schedules vary with season, please call ahead.

Regularly Scheduled Events: None.

Directions: To the city marina, take I–26 to Charleston; take U.S. 17 south toward Savannah. Turn left onto Lockwood Boulevard, then turn right at the first traffic light. City marina is on the right. To Fort Sumter Visitor Education Center at Liberty Square, from 1–26 follow signs for the aquarium, take East Bay Street south to Calhoun. Turn left on Calhoun, and the visitor center will be straight in front of you. For private boaters, Fort Sumter is 3.3 miles from Charleston at the harbor entrance.

96 **MAGNOLIA CEMETERY**

70 Cunnington Avenue, Charleston, SC 29405; (843) 722–8638; magnolia cemetery@aol.com.

Description: Magnolia Cemetery, established in 1850, includes the graves of several prominent Confederate civilian and military leaders. Capt. Horace Hunley and the crew of the CSS *H. L. Hunley,* the Confederate submarine that was the first to sink a warship, are also buried here. A monument to South Carolina's Civil War dead stands in the Confederate section of the cemetery, which contains the graves of several officers and enlisted men, many of whom died during the siege of Charleston.

Admission Fees: Free.

Open to Public: Grounds, winter 8:00 A.M.–5:00 P.M., summer 8:00 A.M.–6:00 P.M.; office, Mon.–Fri. 8:00 A.M.–4:00 P.M.

Visitor Services: None.

Regularly Scheduled Events: Second Saturday in May, Confederate Memorial Day observance; second Friday and Saturday in October, Confederate Ghost Walk (purchase tickets in advance).

Directions: From I–26 take exit 219B (Meeting Street); turn left at second light, then turn right at Cunnington Avenue. Cemetery is at the end of the block.

 WARREN G. LASCH CONSERVATION CENTER

1250 Supply Street, North Charleston, SC 29405; (843) 743–4865; www.hunley .org.

Description: On the night of February 17, 1864, the Confederate submarine *H. L. Hunley* sank the Union sloop USS *Housatonic* near Charleston Harbor. Tragically, *Hunley* never made it back to port, sinking in Charleston Harbor and killing all nine crewmen. The fate of the *Hunley* remained a mystery for more than a century until the wreck was found in May 1995. In the summer of 2000, the submarine was raised and transported to the Warren G. Lasch Conservation Center for archaeological research and restoration. During the week, the center is an active laboratory for preserving the *Hunley,* but on weekends visitors can tour the facility and learn about the fascinating discoveries the wreckage has yielded.

Admission Fees: Tour $12 plus service charge.

Open to Public: Sat. 10:00 A.M.–5:00 P.M., Sun. noon–5:00 P.M. Purchase tickets in advance by calling (877) 448–6539 (877–4HUNLEY) or visiting www.etix.com.

Visitor Services: Handicapped access, information, tours, video, exhibits, gift shop.

Regularly Scheduled Events: None.

Directions: From I–26, take exit 216B, Cosgrove Avenue North. At the third traffic light, turn left onto Spruill Avenue. At the next light, turn right onto McMillan Avenue and proceed through the gate. At the next light, turn right onto Hobson Avenue. Go approximately 1 mile and turn left onto Supply Street. After passing the Charleston Public Works building with its blue roof, the Lasch Center will be immediately on the left. The Lasch Center is located on the campus of the Old Charleston Navy Base, so vehicles may be stopped to identify destination.

CHERAW

 CHERAW CIVIL WAR SITES

c/o Cheraw Visitors Bureau, 221 Market Street, Cheraw, SC 29520; (843) 537–8425; www.cheraw.com; visitcheraw@bell south.net.

Description: Cheraw was the home of John Inglis, who introduced the resolution that South Carolina secede from the Union. This eighteenth-century river town became a place of refuge and a storehouse of valuables, including an official repository of CSA gold. In March 1865 Gen. William T. Sherman visited Cheraw, with more Union troops than occupied any other South Carolina city. They found it "a pleasant town and an old one with the southern aristocratic bearing." Of particular interest are St. David's Church (ca. 1770), used as a hospital during the

Civil War; the cemetery with the earliest known Confederate monument (1867); and the Cheraw Lyceum Museum.

Admission Fees: Free.

Open to Public: Chamber of commerce, Mon.–Thurs. 9:00 A.M.–5:00 P.M., Fri. 9:00 A.M.–noon.

Visitor Services: Lodging, public restrooms, information, food, museum, tour. A free historic district tour brochure and keys to St. David's Church and the museum are available from the Cheraw Chamber of Commerce at 221 Market Street.

Regularly Scheduled Events: April, Cheraw Spring Festival features historic home tours, a Confederate encampment and skirmish for the bridge, a period church service, lantern tours, arts, and entertainment.

Directions: From I–95 at Florence take U.S. 52 north for 35 miles. The chamber of commerce office is located at 221 Market Street, which is also U.S. 1, U.S. 52, and South Carolina 9.

COLUMBIA

SOUTH CAROLINA CONFEDERATE RELIC ROOM AND MUSEUM

301 Gervais Street, Columbia, SC 29201; (803) 737–8095; www.state.sc.us/crr.

Description: The military collection was established in 1896 to honor South Carolina's Confederate veterans. The museum contains exhibits from the American Revolution through Desert Storm, with the focus on South Carolina in the Civil War.

Admission Fees: Adults $4.00.

Open to Public: Tues.–Sat. 10:00 A.M.–5:00 P.M., Mon. by appointment only; closed holidays.

Visitor Services: Handicapped access.

Regularly Scheduled Events: None.

Directions: From I–126 take right onto Huger Street and go past second light. Museum is on right-hand side.

SOUTH CAROLINA STATE HOUSE

1100 Gervais Street, Columbia, SC 29201; (803) 734–2430.

Description: The South Carolina State House, begun in 1855 and unfinished until after the Civil War, witnessed the Federal occupation of Columbia on February 17–18, 1865. Union artillery batteries seeking to find their range fired on this building from across the Congaree River; bronze stars mark the places where their shells hit the statehouse. Gen. William T. Sherman's Federals also raised the United States flag over the unfinished building, looted the existing statehouse, and repealed the Ordinance of Secession. Several Civil War–related monuments are on the statehouse grounds.

Admission Fees: Free.

Open to Public: Mon.–Fri. 9:00 A.M.–5:00 P.M., Sat. 10:00 A.M.–5:00 P.M., first Sun. of month 1:00 P.M.–5:00 P.M.; closed all state holidays.

Visitor Services: Gift shop, tours.

Regularly Scheduled Events: None.

Directions: From I–26 take Elmwood exit and turn right on Assembly Street. Turn left on Gervais Street. From I–77 travel south to Highway 277, which becomes Bull Street. Take Bull Street to Gervais Street, turn right on Gervais Street. The statehouse is on Gervais Street, and parking is available around the corner on Sumter Street.

SOUTH CAROLINA STATE MUSEUM

301 Gervais Street, Columbia, SC 29201; (803) 898–4921; www.museum.state.sc .us; publicrelations@museum.state.sc .us.

Description: On December 20, 1860, South Carolina was the first state to secede from the Union. Beginning with an original signed copy of the Ordinance of Secession, the Civil War exhibit at the South Carolina State Museum focuses on the war as it affected South Carolina. Holdings include period weapons from both sides of the conflict, including the the Morse Carbine, one of the few weapons produced in Greenville, South Carolina. A circa 1960 reproduction of the Confederate submarine *Hunley* is also on display, supplemented by panels that incorporate new evidence from the 1995 discovery of the original off Charleston Harbor.

Admission Fees: Adults $5.00, children three–twelve $3.00, seniors $4.00; group rates available.

Open to Public: Tues.–Sat. 10:00 A.M.–5:00 P.M., Sun. 1:00 P.M.–5:00 P.M.; Memorial Day–Labor Day, open Mon.; closed major holidays.

Visitor Services: Public restrooms, handicapped access, gift shop, information, food, tours.

Regularly Scheduled Events: Third Saturday in February, Columbia Civil War Alliance Tour of Sherman's Route. Call or check Web site for full schedule of events.

Directions: From I–26 take the Elmwood exit and turn right on Assembly Street. Turn left on Gervaise Street. The museum is located beside the historic Gervais Street Bridge and just a few blocks west of the state capitol in downtown Columbia.

EHRHARDT

 RIVERS BRIDGE STATE PARK

325 State Park Road, Ehrhardt, SC 29081; (803) 267–3675; www.south carolinaparks.com; riversbridge @scprt.com.

Description: The only significant engagement in South Carolina during Gen. William T. Sherman's advance through the state in early 1865 took place on February 2 and 3 at the still-intact earthworks overlooking Rivers Bridge, on the Salkehatchie River. Nine hundred Confederates under the overall command of Gen. Lafayette McLaws briefly delayed Sherman's Federals, some

8,000 troops. They soon outflanked the Confederate position upstream at Buford's Bridge and downstream at Broxton's Bridge, forcing a Confederate withdrawal and clearing the way for a Federal advance to Columbia.

Admission Fees: Adults $2.00, seniors $1.25, children fifteen and under free.

Open to Public: Thurs.–Mon. 9:00 A.M.–6:00 P.M.

Visitor Services: Restrooms, handicapped access; battlefield tours, camping, trails.

Regularly Scheduled Events: February, annual battle reenactment and living history exhibit.

Directions: From I–95 take exit 57, South Carolina 64 west to South Carolina 641 west. Follow signs to Rivers Bridge State Park.

FLORENCE

 FLORENCE NATIONAL CEMETERY

803 East National Cemetery Road, Florence, SC 29506; (843) 669–8387; www.cem.va.gov.

Description: This national cemetery was established in 1865 and is associated with the nearby Union prisoner of war camp, Florence Stockade, which held as many as 12,000 prisoners between September 1864 and February 1865. The prisoner cemetery formed the nucleus of the new national cemetery. Some 3,000 Union soldiers who died in the prison, as many as 2,000 of them unknown, are buried here.

Admission Fees: Free.

Open to Public: Office, Mon.–Fri. 8:00 A.M.–4:30 P.M.; grounds, daily from dawn to dusk.

Visitor Services: None.

Regularly Scheduled Events: None.

Directions: From I–95 travel on U.S. 52 (Lucas Street) to North Irby Street and turn right. North Irby Street becomes South Irby Street. Continue on South Irby Street and turn left onto National Cemetery Road.

GEORGETOWN

 BATTERY WHITE

Belle Isle Yacht Club, 1142 Belle Isle Road, Georgetown, SC 29440; (843) 546–1423; biyc@aol.com.

Description: Battery White, a Confederate earthwork constructed in 1862 under the direction of Gen. John C. Pemberton, commander of the Departments of South Carolina and Georgia, was built on Mayrant's Bluff to defend the entrance to Winyah Bay and the Sampit River.
Admission Fees: Free.
Open to Public: Mon.–Fri. 9:00 A.M.–noon and 1:00 P.M.–4:00 P.M.
Visitor Services: None.
Regularly Scheduled Events: None.
Directions: From I–95 take Highway 521 at Alcolu and go east for 50 miles to Highway 17 south and cross the Sampit River. Follow signs to Belle Isle Garden.

HILTON HEAD ISLAND

 COASTAL DISCOVERY MUSEUM

100 William Hilton Parkway, Hilton Head, SC 29926; (843) 689–6767; www .coastaldiscovery.org; info@coastal discovery.org.

Description: The Coastal Discovery Museum offers guided tours of three Civil War–era forts on Hilton Head Island: Fort Walker, Fort Howell, and Fort Mitchel. In addition, historical exhibits and a video are shown at the museum's headquarters.
Admission Fees: Free. Please call ahead to arrange for a tour of the Civil War–era forts: adults $12.00, children $7.00; donation of $2.00 per person is suggested for exhibits.

Open to Public: Mon.–Sat. 9:00 A.M.–5:00 P.M., Sun. 10:00 A.M.–2:00 P.M.
Visitor Services: Public restrooms, information, handicapped access, gift shop.
Regularly Scheduled Events: None.
Directions: From I–95 take exit 8. Follow U.S. 278 to Hilton Head Island, go 1 mile over bridge. Museum is on the right-hand side.

PARRIS ISLAND

 PARRIS ISLAND MUSEUM

Building 111, Panama Street, Parris Island, SC 29902; (843) 228–2951; www .pimuseum.us; visitors@pimuseum.us.

Description: Parris Island was part of the U.S. Army's military department that served as headquarters for the South Atlantic Blockading Squadron and the Department of the South. Parris Island was home to a Quartermaster Coaling Station and a large freedmen's community that was operated by Frances Gage, noted feminist and abolitionist, and Clara Barton. The museum contains extensive displays on the Battles of Port Royal, Port Royal Ferry, Pocotaligo, and Honey Hill, as well as Sherman's March and the beginning of Reconstruction.
Admission Fees: Free.
Open to Public: Mon.–Sun. 10:00 A.M.–4:30 P.M. Closed New Year's Day, Easter, Thanksgiving, and Christmas.
Visitor Services: Public restrooms, handicapped access, gift shop, museum; trails.
Regularly Scheduled Events: None.
Directions: From the south take I–95 to U.S. 278 to South Carolina 170 to South Carolina 802. From the north I–95 to U.S. 21 to South Carolina 280.

SOUTHERN
HEARTLAND

Fort Donelson, Dover, Tennessee. Bob Cross—CWPT files.

❖ ALABAMA ❖

BRIDGEPORT

BRIDGEPORT DEPOT MUSEUM

One Soulard Square, Bridgeport, AL 35740; (256) 495–4020; bridgeporttrain @bellsouth.net.

Description: Bridgeport Depot Museum is on the site of the fourth railroad depot to be located in Bridgeport, Alabama, with the first being destroyed in July 1863 by Confederate forces under Gen. Braxton Bragg. The current depot, constructed in 1917, is used by the Bridgeport Area Historical Association as a museum of local history. The museum features a large display of local Civil War artifacts.

Admission Fees: Free.

Open to Public: By appointment only; call ahead of time.

Visitor Services: Public restrooms, information, handicapped access, gift shop, research library.

Regularly Scheduled Events: September, Annual Bridgeport Jubilee.

Directions: Take I–24 to exit 152 (Kimball, Tennessee). Take Highway 72 west for approximately 5 miles to Bridgeport. Take first exit across Alabama state line. Turn left onto Alabama State Highway 277 south, follow for 3 miles to Seventh Street. Turn left onto Seventh Street and follow signs for Depot Museum.

BRIERFIELD

BRIERFIELD IRONWORKS HISTORICAL STATE PARK

240 Furnace Parkway, Brierfield, AL 35035; (205) 665–1856; www.brierfield ironworks.com.

Description: Brierfield Ironworks began production under direction of the Confederacy in 1862, providing iron to the Selma Arsenal during the Civil War. On March 31, 1865, the furnace was the target of a raid by troops of Gen. James Wilson as part of his campaign in central Alabama. After the war the ironworks was purchased by Gen. Josiah Gorgas, Confederate chief of ordinance, and remained in operation until 1894. The remains are present at the park.

Admission Fees: Adults $2.00, seniors and children $1.00.

Open to Public: Daily from dawn to dusk.

Visitor Services: Public restrooms, information, handicapped access, food, gift shop (CWPT members get a 10 percent discount on all purchases), cabin rentals, historic weapons range, camping, trails.

Regularly Scheduled Events: Third week in March, Civil War living history program.

Directions: From I–65 exit at Cleara/Highway 25; take Highway 25 south to park entrance on County Road 62, approximately 15 miles.

CEDAR BLUFF

CORNWALL FURNACE

2 miles east of Cedar Bluff, Cedar Bluff, AL; (256) 927–8455; www .cherokee-chamber.org; cccoc@tds.net.

Description: The Cornwall Furnace was built in 1863 by the Noble brothers and named for their native Cornwall, England, home. This cold blast furnace furnished iron to the Noble Brothers Foundry in Rome, Georgia, where it was used to manufacture cannon, cannon balls, and other munitions for the Confederate army. Twice ordered destroyed by Sherman, the furnace survived the war but was destroyed in an industrial explosion around 1870. Located on a five-and-one-half-acre county park, the site has one of the best preserved stacks in the southeast.

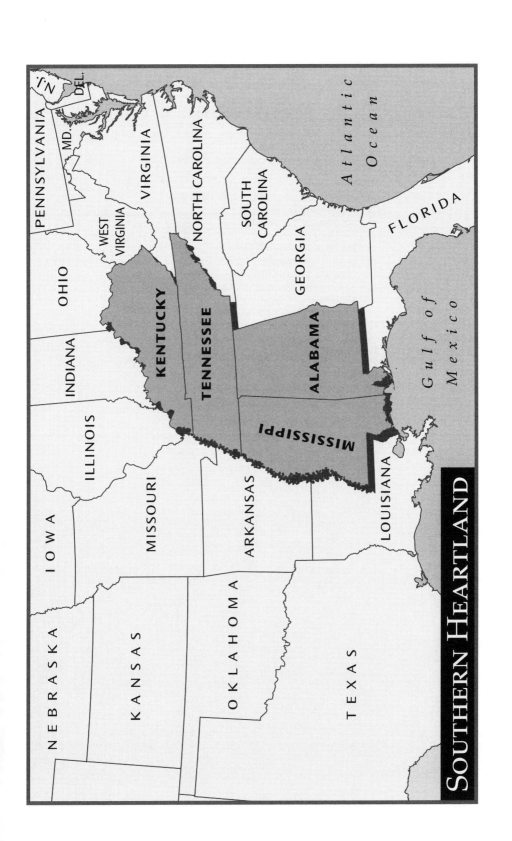

SOUTHERN HEARTLAND

ALABAMA SITES

1   Bridgeport Depot Museum
2   Brierfield Ironworks Historical State Park
3   Cornwall Furnace
4   Fort Gaines
5   Old State Bank and Civil War Walking Tour
6   The Shorter Cemetery
7   Fort Morgan Historic Site
8   Pond Spring
9   The Historic Huntsville Depot
10   Confederate Memorial Park
11   Tannehill Ironworks Historical State Park
12   Alabama Department of Archives and History
13   Alabama State Capitol
14   First White House of the Confederacy
15   Janney Furnace Park
16   Old Cahawba Historic Site
17   Old Depot Museum
18   Old Live Oak Cemetery
19   Selma Historic District
20   Vaughn-Smitherman Museum
21   Historic Blakely State Park

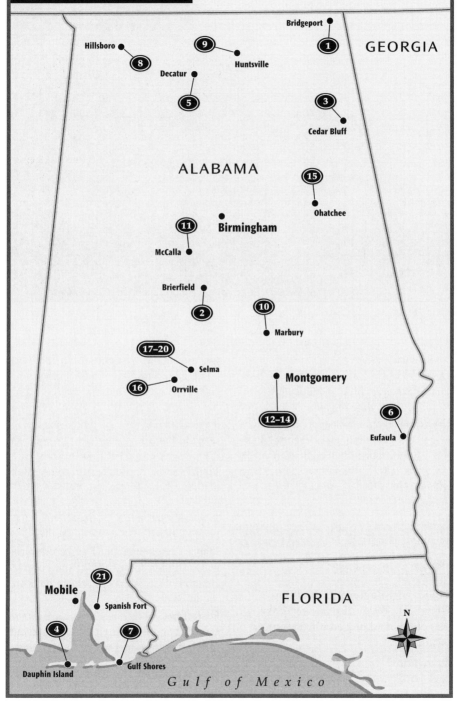

ALABAMA

GEORGIA

ALABAMA

FLORIDA

Bridgeport

Hillsboro
8

9
Huntsville

Decatur

5

1

3
Cedar Bluff

15
Ohatchee

11
McCalla

Birmingham

Brierfield
2

10
Marbury

17–20
Selma

16
Orrville

Montgomery

12–14

6
Eufaula

Mobile

21
Spanish Fort

4

7

Dauphin Island
Gulf Shores

Gulf of Mexico

N

Cornwall Furnace, Cedar Bluff, Alabama. CWPT files.

Admission Fees: Free.
Open to Public: Daily from dawn to dusk.
Visitor Services: Trails, picnic facilities.
Regularly Scheduled Events: None.
Directions: From I–59 take Alabama Highway 68 to Cedar Bluff. Take Alabama Highway 9 when 68 turns to the left; turn left on County Road 92. When 92 turns right, go straight ahead on County Road 251 to end of road.

Dauphin Island

 FORT GAINES

51 Bienville Boulevard, Dauphin Island, AL 36528; (251) 861–6992; www .dauphinisland.org; admin@dauphin island.org.

Description: Fort Gaines is a pre–Civil War brick fort set within a few feet of the Gulf of Mexico. The fort was a key element in the Battle of Mobile Bay, and after its capture, it was used in planning and staging the attack on Mobile. Many of the Civil War structures and courtyard buildings remain.

Admission Fees: Adults $5.00, children five–twelve $3.00, group rates available.
Open to Public: Winter, daily 9:00 A.M.–5:00 P.M.; summer, daily 9:00 A.M.–6:00 P.M.
Visitor Services: Public restrooms, information, food, gift shop, museum, camping, trails.
Regularly Scheduled Events: February, Battle of Mobile Bay 5K Race; August, Battle of Mobile Commemoration Day; second week in December, Christmas at the Fort, recreation of Christmas as celebrated at the fort in 1861.
Directions: From I–10 at exit 17, go south on Highway 193. Once on Dauphin Island, turn left at the water tower and proceed 3 miles to Fort Gaines.

DECATUR

 OLD STATE BANK AND CIVIL WAR WALKING TOUR

925 Bank Street NE, Decatur, AL 35602; (256) 350–2028 or (800) 232–5449; www .decaturcvb.org; info@decaturcvb.org.

Description: A 13-block self-guided walking tour through the Old Decatur and New Albany Historic Districts of Decatur chronicles noteworthy events in the community during the Civil War. The tour includes eleven historical markers with detailed narratives about local events that occurred between 1860 and 1865 and, particularly, events during the four-day Battle of Decatur that began on October 26, 1864.

Admission Fees: Free.

Open to Public: Daily from dawn to dusk; Old State Bank, Mon.–Fri. 9:30 A.M.–noon and 1:00 P.M.–4.30 P.M.

Visitor Services: Information, handicapped access, gift shop, museum.

Regularly Scheduled Events: September, Civil War Reenactment.

Directions: From I–65 take exit 340, travel west 4 miles on Highway 20, crossing the Tennessee River. Turn right on Church Street at second traffic light; Church Street dead-ends into Bank Street. The Old State Bank is on the right and is the first stop on the walking tour.

EUFAULA

 THE SHORTER CEMETERY

Riverside Drive, Eufaula, AL 36027; (334) 687–3793.

Description: Cemetery belonging to the Shorter family. The graves include that of John Gill Shorter, Civil War governor of Alabama. The cemetery also has slave plots.

Admission Fees: Free.

Open to Public: Daily from dawn to dusk.

Visitor Services: Brochure available at Shorter Mansion.

Regularly Scheduled Events: None.

Directions: From I–10 go north on U.S. 231 to Dothan, then U.S. 431 north to Eufala.

GULF SHORES

 FORT MORGAN HISTORIC SITE

51 Highway 180 West, Gulf Shores, AL 36542; (251) 540–7127; bricfort@gulftel .com.

Description: Completed in 1834, Fort Morgan was the primary defensive work at the entrance to Mobile Bay. This large brick fort was seized by Alabama troops on January 4, 1861. Following the Battle of Mobile Bay on August 5, 1864, the fort was besieged and forced to surrender on August 23, 1864.

Admission Fees: Adults $5.00, children six–eighteen $3.00, seniors $4.00; group rates for fifteen or more.

Open to Public: Museum, Sun.–Sat. 9:00 A.M.–5:00 P.M.; fort, Nov.–Feb., 8:00 A.M.–5:00 P.M.; Mar.–Apr., 8:00 A.M.–7:00 P.M.; May–Oct., 8:00 A.M.–7:00 P.M.; closed Thanksgiving, Christmas, and New Year's Day.

Visitor Services: Public restrooms, information, handicapped access, gift shop, museum.

Regularly Scheduled Events: First weekend in August, living history encampment commemorating the Battle of Mobile Bay and siege of Fort Morgan in 1864; every Tuesday in June and July, candlelight tours.

Directions: Exit I–10 at Loxley exit, travel south on Highway 59 to Gulf Shores. Take Highway 180 west to the fort.

HILLSBORO

 POND SPRING

12280 Alabama Highway 20, Hillsboro, AL 35643; (256) 637–8513; www.wheeler plantation.org; wheplan@hiwaay.net.

Description: Gen. Joseph Wheeler came to Alabama in 1863 during the Civil War, and

SOUTHERN HEARTLAND

met Daniella Sherrod, a young widow, whom he married in 1866. Pond Spring was the postwar home of General Wheeler and his family. The site consists of fifty acres, which are home to ten historic buildings, formal gardens, and three cemeteries. The home is undergoing restoration.

Admission Fees: Adults $4.00, college students, seniors $3.00, children six–eighteen $2.00, under six free.

Open to Public: Open for group tours (ten or more). Call for appointment.

Visitor Services: Information, museum; gardens, trails.

Regularly Scheduled Events: None.

Directions: From I–65 take Alabama Highway 20 west; site entrance is at mile marker 53 on Highway 20/U.S. Alternate 72.

 THE HISTORIC HUNTSVILLE DEPOT

320 Church Street, Huntsville, AL 35801; (256) 564–8100 or (800) 678–1819; www.earlyworks.com; info@early works.com.

Description: The Huntsville Depot was built in 1860 as the eastern division headquarters of the Memphis to Charleston Railroad. As a vital east–west Confederate rail line, it was captured by the Federals in 1862 and used as a prison. There is legible graffiti on the third-floor walls left by Civil War soldiers.

Admission Fees: Adults $7.00, students and seniors $6.00.

Open to Public: Wed.–Sat. 10:00 A.M.–4:00 P.M.; closed Jan. and Feb.

Visitor Services: Public restrooms, information, handicapped access, gift shop, museum, picnic area.

Regularly Scheduled Events: None.

Directions: From I–565 east take exit 19A; from I–565 west take exit 19C; you will see the depot as you exit I–565. Proceed to the free parking lot.

 CONFEDERATE MEMORIAL PARK

437 County Road 63, Marbury, AL 36051; (205) 755–1990; www.preserve ala.org; alacmp@bellsouth.net.

Description: Confederate Memorial Park, site of Alabama's only Old Soldiers Home for Confederate Veterans (1902–39), is dedicated to preserving the memory of Confederate soldiers from Alabama. The museum houses uniforms, weapons, equipment, and documents that emphasize Alabama's participation in the war. It also displays artifacts illustrating the postwar lives of the veterans.

Admission Fees: Adults $5.00, children six–eighteen $3.00, seniors $4.00; group rates available.

Open to Public: Park, daily 6:00 A.M.–sunset; museum, daily 9:00 A.M.–5:00 P.M.

Visitor Services: Public restrooms, information, handicapped access, gift shop, museum, trails.

Regularly Scheduled Events: April, Confederate Memorial Day observance.

Directions: From I–65 south take exit 205; take U.S. 31 south for 9 miles, following signs for site. From I–65 north take exit 186; take U.S. 31 north for 13 miles, following signs.

 TANNEHILL IRONWORKS HISTORICAL STATE PARK

12632 Confederate Parkway, McCalla, AL 35111; (205) 477–5711; www .tannehill.org; tannehil@dbtech.net.

Description: This 1,500-acre park was created around Civil War–era iron-making furnaces. The furnaces were a major producer of iron for the Selma Arsenal and were destroyed by Union cavalry raiders in 1865. The park includes a museum, more than forty restored log cabins, and other period buildings, including a working gristmill, church, and school.

Admission Fees: Park, adults $3.00, children six–eleven $1.00, seniors $2.00; museum, adults $2.00, children and seniors $1.00.

Open to Public: Museum, Mon.–Fri. 9:00 A.M.–4:30 P.M., Sat. 10:00 A.M.–4:30 P.M., Sun. 12:30 P.M.–4:30 P.M.; park, daily 7:00 A.M.–dusk.

Visitor Services: Lodging, public restrooms, information, handicapped access, food, gift shop, museum, camping, trails.

Regularly Scheduled Events: Third weekend, March–November, Tannehill Trade Days; Memorial Day weekend, Civil War reenactment; September, blacksmith demonstration, Labor Day celebration; December, candlelight walking tour.

Directions: From I–59 take exit 100 and follow signs (2 miles). From I–459 take exit 1 and follow signs (7 miles).

MONTGOMERY

 ### ALABAMA DEPARTMENT OF ARCHIVES AND HISTORY

624 Washington Avenue, Montgomery, AL 36130-0100; (334) 242–4435; www .archives.alabama.gov.

Description: Located across the street from the state capitol, which served as the provisional capitol of the Confederate States of America, the museum and archives contain the largest collection of Civil War materials in the state. Significant among these is the department's collection of Civil War flags, which are displayed on a rotational basis.

Admission Fees: Free.

Open to Public: Mon.–Sat. 8:30 A.M.–4:30 P.M.; research room closed Mon.

Visitor Services: Public restrooms, information, handicapped access, museum.

Regularly Scheduled Events: Every third Thursday, Architreats, a lunchtime lecture series.

Directions: From I–85 south exit right on Union Street. Turn left at third traffic light (Washington Avenue). From Birmingham or Mobile on I–65, take interstate to I–85 north;

exit right onto Court Street. Stay on service road. At the seventh traffic light, turn left (Union Street). Turn left at the fourth traffic light (Washington Avenue).

 ### ALABAMA STATE CAPITOL

600 Dexter Avenue, Montgomery, AL 36104; (334) 242–3935; www.preserve ala.org.

Description: In 1861 Southern delegates met in the House Chamber to form the Confederate States of America. Earlier the House of Representatives of the state of Alabama had voted for secession in the same chamber. Jefferson Davis was sworn in on the capitol steps as the first and only president of the Confederate States of America.

Admission Fees: Free.

Open to Public: Mon.–Fri. 8:00 A.M.–5:00 P.M., Sat. 9:00 A.M.–4:00 P.M.; guided tours available on Sat. and by group appointment.

Visitor Services: Public restrooms, information, gift shop, museum.

Regularly Scheduled Events: None.

Directions: From I–85 take Union Street exit; travel 4 blocks to Washington Avenue. The State Capitol is at the eastern end of Dexter Avenue, bounded by Bainbridge, Monroe, Union, and Washington Streets. Enter during the week from either Dexter Avenue or Union Street. On Saturdays only the Union Street entrance is open.

 ### FIRST WHITE HOUSE OF THE CONFEDERACY

644 Washington Avenue, Montgomery, AL 36104; (334) 242–1861.

Description: Built in 1835, this house was used by the provisional government of Confederate president Jefferson Davis and his family from February until May 1861.

Admission Fees: Free.

Open to Public: Mon.–Fri. 8:00 A.M.–4:30 P.M.

Visitor Services: Public restrooms, information, handicapped access, museum.

Regularly Scheduled Events: January,

SOUTHERN HEARTLAND

First White House of the Confederacy, Montgomery, Alabama. CWPT files.

Robert E. Lee's birthday; April, Confederate Memorial Day; June, Jefferson Davis's birthday.

Directions: From I–85 take Union Street exit; go 4 blocks to Washington Street and turn left. Look for first house on the left.

OHATCHEE

 JANNEY FURNACE PARK

53 Janney Road, Ohatchee, AL 36271; (256) 241–2800; www.janneyfurnace .org; ccc@calhouncounty.org.

Description: Janney Iron Furnace was built in 1863 to produce iron for use by the Confederate army. A memorial to honor the 5,218 Confederate veterans from Calhoun County who served in the conflict is located adjacent to Janney Furnace.

Admission Fees: Free.

Open to Public: Daily from dawn to dusk; call to arrange a tour.

Visitor Services: Information, public restrooms, camping.

Regularly Scheduled Events: May, Battle of Janney Furnace reenactment; October, Janney Furnace 5K Run and Ohatchee Fest.

Directions: From I–29 take exit 168 north onto Highway 77. Turn right onto Highway 144 in Ohatchee and take the first left onto Big Oaks Road, which dead-ends into Spring Road. Turn left and left again onto Janney Road.

ORRVILLE

 OLD CAHAWBA HISTORIC SITE

9518 Cahawba Road, Orrville, AL 36767; (334) 872–8058; www.preserveala .org/; cahawba@bellsouth.net.

Description: Alabama's first state capital and Civil War boomtown is now Alabama's most famous ghost town. This historic town was home to the Cahawba Rifles, Fifth Alabama Regiment, and also the site of Castle Morgan, a prison for captured Union soldiers. Tragically, many of the prisoners lost their lives on the steamboat *Sultana* after being released at the end of the war. While traveling north toward their homes and families, the boiler on the *Sultana* exploded, killing or mortally wounding many of Castle Morgan's former inmates.

Admission Fees: Adults $5.00, children $3.00, seniors $4.00; group rates available.

Open to Public: Daily 9:00 A.M.–5:00 P.M.; welcome center, daily noon–5:00 P.M.

Visitor Services: Public restrooms, information, handicapped access, gift shop, trails.

Regularly Scheduled Events: May, Old Cahawba Festival.

Directions: From I–85 and I–65 in Montgomery, take Highway 80 west to Selma 48 miles. From Selma take Highway 22 west for 8 miles, turn onto County Road 5, and follow signs to park.

SELMA

 OLD DEPOT MUSEUM

Confederate Navy Ordnance Works, 4 Martin Luther King Jr. Street, Selma, AL 36703; (334) 874–2197; www.selma alabama.org; olddepot@wwwisp.com.

Description: Housed in a historic former railing depot on the site of the Greater Confederate Naval Ordinance Works, which was second only to Tredegar Iron Works in Richmond, Virginia, in manufacture of arms and munitions. Four Confederate "rams," including the CSS *Tennessee,* were built here. Civil War–era artifacts are found in abundance at this museum, as well as other artifacts dating from 7000 B.C. through the Gulf War.

Admission Fees: Adults $4.00, seniors $3.00, children six–eighteen $1.00, under six 50 cents, college students $2.00; groups of fifteen or more receive a discount.

Open to Public: Mon.–Sat. 10:00 A.M.–4:00 P.M. or by appointment; closed Sun.

Visitor Services: Public restrooms, information, handicapped access.

Regularly Scheduled Events: None.

Directions: From I–65 take Selma exit. Take Highway 80, cross over the Alabama River on the Pettus Bridge, then turn right on Water Avenue. Street dead-ends at museum. Located at the corner of Water Avenue and Martin Luther King Jr. Street.

 OLD LIVE OAK CEMETERY

110 West Dallas Avenue, Selma, AL 36701; (334) 874–2160; www.selma alabama.com.

Description: Site of the graves of Confederate soldiers and prominent Selma residents. Features a statue of Elodie B. Todd, half-sister of Mary Todd Lincoln; mausoleum of Vice President William Rufus King; and grave of Benjamin Sterling Turn-

er, the former slave who went on to become the first African-American U.S. congressman from Alabama.

Admission Fees: Free.

Open to Public: Grounds, daily 6:00 A.M. to 6:00 P.M.; summer, 6:00 A.M. to 7:00 P.M.; office, Mon.–Thurs. 8:00 A.M.–4:00 P.M., Fri. 8:00 A.M.–3:30 P.M.

Visitor Services: Information.

Regularly Scheduled Events: March, cemetery tours and living history during Pilgrimage; April, memorial service during Battle of Selma reenactment.

Directions: From Montgomery take Highway 80 west to Selma. From I–65 in Birmingham take exit 22 at Clanton; follow Highway 22 to Selma. In Selma follow Highway 22 (West Dallas Avenue) to cemetery.

 SELMA HISTORIC DISTRICT

Chamber of Commerce, 912 Selma Avenue, Selma, AL 36701; P.O. Box 467, Selma, AL 36702; (334) 875–7241 or (800) 45–SELMA; www.selmaalabama.com; selmacofc@us.inter.net.

Description: The war was almost over when Union troops under the leadership of Gen. James H. Wilson and 13,500 cavalry and mounted infantry (the Raiders) invaded Alabama. Anticipating the invasion, Selma prepared as best it could. But Lt. Gen. Nathan Bedford Forrest's highly outnumbered 2,000 men, mostly old men and boys, could not hold back Wilson's Raiders when the battle began on April 2, 1865. Selma has the largest historic district in Alabama, and it is the second-oldest surviving city in the state. The Windshield Tour, a self-guided driving tour of Selma, features Civil War–era homes and buildings and their history. The map is available from the Selma Chamber of Commerce or the Selma Visitor Information Center.

Admission Fees: Free.

Open to Public: Chamber of Commerce,

Fort Blakeley, Spanish Fort, Alabama. Joann Flirt.

Mon.–Fri. 8:30 A.M.–4:30 P.M.; Selma Visitor Information Center (2207 Broad Street), daily 8:00 A.M.–8:00 P.M.

Regularly Scheduled Events: March, Historic Selma Pilgrimage tour of homes; April, Battle of Selma reenactment; May, Old Cahawba Festival.

Directions: From Montgomery take Highway 80 west to Selma. From I–65 in Birmingham exit at Clanton; take Highway 22 to Selma.

 VAUGHAN-SMITHERMAN MUSEUM

109 Union Street, Selma, AL 36701; (334) 874–2174; www.selmaalabama .com.

Description: Built in 1847 by the Selma Masonic Order to serve as a university, the building served as a hospital for Confederate soldiers during the Civil War and later as the county courthouse and as a military school.

Admission Fees: Age twelve and over $3.00; group rates available.

Open to Public: Tues.–Sat. 9:00 A.M.–4:00 P.M.; other times by appointment.

Visitor Services: Public restrooms, tours, information, handicapped access, museum.

Regularly Scheduled Events: March, Historic Selma Pilgrimage and Antique Show.

Directions: From Montgomery take Highway 80 west to Selma. From I–65 in Birmingham take exit 22 at Clanton; follow Highway 22 to Selma. Take Alabama Avenue to Smitherman Building.

SPANISH FORT

 HISTORIC BLAKELEY STATE PARK CWPT

34745 State Highway 225, Spanish Fort, AL 36527; (251) 626–0798; www.blakeley park.org; blakelypark@aol.com.

Description: The last major battle of the Civil War was fought at Blakeley. It was fought

on April 9, 1865, the same day as the surrender of Gen. Robert E. Lee miles away in Virginia. The Battle of Blakeley was a major news event in the coverage of the Civil War.
Admission Fees: Adults $3.00, children six–twelve $1.50.
Open to Public: Daily 9:00 A.M.–5:00 P.M.
Visitor Services: Public restrooms, information; camping, trails.

Regularly Scheduled Events: Call for dates of Civil War demonstrations and living history demonstrations.
Directions: From I–10 go north on U.S. 98 to U.S. 31 and take a right. Turn left on Highway 225 and go north 4.5 miles. The park is on the left. From I–65 take Highway 225 south 15 miles.

❖ KENTUCKY ❖

BARDSTOWN

 OLD BARDSTOWN VILLAGE CIVIL WAR MUSEUM

310 East Broadway, Bardstown KY 40004; (502) 349–0291; www.civil-war-museum.org.

Description: This museum focuses on "the War in the West," which witnessed the military beginnings of such famous Union generals as Grant, Sherman, and Sheridan. A new museum dedicated to the women of the Civil War is located adjacent to the Civil War Museum in the historic Wright Talbott House.
Admission Fees: Adults, $6.00, seniors, $5.00, children seven–fifteen, $2.50; group rates available.
Open to Public: Mon.–Sat. 10:00 A.M.–5:00 P.M., Sun. noon–5:00 P.M.; Jan. and Feb. open weekends only.
Visitor Services: Public restrooms, handicapped access, gift shop.
Regularly Scheduled Events: None.
Directions: From the Bluegrass Parkway, take exit 25; travel west on U.S. 150. Proceed through two traffic lights and turn right on Old Bloomfield Road after the second. Turn left at stop sign and follow signs to the museum.

 SPALDING HALL

Bardstown Historical Museum, 114 North Fifth Street, Bardstown, KY 40004; (502) 348–2999.

Description: Spalding Hall is a large, five-story, Federal-style brick building erected in 1826 as part of the former St. Joseph's College. It was used as a hospital during the Civil War. Now a museum, Spalding Hall includes a room featuring Civil War artifacts and memorabilia. The museum guide can provide information on Bardstown's role in the Civil War.
Admission Fees: Free.
Open to Public: May–Oct., Mon.–Sat. 10:00 A.M.–5:00 P.M., Sun. noon–4:00 P.M.; Nov.–Apr., Tues.–Sat. 10:00 A.M.–4:00 P.M., Sun. noon–4:00 P.M.
Visitor Services: Public restrooms, museum.
Regularly Scheduled Events: None.
Directions: From southbound Bluegrass Parkway take exit 25; turn right onto U.S. 150, which becomes Stephen Foster Avenue. Turn right at the fourth traffic light (circle halfway around the county courthouse in the center of town) onto North Fifth Street. From northbound Bluegrass Parkway take exit 21; travel north (turn left) on U.S. 31 east. Turn right on West Stephen Foster Avenue, proceed to first traffic light, and turn left onto North Fifth Street.

KENTUCKY SITES

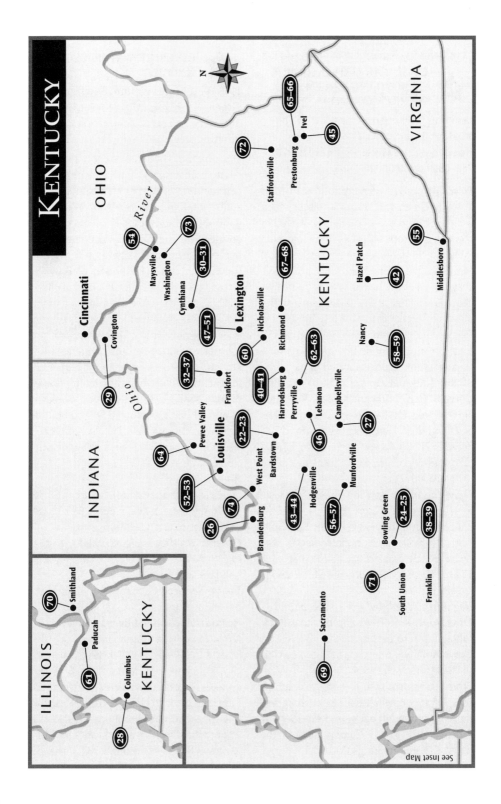

BOWLING GREEN

CIVIL WAR DRIVING TOUR OF BOWLING GREEN AND WARREN COUNTY

Bowling Green Area Convention and Visitors Bureau, 352 Three Springs Road, Bowling Green, KY 42104; (270) 782–0800 or (800) 326–7465.

Description: This driving tour of historic Bowling Green and Warren County, which both the Union and Confederacy wanted to control, is composed of eleven sites. Notably, Bowling Green served as the capital of Confederate Kentucky.

Admission Fees: A free driving tour brochure is available at the visitor center of the Bowling Green/Warren County Tourist and Convention Commission, located at 352 Three Springs Road, Bowling Green; a branch visitor center is located in the lobby of the National Corvette Museum, 350 Corvette Drive, Bowling Green. Tour sites are scattered. Of the eleven sites, admission is charged at Kentucky Museum (270–745–2592), Riverview at Hobson House (270–843–5565), and Lost River Cave Valley (270–393–0077).

Open to Public: Bowling Green Area Visitors Center, all year Mon.–Fri. 8:00 A.M.–5:00 P.M.; Memorial Day–Labor Day, Sat.–Sun. 9:00 A.M.–5:00 P.M.; National Corvette Museum branch, daily 9:00 A.M.–5:00 P.M.

Visitor Services: See brochure for individual site services.

Regularly Scheduled Events: None.

Directions: From I–65 south take exit 28; follow ramp to first light and turn left on Corvette Drive. Branch visitor center is in the lobby of the National Corvette Museum. From I–65 north take exit 22, turn left on U.S. 231 (Scottsville Road) for a short distance and then left again on Kentucky 884 (Three Springs Road). Visitor center is on the left at 352 Three Springs Road.

RIVERVIEW AT HOBSON GROVE

1100 West Main Avenue, Bowling Green, KY 42101; (270) 843–5565; www.bgky.org/riverview.htm; rivervw@bowlinggreen.net.

Description: The Hobson House, an Italianate mansion, was partially constructed before the Civil War. Col. William Hobson, son of builder Atwood Hobson and the youngest Union colonel on record, requested that Brig. Gen. Simon Bolivar Buckner, commanding Southern officer during the Confederate occupation of Bowling Green, spare the property. Buckner filled the basement of the unfinished mansion with Confederate ammunition. Atwood Hobson, one of the most ardent Union supporters in southern Kentucky, brought a French military professor to his home for the purpose of instructing William and his contemporaries in French military tactics. Atwood, president of a local bank, borrowed $30,000 to advance the Union cause. He also purchased 300 rifles to arm local citizens against the Confederates.

Admission Fees: Adults $5.00 (CWPT members $1.00 off admission), students $2.50, children under six free, families $10.00; call in advance to arrange group tours.

Open to Public: Tue.–Sat. 10:00 A.M.–4:00 P.M., Sun. 1:00 P.M.–4:00 P.M.; closed Mon., holidays, and Jan.

Visitor Services: Public restrooms, gift shop, museum, tours.

Regularly Scheduled Events: None.

Directions: From southbound I–65 take exit 28 and follow signs to Bowling Green via U.S. 68/Highway 80. Turn right on Sixth Avenue, which becomes Veterans Memorial Lane and leads to Hobson Grove Park; follow signs. From northbound I–65 take exit 20 onto the Green River Parkway. Take Morgantown Road exit onto U.S. 231. Turn right toward Bowling Green. Turn left onto Veterans Memorial Lane and follow signs.

CIVIL WAR TECHNOLOGY

"In the arts of life, man invents nothing; but in the arts of death he outdoes nature herself, and produces by chemistry and machinery all the slaughter of plague, pestilence and famine."

—George Bernard Shaw

The Civil War in the United States has often been called "the first modern war." There were so many technological advances during this period that the war truly did bring in a new era of warfare.

In naval warfare the Confederate navy made a successful submarine attack, and the first ironclad ships were engaged in ship-to-ship combat. During this time naval mines, called "torpedoes" (though they are a bit different from what we currently refer to as torpedoes), were used as well.

The railroad also led to new war developments. For the first time artillery was mounted on rail cars, and the railroads became a major means of transporting both troops and supplies. The railroad was also used for moving the wounded on "hospital trains."

Some other "firsts" include the use of portable telegraph units on the battlefield, the use of hot-air balloons for military reconnaissance, and the use of machine guns and repeating rifles and carbines in battle. Large numbers of photographs were taken on battlefields, and American soldiers and naval personnel received the first Congressional Medals of Honor.

CWPT *CIVIL WAR EXPLORER*

SOUTHERN HEARTLAND

BRANDENBURG

 GENERAL JOHN HUNT MORGAN'S BRANDENBURG RAID

P.O. Box 483, Brandenburg, KY 40108; (270) 422–3626 (Chamber of Commerce); www.visitmeadecounty.org; tourism @bbtel.com.

Description: Follow the four-day action of Gen. John Hunt Morgan's raid on this scenic Ohio River community—a well-known shipping and trading place throughout much of the nineteenth century. A free brochure chronicles the Confederate leader's July 6–9, 1863, time here, which included a skirmish on the river and burning of the steamer *Alice Dean*. Pick up the brochure from the local chamber of commerce office or the public library.

Admission Fees: Free.

Open to Public: Chamber of Commerce office, Mon.–Fri. 9:00 A.M.–4:00 P.M.; Meade County Public Library, Mon., Wed., Fri. 9:00 A.M.–5:30 P.M., Tues. and Thurs. 9:00 A.M.–8:00 P.M., Sat. 9:00 A.M.–4:00 P.M.; closed Sun.

Visitor Services: Chamber of Commerce office, public restrooms, handicapped access; Meade County Public Library, public restrooms.

Regularly Scheduled Events: None.

Directions: From I–64 at Corydon, Indiana, take exit 62; travel on Highway 135 south (approximately 20 miles) and cross Ohio River. Take Highway 1051; at four-way stop, turn left on High Street/Highway 79 and proceed 2 miles. Chamber office is inside City Hall at 735 High Street. The library is located at 400 Library Place (off Broadway/Highway 448).

CAMPBELLSVILLE

 27 TEBBS BEND BATTLEFIELD

Tebbs Bend Road, Campbellsville, KY 42719; (800) 738–4719 or (270) 465–8726; www.campbellsville.com; taylorcounty tourism@juno.com.

Description: The 1863 Battle of Tebbs Bend/ Green River Bridge took place on a bend in the Green River 8 miles from Campbellsville and was an early omen of the disaster to befall Gen. John Hunt Morgan on his Great Indiana and Ohio Raid. The engagement was one of the bloodiest battles in the western theater for the small number of troops involved. Adjacent to the battlefield is the Atkinson-Griffin Log House, which served as a Confederate hospital; bloodstains are still visible on the floor. A self-guided driving tour brochure of the battlefield is available at the tourist commission or at Green River Lake Corps of Engineers Visitor Center.

Admission Fees: Free.

Open to Public: Battlefield, daily from dawn to dusk. Taylor County Tourist Commission, Mon.–Fri. 8:30 A.M.–4:30 P.M.; Green River Visitor Center, Mon.–Fri. 8:00 A.M.–4:00 P.M., extended summer hours.

Visitor Services: Public restrooms, picnic area, Atkinson-Griffin House and Confederate Hospital at Green River Lake Corps of Engineers Visitors Center, adjacent to battlefield.

Regularly Scheduled Events: Call for events.

Directions: From Campbellsville obtain driving tour brochure at the tourist commission, located on the courthouse square that is on Highway 55. Take Highway 55 south for 8 miles and turn right on Morgan-Moore Trail to begin tour. From the south take exit 49 off Cumberland Parkway to Columbia and follow Highway 55 north for 12 miles to Green River Lake Corps of Engineers Visitor Center. Obtain brochure at the interpretive center. Return to park entrance, turn right on Highway 55, and travel 2 miles. Turn left on the Morgan-Moore Trail to begin tour.

Atkinson-Griffin Log House, Tebbs Bend Battlefield, Campbellsville, Kentucky. Courtesy of Taylor County Tourist Commission–CWPT files.

COLUMBUS

 COLUMBUS-BELMONT STATE PARK

Kentucky 58 and Kentucky 123/80, Columbus, KY 42032; (270) 677–2327; www.parks.ky.gov.

Description: Columbus-Belmont State Park played a fascinating role in the Civil War. The 1861 Battle of Belmont, fought to overtake the Confederate stronghold here, marked the opening of the Union's western campaign. It was also Union Gen. Ulysses S. Grant's first active engagement of the Civil War. Some of the artillery that shelled the Union troops and the six-ton anchor that held the great chain stretching across the river are on display in the park.

Admission Fees: Adults $2.00, children $1.50; group rates available.

Open to Public: May–Oct., daily 9:00 A.M.–5:00 P.M.; Apr., open weekends or by appointment.

Visitor Services: Public restrooms, food, gift shop, museum, picnic area, camping, trails.

Regularly Scheduled Events: Second weekend in October, Civil War Days.

Directions: From Purchase Parkway take exit 1, U.S. 51 north to Clinton; go northwest on Kentucky 58 to Columbus and the park.

COVINGTON

 BEHRINGER-CRAWFORD MUSEUM

1600 Montague Road/Devou Park, Covington, KY 41011; (859) 491–4003; www.bcmuseum.org; info@bcmuseum .org.

Description: The Covington Behringer-Crawford Museum preserves northern Kentucky's natural and cultural history. It is located in the 1848–80 Devou family home in the 700-acre Devou Park. The museum's Civil War collection focuses on the Siege of Cincinnati, the story of Gen. John Hunt Morgan, and the significance of the Under-ground Railroad. A battery in the park offers interpretive Civil War signage.

Admission Fees: Adults $5.00, children $3.00, seniors $4.00.

Open to Public: Tues.–Fri. 10:00 A.M.–5:00 P.M., Sat.–Sun. noon–5:00 P.M.; closed Jan.

Visitor Services: Public restrooms, information, handicapped access, gift shop, private research library, tours upon request.

Regularly Scheduled Events: June, periodic Civil War reenactments; November–December, holiday trains and Victorian house decorations.

Directions: From I-71/75 take exit 191 (Covington's Pike Street/12th Street). Go west on Pike Street and bear right on Lewis Street immediately past the interstate. Just after the third stop sign, bear right up the hill onto Montague Road; at the three-way stop, turn right; go through a four-way stop; the parking lot is on the left as you head down the hill.

CYNTHIANA

 JEFFERSON DAVIS MONUMENT STATE HISTORIC SITE

U.S. 68 East, Cynthiana, KY 41642; (270) 889–6100; www.parks.ky.gov; jefferson davis@ky.gov.

Description: The monument is a 351-foot-high stone obelisk that marks the site where, on June 3, 1808, Jefferson Davis, the only president of the Confederacy, was born. There is an elevator to an observation room high atop the structure for a panoramic view of the western Kentucky countryside.

Admission Fees: Adults and children $2.00, school groups $1.00 per student.

Open to Public: May–Oct., daily 9:00 A.M.–5:00 P.M.; closed Nov.–Apr.

Visitor Services: Public restrooms, handicapped access, gift shop.

Regularly Scheduled Events: First weekend in June, Jefferson Davis birthday celebration, Miss Confederacy pageant, living history camps, artillery and infantry demonstrations.

Directions: Take Pennyrile Parkway south to Hopkinsville, where it ends; go approximately 10 miles east on U.S. 68 to Fairview.

 **MORGAN'S RAIDS AT CYNTHIANA**

203 West Pike Street, Cynthiana, KY 41031; (859) 234–5236; www.cynthiana ky.com; cynchamber@se-tel.com.

Description: Rebel raider John Hunt Morgan's two famous Kentucky raids in 1862 and 1864 included significant engagements with Union forces at Cynthiana. Morgan's mission was to destroy railroad facilities, disrupt communications, acquire supplies, recruit, and threaten the community of Cincinnati.

Admission Fees: Free.

Open to Public: Cynthiana Chamber of Commerce office, Mon.–Fri. 9:00 A.M.–4:00 P.M.

Visitor Services: Brochure available from the Cynthiana Chamber of Commerce.

Regularly Scheduled Events: Fourth weekend of September, Battle of Cynthiana reenactment.

Directions: From I–75 take exit 126; travel northeast on U.S. 62 to U.S. 27 (approximately 15 miles) and into Cynthiana. Chamber of Commerce office is on Pike Street, behind courthouse.

FRANKFORT

 FRANKFORT CEMETERY

215 East Main Street, Frankfort, KY 40601; (502) 227–2403.

Description: Frankfort Cemetery is a highly scenic cemetery whose southern edge overlooks the Kentucky River, the state capitol, and the town of Frankfort. The cemetery has been described as "Kentucky's Westminster" because so many famous people are buried here. A brochure gives the location of the graves of many Civil War notables, the Confederate monument and surrounding unknown graves, and the state military monument that tells about Kentucky's role in the Civil War.

Admission Fees: Free.

Open to Public: Brochures available at the Frankfort Cemetery office Mon.–Fri. 8:00 A.M.–4:00 P.M. or the Frankfort Tourist Information Center (100 Capitol Avenue) on weekends. Cemetery, Mon.–Sat. 7:30 A.M.–dusk, Sun. 8:00 A.M.–dusk. (*NOTE:* Buses and motor coaches are not allowed in the Frankfort Cemetery.)

Visitor Services: Information.

Regularly Scheduled Events: None.

Directions: From I–64 take exit 58 (Frankfort/Versailles). Travel on U.S. 60 toward Frankfort and follow signs for downtown Frankfort and East Main Street. U.S. 60 turns left at the intersection with U.S. 460 and becomes East Main Street. Turn left onto East Main Street. To proceed to Frankfort Cemetery, turn left at traffic light onto Glenn's Creek Road; immediately turn right into cemetery. To reach the tourist center, continue on East Main past the turn to Frankfort Cemetery. Turn left onto Capitol Avenue. Tourist center is at 100 Capitol Avenue on the right.

 GREEN HILL CEMETERY

Located on Atwood Avenue, off East Main Street, Frankfort, KY 40601; (502) 564–1792.

Description: The ladies of the George M. Monroe Chapter 8, Kentucky Colored Corps, a division of the Women's Relief Corps of the Grand Army of the Republic, erected a simple yet noble monument in 1924. It honors the 141 black men from central Kentucky who fought for the Union, all of whom mustered into Federal service at Camp Nelson, Kentucky.

Admission Fees: Free.
Open to Public: Daily from dawn to dusk.
Visitor Services: None.
Regularly Scheduled Events: None.
Directions: From I–64 take exit 58 (Frankfort/Versailles); travel on U.S. 60 west, which turns left at its intersection with U.S. 460 and becomes East Main Street. Turn left between a Chevron station (859 East Main Street) and the sign EAST SIDE SHOPPING CENTER (863 East Main) onto a paved way. This way becomes Atwood Avenue. Follow it around a curve to Green Hill Cemetery on the left. Turn into the cemetery's circular lane and go one-third around the circle; the monument is approximately 75 feet away to the right.

 KENTUCKY MILITARY HISTORY MUSEUM

125 East Main Street, Frankfort, KY 40601; (502) 564–3265 or (502) 564–1792; www.history.ky.gov; khstours@ky.gov.

Description: The Kentucky Military History Museum is housed in the 1850 State Arsenal and has a large collection of Kentucky Union and Confederate memorabilia, including identified uniforms, flags, guns, and other equipment. During the war the arsenal was a cartridge factory for the Union army as well as a regional supply center for Northern troops from midwestern states.
Admission Fees: Adults $4.00, children six–twelve $2.00.
Open to Public: Tues.–Sat. 10:00 A.M.–5:00 P.M.
Visitor Services: Public restrooms, handicapped access.
Regularly Scheduled Events: None.
Directions: From I–64 take exit 58B. Follow U.S. 127 to Clinton Street, continue on Clinton Street to Ann Street, and turn right. Continue on to East Main. Turn left on East Main to museum.

Kentucky Military History Museum, Frankfort. CWPT files.

 KENTUCKY STATE CAPITOL

c/o Information Desk, 700 Capitol Avenue, Frankfort, KY 40601; (502) 564–3449; www.lcr.ky.gov; capitoltours desk@ky.gov.

Description: The rotunda of Kentucky's handsome 1910 state capitol features statues of prominent Kentuckians, including Abraham Lincoln, sculpted by A. Weinman, and Jefferson Davis, sculpted by Frederick C. Hibbard. Both leaders were born in Kentucky, less than a year and 100 miles apart. In 1904 the Kentucky legislature appropriated $1 million, a debt collected from the U.S. War Department as reparations for damages inflicted by Federal soldiers during the Civil War, to build the new capitol.
Admission Fees: Free.
Open to Public: Mon.–Fri. 8:00 A.M.–4:30 P.M., Sat. 10:00 A.M.–2:00 P.M., Sun. 1:00 P.M.–4:00 P.M.; tours given on the half-hour.
Visitor Services: Information, handicapped access, food, gift shop, tours.

Regularly Scheduled Events: None.
Directions: From I–64 west take exit 58; go 5 miles west on U.S. 60 (East Main Street) to bridge; follow U.S. 60 up Capitol Avenue to building. From I–64 east take exit 52; go north on U.S. 127, east on U.S. 60, and follow signs.

 LESLIE MORRIS PARK AT FORT HILL

400 Clifton Avenue, Frankfort, KY 40601; (502) 696–0607; frankforthistory @yahoo.com.

Description: Within the park is Fort Boone, an 1863 earthen fort attacked by a detachment of Gen. John Morgan's cavalry. Adjacent is the New Redoubt, a second and larger fortification built to protect Kentucky's pro-Union government. The park's visitor center in the Sullivan House, named after the family that lived there for generations, portrays a Civil War–era roadside inn.
Admission Fee: Free.
Open to Public: Park, daily from dawn to dusk; visitor center and tours, Memorial Day–Oct. 31, Tues., Thurs., and Sat. 11:00 A.M.–4:00 P.M.
Visitor Services: Handicapped access, museum, tours, trails.
Regularly Scheduled Events: July, Central Kentucky CW Trail Tour; October, Ghosts of Frankfort.
Directions: To Old State Capitol from I–64, go to U.S. 127 north; turn right onto Holmes Street, right onto Henry Street, left onto Hillside Drive, right at Y onto Clifton, and park gate is straight ahead.

 OLD STATE CAPITOL

c/o Kentucky Historical Society, 100 West Broadway, Frankfort, KY 40601; (502) 564–1792; www.history.ky.gov; khstours@ky.gov.

Description: This 1829 Greek Revival masterpiece was the only Union capitol captured by Southern troops. Here Kentucky's legislature voted first to maintain official neutrality, although the state later became bitterly divided. So resentful of wrongful Union treatment, Kentucky—following the war's end—became so sympathetic to the South that it was observed, "Kentucky seceded after the war!"
Admission Fees: Adults $4.00, children six–twelve $2.00.
Open to Public: Tues.–Sat. 10:00 A.M.–5:00 P.M.; guided tours leave on the hour from the history center.
Visitor Services: Public restrooms, handicapped access, gift shop.
Regularly Scheduled Events: None.
Directions: From I–64 take exit 58, go 5 miles west on U.S. 60 (U.S. 60 becomes East Main Street) to downtown; follow signs.

FRANKLIN

 OCTAGON HALL MUSEUM/ KENTUCKY CONFEDERATE STUDIES ARCHIVE

6040 Bowling Green Road; Franklin, KY 42134; (270) 586–9343; www .octagonhall.com; kycsa@accessky.net.

Description: Octagon Hall was used extensively during the Civil War. An antebellum octagonal structure, the site was used as a campsite and as an observation post to monitor the L & N Railroad for troop movements. The owner, a Southern sympathizer, hid Confederate troops in the building late in the war.
Admission Fees: Adults $3.00, children under thirteen free.
Open to Public: Wed.–Sat. 8:00 A.M.–3:30 P.M.; tours on the hour.
Visitor Services: Public restrooms, information, gift shop, tours, research archives, trails.
Regularly Scheduled Events: Quarterly living history programs.
Directions: From I–65 take exit 2, travel on

U.S. 31W 6 miles north of Franklin. Octagon Hall Museum is on the east side of U.S. 31W.

SIMPSON COUNTY ARCHIVES AND MUSEUM

(Old Simpson County Jail and Jailer's Residence)
206 North College Street, Franklin, KY 42134; (270) 586–4228; www.rootsweb .com/~kyschs; oldjail@comcast.net.

Description: Confederate prisoners, or Union officers, or maybe both, executed drawings (thought to be in charcoal) on plaster walls in a second-story room of this circa 1835 brick house. The drawings portray soldiers on both sides, one bearing a striking resemblance to the "Thunderbolt of the Confederacy," Brig. Gen. John Hunt Morgan. One of the displays tells of Franklin native Marcellus Jerome Clarke, the best-known of Kentucky's Civil War guerrillas, who went by the nom de guerre "Sue Mundy."

Admission Fees: Free.

Open to Public: Mon.–Fri. 9:00 A.M.–4:00 P.M., Sat. 10:00 A.M.–2:00 P.M.; or by appointment.

Visitor Services: Public restrooms, research archives, tours, handicapped access to first floor only.

Regularly Scheduled Events: None.

Directions: From I–65 southbound take exit 6 and travel west on Kentucky 100 to Franklin. Turn right on U.S. 31W (Main Street); turn left on Kentucky Avenue. Go 1 block and turn right on North College to stone jail and brick house. From I–65 northbound take exit 2; turn left onto U.S. 31W north and travel into Franklin, where U.S. 31W becomes Main Street. Turn left onto Kentucky Avenue. Go 1 block to North College Street and turn right.

HARRODSBURG

OLD FORT HARROD STATE PARK

U.S. 68 and U.S. 127, Harrodsburg, KY 40330-0156; (859) 734–3314; www.parks .ky.gov; fortharrod@kentucky.gov.

Description: Located on the grounds of this state park is the Lincoln Marriage Temple, a brick pavilion enshrining the cabin in which the parents of President Abraham Lincoln were wed on June 12, 1806. Also, the "Mansion Museum" features Confederate and Union rooms. Exhibits include paintings, photographs, newspapers, documents, and firearms.

Admission Fees: Adults $4.50, children $2.50, seniors $4.00; group rates available.

Open to Public: Fort open year-round; closed Thanksgiving, Christmas week, and weekends December–March. Open to the public Mar. 16–Oct. 31, 9:00 A.M.–5:00 P.M.; Nov. 1–Mar. 15, 8:30 A.M.–4:30 P.M.

Visitor Services: Public restrooms, handicapped access, gift shop, museum.

Regularly Scheduled Events: June, Old Fort Harrod Festival; mid-November, holiday gala tour.

Directions: From Bluegrass Parkway take I–64 to U.S. 127; go 15 miles south on U.S. 127 to intersection of U.S. 127 and U.S. 68.

THE SHAKER VILLAGE OF PLEASANT HILL

3501 Lexington Road (on U.S. 68, 7 miles northeast of Harrodsburg), Harrodsburg, KY 40330; (859) 734–5411 or (800) 734–5611; www.shakervillageky.org; services@shakervillageky.org.

Description: The Shaker Village of Pleasant Hill is a restored indoor and outdoor living history museum that interprets the lives of the Shakers. This unique American religious community is located on a turnpike that was a strategic conduit for Union and Confederate soldiers throughout the Civil War, but

SOUTHERN HEARTLAND

especially during the 1862 Kentucky campaign. The Shakers were Unionists and emancipationists, but their dedication to pacifism prevented their participation in the conflict. The Shakers extended generous hospitality to both armies as they marched through the village. The only non-Shaker buried in the cemetery is a Confederate soldier who died there shortly after the nearby Battle of Perryville, on October 8, 1862. Also, the Shaker Landing on the Kentucky River was critical to the Union effort throughout the war.

Admission Fees: Adults $14.00, youths twelve–seventeen $7.00, children six–eleven $5.00; call for group and reduced winter rates.

Open to Public: Apr.–Oct. 10:00 A.M.–5:00 P.M.; Nov.–Mar., daily 10:00 A.M.–4:30 P.M.

Visitor Services: Lodging, public restrooms, partially handicapped accessible, food, gift shop, riverboat excursions, conference facilities, museum, tours, trails.

Regularly Scheduled Events: Even-numbered years, Civil War living history weekend.

Directions: From I–64/75 near Lexington, access New Circle Road (Kentucky 4) from exit 115 (Newtown Pike), exit 113 (Paris Pike/North Broadway), or exit 110 (Winchester Road) and go east or south to U.S. 68. Travel south on U.S. 68, a Kentucky Scenic Byway, for 21 miles to the Shaker Village of Pleasant Hill.

HAZEL PATCH

CAMP WILDCAT CIVIL WAR BATTLEFIELD CWPT

Old Wilderness Road, London, KY 40741; (800) 348–0095 or (606) 864–9776; www.campwildcatpreservation foundation.org; laurelsect8@sunspot .com.

Description: The October 1861 Battle of Wildcat Mountain was the earliest major Civil War battle as well as the first Union victory in Kentucky. This action was part of

Confederate Gen. Felix Zollicoffer's Mill Springs campaign.

Admission Fees: Free.

Open to Public: Daily from dawn to dusk.

Visitor Services: Interpretive signs.

Regularly Scheduled Events: October, battle reenactment.

Directions: From I–75 take exit 49; proceed north on Kentucky 909 to U.S. 25. Turn right (south) on U.S. 25 and proceed approximately 1 mile. Turn left on Hazel Patch Road. Travel approximately 1 mile to a graveled county road and turn left. This road is marked with a directional sign to the battlefield. Proceed approximately 2 miles to the battlefield site.

HODGENVILLE

ABRAHAM LINCOLN BIRTHPLACE NATIONAL HISTORIC SITE

2995 Lincoln Farm Road, Hodgenville, KY 42748; (270) 358–3137; www.nps.gov/ abli.

Description: Born in a one-room log cabin near Hodgen's Mill, Abraham Lincoln lived in Kentucky from 1809 to 1816. The site incorporates the birthplace and boyhood home of the sixteenth president of the United States, who successfully preserved the Union through the turmoil of the Civil War. The 116-acre park features the cabin typically thought to be Lincoln's birthplace, enshrined in the neo-classical Memorial Building on the site where he was born, and the spring where the Lincoln family drew water.

Admission Fees: Free.

Open to Public: Daily 8:00 A.M.–4:45 P.M.; call for extended summer hours.

Visitor Services: Public restrooms, handicapped access, gift shop, visitor center, exhibits, orientation film, picnic area, trails.

Regularly Scheduled Events: Sunday before the Monday holiday in January, Martin Luther King Jr.'s Birthday; February 12, Lincoln's Birthday; September, Constitutional

Week; second week in October, Lincoln Days festival; second Thursday in December, Christmas in the Park.

Directions: From the south on I–65, take exit 81; go east on Kentucky 84 (Sonora), approximately 9 miles. From the north on I–65, take exit 91 (Elizabethtown) and go south on Kentucky 61 for approximately 12 miles.

 THE LINCOLN MUSEUM

66 Lincoln Square, Hodgenville, KY 42748; (270) 358–3163; www.lincoln museum-ky.org; abe@lincolnmuseum-ky.org.

Description: On the square in the downtown Hodgenville Historic District, the Lincoln Museum relates major events in Lincoln's life through twelve detailed dioramas featuring a collection of twenty-one realistic wax figures. Includes art collections, film, Civil War artifacts, and a children's room.

Admission Fees: Adults $3.00, children $1.50, seniors and military $2.50; groups of twelve or more, adults $2.00, children $1.00.

Open to Public: Mon.–Sat. 8:30 A.M.–4:30 P.M., Sun. 12:30 P.M.–4:30 P.M.

Visitor Services: Public restrooms, handicapped access, gift shop.

Regularly Scheduled Events: February, Lincoln's Birthday; October, Lincoln Days festival.

Directions: From I–65 at Elizabethtown, take the Hodgenville exit to Highway 61 south and drive 12 miles. Turn left onto Highway 3204, then turn right onto Lincoln Boulevard. Museum is on the right side of town square.

IVEL

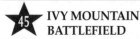 **IVY MOUNTAIN BATTLEFIELD**

Kentucky Highway 23, Ivel, KY 42642; (606) 886–3863; www.geocities.com/ heartland/9999/ivymountainpage.html.

Description: In the fall of 1861, Gen. William "Bull" Nelson, Union commander in northeastern Kentucky, was ordered to break up a large Confederate recruiting camp in Prestonsburg. In what would be the first major clash in eastern Kentucky, Confederate Capt. Andrew Jackson May's recruits would take up positions at this site, where they waited in ambush. The Battle of Ivy Mountain ended the first phase of the struggle for the Big Sandy Valley.

Admission Fees: Free.

Open to Public: Daily from dawn to dusk.

Visitor Services: Information.

Regularly Scheduled Events: November, Battle Anniversary Program.

Directions: From I–64 take exit 191; travel south on Highway 23 for approximately 45 miles to Ivel. The site is on the right-hand side of Highway 23.

LEBANON

 HISTORIC HOMES AND LANDMARKS TOUR OF LEBANON

c/o Lebanon Tourist and Convention Commission, 239 North Spaulding Avenue, Lebanon, KY 40033; (207) 692–0021; www.visitlebanonky.com; visitlebanonky@alltel.net.

Description: This self-guided tour offers a significant glimpse at a town where the Civil War came as a severe blow. Lebanon was the site of three battles in 1861, 1862, and 1863. Its railway location made it susceptible to attack. A free tour brochure may be obtained at the Lebanon Tourist and Convention Commission.

Admission Fees: Free.

Open to Public: Lebanon Tourist and Convention Commission office, Mon.–Fri. 8:30 A.M.–5:00 P.M. The brochure may also be obtained at the library, 201 East Main Street.

Visitor Services: Lebanon Tourist and Convention Commission office, public restrooms, information.

Regularly Scheduled Events: None.

Directions: From the Bluegrass Parkway, take exit 42; travel south on Kentucky 555 South, bypassing Springfield and crossing U.S. 150. The road turns into Kentucky 55. Proceed 9 miles into Lebanon and to U.S. 68 and Centre Square. From I–65 south take exit 112 (16 miles south of Louisville); proceed southeast on Kentucky 245 bypassing Bardstown, taking U.S. 150 to Springfield to Kentucky 55 and then follow directions as above.

LEXINGTON

 ### ASHLAND: THE HENRY CLAY ESTATE

120 Sycamore Road, Lexington, KY 40502; (859) 266–8581; www.henryclay .org; info@henryclay.org.

Description: Ashland, a National Historic Landmark, was the home of "the Great Compromiser," Henry Clay, from 1811 until his death in 1852. Clay was a U.S. senator, Speaker of the House, secretary of state, and a three-time presidential candidate. He is especially noted for his devotion to the Union, and during his time he tried valiantly to prevent the coming Civil War. Clay's son rebuilt Ashland in the 1850s. A Civil War skirmish took place near Ashland, and the house was used as a hospital afterward. The estate includes nineteen acres, several antebellum dependencies, a formal garden, and a new monument describing the action at Ashland.

Admission Fees: Adults $7.00, students $3.00, children five and under free.

Open to Public: Mon.–Sat. 10:00 A.M.–4:30 P.M., Sun. 1:00 P.M.–4:30 P.M.; closed Mon. in Feb., Mar., Nov., and Dec.; closed the month of Jan. and on holidays. Tours on the hour; last tour at 4:00 P.M.

Visitor Services: Public restrooms, food, gift shop, museum, tours.

Regularly Scheduled Events: Summer, reenactments; December, Christmas events.

Directions: Accessible from I–75 and I–64.

Located at the corner of Richmond Road (also East Main Street) and Sycamore Road.

 ### HUNT-MORGAN HOUSE

201 North Mill Street, Lexington, KY 40507; (859) 253–0362; www.bluegrass trust.org; jgood@bluegrasstrust.org.

Description: Built in 1814 for John Wesley Hunt, possibly the first millionaire west of the Alleghenies, this outstanding example of regional Federal architecture is interpreted as an urban antebellum (1814–40) dwelling set in historic Gratz Park, where Civil War divisions among neighbors are dramatically pointed out. It was the family home of Gen. John Hunt Morgan, "Thunderbolt of the Confederacy," and the birthplace of Nobel laureate Dr. Thomas Hunt Morgan, pioneer geneticist. See family and period furnishings throughout and a delightful city garden. The Alexander T. Hunt Civil War Museum occupies several rooms.

Admission Fees: Adults $7.00 ($2.00 off admission for CWPT members), students $5.00; group rates available.

Open to Public: Wed.–Fri. 1:00 P.M.–5:00 P.M., Sat. 10:00 A.M.–4:00 P.M., Sun. 1:00 P.M.–5:00 P.M.; closed mid. Dec.–mid. Apr. Tours begin on the hour, with the last tour at 4:00 P.M.

Visitor Services: Public restrooms, information, limited handicapped access, gift shop, museum. Facilities available for catered meetings and events; call or visit the Web site for more information.

Regularly Scheduled Events: October, ghost tours; December, candlelight tours.

Directions: From I–75 take exit 113; turn right off of the exit and continue until the road turns into Broadway; turn left on West Third Street and almost immediately right on Mill Street; the house is at the corner of Mill and Second Streets, with parking off Second Street.

 **LEXINGTON CEMETERY**

833 West Main Street, Lexington, KY
40508; (859) 255–5522; www.lexcem.org;
info@lexcem.org.
Description: Two self-guided tours are
available: one for trees and the other for historical interest. The latter points out grave
sites of Civil War luminaries such as Confederate Gens. John Hunt Morgan and John
C. Breckinridge. Also, relatives of Mary Todd
Lincoln are interred here, as are Union and
Confederate soldiers, the latter being honored by two notable monuments.
Admission Fees: Free.
Open to Public: Daily 8:00 A.M.–5:00 P.M.
Visitor Services: Information, public restrooms.
Regularly Scheduled Events: None.
Directions: From I–75 take exit 115; travel
south on Newtown Pike (Highway 922) to
West Main Street (Highway 421). Go right
on West Main and turn toward the large
stone cemetery gatehouse on the right. In-
formation is available at offices in gatehouse
or at the Lexington Convention and Visitors
Bureau on Vine Street.

 **MARY TODD LINCOLN
HOUSE**

578 West Main Street, Lexington, KY
40507; (859) 233–9999; www.mtlhouse
.org; mtlhouse@iglou.com.
Description: First Lady Mary Todd Lincoln
resided in this fashionable brick residence
between the ages of fourteen and twenty-
one, and Abraham Lincoln was a guest here
following their marriage. Personal articles
from the Lincoln and Todd families are on
display. Restored garden to the rear.
Admission Fees: Adults $7.00, children six–
twelve $4.00; group rates available.
Open to Public: Mon.–Sat. 10:00 A.M.–4:00
P.M.; last tour 3:15 P.M.; closed Dec. 1–Mar. 15.
Visitor Services: Handicapped access, gift
shop, museum.

Regularly Scheduled Events: None.
Directions: From I–64/75 take exit 115; go
south on Newtown Pike (Highway 922),
cross New Circle Road (Highway 4), and go
to West Main Street (Highway 421). Go left
on West Main; the Mary Todd Lincoln
House is on the right on the corner of West
Main and Tucker, just before Rupp Arena.

 **WAVELAND**

225 Waveland Museum Lane, Lexington,
KY 40515; (859) 272–3611; waveland
@ky.gov.
Description: Both Confederate and Union
armies prized the Standardbred horses
raised on this plantation, which primarily
grew tobacco and hemp. Everyday antebellum life of the Bryan family—including that
of their slaves—is interpreted here. The 1847
brick residence is of classic Greek Revival
design; three original outbuildings, including slave quarters, remain.
Admission Fees: Adults $7.00, students
$4.00, seniors $6.00.
Open to Public: Mar.–mid. Dec., Mon.–Sat.
10:00 A.M.–5:00 P.M., Sun. 1:00 P.M.–5:00 P.M.;
mid. Dec.–Feb., Wed.–Sat. 10:00 A.M.–3:00
P.M.; last tour begins one hour prior to closing.
Visitor Services: Public restrooms, limited
handicapped accessible, tours, picnic area.
Regularly Scheduled Events: December,
Christmas candlelight tours.
Directions: From New Circle Road (Kentucky 4): travel south on Nicholasville Road
(U.S. 27) for 2 miles and turn right on Waveland Museum Lane; parking is on the right.

LOUISVILLE

**CAVE HILL CEMETERY AND
ARBORETUM**

701 Baxter Avenue, Louisville, KY
40204; (502) 451–5630; www.cavehill
cemetery.com; cavehill@bellsouth.net.
Description: Cave Hill Cemetery contains

SOUTHERN HEARTLAND

the remains of many Union soldiers, including three Union generals. Local Southern sympathizers provided a separate section for Confederate dead, also including three generals.

Admission Fees: Free.

Open to Public: Office and grounds, daily 8:00 A.M.–4:45 P.M. (gates are locked promptly at 5:00 P.M.).

Visitor Services: Public restrooms, information.

Regularly Scheduled Events: Summer, monthly historical and horticultural tours.

Directions: From I–64 take exit 8; follow Grinstead Drive west approximately 0.5 mile to Grinstead Drive entrance to Cave Hill Cemetery.

 FARMINGTON HISTORIC HOME

3033 Bardstown Road, Louisville, KY 40205; (502) 452–9920; www.farmington historichome.org.

Description: Farmington is an 1815 house that was based on plans designed by Thomas Jefferson. The site interprets life on the plantation from 1815 through the Civil War, including the roles of African Americans who lived at Farmington. Joshua Fry Speed, son of the original owners, went to Springfield, Illinois, in 1835 and later shared living quarters in Springfield with future president Abraham Lincoln. Speed became Lincoln's most trusted friend and confidant, and Lincoln spent three weeks as a guest at Farmington in 1841. Speed served as Lincoln's advisor on western affairs during the Civil War but declined the president's offer to appoint him secretary of state. However, his brother, James Speed, did serve as attorney general during Lincoln's second term.

Admission Fees: Adults $6.00, children six–seventeen $3.00, under six free, seniors $5.00; call for group rates.

Open to Public: Tues.–Sat. 10:00 A.M.–4:30 P.M., Sun. 1:30–4:30 P.M.; guided tours on the hour; closed New Year's Day, Easter, Derby (first Sat. in May), Thanksgiving, Christmas Eve, and Christmas Day.

Visitor Services: Public restrooms, information, gift shop, museum, tours, visitor center.

Regularly Scheduled Events: April, plant sale; December, candlelight tours; call for additional events.

Directions: From I–64 take I–264 west to Bardstown Road exit. Turn right (north) onto Bardstown Road. Turn right on Wendell Avenue, then immediately right again onto Farmington Lane.

Maysville

 KENTUCKY GATEWAY MUSEUM CENTER

215 Sutton Street, Maysville, KY 41056-1109; (606) 564–5865 (museum), (606) 564–9411 (Maysville Tourism); www .kygmc.org; museum@kygmc.org.

Description: A permanent exhibit, book collection, and video shown here offer a significant glimpse into the region's Civil War heritage. Maysville was a divided community throughout the conflict: It had economic ties to the free and neighboring North, as well as cultural ties to the slave-holding South. Take time also to see the impressive 1887 Union monument in the Maysville Cemetery (on Kentucky 10, near the city limits).

Admission Fees: Adults $2.50, children 50 cents.

Open to Public: Mon.–Fri. 9:00 A.M.–4:00 P.M., Sat. 10:00 A.M.–4:00 P.M.; Jan., closed; Feb.–Mar., closed Mon.

Visitor Services: Information, gift shop, tours, research assistance, public restrooms.

Regularly Scheduled Events: None.

Directions: From the Alexandria-Ashland ("AA") Highway (Kentucky 9), exit at U.S. 68 and follow U.S. 68 north to Bridge Street; turn right on Bridge Street and take the next left onto Second Street. Proceed to Sutton

Street (third traffic light). The museum is the second building on the right.

MIDDLESBORO

 CUMBERLAND GAP NATIONAL HISTORICAL PARK

Located on U.S. Highway 25E South, P.O. Box 1848, Middlesboro, KY 40965; (606) 248–2817; www.nps.gov/cuga; superintendent@cuga.nps.

Description: Cumberland Gap is the historic mountain pass on the Wilderness Road that opened the pathway for westward migration. During the Civil War, Cumberland Gap was first held by the South, then captured by Union troops. Each side held the gap twice.

Admission Fees: Free.

Open to Public: Park, daily from dawn to dusk. Visitor center, daily 8:00 A.M.–5:00 P.M.; closed Christmas.

Visitor Services: Public restrooms, information, handicapped access, gift shop, museum, camping, trails.

Regularly Scheduled Events: May–October, tours of Hensley settlement; call or check Web site for full schedule of events.

Directions: From I–75 take exit 29 at Corbin; follow signs on U.S. 25E (Cumberland Gap Parkway) through Middlesboro. The park is 0.25 mile south of Middlesboro. From I–81 in Tennessee access U.S. 25E going north at Morristown. Park is approximately 50 miles north of Morristown.

MUNFORDVILLE

 HART COUNTY HISTORICAL SOCIETY MUSEUM

109 Main Street, P.O. Box 606, Munfordville, KY 42765; (207) 524–0101; www.historichart.org.

Description: Hart County's seat of government is Munfordville, site of a Civil War battle in 1862. The museum includes Civil War memorabilia related to the Battle of Munfordville and to Munfordville natives, Confederate Brig. Gen. Simon Bolivar Buckner (later governor of Kentucky) and Union Maj. Gen. Thomas Wood. Buckner and Wood were childhood friends and classmates at West Point, an association that well illustrates Kentucky's deep divisions during the Civil War. Museum staff can direct you to sites of the Battle of Munfordville.

Admission Fees: Free.

Open to Public: Tues.–Fri. 9:00 A.M.–4:00 P.M., Sat. 9:00 A.M.–1:00 P.M.

Visitor Services: Public restrooms, gift shop.

Regularly Scheduled Events: September, Battle of Munfordville reenactment.

Directions: From I–65 take exit 65 (U.S. 31W) 1 mile south into Munfordville. U.S. 31W becomes Main Street. Museum is in two-story brick building next to city hall.

 MUNFORDVILLE BATTLEFIELD CWPT

c/o Civil War Preservation Trust, 1331 H Street NW, Suite 1001, Washington, DC 20005; (800) 298–7878; www.civilwar.org.

Description: In September 1862, Gen. Braxton Bragg led his Confederate offensive into Kentucky from Chattanooga, Tennessee, followed by Maj. Gen. Don Carlos Buell's Army of the Ohio. On September 14, Bragg's advanced forces under Brig. Gen. James R. Chalmers met the solid resistance of Col. John T. Wilder's garrison troops at Fort Craig. The Union garrison guarded the strategic Louisville & Nashville Railroad and the location of the railroad bridge crossing the Green River at Munfordville. By September 17, the undermanned redoubt was surrendered to the Confederates, in an important blow to Union supply lines in the west.

Admission Fees: Free.

Open to Public: Daily from dawn to dusk.

Visitor Services: Interpretive signage.

Regularly Scheduled Events: None.

Directions: From I–65 south take exit 65

SOUTHERN HEARTLAND

onto U.S. 31W, heading south into Munfordville. Fort Craig sits on the south side of the Green River Bridge. Turning right onto Craig Avenue leads west to the Louisville & Nashville Railroad and the adjacent battlefield. The site entrance is on the old Woodsonville Road.

NANCY

 MILL SPRINGS BATTLEFIELD CWPT
Highway 235, Nancy, KY 42544; (606) 636–4045; www.millsprings.net; administrator@millsprings.net.

Description: The Battle of Mill Springs was one of the earliest Union victories of the Civil War. This victory turned the Confederate flank in Kentucky and opened up an invasion route into east Tennessee and even Nashville. Confederate Gen. Felix K. Zollicoffer was killed in this battle; he was the first general killed in the west. Gen. George H. Thomas, who would later gain fame as the "Rock of Chickamauga," commanded the Union forces. After viewing the twenty-minute video depicting the Battle of Mill Springs, take an 8-mile driving tour from the visitor center to the Confederate encampment on the banks of Lake Cumberland.

Admission Fees: Free.

Open to Public: Daily from dawn to dusk; visitor center, Mon.–Sat. 9:00 A.M.–4:00 P.M., Sun. 1:00 P.M.–4:00 P.M.

Visitor Services: Information, public restroom, gift shop, handicapped access, driving tour, guided tours by appointment.

Regularly Scheduled Events: Weekend closest to January 19, battle commemoration ceremony; May, Memorial Day services; call for other events.

Directions: From I–75 take the London/U.S. 80 exit; follow U.S. 80 west to Somerset. At Somerset take the Cumberland Parkway west. (U.S. 80 and the parkway are the same

route briefly in Somerset.) From the Cumberland Parkway take the second left and then the first right. Proceed approximately 9 miles on Kentucky 80 to Nancy. At Nancy turn left (south) on Kentucky 235. Proceed approximately 1 mile to Zollicoffer Park on the left. Watch for the brown signs for Mill Springs Battlefield.

 ZOLLICOFFER PARK

Highway 235, 1 mile south of Nancy, Nancy, KY 42544; (606) 636–4045; www.millsprings.net; administrator@mill springs.net.

Description: Zollicoffer Park marks the site of the fiercest fighting in the Battle of Mill Springs, an important early Civil War conflict. The park is named for Confederate Gen. Felix K. Zollicoffer, mortally wounded in the battle. The park contains a 0.5-mile walking trail, interpretive signs, a Confederate mass grave, and the Zollicoffer Confederate Memorial Cemetery.

Admission Fees: Free.

Open to Public: Daily from dawn to dusk.

Visitor Services: Information, handicapped access, driving tour, guided tours by appointment.

Regularly Scheduled Events: Weekend closest to January 19 and Memorial Day, Battle of Mill Springs commemoration ceremony; call for other events.

Directions: From I–75 take the London/ U.S. 80 exit; follow U.S. 80 west to Somerset. At Somerset take the Cumberland Parkway west. (U.S. 80 and the parkway are the same route briefly in Somerset.) From the Cumberland Parkway take the second left and then the first right. Proceed approximately 9 miles on Kentucky 80 to Nancy. At Nancy turn left (south) on Kentucky 235. Proceed approximately 1 mile to Zollicoffer Park on the left. Watch for the brown signs for Mill Springs Battlefield.

NICHOLASVILLE

 CAMP NELSON

6612 Danville Road, Nicholasville, KY 40356; (859) 881–5716; www.campnelson .org.

Description: Camp Nelson was a major Union supply depot for the armies of the Ohio and Cumberland. It supplied the Union invasion of Knoxville and the Battles of Saltville in southwest Virginia. It was also the third-largest recruiting base for African-American soldiers in the United States, with more than 10,000 black soldiers recruited here. More than 400 acres of the 4,000-acre campsite have been purchased and are being preserved for interpretation. The only structure (the white house that served as the officers' quarters) of the 300 that were part of the camp has been meticulously restored and serves as a visitor center and museum.

A 3-mile interpretive trail goes through the depot section and the northern line of fortifications.

Admission Fees: Free.

Open to Public: Camp Nelson Visitor Center, Tues.–Sat. 10:00 A.M.–4:00 P.M. The trail system and grounds are open daily, dawn to dusk.

Visitor Services: Public restrooms, information, handicapped access, food, gift shop, museum, archaeological lab, driving tour; trails.

Regularly Scheduled Events: April and September, living history events.

Directions: From I–75 take exit 110 (U.S. 60) west to New Circle Road (Kentucky 4) in Lexington. Follow Kentucky 4 east to the Nicholasville Road exit; take Nicholasville Road (U.S. 27) south approximately 10 miles to Nicholasville; proceed on the Nicholasville Bypass 5 miles south of the city. From U.S. 27 turn east (left) onto Kentucky 1268

SOUTHERN HEARTLAND

Camp Nelson, Nicholasville, Kentucky. Kentucky Heritage Council.

and make an immediate right onto old U.S. 27. Proceed about 1 mile to Camp Nelson, which is on the left.

PADUCAH

 61 DOWNTOWN PADUCAH CIVIL WAR WALKING TOUR

c/o Paducah Convention and Visitors Bureau, 128 Broadway, P.O. Box 90, Paducah, KY 42002; (270) 443–8783, (800) PADUCAH; www.paducah.travel.

Description: The tour map is based on one drawn in 1861 by a Federal captain who was among the troops occupying Paducah by order of Gen. U. S. Grant. Also, one of the magnificent murals adorning the city floodwall concerns the Civil War in Paducah. The eight sites are scattered throughout downtown Paducah, based around U.S. 45 and U.S. 60.

Admission Fees: Free.

Open to Public: Paducah Visitors Center, Mon.–Fri. 9:00 A.M.–5:00 P.M.

Visitor Services: At Paducah Visitors Center, public restrooms, information.

Regularly Scheduled Events: None.

Directions: From I–24 take exit 4 (this route is called the I–24 Downtown Loop), follow signs for Quilter's Museum—with street numbers descending—into downtown area; turn left on Broadway to visitor center.

PERRYVILLE

 62 PERRYVILLE BATTLEFIELD STATE HISTORIC SITE CWPT

1825 Battlefield Road, P.O. Box 296, Perryville, KY 40468; (859) 332–8631; www.perryvillereenactment.org.

Description: Kentucky's greatest Civil War battle took place outside Perryville on October 8, 1862. It was the South's last serious attempt to gain possession of the state. A museum on the grounds interprets the battle and its aftermath.

Admission Fees: Museum, adults $2.00, children $2.00; group rates available.

Open to Public: Apr.–Oct., Mon.–Sat. 9:00 A.M.–5:00 P.M., Sun. 10:00 A.M.–5:00 P.M.; Nov.–Mar., Wed.–Sat. 9:00 A.M.–3:00 P.M.

Visitor Services: Public restrooms, handicapped access, gift shop, museum, trails.

Regularly Scheduled Events: October, annual living history.

Directions: From Bluegrass Parkway take exit 59; go 24 miles south on U.S. 127 through Harrodsburg to Danville. Take U.S. 127/150 bypass; go west (turn right) on U.S. 150; go 9 miles to Perryville; north (turn right) on Kentucky 1920.

 63 TOWN OF PERRYVILLE

U.S. 68 and U.S. 150, P.O. Box 65, Perryville, KY 40468; (859) 332–1862; www.perryville.net; info@perryville .net.

Description: The town of Perryville has been a National Historic Register District since 1976. Looking much as it did during the 1862 Battle of Perryville, this is one of the most intact nineteenth-century communities in the state. The 1840s commercial district, "Merchants' Row," still stands. Numerous homes and churches served as field hospitals, and remnants of the battle's aftermath remain.

Admission Fees: Free.

Open to Public: Daily from dawn to dusk.

Visitor Services: Lodging, public restrooms, gas, food, gift shop.

Regularly Scheduled Events: October, annual living history.

Directions: From Bluegrass Parkway take exit 59; go 24 miles south on U.S. 127 through Harrodsburg to Danville. Take U.S. 127/150 bypass; go west (turn right) on U.S. 150 for 9 miles to Perryville.

PEWEE VALLEY

PEWEE VALLEY CONFEDERATE CEMETERY AND MONUMENT

P.O. Box 792, Pewee Valley, KY 40056; (502) 241–8049; http://johnhuntmorgan .scv.org.

Description: The Pewee Valley Confederate Cemetery and Monument are all that remain from the Kentucky Confederate Home, established in 1904. Interred here are 313 Confederate veterans—most of whom had been residents of the former institution.

Admission Fees: Free.

Open to Public: Daily from dawn to dusk.

Visitor Services: None.

Regularly Scheduled Events: First Saturday in June, Confederate Memorial Day service—includes Confederate reenactors and the firing of period artillery.

Directions: Take I–265 (Gene Synder Freeway) to exit 30. Turn right on CR 146, travel approximately 2 miles, turn left onto Maple Avenue. The cemetery and monument are located on Maple Avenue 0.8 mile beyond the intersection.

PRESTONSBURG

MIDDLE CREEK NATIONAL BATTLEFIELD

P.O. Box 326, Prestonsburg, KY 41653-0326; (606) 886–1312; www.middlecreek .org; fdfitz@mail.com.

Description: On January 10, 1862, unknown colonel (and future president of the United States) James A. Garfield led Union soldiers against the experienced Brig. Gen. Humphrey Marshall and his Confederate troops in what would become the largest and most significant Civil War battle in eastern Kentucky.

Admission Fees: Free.

Open to Public: Daily from dawn to dusk.

Visitor Services: None.

Regularly Scheduled Events: None.

Directions: Located at the intersection of Kentucky Route 114 and Kentucky Route 404.

THE SAMUEL MAY HOUSE LIVING HISTORY MUSEUM

1135 North Lake Drive, Prestonsburg, KY 41653; (606) 889–9608; (606) 866–1341 or (800) 844–4704; www.mayhouse.org; smayhouse@mikrotec.com.

Description: This restored Federal-style house was the boyhood home of Col. Andrew Jackson May, the leading Confederate organizer in eastern Kentucky. In the meadow below the house, Colonel May and Col. Hiram Hawkins organized the Fifth Kentucky Infantry Regiment. From time to time during the Civil War, the house served as a Confederate recruiting station.

Admission Fees: Tour $2.00 per person.

Open to Public: Tours by appointment only.

Visitor Services: Public restrooms, handicapped access, gift shop, tours.

Regularly Scheduled Events: None.

Directions: From the Mountain Parkway, continue on Kentucky 114 20 miles past the termination of the Mountain Parkway (in Salyersville) to Prestonsburg. After crossing the bridge over the Big Sandy River, turn left (north) on U.S. 23/460; drive 1 mile, past a Wendy's restaurant on the right. The May House is on the left. Turn left on Porter Drive; the parking lot is below the house.

RICHMOND

BATTLE OF RICHMOND
CWPT

c/o Tourism Commission, Visitor Center, 345 Lancaster Avenue, Richmond, KY 40475; (800) 866–3705; www.richmond ky.com; tourism@richmond.ky.us.

Description: The Battle of Richmond was part of the important 1862 Perryville campaign. Richmond was the site of one of the Confederacy's greatest victories. A self-guided tour brochure and taped narrative

White Hall, Richmond, Kentucky. CWPT files.

are available at the Richmond Visitor Center. The eight "stations" of the driving tour begin at the top of Big Hill southeast of Berea and end at the Madison County Courthouse in Richmond.

Admission Fees: Refundable deposit for tape, $5.00.

Open to Public: Tourism office, Mon.–Fri. 8:00 A.M.–4:00 P.M.

Visitor Services: Public restrooms, information.

Regularly Scheduled Events: None.

Directions: From I–75 take exit 87; follow signs to Richmond Visitor Center (near Eastern Kentucky University campus) on Lancaster Avenue.

 WHITE HALL STATE HISTORIC HOUSE

500 White Hall Shrine Road, Richmond, KY 40475-9159; (859) 623–9178; www .kystateparks.com; whitehall@ky.gov.

Description: Cassius Marcellus Clay, "the Lion of White Hall," was an outspoken emancipationist, newspaper publisher, and minister to Russia under his friend Abraham Lincoln. This Italianate mansion, furnished in period pieces, was built for Clay and has many noteworthy features.

Admission Fees: Adults $6.00, children $3.00; group rates available.

Open to Public: Apr.–Labor Day, daily 9:00 A.M.–5:00 P.M.; Labor Day–Oct., Wed.–Sun. 9:00 A.M.–5:00 P.M.; closed Mon. and Tues.; closed Nov.–Mar.

Visitor Services: Handicapped access, gift shop, tours.

Regularly Scheduled Events: September, living history weekend; October, Ghost Walk; December, A Victorian Christmas.

Directions: From I–75 take exit 95; travel on Highway 627; cross U.S. 25. The house is located at the end of Highway 627.

SACRAMENTO

 BATTLE OF SACRAMENTO DRIVING TOUR

c/o City Clerk, P.O. Box 245, Sacramento, KY 42372; (270) 736–5114; www.battleof sac.com; battleofsac@dynasty.net.

Description: The Battle of Sacramento took

place early in the Civil War, in December 1861. The ten-stop driving tour recreates its daring action and introduces the combat's participants. Confederate Lt. Col. Nathan Bedford Forrest emerged the victor. A free driving-tour brochure is available at the Sacramento City Hall, located at 210 West Third Street.

Admission Fees: Free.

Open to Public: The free brochure is available at the Sacramento City Hall, open Mon.–Fri. 8:00 A.M.–4:00 P.M.

Visitor Services: City Hall, public restrooms, information.

Regularly Scheduled Events: Third weekend in May, annual reenactment.

Directions: From Western Kentucky Parkway take exit 58; travel north on U.S. 431 5 miles to unincorporated community of South Carrollton; turn left on Kentucky 81 and proceed to Sacramento. City Hall is located at 210 West Third Street.

SMITHLAND

 FORT SMITH

c/o Smithland City Hall, 310 Wilson Avenue, P.O. Box 287, Smithland, KY 42081; (270) 928–2446.

Description: Union forces constructed the star-shaped, earthen Fort Smith after Gen. Ulysses S. Grant seized Paducah in 1861. The fort was part of a larger complex designed to protect the mouth of the Cumberland River at the Ohio River. From this location soldiers were sent down the Cumberland River to participate in the expedition against Forts Henry and Donelson near the Tennessee-Kentucky border. As many as 2,000 Union troops were stationed in Smithland during the Civil War. By 1864 the fort was manned by a contingent of the Thirteenth U.S. Colored Heavy Artillery. Several of these men are buried in the cemetery adjacent to the fort.

Admission Fees: Free.

Open to Public: Daily from dawn to dusk; obtain brochure at the Smithland City Hall, Mon.–Fri. 9:00 A.M.–noon, 1:00 P.M.–4:30 P.M.

Visitor Services: City Hall, information, rest rooms, trails.

Regularly Scheduled Events: First weekend in May, Civil War living history, artillery demonstration, Grand Ball, and sutlers.

Directions: From I–24 take exit 31 onto Highway 453. Travel approximately 15 miles to Smithland. To city hall, at caution light in Smithland, turn left; proceed 3 blocks; turn right onto Wilson Avenue. Smithland City Hall is located at 310 Wilson Avenue. To Fort Smith, at the caution light in Smithland, turn left; proceed 1 block and turn left; cross intersection of Wilson Avenue and proceed up steep hill into Smithland Cemetery. Follow the road to the water tower. Travel on foot on the trail to the right (west) of the tower approximately 50 feet; the fort is on the right of the trail.

SOUTH UNION

 SHAKER MUSEUM AT SOUTH UNION

850 Shaker Museum Road, South Union, KY 42283; (270) 542–4167; www.shakermuseum.com

Description: Scores of encampments occurred within this pacifist village. Afterward, it was estimated that more than 100,000 meals had been provided to soldiers on both sides.

Admission Fees: Adults $5.00, children $1.50; group rates are available, please call ahead.

Open to Public: Dec.–Feb., Tues.–Sat. 9:00 A.M.–4:00 P.M.; Mar.–Nov., Mon.–Sat. 9:00 A.M.–5:00 P.M., Sun. 1:00 P.M.–5:00 P.M.; closed major holidays.

Visitor Services: Gift shop, tours, lodging.

Regularly Scheduled Events: April, South Union Seminar; November, Shaker Breakfast; December, Christmas at Shaker with candlelight tours.

Directions: Located on U.S. 68, 10 miles west of Bowling Green. From I–65 take exit 20 (Natcher Parkway) to exit 5 (U.S. 68/80). Turn left and follow signs, approximately 10 miles to South Union.

STAFFORDSVILLE

72 MOUNTAIN HOMEPLACE

745 Kentucky Route 2275, P.O. Box 1850, Staffordsville, KY 41256; (606) 297–1850; www.mountainhomeplace .com; mthome@foothills.net.

Description: Mountain Homeplace re-creates life in Johnson County from 1850 to 1875. The historic buildings that have been assembled here include a one-room school-house, a blacksmith shop, and other build-ings and implements used to operate a farm. Interpreters provide information about the Civil War in this area of Kentucky. An award-winning video shown at the visitor center features actor Richard Thomas, who spent summers with his family in Johnson County during his youth. The video includes a segment about Johnson County's tenuous situation during the Civil War. Both sides had ardent sympathizers here, and neither the Union nor the Confederate flags were allowed to fly above the county courthouse.

Admission Fees: Adults $6.00, children $4.00, seniors $5.00; call in advance for spe-cial group rates.

Open to Public: Tues.–Sat. 8:30 A.M.–5:00 P.M.; call to confirm winter hours.

Visitor Services: Public restrooms, infor-mation, gift shop, museum, tours, trails.

Regularly Scheduled Events: Call or check Web site for events.

Directions: From the west on I–64, take exit 98 (several miles east of Winchester) and travel south on Mountain Parkway for ap-proximately 70 miles to Salyersville. Turn left on U.S. 460 and proceed 15 miles to Kentucky 40. Turn left onto Kentucky 40

and proceed approximately 1.5 miles. Turn right on Paintsville Lake Road (Route 2275) past intersection with Highway 172 and fol-low signs. From the east on I–64, take exit 191 (south of Catlettsburg); proceed south on U.S. 23 for 59 miles to the intersection with U.S. 460; turn right on U.S. 460 and travel approximately 3.5 miles. Turn right on Paintsville Lake Road (Route 2275) past in-tersection with Highway 172 and follow signs.

WASHINGTON

73 OLD WASHINGTON

2215 Old Main Street, Washington, KY 41056; (606) 759–7411 or (606) 564–9419; www.washingtonky.com.

Description: Civil War–associated sites within this 1785 outpost for pioneers trav-eling the Buffalo Trace include the birthplace and childhood home of Confederate Gen. Albert Sidney Johnston; the Methodist Epis-copal Church South, significant to African-American history; the Paxton Inn, a docu-mented Underground Railroad station; and the site of the slave auction that inspired Harriet Beecher Stowe to write *Uncle Tom's Cabin,* now the Harriet Beecher Stowe Slav-ery to Freedom Museum.

Admission Fees: Historical tour, adults $10.00, children $4.00; other tours available.

Open to Public: Mon.–Sat. 11:00 A.M.–3:00 P.M., Sun. noon–3:00 P.M.; closed Mon.–Fri. first weekend in Dec.–Mar. 15, but open on weekends. Will open for special tours on weekdays; please call ahead to schedule.

Visitor Services: Public restrooms, infor-mation, limited handicapped access, gift shop (CWPT members receive a 10 percent discount), visitor center, tours.

Regularly Scheduled Events: None.

Directions: From I–75 in Cincinnati take Highway 275 to Ashland-Alexandria High-way (AA Highway/Kentucky 9); exit at U.S.

68 and travel 2 miles south. Old Washington borders old U.S. 68 to the east of U.S. 68. From I–75 and I–64 in Lexington, take U.S. 68 north; Old Washington borders old U.S. 68 to the east of U.S. 68.

WEST POINT

 74 FORT DUFFIELD

16706 Abbott's Beach Road, West Point, KY 40177; (502) 922–4574; members.aol. com/ftduffield/fort.html; duffield@iglou .com.

Description: This 1861 Union fortification was built to protect the supply base at West Point, Kentucky, and supply routes over the Old L&N Turnpike. From its strategic vantage point high above the city, defenders could also control the Ohio and Salt Rivers.

Fort Duffield is one of the best-preserved and largest forts in Kentucky.

Admission Fees: Free; donations welcome.
Open to Public: Daily 9:00 A.M.–dusk.
Visitor Services: Information, handicapped access; trails.
Regularly Scheduled Events: Memorial Day, reenactment.
Directions: From I–65 take exit 125 west on Gene Snyder Freeway/Highway 841 to U.S. 31W; take exit 1 and turn left onto U.S. 31 south toward Fort Knox. West Point is approximately 16 miles. Entrance to park is at Salt River Drive on the right. Watch for signs. From the south take I–65, exit 102, Highway 313 west approximately 9.1 miles to Dixie Highway/U.S. 31W. Turn right onto U.S. 31W; West Point is approximately 16 miles. Entrance to park is at Salt River Drive on the right. Watch for signs.

❖ MISSISSIPPI ❖

BALDWYN

 75 BRICE'S CROSSROADS BATTLEFIELD VISTOR AND INTERPRETIVE CENTER
CWPT

607 Grisham Street, Baldwyn, MS 38824; (662) 365–3969; www.brices crossroads.com; bcr@dixie-net.com.

(The National Park Service owns one acre of property at the battlefield and can be contacted at (662) 680–4025.)
Description: At Brice's Crossroads in June 1864, a battle was fought that served to divert Confederate Gen. Nathan Bedford Forrest from the railroad supply line that was essential to the success of Union Gen. William T. Sherman. Although considered a Confederate victory, Forrest's forces were diverted and Sherman persevered and went on to win the Atlanta campaign. Brice's

Crossroads was the greatest strategic battle the war would produce and ranks with such battles in military history as Cannae, the Cowpens, and Tobruk.

Admission Fees: Adults $3.00, children and seniors $1.00; group rates available.
Open to Public: Museum, Tues.–Sat. 9:00 A.M.–5:00 P.M., Sun. 12:30 P.M.–5:00 P.M.; site, daily from dawn until dusk.
Visitor Services: Public restrooms, information, handicapped access, gift shop (10 percent discount to all CWPT members), museum, video and audio tour, trails.
Regularly Scheduled Events: June, biennial battle reenactment.
Directions: From I–45 proceed north to Baldwyn; exit Mississippi 370. To go to the museum, turn east on 370 and turn south on Grisham Road. To get to battlefield site, go west on Mississippi 370 about 6 miles to park.

MISSISSIPPI SITES

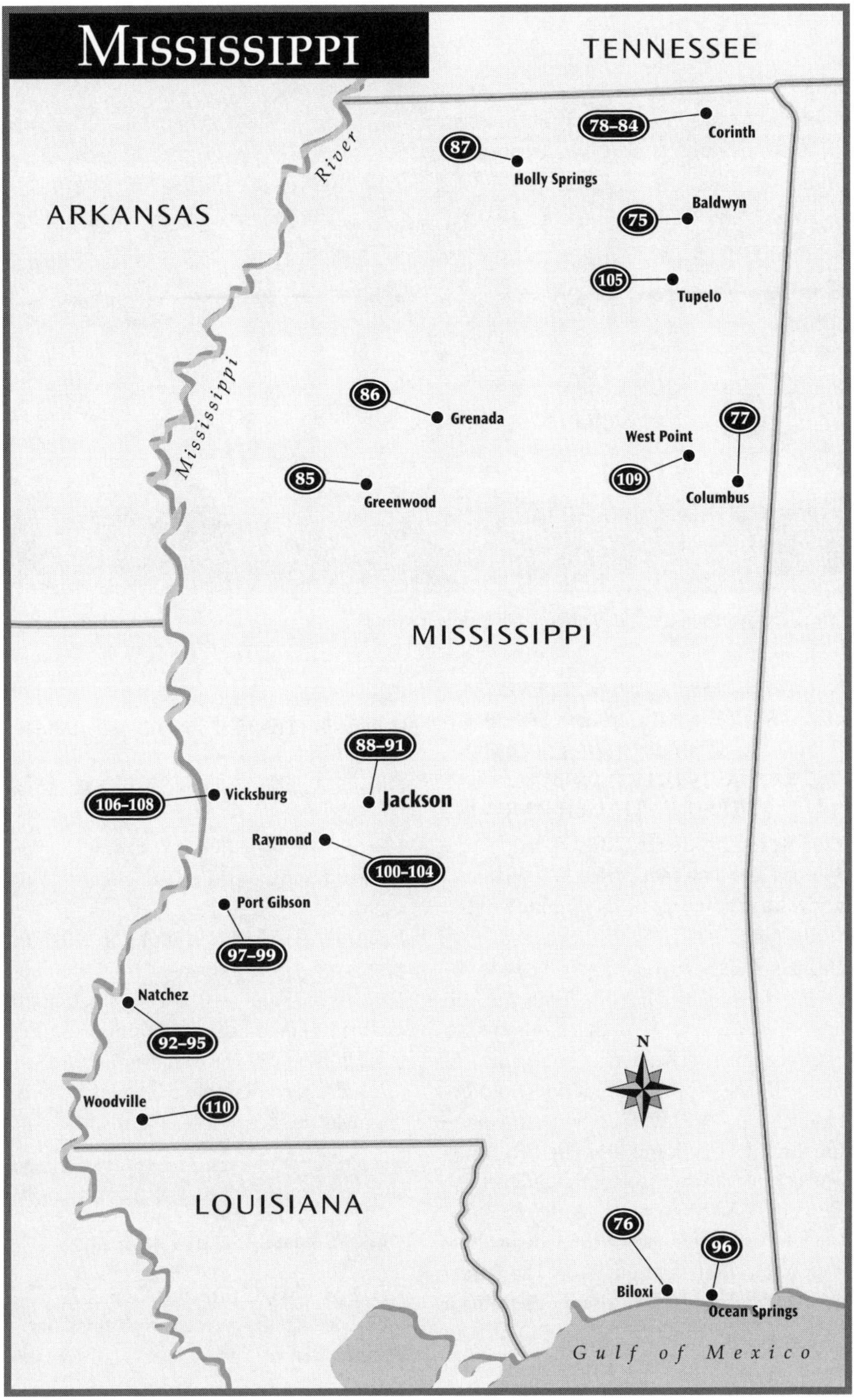

MISSISSIPPI

TENNESSEE

ARKANSAS

Mississippi River

78–84 • Corinth

87 • Holly Springs

75 • Baldwyn

105 • Tupelo

86 • Grenada

77

West Point
109 •
• Columbus

MISSISSIPPI

88–91

106–108 • Vicksburg   • Jackson

Raymond •
100–104

• Port Gibson
97–99

• Natchez
92–95

Woodville   110
•

LOUISIANA

85 • Greenwood

N

76

96

Biloxi •
• Ocean Springs

Gulf of Mexico

Brice's Crossroads Battlefield, Baldwyn, Mississippi. CWPT files.

BILOXI

 BEAUVOIR: THE JEFFERSON DAVIS HOME AND PRESIDENTIAL LIBRARY

2244 Beach Boulevard, Biloxi, MS 39531; (228) 388–4400, (800) 570–3818; www.beauvoir.org; bjdaivshome@bell south.net.

Description: Beauvoir was the seaside retirement estate of Jefferson Davis, the one and only president of the Confederate States of America. Beauvoir was also the site of the Mississippi Confederate Soldiers Home from 1903 to 1957. The restored antebellum home dominates the fifty-one-acre complex that includes outbuildings, the Confederate Museum, a historic cemetery, the Tomb of the Unknown Confederate Soldier, nature trail, and gift shop. The Jefferson Davis Presidential Library contains a biographical exhibit on Jefferson Davis in addition to the research library's collection on nineteenth-century Southern history. *NOTE:* Site is currently closed due to severe damage from Hurricane Katrina.

Admission Fees: Call for rates when site reopens.

Open to Public: Call for times when site reopens.

Visitor Services: Public restrooms, information, handicapped access, gift shop, museum.

Regularly Scheduled Events: Call for events when site reopens.

Directions: From I–10 east exit south at exit 46 (I–110/Biloxi Beach), continue south to exit Highway 90 west/Gulfport. Beavoir is located approximately 5.5 miles west on Highway 90 (Beach Boulevard).

COLUMBUS

 FRIENDSHIP CEMETERY

P.O. Box 1408, Columbus, MS 39703; (662) 328–4164; www.columbusms.org/cemetery.htm.

Description: Burial site of four Confederate generals, more than 2,000 Confederate soldiers, and veterans from every war the United States has fought, as well as distinguished authors, legislators, and people from all walks of life. Site of America's first Decoration Day (1866), inspiring the writing of the poem "The Blue and the Gray." This site relates to the theme of reconciliation after the Civil War, because the Ladies of Columbus put flowers on the graves of Confederate and Union soldiers who had been buried there during the war.

Admission Fees: Free.

Open to Public: Daily 7:00 A.M.–sunset.

Visitor Services: Locator service is available.

Regularly Scheduled Events: Early spring, Spring Pilgrimage, includes "Tales from the Crypt."

Directions: Go 69 miles from I–55 on U.S. 82 east; 68 miles from I–20 on U.S. 45 north. Located on Fourth Street, just south of the city of Columbus.

CORINTH

 BATTERY F

P.O. Box 2158, Corinth, MS 38835; (662) 287–9501 or (800) 748–9048; www .corinth.net; tourism@corinth.net.

Description: Battery F is one of the six outer batteries built by the Union army in a position to provide support fire on October 3, 1862. Facing northwest, Battery F protected the Memphis and Charleston Railroad. The battery was the northernmost of the detached batteries protecting approaches along roads and railroads. It was captured the evening of October 3. Battery F is a well-preserved earthwork about 150 feet long, with a parapet between 3 and 6 feet high.

Admission Fees: Free.

Open to Public: Daily during daylight hours.

Visitor Services: Information.

Regularly Scheduled Events: None.

Directions: From I–40 at Jackson, Tennessee, exit onto U.S. 45 south to Corinth (50 miles). From U.S. 45 take Memphis exit

onto U.S. 72 east. Turn north at the intersection of U.S. 72 and Alcorn Drive; turn at the first right onto Smithbridge Road to Pinelake subdivision. Battery F is located at the corner of Bitner and Davis Streets in the subdivision.

 BATTERY ROBINETT

P.O. Box 2158, Corinth, MS 38835; (662) 287–9501 or (800) 748–9048; www .corinth.net; tourism@corinth.net.

Description: Battery Robinett is a reconstruction of one of seven batteries constructed by the Federal army following the siege of Corinth in the spring of 1862. It was the scene of the most famous event of the Battle of Corinth.

Admission Fees: Free.

Open to Public: Daily from dawn to dusk.

Visitor Services: Information; trails.

Regularly Scheduled Events: None.

Directions: From I–40 at Jackson, Tennessee, exit onto U.S. 45 south to Corinth (50 miles). From U.S. 45, take Memphis exit onto U.S. 72 east. From U.S. 72 east turn left onto Fulton Drive at shopping center with the Kroger store. Follow Fulton Drive to Linden Street; turn left at this intersection. Battery Robinett will be on the left. Entrance at top of hill approximately .25 mile from Fulton Drive/Linden Street intersection on left.

 CORINTH CIVIL WAR INTERPRETIVE CENTER, SHILOH NATIONAL MILITARY PARK CWPT

501 West Linden Street, Corinth, MS 38834; (662) 287–9273; www.nps.gov .shil.

Description: For six months in 1862, the critical railroad junction of Corinth, Mississippi, captured the full attention of a divided nation. As one of the National Park Service's newest visitor centers, the Corinth Civil War Interpretive Center explains the key role of Corinth in the Civil War's west-

Bronze Relief at the Civil War Interpretive Center, Corinth, Mississippi. CWPT files.

ern theater. The center stands near the site of Battery Robinett, a Union fortification witness to bloody fighting during the October 1862 Battle of Corinth. The 15,000-square-foot facility features interactive exhibits, a multimedia presentation on the Battle of Shiloh, and a video on the Battle of Corinth. Maps for a self-guided walking tour and the Corinth campaign driving tour, as well as information about the surrounding siege and Battle of Corinth sites, are available at the Interpretive Center.

Admission Fees: Free.

Open to Public: Interpretive Center, daily 8:30 A.M.–4:30 P.M.; walking and driving tours, daily during daylight hours.

Visitor Services: Public restrooms, information, handicapped access, gift shop.

Regularly Scheduled Events: None.

Directions: From I–40 at Jackson, Tennessee, exit onto U.S. 45 south; drive to Corinth (50 miles) and exit onto U.S. 72 (Memphis exit) east. The Interpretive Center is located near the junction of U.S. 72 and U.S. 45.

 **CORINTH NATIONAL CEMETERY**

1551 Horton Street, Corinth, MS 38834; (901) 386–8311; www.cem.va.gov.

Description: On April 13, 1866, the secretary of war authorized immediate action to provide a final resting place for the honored dead killed in Civil War battles for control of the railroad in and around Corinth. This beautiful twenty-acre cemetery is the resting place for 1,793 known and 3,895 unknown Union soldiers.

Admission Fees: Free.

Open to Public: Grounds, daily from dawn until dusk; office, Mon.–Fri. 8:00 A.M.–4:30 P.M.

Visitor Services: Public restrooms, information.

Regularly Scheduled Events: Veterans Day and Memorial Day events.

Directions: From I–40 at Jackson, Tennessee, exit onto U.S. 45 south, drive to Corinth (50 miles), and exit onto U.S. 72 (the Memphis exit) east. Follow signs off U.S. 72 in Corinth.

THE BATTLE OF CORINTH

As the 150th anniversary of the outbreak of the Civil War approaches, we as Americans reflect on the complexity and tragedy of the conflict that divided our nation. As Mississippians, we remember the impact of this war on our home state, of the burning of many of our towns, and of the blood that was shed in small skirmishes and major battles across the state. From Corinth to Brice's Crossroads to Raymond to Vicksburg and countless points between, the Civil War left an indelible mark on Mississippi.

Of particular significance to Mississippians is the Battle of Corinth. In 1862, this small northeastern Mississippi town of 1,200 was vital to the Union because of its location at the junction of the Memphis and Charleston and the Mobile and Ohio Railroads. Over the next four years, the people of Corinth would see their town switch between Union and Confederate control and be overrun with more than 300,000 troops. This beautiful and once tranquil town would also see its homes turned into hospitals and its peaceful pastures turned into burial grounds. History has shown that the battles for Corinth eventually led to the end of the western theater of the Civil War.

The events in this small town nearly a century and a half ago shaped the America that we know today. With its Civil War–era homes, its historic cemetery, and its extraordinary Civil War Interpretive Center, Corinth is a testament to the conflict that ultimately brought restoration and unity for those of us who remember it today.

— Gov. Haley Barbour, Mississippi

SOUTHERN HEARTLAND

 CROSSROADS MUSEUM

221 North Fillmore Street, Corinth, MS 38834; (662) 287–3120; www.crossroads museum.com; nemma@corinth.ms.

Description: The Crossroads Museum is located in the newly renovated 1918 Corinth Depot. This depot sits adjacent to one of the most important patches of land in the western theater of the Civil War—the Corinth Railroad Crossroads. Here the Memphis and Charleston and the Mobile and Ohio Railroads crossed, making Corinth in 1862 an important location for troop movement and supply and communication lines. The Battle of Shiloh was fought as an offensive measure to keep the Federal army from controlling the railroad. After the siege of Corinth, the Federals gained control, and the subsequent Battle of Corinth was fought in the Confederates' last effort to retake the crossing from the Federals. The fall of Corinth's railroad crossing was the beginning of the end of the war in the west. Also located on the museum property is the site of the Tishomingo Hotel, which served as a hospital during the war.

Admission Fees: Adults $5.00, seniors and students seventeen and up $3.00, children sixteen and under free.

Open to Public: Tues.–Sat. 9:00 A.M.–5:00 P.M., Sun. 1:00 P.M.–5:00 P.M.

Visitor Services: Public restrooms, handicapped access, gift shop, library, tours.

Regularly Scheduled Events: None.

Directions: From U.S. 72 turn left onto Tate Street. Follow Tate Street to Fillmore Street

---

THE CORINTH CAMPAIGN TRAIL

Points of interest located in northeast Mississippi and central Tennessee are as follows:

- Corinth Civil War Interpretive Center, Corinth
- The Verandah-Curlee House, Corinth
- Shiloh National Military Park, Shiloh, Tennessee
- Fallen Timbers, Tennessee
- Confederate Fieldwork, Corinth (siege)
- Union Siege Lines, Sherman and Davies, Corinth (siege)
- Union Siege Lines, Army of the Mississippi, Corinth (siege)
- Union Siege Lines, Army of the Tennessee, Corinth (siege)
- Union Fieldworks, Davies Line, Corinth (siege)
- Rienzi—Sheridan Raid
- Booneville—Sheridan Raid
- Iuka Battlefield Sites
- Shady Grove Cemetery, Iuka
- Corinth Battlefield—Battery D
- Corinth Battlefield—Battery F
- Corinth Battlefield—Battery Robinett
- Corinth Battlefield—Historic Railroad Crossing/Trailhead Park
- Corona College Site—Corinth (battlefield)
- Hatchie (or Davis's) Bridge Battlefield, Tennessee

These are nationally significant sites associated with the struggle between Union and Confederate forces for control of the vital crossroads of the Memphis and Charleston and the Mobile and Ohio Railroads at Corinth, Mississippi (April–October 1862).

Find directions in "A Guide to the Corinth Campaign," which provides a self-guided driving tour of these sites. The guide is available free from the Corinth Civil War Interpretive Center, Shiloh National Military Park, 1055 Pittsburg Landing Road, Shiloh, TN 38376; (662) 287–9273.

---

and turn left again. At Tate and Wick Streets, turn left. Wick Street ends at the museum.

 HISTORIC RAIL CROSSING/ TRAILHEAD PARK

P.O. Box 2158, Corinth, MS 38835; (662) 287–9501 or (800) 748–9048; www.corinth .net; tourism@corinth.net.

Description: Viewing area for the crossing of the historic Memphis and Charleston and Mobile and Ohio Railroads in 1862. The Battle of Shiloh was fought for control of this crossing. The park serves as the trailhead for the historic Corinth hiking and biking trail that connects many of the Civil War Corinth National Historic Landmark sites.

Admission Fees: Free.

Open to Public: Daily during daylight hours.

Visitor Services: Public restrooms, handicapped access, drinking fountain, picnic area.

Regularly Scheduled Events: None.

Directions: From I–40 at Jackson, Tennessee, exit onto U.S. 45 south; drive to Corinth (50 miles) and exit onto U.S. 72 (Memphis exit) east. Turn left on Fulton Drive at shopping center with the Kroger store. Follow the brown Civil War Center banners mounted on light posts to Waldron Street. Turn right on Waldron; continue to follow banners to the park located at the corner of Jackson and Waldron Streets in downtown Corinth.

 THE VERANDAH-CURLEE HOUSE

705 Jackson Street, Corinth, MS 38834; (662) 287–9501 or (800) 748–9048; www .verandahhouse.net; tourism@corinth .net.

Description: Built in 1857 by one of Corinth's founders, the home is a significant example of Greek Revival architecture. The house was used in the Civil War as headquarters for Gens. Braxton Bragg, H. W. Halleck, and John B. Hood. The restored home/museum contains a collection of Boehme-edition Audubon prints, eighteenth- and nineteenth-century antiques, paintings, and an exhibit of replicas of Civil War soldiers' furnishings made by Corinth's C and D Jarnigan Company.

Admission Fees: Suggested donation $5.00.

Open to Public: Tours currently by appointment only.

Visitor Services: Information, tour.

Regularly Scheduled Events: None.

Directions: From I–40 at Jackson, Tennessee, exit onto U.S. 45 south; drive to Corinth (50 miles) and exit onto U.S. 72 (Memphis exit) east. Turn left on Fulton Drive at shopping center with the Kroger store. Follow the brown Civil War Center banners mounted on light posts to Waldron Street. Turn right on Waldron; continue to follow banners to Jackson Street. Turn left on Jackson Street and proceed 2 blocks to Childs Street. The house is at the corner of Jackson and Childs Streets.

FOR MORE INFORMATION

Mississippi's annual *Travel Planner* contains a Civil War section, organized regionally, that gives visitor contact information for approximately seventy-five sites, including battlefields and fortifications, cemeteries, historic communities, homes, and sites associated with the political history of the war. The guide also contains a general essay on the war in the state, a chronology of significant events from secession to surrender, a selected reading list, and photographs. It is available free by writing Mississippi Department of Tourism Development, P.O. Box 849, Jackson, MS 39205; or call (800) WARMEST.

GREENWOOD

 FORT PEMBERTON

c/o Greenwood Convention and Visitors Bureau, P.O. Drawer 739, Greenwood, MS 38935; (662) 453–9197; www .greenwoodms.org.

Description: Located on U.S. 82 west on the banks of the Yazoo Pass connecting the Yazoo and Tallahatchie Rivers, Fort Pemberton was a hastily constructed fortification consisting of cotton bales and timber logs. A significant military battle occurred here when Confederate forces successfully drove back three Union ironclads, forcing Gen. Ulysses Grant to seek another route to Vicksburg. A historical marker is located on U.S. 82. The nearby Cottonlandia Museum contains artifacts from the Union sidewheel steamship *Star of the West*, which fired the first shots of the Civil War as it unsuccessfully tried to resupply the Union forces at Fort Sumter.

Admission Fees: Free.

Open to Public: Daily during daylight hours.
Visitor Services: Information, trails.
Regularly Scheduled Events: None.
Directions: From I–55 take Greenwood/ Winona exit. Take U.S. 82 west to Greenwood. Pick up brochure at Greenwood Convention and Visitors Bureau located on U.S. 82 at Leflore Avenue on left. To Cottonlandia Museum, travel west on U.S. 82; the museum is located on the right, east of Fort Pemberton. To Fort Pemberton, travel west on U.S. 82 and proceed past Wal-Mart. Fort is located on the right, just east of the U.S. 49E intersection.

GRENADA

 GRENADA LAKE

2151 Scenic Loop 333, Grenada, MS 38901; field office (662) 226–5911; visitor center (662) 226–1679; www.mvk.usace .army.mil/lakes/grenadalake.

Description: Grenada was to be Gen. John Pemberton's defense line against Grant's approach to Vicksburg on the Mississippi Central Railroad. Eight fortifications were built here; two of them are restored on Grenada Lake property. Only a skirmish was actually fought because Grant turned back due to Gen. Earl Van Dorn's raid on Grant's camp.
Admission Fees: Free.
Open to Public: Forts, daily during daylight hours; visitor center, Mon.–Fri. 9:30 A.M.– 1:00 P.M. and 1:30 P.M.–5:00 P.M., Sat.–Sun. 8:30 A.M.–5:00 P.M.
Visitor Services: Lodging, public restrooms, information, gas, handicapped access, food, gift shop, museum, camping, trails.
Regularly Scheduled Events: June, Thunder on Water music festival and boat race.
Directions: From I–55 take Grenada exit for Highway 8. Take Highway 8 east from Grenada to Scenic Loop 333 that goes to Grenada Lake.

HOLLY SPRINGS

 MARSHALL COUNTY HISTORICAL MUSEUM

220 East College, P.O. Box 806, Holly Springs, MS 38635; (662) 252–3669; www.marshallcountyhistoricalmuseum .org; marshallcomuseum@bellsouth.net.

Description: The Civil War hit Holly Springs hard. The town experienced sixty-two raids, the most famous being Gen. Earl Van Dorn's December 20, 1862, raid on Gen. Ulysses S. Grant's camp, in the course of which his troops destroyed millions of dollars worth of Federal supplies. Holly Springs served as a headquarters for General Grant. Marshall County produced ten Confederate generals, eight adjutant generals, and nine members of the Confederate Congress. The town boasts sixty-one antebellum homes. Arms for the Confederacy were manufactured at the armory in Holly Springs. The Marshall County Museum features a Civil War room with a variety of exhibits and artifacts.
Admission Fees: $4.00.
Open to Public: Mon.–Fri. 10:00 A.M.–5:00 P.M.
Visitor Services: Public restrooms, information, handicapped access, gift shop.
Regularly Scheduled Events: Annual history tours of local Civil War sites, call for schedule; April, Spring Pilgrimage; December, Christmas Pilgrimage.
Directions: From I–55 at Senatobia, travel east on Highway 4, 45 miles to Holly Springs and the museum. Located 42 miles southeast of Memphis on U.S. 78, 60 miles northwest of Tupelo on U.S. 78, 17 miles southwest of Ashland on Highway 4, and 30 miles north of Oxford on Highway 7.

JACKSON

 88 MANSHIP HOUSE MUSEUM

420 East Fortification Street, Jackson, MS 39202; (601) 961–4724; www.mdah .state.ms.us/museum/manship.html; manship@mdah.state.ms.us.

Description: Charles Henry Manship, a decorative painter and craftsman by trade, built the Manship House. Manship served Jackson as its first mayor for two terms during the Civil War in 1862 and 1863. The Confederate fortification protecting the city from invasion from the north was located nearby. Two of Manship's sons, David Daley and Charles Henry Jr., served the Confederacy.
Admission Fees: Free.
Open to Public: Tues.–Fri. 9:00 A.M.–4:00 P.M., Sat. 10:00 A.M.–4:00 P.M.; group tours by appointment.
Visitor Services: Public restrooms, information, handicapped access.
Regularly Scheduled Events: Seasonal interpretations; call or check Web site for information.
Directions: From I–55 take Fortification Street exit; continue west on Fortification and turn right (north) onto Congress Street. The first driveway on the left belongs to the Manship House parking lot. Visitors should enter the cream-colored visitor center for information and a guided tour.

 89 MISSISSIPPI GOVERNOR'S MANSION

300 East Capitol Street, Jackson, MS 39201; (601) 359–6421; www.mdah.state .ms.us.

Description: During the Civil War, Jackson was occupied four times by Union troops. Although there is no evidence that either Gen. Ulysses S. Grant or Gen. William T. Sherman ever used the mansion as headquarters, a letter written by General Sherman dated July 19, 1863, indicates that Union officers entertained themselves at the mansion on a least one occasion: "Last night, at the Governor's Mansion, in Jackson, we had a beautiful supper and union of the generals of the army." A letter from Dr. R. N. Anderson to Gov. John J. Pettus documents the fact that wounded soldiers were housed in the mansion.
Admission Fees: Free.
Open to Public: Tues.–Fri. 9:30 A.M.–11:00 A.M. Tours begin on the half hour; call ahead to confirm availability.
Visitor Services: Handicapped access, museum, public restrooms, gift shop.
Regularly Scheduled Events: First Friday in December, candlelight tour.
Directions: From I–55 take Pearl Street exit onto Pearl Street viaduct. Cross South State Street, drive west to the intersection with West Street, and turn right. The mansion is at the corner of West and Capitol Streets. No public parking on grounds except for handicapped visitors.

 90 THE OAKS HOUSE MUSEUM

823 North Jefferson Street, Jackson, MS 39202; (601) 353–9339; www.greater belhaven.com.

Description: This house museum interprets the life of the James Boyd family from the 1840s to the 1860s. Gen. Ulysses Grant's troops raided the house, and Gen. William Sherman and his troops briefly used the house as a headquarters.
Admission Fees: Adults $4.50, children $3.00, seniors $3.50; group rates available.
Open to Public: Tues.–Sat. 10:00 A.M.–3:00 P.M.
Visitor Services: Information.
Regularly Scheduled Events: None.
Directions: From I–55 take High Street exit (96B) west to North Jefferson Street. Turn north on Jefferson Street; the museum is at

823, on the west side of the street. There is a white picket fence in front of the house.

 OLD CAPITOL MUSEUM OF MISSISSIPPI HISTORY

Mississippi Department of Archives and History, 100 South State Street, Jackson, MS 39205-0571; (601) 359–6920; www.mdah.state.ms.us; ocmuseum@mdah.stae.ms.us.

Description: This building was the site of Mississippi's Secession Convention, January 1861. It continued as the seat of state government until May 1863, when it was evacuated before the Battle of Jackson and later vandalized by Federal troops. For the remainder of the war, it remained in Confederate hands, although legislative and state offices were removed to Macon. In October 1864 it served as a Confederate military headquarters. *NOTE:* Site was damaged by Hurricane Katrina and is expected to remain closed until January 2009.

Admission Fees: Free.

Open to Public: Call for information.

Visitor Services: Public restrooms, information, handicapped access, gift shop.

Regularly Scheduled Events: Call for events.

Directions: From I–55 take Pearl Street exit to downtown Jackson; turn right at first light onto State Street; pass in front of building; turn right on Amite Street to enter parking lot behind building.

NATCHEZ

 LONGWOOD

140 Lower Woodville Road, Natchez, MS 39120; (601) 442–5193; www.natchezpilgrimagetours.com.

Description: Longwood provides the visitor with eloquent testimony to the devastating impact of the Civil War on the cotton economy of the American South. The tragic story of the hardships of the family who lived there, "reared in the lap of luxury and reduced to poverty," has all the tragedy and pathos of *Gone With the Wind* but with a double reverse twist. First, it is true. Second, the family that lost everything was loyal to the Union. Work on the house, begun in 1860, stopped after war was declared in 1861. The Northern workmen made their way through the blockade that was put on the South and home to Philadelphia, leaving their tools on the workbench, where they remain.

Admission Fees: Adults $8.00, children $6.00. Group rates are available.

Open to Public: Tours, daily 9:00 A.M.–4:30 P.M.

Visitor Services: Public restrooms, information, handicapped access, gift shop.

Regularly Scheduled Events: Spring and fall pilgrimages; call for dates.

Directions: From I–120 at Vicksburg turn south on U.S. 61; go approximately 75 miles to Natchez. From I–55 at Brookhaven turn west on U.S. 84; go approximately 60 miles to Natchez.

 MELROSE

c/o Natchez National Historical Park, 640 South Canal Street, Box E, Natchez, MS 39120; (601) 446–7970; www.nps.gov/natc; natc_information@nps.gov.

Description: The home of John T. McMurran, Melrose is an excellent example of an antebellum Greek Revival estate. McMurran was a well-known Natchez lawyer and planter from the 1830s to 1865 who controlled cotton plantations in Mississippi, Arkansas, Louisiana, and Texas. Melrose's story is of the effect of the cotton-based economy on the political and social life of the South and of the Civil War on that economy.

Admission Fees: Admission to the grounds is free; guided tours of mansion, adults

$8.00, children and seniors $4.00.

Open to Public: Daily 8:30 A.M.–5:00 P.M.; tours begin on the hour, with final tour at 4:00 P.M.

Visitor Services: Public restrooms, information, handicapped access, gift shop, museum.

Regularly Scheduled Events: March, spring pilgrimage; October, fall pilgrimage; December, Christmas program.

Directions: From I–20 at Vicksburg take U.S. 61 to Natchez. Turn right on Melrose Parkway and follow signs. From I–10 at Baton Rouge, take U.S. 61 to Natchez. Turn left on Melrose Parkway and follow signs.

 NATCHEZ NATIONAL CEMETERY

41 Cemetery Road, Natchez, MS 39120; (601) 445–4981; www.cem.va.gov.

Description: The town of Natchez was spared extensive damage by surrendering early to Union troops during two military engagements fought in 1863 and 1864. Some of the first internments in the original cemetery, created in 1866, were Federal troops who had died at "The Gardens," a Natchez home converted into a military hospital. Other interments were brought from sites in Louisiana and Mississippi, including many bodies that had been buried in the levees near the west shore of the Mississippi River.

Admission Fees: Free.

Open to Public: Grounds, daily from dawn to dusk; office, Mon.–Fri. 8:00 A.M.–4:30 P.M.; closed federal holidays except Memorial Day and Veterans Day.

Visitor Services: Information.

Regularly Scheduled Events: None.

Directions: From U.S. 61 south, turn right on Canal Street (near Mississippi River bridge) and proceed north to the end of the street. Turn left, then immediately right onto Linton Avenue. Follow Linton Avenue to stop sign and continue straight to Cemetery Road. The entrance to the cemetery is on the right.

 THE WILLIAM JOHNSON HOUSE

c/o Natchez National Historical Park, 640 South Canal Street, Box E, Natchez, MS 39120; (601) 446–5790; www.nps .gov/natc; natc_information@nps.gov.

Description: The home of a free African-American entrepreneur and diarist in antebellum Natchez, the William Johnson House provides a unique opportunity to glimpse a seldom-interpreted part of Southern history. Born a slave, Johnson was freed by his father. He was educated and became a well-known Natchez businessman and slaveholder himself.

Admission Fees: Free.

Open to Public: Daily 9:00 A.M.–4:30 P.M.

Visitor Services: Information, public restrooms, handicapped access, museum, gift shop.

Regularly Scheduled Events: None.

Directions: From I–20 at Vicksburg take U.S. 61 to Natchez. Turn right on U.S. 84 toward the bridge. At Canal Street (just before the bridge) turn right. Follow Canal Street to State Street and turn right. Johnson House is on the right. From I–10 at Baton Rouge, take U.S. 61 to Natchez. Turn left on U.S. 84; follow it to Canal Street and turn right. Follow Canal Street to State Street and turn right. Johnson House is on the right.

Ocean Springs

 FORT MASSACHUSETTS

Gulf Islands National Seashore, 3500 Park Road, Ocean Springs, MS 39564; (228) 875–0821; www.nps.gov/guis.

Description: With hostilities underway in 1861, Ship Island and Fort Massachusetts underwent Confederate occupation; a brief

SOUTHERN HEARTLAND

Grand Gulf Military Monument, Port Gibson, Mississippi. Courtesy of the Grand Gulf Military Monument.

land and naval battle; Federal occupation; creation of western Gulf Union navy headquarters and depot and military prisons, including a prisoner-of-war camp; and the staging of 20,000 troops used to capture Confederate New Orleans and Mobile.

Admission Fees: Ferry charges fee; no fee to visit Fort Massachusetts.

Open to Public: Fort Massachusetts is normally open from the arrival of the first ferry to the departure of the last vessel. This includes four hours at midday during spring and autumn and approximately eight hours in summer. Call for schedule.

Visitor Services: Public restrooms, limited handicapped access, ranger station, picnic area.

Regularly Scheduled Events: None.

Directions: From I–10 take U.S. 49 south to Gulfport, Mississippi, Small Craft Harbor. Board the ferry to Ship Island via Pan Isles Excursions; travel time is approximately one hour.

PORT GIBSON

 GRAND GULF MILITARY MONUMENT PARK

12006 Grand Gulf Road, Port Gibson, MS 39150; (601) 437–5911; www.grand gulfpark.state.ms.us; grandgulfpark @aol.com.

Description: The river batteries at Grand Gulf were the southernmost leg of the Vicksburg defenses. Grant tried to land his army at Grand Gulf but was driven off by the Confederate batteries. After the Battle of Port Gibson, Grand Gulf became Grant's base of operations.

Admission Fees: Adults $3.00, children $1.00, seniors $2.00; group rates available.

Open to Public: Mon.–Sun. 8:00 A.M.–5:00 P.M.; closed major holidays.

Visitor Services: Public restrooms, information, handicapped access, gift shop, museum, camping, trails.

Regularly Scheduled Events: Several times a year, Civil War artillery demonstrations.

Directions: From I–20 at Vicksburg take U.S. 61 south for 22 miles, turn right at Grand Gulf Road, and proceed 7.5 miles to the site.

98 PORT GIBSON BATTLEFIELD

Department of Archives and History, 400 Jefferson Davis Boulevard, Natchez, MS 39120; (601) 446–6502; www.mdah.state.ms.us.

Description: The Shaifer House was the site of the opening shots in the Battle of Port Gibson. The house was used by Maj. Gen. John A. McClernand for his headquarters and later used as a hospital. Confederate forces were entrenched at Magnolia Church. Part of the battle was fought on the Bruinsburg Road at Point Lookout. Restoration of the site is in progress, and the majority of the battlefield is privately owned.

Admission Fees: Free.

Open to Public: Daily from dawn to dusk.

Visitor Services: None.
Regularly Scheduled Events: None.
Directions: From I–20 at Vicksburg travel south on U.S. 61, 28 miles to Port Gibson. Turn right on Carrol Street, continue on Rodney Road, then Bessie Weathers Road to Shaifer Road, a distance of 4.5 miles.

 WINDSOR RUINS

(10 miles outside of Port Gibson)
Department of Archives and History,
400 Jefferson Davis Boulevard,
Natchez, MS 39120; (601) 446–6502;
www.mdah.state.ms.us.

Description: The Windsor Ruins are located near the abandoned town of Bruinsburg, where Gen. Ulysses Grant's army crossed the Mississippi River from April 30 to May 1, 1863, to begin the campaign for the capture of Vicksburg. The mansion was located along the route of Grant's army on its march inland toward Jackson. Windsor Mansion was destroyed by accidental fire in 1890.
Admission Fees: Free.
Open to Public: Daily from dawn to dusk.
Visitor Services: Interpretive sign.
Regularly Scheduled Events: None.
Directions: From I–20 take the Natchez Trace Parkway south to the exit for County Highway 552. Follow Highway 552 past the turnoff for Alcorn State University; follow the signs to the site entrance.

RAYMOND

 CONFEDERATE CEMETERY

Port Gibson Street, Raymond, MS
39154; (601) 857–8041; www.raymond
ms.com.

Description: The cemetery contains the graves of soldiers mortally wounded in the Battle of Raymond, fought May 12, 1863. The soldiers are mostly from the Third Tennessee and the Seventh Texas. In 1985 a total of 109 Confederate dead were

identified, the remaining graves hold unknown soldiers.
Admission Fees: Free.
Open to Public: Daily from dawn to dusk.
Visitor Services: None.
Regularly Scheduled Events: None.
Directions: From I–20 at Jackson take exit 40A (Highway 18 south) 8 miles to Raymond.

 DRIVING TOUR OF HISTORIC RAYMOND

Raymond City Hall, 110 Courtyard
Square, P.O. Box 10, Raymond, MS
39154; (601) 857–8041; www.raymond
ms.com; mayor@raymondms.com.

Description: The Raymond Driving Tour features three structures that stand as a reminder of the Battle of Raymond, fought outside this small community. The Raymond Courthouse, built in 1857–59 by the Weldon Brothers' skilled slave crew, is on the National Register of Historic Places and is an excellent example of Greek Revival architecture. It was used as a hospital for Union wounded following the six-hour Battle of Raymond. The tour also includes 1831–34 Waverly, used as a temporary headquarters for Generals James McPherson and Ulysses Grant, and the Confederate cemetery.
Admission Fees: Free.
Open to Public: Brochure and map available at city hall, Mon.–Fri. 8:00 A.M.–noon, 1:00 P.M.–5:00 P.M.; driving tour, daily during daylight hours; interior tours of the church and courthouse by appointment.
Visitor Services: Information.
Regularly Scheduled Events: First Saturday of May, Raymond Country Fair (revival of Southern culture with food, entertainment, crafts, and history).
Directions: From I–20 at Jackson take exit 40A (Highway 18 south) 8 miles to Raymond. Turn right on Hinds Boulevard, turn left on Main Street, and proceed to courthouse. City hall is a small building behind the courthouse. Park near the water tower; pick up a brochure at city hall.

SOUTHERN HEARTLAND

 **RAYMOND BATTLEFIELD** CWPT

Fourteen Mile Creek, Highway 18, Raymond, MS 39154; (601) 857–8041; www.raymondms.com.

Description: A corps of the Army of Tennessee was attacked just south of the town on May 12, 1863, by Brig. Gen. John Gregg's brigade, causing Maj. Gen. U. S. Grant to abandon his plan to attack Vicksburg and march east toward Jackson instead to eliminate the perceived threat to his army's rear.
Admission Fees: Free.
Open to Public: Daily from dawn to dusk.
Visitor Services: None.
Regularly Scheduled Events: None.
Directions: From I–20 at Jackson take exit 40A (Highway 18 south) 8 miles to Raymond.

 RAYMOND COURTHOUSE

Main Street, Raymond, MS 39154; (601) 857–8041; www.raymondms.com.

Description: Weldon Brothers built Hinds County Courthouse in 1857–59 with skilled slave labor. Following the Battle of Raymond, Union troops occupied the town and removed Confederate flags from the cupola. They hoisted the Union flag, singing the chorus for "The Battle Cry for Freedom," ("The Union forever . . . "). The courthouse was used as a hospital for Confederate wounded.
Admission Fees: Free.
Open to Public: Mon.–Fri. 8:00 A.M.–5:00 P.M.; closed state holidays.
Visitor Services: Public restrooms, information, handicapped access.
Regularly Scheduled Events: None.
Directions: From I–20 at Jackson take exit 40A (Highway 18 south) 8 miles to Raymond.

 ST. MARKS EPISCOPAL CHURCH

Main Street, Raymond, MS 39154; (601) 857–8041; www.raymondms.com.

Description: Organized in 1837 and built in 1854, St. Marks is the only antebellum church remaining in Raymond. After the Battle of Raymond, it was taken by the Union army and used for a hospital. Cotton was spread on the floors of the sanctuary for the wounded. Bloodstains remain visible today.
Admission Fees: Free.
Open to Public: By appointment.
Visitor Services: None.
Regularly Scheduled Events: None.
Directions: From I–20 at Jackson take exit 40A (Highway 18 south) 8 miles to Raymond.

TUPELO

 TUPELO NATIONAL BATTLEFIELD

c/o Natchez Trace Parkway, 2680 Natchez Trace Parkway, Tupelo, MS 38804; (662) 680–4025 or (800) 305–7147; www.nps.gov/natr.

Description: Tupelo National Battlefield is a one-acre site off the Natchez Trace Parkway where, from July 13 to 15, 1864, a battle was fought that served to keep Confederate Gen. Nathan Bedford Forrest from altering the supply line that was essential to the success of Union Gen. William T. Sherman. Neither side could claim victory.
Admission Fees: Free.
Open to Public: Daily from dawn to dusk.
Visitor Services: Interpretive signs, brochure.
Regularly Scheduled Events: None.
Directions: Take Highway 78 to the Natchez Trace Parkway; go south on the Natchez Trace Parkway for 4 miles to Mississippi Highway 6 (Main Street) exit; turn left onto Mississippi Highway 6 and go 1 mile to battlefield site.

VICKSBURG

OLD COURT HOUSE MUSEUM—EVA W. DAVIS MEMORIAL

1008 Cherry Street, Vicksburg, MS 39183; (601) 636–0741; www.oldcourt house.org; societyhistorica@bellsouth .net.

Description: Completed in 1860, the Old Court House was the site of the raising of the U.S. flag over Vicksburg following the surrender on July 4, 1863. The building was the county courthouse until 1939 and has been a musem of local history since 1948. In 1843 Jefferson Davis made the first speech of his political career on the grounds.

Admission Fees: Adults $5.00, children $3.00, seniors $4.50; group rates available.

Open to Public: Mon.–Sat. 8:30 A.M.–4:30 P.M., Sun. 1:30 P.M.–4:30 P.M.

Visitor Services: Public restrooms, information, handicapped access, gift shop.

Regularly Scheduled Events: December, Confederate Christmas Ball.

Directions: From I–20 take Clay Street exit to Cherry Street and turn right.

VICKSBURG BATTLEFIELD MUSEUM

4139 North Frontage Road, Vicksburg, MS 39183; (601) 638–6500; www .vicksburgbattlefield.net; thegunboat @bellsouth.net.

Description: Houses the world's largest collection of Civil War gunboat models, plus an 8-by-20-foot diorama of the siege of Vicksburg, thirty original paintings depicting the Inland Water War, and the thirty-minute documentary *Vanishing Glory.*

Admission Fees: Adults $5.50, children $3.25, seniors $5.00; family maximum $20.00.

Open to Public: Mon.–Sat. 9:00 A.M.–5:00 P.M.

Visitor Services: Handicapped access, gift

SOUTHERN HEARTLAND

Union Cavalry Monument, Vicksburg National Military Park, Mississippi. Michael Terry, CWPT files.

THE CAMPAIGN FOR VICKSBURG

Between Cairo, Illinois, and the Gulf of Mexico, the Mississippi River meanders over a course nearly 1,000 miles long. During the Civil War, control of this stretch was of vital importance to the Federal government. Command of the waterway would allow uninterrupted flow of Union troops and supplies into the South. It would also have the desired effect of isolating the states of Texas, Arkansas, and most of Louisiana, comprising nearly half the land area of the Confederacy, a region on which the South depended heavily for supplies and recruits.

From the beginning of the war in 1861, the Confederates, to protect this vital lifeline, erected fortifications at strategic points along the river. Federal forces, however, fighting their way southward from Illinois and northward from the Gulf, captured post after post, until by late summer 1862 only Vicksburg and Port Hudson posed major obstacles to complete Union control of the Mississippi. Of the two posts, Vicksburg was the stronger and more important. It sat on a high bluff overlooking a bend in the river, protected by artillery batteries along the riverfront and by a maze of swamps and bayous to the north and south. President Lincoln called Vicksburg "the key" and believed that "the war can never be brought to a close until that key is in our pocket." So far the city had defied Union efforts to force it into submission.

In October 1862 Ulysses S. Grant was appointed commander of the Department of the Tennessee and charged with clearing the Mississippi of Confederate resistance. That same month, Lt. Gen. John C. Pemberton, a West Point graduate and a Pennsylvanian by birth, assumed command of the 50,000 widely scattered Confederate troops defending the Mississippi. His orders were to keep the river open. Vicksburg became the focus of military operations for both men.

During the winter of 1862–63, Grant conducted a series of amphibious operations (often referred to as bayou expeditions) aimed at reducing Vicksburg. All of them failed. By spring Grant had decided to march his army of approximately 45,000 men down the west (Louisiana) bank of the Mississippi, cross the river well below Vicksburg, and then swing into position to attack the city from the south.

On March 31, 1863, Grant moved his army south from its encampments at Milliken's Bend, 20 miles northwest of Vicksburg. By April 28 the Northerners were established at Hard Times on the Mississippi above Grand Gulf. On April 29, Adm. David D. Porter's gunboats bombarded the Confederate forts at Grand Gulf to prepare the way for a crossing, but the attack was repulsed. Undaunted, Grant marched his troops a little farther south and, on April 30, stormed across at Bruinsburg.

Striking rapidly eastward to secure the bridgehead, the Northerners met elements of Pemberton's Confederate forces near Port Gibson on May 1. The Southerners fought a gallant holding action, but they were overwhelmed and fell back toward Vicksburg. After meeting and defeating a small Confederate force near Raymond on May 12, Grant's troops attacked and captured Jackson, the state capital, on May 14, scattering the Southern defenders.

Turning his army westward, Grant moved toward Vicksburg along the line of the Southern Railroad of Mississippi. At Champion Hill on May 16 and at Big Black River Bridge on May 17, his soldiers attacked and overwhelmed Pemberton's disorganized Confederates, driving them back into the Vicksburg fortifications. By May 18 advance units of the Federal army were approaching the bristling Confederate defenses.

Believing that the battles of Champion Hill and Big Black River Bridge had broken the Confederate morale, Grant immediately scheduled an assault on the Vicksburg lines. The first attack took place against the Stockade Redan on May 19. It failed. A second attack, launched on the morning of May 22, was also repulsed.

Realizing that it was useless to expend further lives in attempts to take the city by storm, Grant reluctantly began formal siege operations. Batteries of artillery were established to hammer the Confederate fortifications from the land side, while Admiral Porter's gunboats cut off communications and blasted the city from the river. By the end of June, with little hope of relief and no chance to break out of the Federal cordon, Pemberton knew that it was only a matter of time before he must "capitulate upon the best attainable terms." On the afternoon of July 3, he met with Grant to discuss terms for the surrender of Vicksburg.

Grant demanded unconditional surrender; Pemberton refused. The meeting broke up. During the afternoon the Federal commander modified his demands and agreed to let the Confederates sign paroles not to fight again until exchanged. In addition, officers could retain sidearms and a mount. Pemberton accepted these terms, and at 10:00 A.M. on July 4, 1863, Vicksburg was officially surrendered.

When Port Hudson surrendered five days later, the great Northern objective of the war in the West—the opening of the Mississippi River and the severing of the Confederacy—was at last realized. For the first time since the war began, the Mississippi was free of Confederate troops and fortifications. As President Lincoln put it, "The Father of Waters again goes unvexed to the sea."

NATIONAL PARK SERVICE

shop, guided tours for groups (individuals are given a self-guided tour book for the museum).

Directions: From I–20 take Clay Street west; turn right on Washington Street, travel north 2 blocks. Museum will be on the left-hand side.

108 VICKSBURG NATIONAL MILITARY PARK

3201 Clay Street, Vicksburg, MS 39183-3495; (601) 636–0583; www.nps.gov/vick; vick_interpretation@nps.gov.

Description: Vicksburg National Military Park is a 1,800-acre military park established in 1899 that commemorates the campaign and siege of Vicksburg. The focus of Union land and naval operations along the Mississippi River, the city fell to Gen. Ulysses S. Grant after a lengthy campaign and forty-seven-day siege on July 4, 1863. The fall of

Gunboat Cairo, *Vicksburg, Mississippi.* Courtesy Vicksburg National Military Park.

Vicksburg National Military Cemetery, Mississippi. Mary Louise Nosser–CWPT files.

Vicksburg gave the North control of the river; severed a major Confederate supply line that ran east–west through Vicksburg; achieved a major objective of the Anaconda Plan, cutting the Confederacy in two and sealing it off from the rest of the world; and effectively sealed the doom of Richmond. The park boasts more than 1,300 monuments, the historic Shirley House, Confederate forts, Union approaches, the restored Union ironclad gunboat *Cairo,* and Vicksburg National Cemetery, which is the final resting place for 18,000 American soldiers and sailors.

Admission Fees: Cars $8.00, school groups free with reservation.

Open to Public: Daily 8:00 A.M.–5:00 P.M.; hours vary by season.

Visitor Services: Public restrooms, handicapped access, gift shop, visitor center, USS *Cairo* Gunboat and Museum, licensed tour guides available.

Regularly Scheduled Events: June–August, living history programs, featuring rifle and cannon firing demonstrations.

Directions: From I–20 take exit 4B; follow signs.

WEST POINT

 WAVERLEY PLANTATION MANSION

1852 Waverley Mansion Road, West Point, MS 39773; (662) 494–1399.

Description: Waverley is a National Historic Landmark Greek Revival home that commemorates the antebellum South. The plantation was a self-sustaining community, complete with gardens, orchards, and livestock. In later years Waverley had its own lumber mill, tannery, and hat-manufacturing operation. Gen. Nathan Bedford Forrest was a friend and frequent visitor of the owner, Col. George Hampton Young. General Forrest spent three weeks recuperating at Waverley during the Civil War. He resided in the Egyptian Room and used the home as a headquarters. The octagonal cupola of the home served as an observation point for watching the river and the prairie for troop movement. Waverley features twenty acres of landscaped gardens with peacocks and black swans.

Admission Fees: Adults $7.50, children under six free; group rates available.

Open to Public: Daily 9:00 A.M.–5:00 P.M.

Visitor Services: Public restrooms, information, gift shop, tours, trails.

Regularly Scheduled Events: Spring pilgrimage of homes, call for schedule.

Directions: Located 15 minutes from Columbus, 1 mile off Highway 50 between Columbus and West Point, near the Tenn-Tom Waterway on the west side of river.

WOODVILLE

 ROSEMONT PLANTATION/ HOME OF JEFFERSON DAVIS

Highway 24 East, Woodville, MS 39669; (601) 888–6809; www.rosemont plantation.com; janlou3@bellsouth.net.

Description: This is the family home of Confederate president Jefferson Davis, built by his parents in 1810 and the family home until 1895. Many articles of furniture and family portraits of the Davis family are still in the home. Rosemont is the headquarters of the Davis Family Association, and reunions are held there biannually. The home is an early "cottage style" planter's home. Five generations of Davis's family lived here. His mother, Jane Davis, is buried in the family cemetery on the grounds.

Admission Fees: Adults $10.00, children $4.00.

Open to Public: Mar.–Dec. 15, Tues.–Sat. 10:00 A.M.–4:00 P.M. Open Tues.–Sun. during the Natchez Spring Pilgrimage and during October.

Visitor Services: Public restrooms, information, gift shop, museum.

Regularly Scheduled Events: None.

Directions: One mile off U.S. 61 on Highway 24 east, marked by state highway signs.

❖ TENNESSEE ❖

CHATTANOOGA/LOOKOUT MOUNTAIN

 BATTLES FOR CHATTANOOGA MUSEUM

1110 East Brow Road, Lookout Mountain, TN 37350; (423) 821–2812; www .battlesforchattanooga.com.

Description: Experience the battles for Chattanooga through the sights and sounds of a three-dimensional, 480-square-foot electronic battle map. More than 5,000 miniature soldiers and dramatic sound effects show troop movements during the 1863 battles.

Admission Fees: Adults $6.95, children $4.95; group rates available.

Open to Public: Daily 10:00 A.M.–5:00 P.M., summer 9:00 A.M.–6:30 P.M.

Visitor Services: Public restrooms, handicapped access, gift shop.

Regularly Scheduled Events: None.

Directions: From I–24 take exit 178; follow signs to Point Park atop Lookout Mountain.

 CHATTANOOGA NATIONAL CEMETERY

1200 Bailey Avenue, Chattanooga, TN 37404; (423) 855–6590; www.cem.va.gov.

Description: Chattanooga National Cemetery was established during the Civil War in December 1863 by an order from Gen. George Thomas to provide a proper burial for Union soldiers killed in the battles around Chattanooga. Eight of Andrews's Raiders are buried in the cemetery, four of whom were the first to receive the Congressional Medal of Honor.

Admission Fees: Free.

Open to Public: Office, Mon.–Fri. 8:00 A.M.– 4:30 P.M.; gates are always open.

TENNESSEE SITES

111 Battles for Chattanooga Museum
112 Chattanooga National Cemetery
113 Chattanooga Regional History Museum
114 Chickamauga and Chattanooga National Military Park/Lookout Mountain
115 Fort Defiance/Fort Sevier/Fort Bruce
116 The Athenaeum Rectory
117 Abraham Lincoln Library and Museum
118 Dover Hotel (Surrender House), Fort Donelson National Battlefield
119 Fort Donelson National Battlefield
120 Homeplace 1850
121 Nathan Bedford Forrest State Park
122 Carnton Plantation
123 The Carter House
124 Confederate Memorial Park at Winstead Hill
125 Fort Granger
126 McGavock Confederate Cemetery
127 Andrew Johnson National Historic Site
128 Dickson-Williams Mansion
129 Battle of Hartsville Driving Tour
130 Fort Pillow State Historic Site
131 Britton Lane Battlefield
132 Salem Cemetery Battlefield
133 Confederate Memorial Hall (Bleak House)
134 East Tennessee History Center
135 Fort Dickerson
136 Knoxville Driving Tour, Siege of Knoxville and Battle of Fort Sanders
137 Mabry-Hazen House Museum and Bethel Cemetery
138 Old Gray Cemetery
139 Town of La Grange
140 Nashville National Cemetery
141 Forrest Park
142 The Inn at Hunt Phelan
143 Memphis National Cemetery
144 Memphis Pink Palace Museum
145 Mississippi River Museum at Mud Island
146 From Bridge to Bridge Driving Tour Brochure
147 Fortress Rosecrans, Stones River National Battlefield
148 Oaklands Historic House Museum
149 Stones River National Battlefield
150 Battle of Nashville Tour Map
151 Belle Meade Plantation
152 Belmont Mansion
153 Mount Olivet Cemetery
154 Tennessee State Museum and State Capitol
155 Travellers Rest Plantation and Museum
156 Johnsonville State Historic Area
157 Parker's Crossroads Battlefield Self-Guided Tour
158 Davis Bridge Battlefield
159 Tennessee River Museum
160 Shiloh National Military Park
161 Sam Davis Home
162 Rippavilla Plantation
163 Spring Hill Battlefield
164 Tennessee Antebellum Trail
165 Tullahoma Campaign Civil War Trail
166 Historic Chockley Tavern

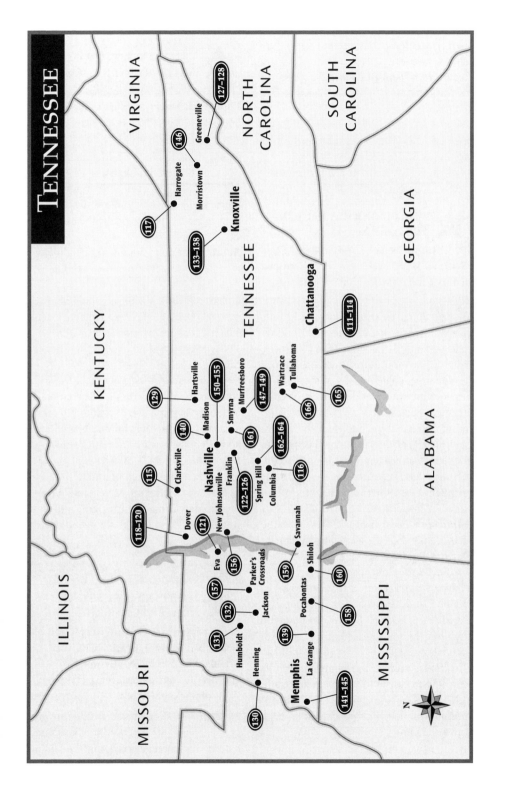

Visitor Services: Public restrooms, information, handicapped access.

Regularly Scheduled Events: May, Memorial Day ceremony; November, Veterans Day ceremony.

Directions: From I–24 take the Fourth Avenue exit. Go north to 23rd Street (second stoplight) and turn left on 23rd. Second stoplight is Holtzclaw, turn right; cemetery is 0.5 mile on left-hand side.

 CHATTANOOGA REGIONAL HISTORY MUSEUM

400 Chestnut Street, Chattanooga, TN 37402; (423) 265–3247; www.chattanooga history.com; dblack@chattanoogahistory .com.

Description: The Chattanooga Regional History Museum has an extensive Civil War collection numbering more than 500 pieces, including a mountain howitzer; Grant's headquarters chair; dozens of muskets, rifles, swords, knives, and pistols; projectiles and minié balls; various accoutrements; uniforms; original photographs taken by R. M. Linn, George N. Bernard, and others; diaries and letters; and veterans' and national park memorabilia. These artifacts are on display in the museum's permanent collection or stored in its archives.

Admission Fees: Adults $4.00, children $3.00, seniors $2.50; group rates available.

Open to Public: Mon.–Fri. 10:00 A.M.–4:30 P.M., Sat.–Sun. 11:00 A.M.–5:00 P.M.

Visitor Services: Public restrooms, information, handicapped access, gift shop.

Regularly Scheduled Events: Programs on Civil War history and bus tours; call for schedule.

Directions: From I–24 to Highway 27 north; take 4th Street exit; turn right at first traffic light onto Chestnut Street. CRHM is immediately on left, with parking in lot adjacent to building.

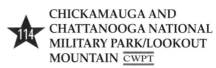 **CHICKAMAUGA AND CHATTANOOGA NATIONAL MILITARY PARK/LOOKOUT MOUNTAIN** ⟨CWPT⟩

Point Park Visitor Center, Lookout Mountain, TN 37350; (423) 821–7786; www.nps.gov/chch.

Description: The Lookout Mountain district of Chickamauga and Chattanooga National Military Park preserves land on which the Battle of Lookout Mountain was fought, November 24, 1863, as part of the battles for Chattanooga.

Admission Fees: Adults $3.00, children fifteen and under free, seniors with Golden Age Pass $1.50.

Open to Public: Visitor center, daily 8:30 A.M.–5:00 P.M.; Point Park, daily 9:00 A.M.–6:00 P.M.; call for extended summer hours.

Visitor Services: Public restrooms, handicapped access, gift shop.

Regularly Scheduled Events: November, anniversary of the battles for Chattanooga, including living history regiment demonstrations, special tours of Missionary Ridge and other battle sites; call for schedule.

Directions: From I–24 take exit 74; turn onto U.S. 41 east, then onto Highway 148 up Lookout Mountain. After ascending approximately 3 miles, turn right onto East Brow Road. Point Park is at the end of East Brow Road.

CLARKSVILLE

 FORT DEFIANCE/FORT SEVIER/FORT BRUCE

c/o Clarksville Parks and Recreation, 104 Public Square, Clarksville, TN 37040; (931) 645–7476; www.cityof clarksville.com/parks&rec; parks&rec @cityofclarksville.com.

Description: Constructed on the property of Clarksville pioneer Valentine Sevier and renamed on completion. During the capture of Clarksville, Fort Defiance was abandoned by Confederate forces, leading to the fall of Nashville. Confederate troops briefly reoccupied Fort Defiance in the summer of 1862. During the remainder of the war, Col. Sanders D. Bruce of Kentucky, for whom it was renamed, commanded and expanded the fort. A new exhibit center with information on the fort and the occupation of the city of Clarksville from 1862 to 1865 is planned for 2008.

Admission Fees: Free.

Open to Public: Daily 8:00 A.M.–dusk.

Visitor Services: For tours call Clarksville Parks and Recreation at (931) 645–7476.

Regularly Scheduled Events: None.

Directions: From I–24 west from Clarksville, take exit 4; turn left onto Highway 79; cross bridge to Kraft Street and turn right (41A north); turn left onto B Street, then turn left onto Walker Street; turn left at A Street.

COLUMBIA

 THE ATHENAEUM RECTORY

808 Athenaeum Street, Columbia, TN 38401; (931) 381–4822; www.athenaeum rectory.com; info@anthaeumrectory .com.

Description: The Athenaeum Rectory was headquarters for Generals James Negley and John Schofield during the Civil War. Gen. Nathan Bedford Forrest was a frequent visitor. The owner of the house, the Rev. F. G. Smith, the rector of a girls' school, outfitted a company of Confederate soldiers, the Maury Rifles. The Reverend Smith also designed a submarine and worked on a hot-air balloon for the South. Owned and operated by the Association for the Preservation of Tennessee Antiquities.

Admission Fees: Adults $6.00, students grades one–five $1.00, grades six–twelve $2.00, seniors $5.00; group rates available.

Open to Public: Feb.–Dec., Tues.–Sat. 10:00 A.M.–4:00 P.M.

Visitor Services: Public restrooms, handicapped access, gift shop, museum, tours.

Regularly Scheduled Events: First weekend in May, Ladies' 1861 weekend; first full week after the Fourth of July, 1861 girls' summer school; December, Majestic Middle Tennessee Christmas.

Directions: From I–65 south to exit 53, take Saturn Parkway to Highway 31 south (take Columbia exit from Saturn Parkway). Travel approximately 8 miles into Columbia to West Seventh Street and turn right. Proceed 3 blocks to West Seventh Street Church of Christ. Turn left immediately past the church on Athenaeum Street. The house is at the end of the street and is designated by a blue sign.

CUMBERLAND GAP/ HARROGATE

 ABRAHAM LINCOLN LIBRARY AND MUSEUM

Lincoln Memorial University, 6965 Cumberland Gap Parkway, Harrogate, TN 37752; (423) 869–6235; www.lmunet .edu/museum/index.html.

Description: The Abraham Lincoln Library and Museum houses one of the largest and most complete Lincoln and Civil War collections in the country. Exhibited are many rare items—the silver-topped cane Lincoln carried the night of his assassination, a lock of his hair clipped as he lay on his death bed, two life masks made of Lincoln, and numerous personal belongings. Approximately 30,000 books, manuscripts, paintings, and sculptures tell the story of President Lincoln and the Civil War period in America.

Admission Fees: Adults $5.00, children six–twelve $3.00, seniors $3.50; group rates available.

Open to Public: Museum, Mon.–Fri. 9:00 A.M.–4:00 P.M., Sat. 11:00 A.M.–4:00 P.M., Sun. 1:00 P.M.–4:00 P.M.; library, call (423) 869–6304 for an appointment.

Visitor Services: Public restrooms, information, gift shop.
Regularly Scheduled Events: None.
Directions: From I–75 north exit at Caryville; follow Highway 63 to U.S. 25 east; go north on U.S. 25 approximately 1.5 miles, museum is on left. From I–75 south exit at Corbin, Kentucky; follow U.S. 25E south to Harrogate. Museum will be on right.

DOVER

 DOVER HOTEL (SURRENDER HOUSE), FORT DONELSON NATIONAL BATTLEFIELD

Highway 79, P.O. Box 434, Dover, TN 37058; (615) 232–5706; www.nps.gov/ fodo; fodo_administration@nps.gov.

Description: The Dover Hotel was the site where Gen. Ulysses S. Grant demanded "unconditional and immediate surrender" from Gen. Simon B. Buckner after the Battle of Fort Donelson in February 1862. The hotel is the only original major battle surrender structure remaining from the Civil War.
Admission Fees: Free.

Open to Public: June–Sept., Sat.–Sun. noon–4:00 P.M.
Visitor Services: Public restrooms, information, handicapped access.
Regularly Scheduled Events: None.
Directions: From I–24 exit onto Highway 79 south at Clarksville; continue 35 miles to Dover and turn left at Petty Street. The hotel is 2 blocks down on the left.

 FORT DONELSON NATIONAL BATTLEFIELD
CWPT

Highway 79, P.O. Box 434, Dover, TN 37058; (615) 232–5706; www.nps.gov/ fodo; fodo_administration@nps.gov.

Description: Fort Donelson was built by the Confederates to control the Cumberland River. The Union army under the command of Gen. Ulysses Grant captured the fort in February 1862. More than 14,000 Confederate soldiers were captured. The victory secured Union control of the Cumberland River, Nashville, Clarksville, and most of Middle Tennessee.
Admission Fees: Free.

Fort Donelson, Dover, Tennessee. Bob Cross–CWPT files.

FORT DONELSON

On the morning of February 16, 1862, a young Union commander named Ulysses S. Grant made it clear he would accept only "unconditional and immediate surrender" from Confederate leader Simon B. Buckner, whose troops had tried for three days to fight off Northern soldiers attacking the earthen Fort Donelson in Stewart County, Tennessee. Buckner reluctantly entered the Dover Hotel and accepted Grant's terms, which he called "ungenerous and unchivalrous."

Today, the Dover Hotel still stands in Dover, Tennessee, near the Fort Donelson National Battlefield. The hotel and the park's national cemetery, the final resting place of Civil War veterans and many veterans who have served the United States since then, are two of my favorite sites in the area.

The sense of history at the battlefield is overwhelming. When I visit the park, I try to stop and consider the magnitude of what happened here—how I am standing on the very soil where Northern and Southern troops met in battle almost a century and a half ago. It is humbling to walk the path of the actual battle lines, where Union forced took control of the fort, giving them access to the Cumberland River and the heart of the South.

It is, after all, the Fort Donelson battle that allowed young Grant to catch the eye of President Abraham Lincoln, paving his way to Appomattox and, later, the White House. I feel lucky to have such a well-preserved piece of history in my congressional district, providing a great practical lesson for visitors, schoolchildren, and history buffs alike.

—U.S. Congressman John Tanner, Tennessee

SOUTHERN HEARTLAND

Open to Public: Daily 8:00 A.M.–4:30 P.M.
Visitor Services: Public restrooms, information, handicapped access, visitor center, gift shop, museum, trails.
Regularly Scheduled Events: None.
Directions: From I–24 take Highway 79 to Dover; follow signs.

 HOMEPLACE 1850

13 miles north of Dover, on the Trace in Land Between the Lakes, Dover, TN 37058; (270) 924–2000; www.lbl.org; rweakley@fs.fed.us.

Description: Homeplace 1850 is a living history, open-air museum that re-creates life on a mid-nineteenth-century Tennessee farm. Authentically furnished houses and barns and demonstrations of daily chores

bring to life a typical Civil War soldiers' boyhood. In the Civil War the Cumberland and Tennessee Rivers were a gateway to Nashville and the all-important railroads that fed the Confederacy its troops and supplies. Forts Henry and Donelson, located nearby, were critical to the defense of the region. Homeplace 1850 considers the impact the war had on the farmers of Tennessee.

Admission Fees: Age thirteen and over, $3.00, children five–twelve $2.00, four and under free; call for group rates.
Open to Public: Mar., Wed.–Sat. 9:00 A.M.–5:00 P.M., Sun. 10:00 A.M.–5:00 P.M.; Apr.–Oct., Mon.–Sat. 9:00 A.M.–5:00 P.M., Sun. 10:00 A.M.–5:00 P.M.; Nov., Wed.–Sat. 9:00 A.M.–5:00 P.M., Sun. 10:00 A.M.–5:00 P.M.; closed Dec.–Feb.
Visitor Services: Public restrooms, camp-

ing, picnic area, hunting, fishing, Fort Henry Trail, cycling, horseback riding.

Regularly Scheduled Events: May, River Day; July, Independence Day; third weekend in September, Harvest Celebration; third weekend in October, Homeplace Wedding; call for a complete schedule.

Directions: From I–24 take exits 31 or 4 in Tennessee or exit 65 in Kentucky. Follow signs to Land Between the Lakes.

EVA

 NATHAN BEDFORD FORREST STATE PARK

1825 Pilot Knob Road, Eva, TN 38333; (731) 584–6356; www.state.tn.us/ environment/parks/nbforrest.

Description: The park was named for Gen. Nathan Bedford Forrest, the intrepid Confederate cavalry leader who on November 4, 1864, attacked and destroyed the Federal supply and munitions depot at Johnsonville at the mouth of Trace Creek. His operations were concentrated along the river near the park and the town of Eva. The park features a monument to General Forrest and a map delineating the action at Johnsonville.

Admission Fees: Free.

Open to Public: Park, daily from dawn to dusk; museum, daily 8:00 A.M.–4:30 P.M.

Visitor Services: Public restrooms, information, handicapped access, gift shop, museum, camping, trails.

Regularly Scheduled Events: September, folklife festival; November, Civil War skirmish; December, Lighing of the Knob.

Directions: Located north of I–40 on the Tennessee River. From I–40 take exit 126; travel north on Highway 641 (15 miles) to Highway 70 in Camden; go around courthouse. Take Highway 191 north for 9 miles to the park. There are signs from Camden.

FRANKLIN

 CARNTON PLANTATION

1345 Carnton Lane, Franklin, TN 37064; (615) 794–0903; www.carnton.org; info @carnton.org.

Description: Possibly the bloodiest five hours of the Civil War took place at the Battle of Franklin. On November 30, 1864, Carnton was engulfed by Confederate troops moving toward well-entrenched Federal troops and a devastating battle. Later the mansion housed hundreds of the more than 6,000 Confederate casualties, leaving the floors permanently blood stained. Adjoining the property is the McGavock Confederate Cemetery and the recently preserved Eastern Flank Battlefield.

Admission Fees: Adults $10.00, children six–twelve $3.00, seniors $9.00; group rates available.

Open to Public: Mon.–Sat. 9:00 A.M.–5:00 P.M., Sun. 1:00 P.M.–5:00 P.M.; last tour at 4:00 P.M.

Visitor Services: Museum, gift shop, restrooms, guided tours.

Regularly Scheduled Events: None.

Directions: From I–65 take exit 65. Turn right on Highway 96, turn left on Mack Hatcher Parkway, turn right to Lewisburg Avenue (Highway 431), then turn left on Carnton Lane.

 THE CARTER HOUSE CWPT

1140 Columbia Avenue, Franklin, TN 37064; (615) 791–1861; www.carterhouse.org; carterhouse1864@aol.com.

Description: Built in 1830, the Carter House was the location of the 1864 Battle of Franklin. The house and grounds, which served as a Federal command post before the battle and as a hospital after, are today preserved on ten acres. In this evening battle lasting only five hours, more Confeder-

Carnton Plantation, Franklin, Tennessee. Chris E. Heisey–CWPT files.

ate soldiers, including thirteen generals, were lost than in Pickett's Charge at Gettysburg. More than 1,000 bullet holes are still visible from the battle.

Admission Fees: Adults $8.00, children six–twelve $4.00, seniors $7.00; group rates available.

Open to Public: Apr.–Nov., Mon.–Sat. 9:00 A.M.–5:00 P.M., Sun. 1:00 P.M.–5:00 P.M.; remainder of year, closes at 4:00 P.M.; closed Sun. in Jan.

Visitor Services: Public restrooms, gift shop, museum, guided tours, film.

Regularly Scheduled Events: November, battle anniversary events; first weekend in December, candlelight tour of homes.

Directions: From I–65 take exit 65; take Highway 96 into Franklin. At Courthouse Square turn left on Main Street; turn left on Columbia Avenue (Highway 31 south). Entrance off West Fowlkes Street.

 CONFEDERATE MEMORIAL PARK AT WINSTEAD HILL

P.O. Box 305, Franklin, TN 37065; (615) 791–2103; www.franklin-gov.com/parks.

Description: General Hood's troops formed on Winstead Hill before the Battle of Franklin. A memorial to the Army of Tennessee stands on the hill today. The overlook features a large military map and memorials to the Confederate generals who died in the battle in 1864.

Admission Fees: Free.

Open to Public: Daily from dawn to dusk.

Visitor Services: NOTE: Access to the monument requires a climb up stairs to the top of the hill.

Regularly Scheduled Events: Last weekend in November, the Battle of Franklin Memorial March starts here and concludes at the Carter House.

Directions: From I–65 take exit 65 and travel west on Highway 96 for 0.25 mile to Mack Hatcher Bypass; turn left and proceed to the end of the bypass; turn left on High-way 31. Winstead is the first hill on the right.

 **FORT GRANGER**

P.O. Box 305, Franklin, TN 37065; (615) 791–2103; www.franklin-gov.com/parks.

Description: In February 1863 Gen. William Rosecrans, in command of the Federal troops in Middle Tennessee, ordered Maj. Gen. Gordon Granger to fortify Franklin. On November 30, 1864, Confederate Gen. John Bell Hood attacked. The fort was abandoned when the Federals withdrew to Nashville during the night, but it was reoccupied two weeks later as Hood's defeated army withdrew from the state.

Admission Fees: Free.

Open to Public: Daily from dawn to dusk.

Visitor Services: Tours may be arranged through the Carter House Museum by calling (615) 791–1861.

Regularly Scheduled Events: None.

Directions: From I–65 take Franklin exit (Highway 96) west toward downtown Franklin for 2.5 miles. Turn right into Pinkerton Park and follow the signs to the fort. The park is on the right just before the bridge over the Harpeth River, before you get into downtown Franklin.

 McGAVOCK CONFEDERATE CEMETERY

Carnton Lane, Franklin, TN 37064; (615) 794–0903.

Description: McGavock Confederate Cemetery is the largest private Confederate cemetery in the nation and a National Historic Landmark. It adjoins the Carnton Plantation property. The Franklin United Daughters of the Confederacy maintains the cemetery. Also visit the Confederate monument in the Franklin town square, unveiled by the UDC on November 30, 1899, memorializing the Southern men who fought in the Battle of Franklin on November 30, 1864.

Admission Fees: Free.

Open to Public: Daily from dawn to dusk.

Visitor Services: Informational sign; tours available by request; a booklet about the cemetery is available at Carnton Plantation.

Regularly Scheduled Events: November, illumination service.

Directions: From I–65 north take exit 61; turn left on Goose Creek Bypass; at the four-way stop, turn right on Lewisburg Pike; proceed to Carnton Lane and turn left; follow signs to cemetery. From I–65 south take exit 65 (Highway 96); take Highway 96 to Mack Hatcher Bypass and turn left; proceed to Lewisburg Avenue and turn left; travel to Carnton Lane and turn left. Follow signs to cemetery.

GREENEVILLE

 ANDREW JOHNSON NATIONAL HISTORIC SITE

101 North College Street, Greeneville, TN 37743; (423) 639–3551; www.nps .gov/anjo.

Description: The sixteen-acre Andrew Johnson National Historic Site honors the life and work of the nation's seventeenth president and preserves his two homes, tailor shop, and grave site. When Tennessee seceded from the Union, Johnson became an avid opponent of secession and was appointed military governor of Tennessee by President Lincoln in 1862. In this role Johnson reestablished a Union government. While he and his family were in Nashville, both forces occupied his home. His Reconstruction-era presidency, from 1865 to 1869, illustrates the U.S. Constitution at work following Lincoln's assassination and during attempts to reunify a nation that had been torn by war.

Admission Fees: Free.

Open to Public: Daily 9:00 A.M.–5:00 P.M.; reservations requred for tours of the homestead; closed Thanksgiving, Christmas, and New Year's Day.

Visitor Services: Public restrooms, gift shop, museum, visitor center, guided tours.

Regularly Scheduled Events: December 29, Johnson's birthday.

Directions: From I–81N, take exit 23 and follow U.S. 11E north to Greenville, then follow park signs. From I–81S, take exit 36 and follow Route 172 south to Greenville, then follow park signs.

 DICKSON-WILLIAMS MANSION

c/o 130 South Main Street, Greeneville, TN 37743; (423) 787–7746 or (423) 639–7102; www.mainstreetgreeneville.com; mainst@greene.xtn.net.

Description: This mansion, built between 1815 and 1821, hosted many notables: Marquis de Lafayette, Henry Clay, and Presidents Jackson and Polk. During the war it served as headquarters for both Union and Confederate officers while they were in Greeneville. It was in this house that Gen. John Hunt Morgan, the "Rebel Raider," spent his last night before he was killed in the garden on September 4, 1864. The room where General Morgan slept contains the original furniture that was there when he occupied the room.

Admission Fees: Adults $10.00, children $5.00.

Open to Public: By appointment; call (423) 787–0500.

Visitor Services: Tours.

Regularly Scheduled Events: October, reenactment of Battle of Blue Springs; December, Christmas tours.

Directions: From I–81N take exit 23; turn right onto U.S. 11E and continue for 12 miles; take Greeneville Business exit (exit right). At the fourth traffic light, turn left onto Main Street. Turn left at the second light onto Church Street. The General Morgan Inn parking lot is on the left. All tours leave from the lobby of the inn.

HARTSVILLE

 BATTLE OF HARTSVILLE DRIVING TOUR

95 River Valley Court, Hartsville, TN 37074; (615) 449–1890; www.hatton.scv .org; ds1861@charter.net.

Description: The Battle of Hartsville has been called "the most successfully executed cavalry raid of the War Between the States." From this battle Col. John Hunt Morgan received his commission to brigadier general. The seventeen-stop driving tour includes buildings used as hospitals where Morgan rushed 1,834 prisoners after the seventy-five-minute battle; river crossings; rendezvous points; homes; and a cemetery.

Admission Fees: Free.

Open to Public: Daily during daylight hours; Hartsville Chamber of Commerce office, Mon.–Fri. 8:30 A.M.–4:30 P.M.

Visitor Services: Informational brochure available from the Hartsville-Trousdale County Chamber of Commerce, 200 East Main Street, Suite 11, Hartsville, TN 37074 (located in the courthouse); also available on Web site.

Regularly Scheduled Events: None.

Directions: From I–40 at Lebanon take Highway 231 to Highway 25. Turn right on Highway 25 and proceed to Hartsville. At the first traffic light, turn right on Broadway. Proceed 3 blocks and turn left on Main Street. The chamber of commerce is located at 200 East Main.

HENNING

 FORT PILLOW STATE HISTORIC SITE

3122 Park Road, Henning, TN 38041; (731) 738–5731; www.state.tn.us.

Description: Federal forces captured this important Confederate river defense in 1862. On April 12, 1864, Confederate Gen. Nathan Bedford Forrest attacked the fort

SOUTHERN HEARTLAND

and demanded immediate surrender of the garrison, but he was refused. The fort was then stormed and captured. Because of high Union casualties and the presence of African-American troops, controversy surrounding this battle still exists today.

Admission Fees: Free.

Open to Public: Park, daily 8:00 A.M.–sunset; museum, daily 8:00 A.M.–4:00 P.M.

Visitor Services: Public restrooms, information, handicapped access, gift shop, museum, camping, trails.

Regularly Scheduled Events: Every second weekend in April, Living History Weekend; first weekend in November, Civil War lectures.

Directions: From I–40 take Brownsville exit, Highway 19 west to Highway 51 and travel south. Turn right to Highway 87 west. Follow signs to the park.

HUMBOLDT

 BRITTON LANE BATTLEFIELD

c/o 4707 Steam Ferry Mill Road, Medon, TN 38356; (731) 989–7944 or (731) 935–2209; www.brittonlane1862.madison .tn.us; jmweaver@bellsouth.net.

Description: On September 1, 1862, Confederate Col. William H. Jackson's Seventh Tennessee Cavalry, Nathan Bedford Forrest's brigade, attacked the Twentieth and Thirtieth U.S. Infantry, Cavalry, and Artillery under the command of Col. Dennis, near Jackson, Tennessee. The Battle of Britton Lane resulted in the capture of a large Union wagon train, two pieces of artillery, and 213 prisoners. Monuments mark the site, along with a mass grave of Confederates killed in the action. An extant cabin on the site was used as a Federal and a Confederate hospital site. After the battle eighty-seven Union prisoners were imprisoned in the Denmark Presbyterian Church near Britton Lane Battlefield. The structure still contains graffiti left by the Union prisoners.

Admission Fees: Free.

Open to Public: Daily from dawn to dusk.

Visitor Services: Information, handicapped access, museum, trails.

Regularly Scheduled Events: Throughout the year, reenactments, living history, gun shows, Civil War church services; call for information.

Directions: From I–40 take exit 76 (Highway 223 south); travel on Highway 223 south 9 miles to Denmark. Turn left at Denmark Church onto Britton Lane Road.

JACKSON

 SALEM CEMETERY BATTLEFIELD

c/o 379 White Fern Road, Beech Bluff, TN 38313; (731) 424–1279; www.salem cemeterybattlefield.com.

Description: Self-guided tour with brochures available at the cemetery's main gate. The site has three large monuments, a flagpole, two cannons, and a battle map inlay showing the layout of the battle. A historical marker identifies the site. A battle occurred nearby on December 19, 1862, between Gen. Nathan Beford Forrest's cavalry and Union troops. Approximately 1,000 men were engaged in the two-hour battle.

Admission Fees: Free.

Open to Public: Daily during daylight hours.

Visitor Services: Tour brochure.

Regularly Scheduled Events: None.

Directions: From I–40 east of Jackson, take exit 85 (Christmasville Road); travel south on Paul D. Wright Drive (look for Salem Battlefield signs); proceed 4 miles to Bendix Drive; turn left; proceed 2 miles to Cotton Grove Road; turn left and travel 0.75 mile. Cemetery and battlefield entrance are on the left.

KNOXVILLE

133 CONFEDERATE MEMORIAL HALL (BLEAK HOUSE)

3148 Kingston Pike, Knoxville, TN 37919; (865) 522–2371; www.knoxville cemetery.org.

Description: Bleak House is a Victorian mansion built in 1858 by prominent Knoxvillian Robert H. Armstrong, using slave labor to mold the bricks on-site. During the siege of Knoxville and the Battle of Fort Sanders in November and December 1863, the home served as headquarters for Confederate Gens. James Longstreet and Lafayette McLaws. Three soldiers using the house's tower as a sharpshooters' post were killed there by Federal cannon fire. A comrade sketched their likenesses on the wall of the tower. Two cannonballs are still embedded in the walls. Artillery was also set up on the lawn to fire on the Federals.

Admission Fees: Adults $5.00, children seven–twelve $1.50, students $3.00, seniors $4.00.

Open to Public: Tues., Wed., Fri. 1:00 P.M.–4:00 P.M.; group tours by appointment.

Visitor Services: Public restrooms, gift shop, museum, tours.

Regularly Scheduled Events: April, extended hours and gardens open during Knoxville Dogwood Arts Festival; December, Christmas open house.

Directions: From I–40 take Alcoa Highway exit; then take Kingston Pike west exit; turn right (west) on Kingston Pike. Confederate Memorial Hall is on the left at 3148 Kingston Pike.

134 EAST TENNESSEE HISTORY CENTER

601 South Gay Street, Knoxville, TN 37902, (865) 215–8824 or (865) 215–8830; www.east-tennessee-history.org; eths @east-tennessee-history.org.

Description: A visit to the East Tennessee History Center in Knoxville will bring you face to face with the region's history makers. Here you can visit a museum, uncover your family's roots, or learn about historic sites, research facilities, and other historical and genealogical resources in this thirty-five-county region. Housed on the first floor of the center, the East Tennessee Historical Society pursues its educational mission through publications, lectures, conferences, and school programs. The ETHS Museum explores more than two centuries of life in the Tennessee Valley, including extensive collections of East Tennessee–related Civil War and Reconstruction artifacts, memorabilia, uniforms, weaponry, flags, and other items reflecting the divided loyalties of the region. Researchers can trace their own Civil War ancestry through the Civil War Families in Tennessee project and the vast genealogical resources housed in the McClung Historical Collection and Knox County Archives, in the center's upper floors.

Admission Fees: Free.

Open to Public: Museum, Mon.–Fri. 9:00 A.M.–4:00 P.M., Sat. 10:00 A.M.–4:00 P.M., Sun. 1:00 P.M.–5:00 P.M.; McClung Collection, Mon.–Tues. 9:00 A.M.–8:30 P.M., Wed.–Fri. 9:00 A.M.–5:30 P.M., Sat. 9:00 A.M.–5:00 P.M., Sun. 1:00 P.M.–5:00 P.M.

Visitor Services: Public restrooms, information, handicapped access, research library, gift shop (CWPT members eligible for 20 percent discount on on-site purchases).

Regularly Scheduled Events: The East Tennessee Historical Society holds lectures once a month, brown bag lunches in summer, and evening events in autumn and spring; call for details.

Directions: From I–75 north merge onto I–40 east and continue toward downtown Knoxville. Take exit 388 (U.S. 441/Henley Street), keep right at fork in ramp, and turn left onto Western Avenue, which becomes Summit Hill Drive. Turn right onto Gay Street. The History Center is on the corner of Gay Street and Clinch Avenue, directly across from the Tennessee Theatre. From

I–75 south take I–275 to the I–40 east/ Henley Street/U.S. 441 exit. Keep right at the fork in the ramp, turning left onto Western Avenue, and follow directions above. From I–81 south continue onto I–40 west. Take exit 388A (James White Parkway) to Cumberland Avenue. Continue on Cumberland Avenue and turn right on Gay Street.

 135 FORT DICKERSON

c/o Knoxville Visitors Welcome Center, 301 South Gay Street, Knoxville, TN 37902; (423) 523–7263 or (800) 727–8045; www.knoxville.org.

Description: Fort Dickerson was one of sixteen earthen forts and battery emplacements built by the Federal army to protect Knoxville during the Civil War. The fort, atop a 300-foot-high ridge across the Tennessee River from Knoxville, was begun in November 1863 and completed in January or February 1864. The position was attacked by Confederate cavalry under Gen. Joseph Wheeler on November 15, 1863, but the assault was canceled due to the formidable terrain, artillery, and unexpectedly strong force guarding the approaches to Knoxville.
Admission Fees: Free.
Open to Public: Daily from dawn to dusk.
Visitor Services: None.
Regularly Scheduled Events: None.
Directions: From I–40 take the Downtown or U.S. 441 exit; go south on U.S. 441 (Chapman Highway)/Henley Street; cross the Henley Street bridge and continue for approximately 1 mile. There is a Gulf gas station on the left; the drive to the fort is on the right and is marked by a sign.

 136 KNOXVILLE DRIVING TOUR, SIEGE OF KNOXVILLE AND BATTLE OF FORT SANDERS
c/o Knoxville Visitors Welcome Center, 301 South Gay Street, Knoxville, TN 37901; (423) 523–7263 or (800) 727–8045; www.knoxville.org.

Description: Driving tour features sites associated with the November 1863 attempt by Confederate Gen. James Longstreet to capture Knoxville and the army of Union Gen. Ambrose E. Burnside. Tour sites include Longstreet's headquarters, Fort Dickerson, cemeteries, hospitals, site of mortal wounding of Gen. William P. Sanders, and the site of the unsuccessful attack on Fort Sanders.
Admission Fees: Free.
Open to Public: Knoxville Visitors Welcome Center, Mon.–Fri. 7:30 A.M.–6:00 P.M., Sat. 9:00 A.M.–5:00 P.M., Sun. 1:00 P.M.–4:00 P.M.
Visitor Services: Brochure for the self-guided driving tour available at the Knoxville Visitors Welcome Center in the Candy Factory downtown or by writing to the address listed earlier.
Regularly Scheduled Events: None.
Directions: From I–40 take exit 388 to Western Avenue. Turn left on Western Avenue, which becomes Summit Hill Avenue. Turn left onto Gay Street; the visitor center is on the right.

 137 MABRY-HAZEN HOUSE MUSEUM AND BETHEL CEMETERY
1711 Dandridge Avenue, Knoxville, TN 37915; (865) 522–8661; www.mabry hazen.com; info@mabryhazen.com.

Description: The Mabry-Hazen House was occupied by Union and Confederate troops alternately. From 1861 to 1863 Knoxville was occupied by Confederate troops under Gen. Felix Zollicoffer, who set up headquarters in the home. In 1863 Knoxville and the Mabry home were taken over by Union troops, while the family continued to live upstairs. The grounds were fortified, and Mrs. Mabry's sketch of the trenches surrounding the house survives. Hundreds of artifacts help create a personal picture of family life during the Civil War and Reconstruction. The Knoxville Confederate Cemetery contains the remains of 1,600 Confederate troops, plus those of 60 Union soldiers killed between 1861 and 1864. The centerpiece of the cemetery is a 12-foot-square, 48-foot-high monument dedicated in 1891.

Admission Fees: Adults $5.00, children $2.50, seniors $4.50, groups $4.00/person.

Open to Public: Tues.–Sat. 9:00 A.M.–2:00 P.M.

Visitor Services: Public restrooms, information, limited handicapped access, gift shop, museum.

Regularly Scheduled Events: December, Christmas candlelight tour.

Directions: From I–40 take exit 388 to James White Parkway. Take first exit off parkway; turn left on Summit Hill Drive; at second traffic light Summit Hill Drive becomes Dandridge Avenue; turn left on Rosedale; take first gravel drive to the right.

 OLD GRAY CEMETERY

543 North Broadway, Knoxville, TN 37917; (865) 522–1424; www.korrnet.org/oldgray; oldgray@discoveret.org.

Description: Old Gray Cemetery, established in 1850, reflects the sympathies of East Tennessee during the Civil War with gravestones and sculpted monuments honoring Union and Confederate dead. Col. Henry M. Ashby, Gen. William R. Caswell, and Tennessee wartime governor William G. "Parson" Brownlow are among those buried in this Victorian cemetery in the heart of Knoxville.

Admission Fees: Free.

Open to Public: Daily from dawn to dusk.

Visitor Services: Self-guided tour brochure.

Regularly Scheduled Events: None.

Directions: From I–275 take exit 1A east to Baxter Avenue. Proceed up the hill to North Central Avenue. Turn right on North Central and proceed 0.4 mile to North Broadway. Turn right and travel 2 blocks. Old Gray is opposite St. John's Lutheran Church.

La Grange

 TOWN OF LA GRANGE

P.O. Box 621, La Grange, TN 38046; (901) 878–1246; www.lagrangetn.com; lagrange@bellsouth.net.

Description: Not unlike other Southern towns that were occupied by Union troops, La Grange suffered severely at the hands of the thousands of Federals who established a garrison here. The Civil War arrived on the very doorstep of La Grange on June 13, 1862, less than one week after the fall of Memphis to Union troops. From that moment on, either Union or Confederate soldiers occupied the town because of its strategic importance along the Memphis and Charleston Railroad. At one time as many as 30,000 Union soldiers were encamped in and around the town, and more than 3,000 wounded or sick were hospitalized there. By far the most famous Civil War–era event that occurred in La Grange was Grierson's Cavalry Raid. In April 1863 Union Col. Benjamin H. Grierson led 1,700 cavalry from La Grange to Baton Rouge, covering 600 miles in sixteen days. Grierson's daring raid contributed to Grant's success in taking Vicksburg in 1863.

Admission Fees: Free.

Open to Public: Daily from dawn to dusk; city hall, Mon.–Fri. 8:00 A.M.–noon.

Visitor Services: Pick up driving tour brochure at city hall or Cogbill's Store at the Livery. Cogbill's is open Thurs.–Sun. during lunch hours; call (901) 878–1235 for schedule.

Directions: From I–40 take exit 56; drive south toward Somerville on Tennessee Highway 76, which intersects Tennessee Highway 57 in Moscow. Turn east onto Tennessee Highway 57; drive approximately 10 miles to La Grange. Highway 57 becomes Main Street. Cogbill's Store and the city hall are located on the corner of Main Street and La Grange Road.

SOUTHERN HEARTLAND

MADISON

NASHVILLE NATIONAL CEMETERY

1420 Gallatin Road South, Madison, TN 37115-4619; (615) 736–2839; www.cem.va.gov.

Description: In 1867, 16,530 interments were brought from all over the area and reinterred in the Nashville National Cemetery. Of these, 4,006 are unknown. Also, 1,447 U.S. Colored Infantry are interred at Nashville.

Admission Fees: Free.

Open to Public: Office, Mon.–Fri. 7:30 A.M.–5:00 P.M.; grounds, daily from dawn to dusk.

Visitor Services: Public restrooms, information.

Regularly Scheduled Events: Memorial Day ceremony.

Directions: Take I–40 west to Briley Parkway. Follow Briley Parkway north 10 miles to exit 14A (Gallatin Road, Madison). The national cemetery is located 0.25 mile on the left.

MEMPHIS

FORREST PARK

North side of Union Avenue between Dunlap and Manassas Streets, Memphis, TN 38124; (901) 545–4500 (ask for county historian).

Description: Forrest Park, in downtown Memphis, is the site where Gen. Nathan Bedford Forrest is buried. The park features a large, bronze equestrian statue of the general, erected in 1905, as well as the granite monument that serves as the grave marker for the general and his wife, Mary Montgomery Forrest. After the Civil War General Sherman said of Forrest, "He was the most remarkable man our Civil War produced on either side." General Lee, when asked to identify the greatest soldier under his command, said, "a man I have never seen, sir . . . Forrest." The monument is located 2 blocks from the scene of Forrest's death in 1877.

Admission Fees: Free.

Open to Public: Daily twenty-four hours.

Visitor Services: Handicapped access; trails.

Regularly Scheduled Events: Sunday closest to July 13, Forrest's birthday celebration.

Directions: From I–240 north take the Union Avenue westbound exit. Forrest Park is on the north side of Union between Dunlap and Manassas Streets. From I–240 south and I–40, take the Madison Street westbound exit. Forrest Park is on the south side of Madison between Dunlap and Manassas Streets.

 THE INN AT HUNT PHELAN

533 Beale Street, Memphis, TN 38103; (901) 525–8225; www.huntphelan.com; info@huntphelan.com.

Description: The mansion was originally built between the years 1824 and 1828 from the plans of famed architect Robert Mills, whose other works include the U.S. Treasury building, the Washington Monument, and parts of the White House. Distinguished visitors include U.S. presidents Ulysses S. Grant, Andrew Jackson, and Andrew Johnson. Local lore has it that some of the original garden was planted by Varina Davis while her husband, Jefferson, was attending to the affairs of government in the mansion library. The mansion served as Grant's headquarters and as a hospitality lodge and hospital for the troops during the planning of the siege at Vicksburg. It also served as the first Freedmen's Bureau to educate the newly freed slaves.

Admission Fees: Free; call for room and restaurant rates.

Open to Public: Inn, daily twenty-four hours; call for restaurant operating hours.

Visitor Services: Bed-and-breakfast lodging, restaurant, information.

Regularly Scheduled Events: Spring and summer, live music on the patio.

Directions: From East Memphis follow Union Avenue west, turn left on South Lauderdale Street, turn right on Beale Street, then drive 1 block west on Beale Street. From downtown follow Union Avenue east, turn right on South Lauderdale Street, turn right on Beale Street, then drive 1 block west on Beale Street.

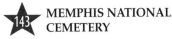

MEMPHIS NATIONAL CEMETERY

3568 Townes Avenue, Memphis, TN 38122; (901) 386–8311; www.cem.va.gov.

Description: Strong Union land and river forces captured Memphis on June 6, 1862, and, with the surrender, the city became the location of several Federal hospitals serving the western theater of war. The dead from these hospitals were buried in private cemeteries, and in 1866 were reinterred in the Mississippi National Cemetery. In 1867 the name was changed to the Memphis National Cemetery. Of the 13,965 soldiers buried at this site, 8,866 are unknown. Other burials include those from the USS *Sultana,* which sank in April 1865 and ranks as one of the nation's deadliest maritime disasters, with 1,700 soldiers and crew lost.

Admission Fees: Free.

Open to Public: Office, Mon.–Fri. 8:00 A.M.–4:30 P.M.; grounds, daily 8:00 A.M.–dusk.

Visitor Services: Public restrooms, information.

Regularly Scheduled Events: May, Memorial Day program; November, Veterans Day program.

Directions: From I–240 take exit 8B/Jackson Avenue. Travel south approximately 2 miles. After crossing railroad viaduct, take first left onto Townes Avenue. Cemetery gate is at the intersection of Jackson and Townes Avenues.

MEMPHIS PINK PALACE MUSEUM

3050 Central Avenue, Memphis, TN 38111-3399; (901) 320–6320; www.memphismuseums.org; info@pink palacemuseums.org.

Description: The Civil War exhibit displays artifacts, documents, and photographs of civilian Memphis; arms and equipment; and currency. It provides material on the war around Memphis, the Battle of Memphis, Gen. Nathan Bedford Forrest, and Confederate veterans. A vignette of an artillery crew serving an ordnance rifle is the centerpiece of the exhibit. The Civil War exhibit is part of a larger museum.

Admission Fees: Adults $8.25, children $5.75, seniors $7.75; call for group rates.

Open to Public: Mon.–Sat. 9:00 A.M.–5:00 P.M., Sun. noon–5:00 P.M.

Visitor Services: Public restrooms, information, handicapped access, food, gift shop.

Regularly Scheduled Events: None.

Directions: From I–40 take Sam Cooper Boulevard to the Highland exit. Travel south on Highland for 2 miles to the Central Avenue intersection. Turn west on Central Avenue and continue for 1 mile. The museum is located on the north side of Central Avenue.

MISSISSIPPI RIVER MUSEUM AT MUD ISLAND

125 North Front Street, Memphis, TN 38103-1713; (901) 576–7241 or (800) 507–6507; www.mudisland.com.

Description: Within the Mississippi River Museum are five galleries dedicated to the significant role of the Mississippi River in the Civil War. A life-size replica of a Union City ironclad gunboat is featured. Also included are a half-dozen boat models, displays of Civil War uniforms, field equipment, weapons, and personal items.

Admission Fees: Adults $8.00, children $5.00, seniors $6.00.

Open to Public: Spring and fall, Tues.–Sun. 10:00 A.M.–5:00 P.M.; summer, daily 10:00 A.M.–6:00 P.M.; closed Nov.–early Apr., call for dates.

Visitor Services: Public restrooms, information, handicapped access, gift shop.

Regularly Scheduled Events: None.

Directions: From I–40 east take Front Street exit; turn right (south) and proceed 2 blocks.

Morristown

 146 FROM BRIDGE TO BRIDGE DRIVING TOUR BROCHURE

(Tour begins at the Knox/Jefferson County Line)

c/o Rose Center, P.O. Box 1976, Morristown, TN 37816; (423) 581–4330.

Description: From Bridge to Bridge is a self-guided tour of historical sites from the Civil War in the East Tennessee Valley. Beginning at the Strawberry Plains Bridge over the Holton River at the Knox/Jefferson County Line, the tour generally follows U.S. 11E and visits twenty-three locations over its 40-mile length to its end at the Lick Creek Bridge in western Green County. Both bridges were burned during the Civil War.

Admission Fees: Free.

Open to Public: Daily from dawn to dusk; Rose Center, Mon.–Fri. 9:00 A.M.–5:00 P.M.

Visitor Services: Brochures are available by calling the Rose Center at (423) 581–4330.

Regularly Scheduled Events: None.

Directions: From I–81 take exit 15 to Morristown. The Rose Center is located at 442 West Second North Street.

Murfreesboro

 147 FORTRESS ROSECRANS, STONES RIVER NATIONAL BATTLEFIELD

3501 Old Nashville Highway, Murfreesboro, TN 37129-3094; (615) 893–9501 or (615) 478–1035; www.nps.gov/stri; stri_information@nps.gov.

Description: After the Confederates had withdrawn from Murfreesboro at the conclusion of the Battle of Stones River in January 1863, the Federal army, under Gen. William Rosecrans, began fortifying Murfreesboro. Fortress Rosecrans became one of the Union's largest earthen fortifications of the Civil War. The features that remain include Redoubt Brannan, Lunettes Palmer and Thomas, and Curtain Wall 2.

Admission Fees: Free.

Open to Public: Redoubt Brannan and Lunette Thomas are open 8:00 A.M.–5:00 P.M. Lunette Palmer and Curtain Wall 2 are open during daylight hours. Closed December 25.

Visitor Services: Handicapped access, exhibits, trail.

Regularly Scheduled Events: First weekend in October, Fortress Rosencrans encampment.

Directions: From I–24 take Exit 76, turn left onto Medical Center Parkway, and left again onto Thompson Lane. Turn right onto the access road to Old Nashville Highway, left at stop sign onto Old Nashville Highway. Park entrance is a quarter of a mile on left. See park officials for the location of Redoubt Brannan.

 148 OAKLANDS HISTORIC HOUSE MUSEUM

900 North Maney Avenue, Murfreesboro, TN 37130; (615) 893–0022; www.oaklandsmuseum.org; info@oaklandsmuseum.org.

Description: Oaklands was one of the largest plantations in Rutherford County during the Civil War. It was the home of the Maney family, one of the wealthiest families in the county. The Union army used the plantation in June 1862 as a camp. On July 13, 1862, Confederate Gen. Nathan Bedford Forrest and his cavalry raided the city of Murfreesboro and recaptured it. The surrender was negotiated at Oaklands. Another houseguest was Confederate president Jefferson Davis, who stayed at Oaklands while visiting his troops prior to the Battle of Stones River.

STONES RIVER NATIONAL BATTLEFIELD

On December 31, 1862, one of the bloodiest battles of the Civil War began at the Stones River near Murfreesboro, Tennessee. Confederate Gen. Braxton Bragg had strategically positioned himself near Murfreesboro to protect the fields that were supplying his men's food and to stop the Union from advancing to Chattanooga.

On the evening before the fighting began, music from each army's band could be heard across the fields as a battle of the bands ensued. Hours later, those refrains would give way to the deafening sounds of weaponry.

At the end of the first day's battle, the Confederates had succeeded in pushing the Union soldiers back, but great losses had occurred on both sides. The corpse-laden battlefield reminded some Union soldiers of the slaughter pens of Chicago's stockyards, a description that stuck.

The battle resumed on the afternoon of January 2, 1863, with devastating results. A force of Union cannons left 1,800 Confederate soldiers dead or wounded in just forty-five minutes. As the Union sent reinforcements, the Army of Tennessee retreated on January 3. Two days later, the Union took Murfreesboro.

When the Battle of Stones River ended, more than 3,000 men had lost their lives and nearly 16,000 more were wounded. In total, nearly 24,000 of the 81,000 men who fought at Stones River were killed, wounded, or captured.

Today, when I visit the hallowed ground of Stones River National Battlefield, it is easy to envision the young men who fought valiantly on both sides. The tradition-steeped ground is home to Hazen's Monument, the oldest intact Civil War memorial in the nation. But the most stirring feature of the vast grounds is the adjoining Stones River National Cemetery, which conveys the true price of war. There, 6,100 Union soldiers are buried alongside an additional 1,000 family members and veterans of later wars.

— *Congressman Bart Gordon, Tennessee*

SOUTHERN HEARTLAND

Admission Fees: Adults $7.00, children $5.00, seniors $6.00.

Open to Public: Tues.–Sat. 10:00 A.M.–4:00 P.M., Sun. 1:00 P.M.–4:00 P.M., last tour at 3:00 P.M.

Visitor Services: Public restrooms, handicapped access, information, gift shop.

Regularly Scheduled Events: December, candlelight tour of homes; call or check Web site for other events.

Directions: From I–24 take exit 81B; proceed to third traffic light; turn right on Broad Street. Proceed to next traffic light and turn left on Maney Avenue; follow Maney Avenue to Oaklands.

 **STONES RIVER NATIONAL BATTLEFIELD** CWPT

3501 Old Nashville Highway, Murfreesboro, TN 37129; (615) 893–9501 or (615) 478–1035; www.nps.gov/stri; stri_information@nps.gov.

Description: From December 31, 1862, through January 2, 1863, the Union Army of the Cumberland and the Confederate Army of Tennessee struggled here for control of Middle Tennessee. More than 81,000 soldiers fought in this midwinter battle; with more than 23,000 casualties, it was one of the bloodiest battles fought west of the

Destroyed Union Artillery, Stones River National Battlefield, Murfreesboro, Tennessee. Chris E. Heisey–CWPT files.

Appalachians. The Union victory allowed the army to construct Fortress Rosecrans and set the stage for the advance on Chattanooga.

Admission Fees: Free.

Open to Public: Daily 8:00 A.M.–5:00 P.M.; closed Christmas.

Visitor Services: Public restrooms, information, handicapped access, gift shop, museum.

Regularly Scheduled Events: May–October, ranger programs; May, Memorial Day ceremony; third weekend in July, artillery battery programs; December 26–January 3, anniversary programs.

Directions: From I–24 take exit 76 and turn right (westbound) or left (eastbound) onto Medical Center Parkway. Turn left at Thompson Lane (first light). Drive 2 miles and turn right onto access road. Turn left at stop sign (Old Nashville Highway). Visitor center is 0.75 mile up the road on the left.

NASHVILLE

150 BATTLE OF NASHVILLE TOUR MAP

c/o Metropolitan Historical Commission, 3000 Granny White Pike, Nashville, TN 37204; (615) 862–7970; www.nashville.gov/mch.

Description: The Battle of Nashville was one of the most strategic of the Civil War. Union forces had held this important city since February 1862. After losing Atlanta to Sherman, Gen. John Bell Hood moved his Army of Tennessee north, hoping to reclaim Nashville. On December 15–16, 1864, the Confederacy's last offensive action in Tennessee ended in the loss of the Army of Tennessee as an effective fighting force. The tour brochure includes a map and pertinent background information.

Admission Fees: Free.

Open to Public: Daily from dawn to dusk; Historical Commission office, Mon.–Fri. 8:00 A.M.–4:30 P.M.

Visitor Services: Information.

Regularly Scheduled Events: None.

Directions: Contact or visit the Metropolitan Historical Commission for a free brochure. From downtown Nashville take 12th Avenue South (Granny White Park) approximately 2.5 miles to Sevier Park. The Historical Commission is located in a historic yellow house inside the city park, at the corner of 12th and Kirkwood Avenue.

151 BELLE MEADE PLANTATION

5025 Harding Road, Nashville, TN 37205; (615) 356–0501 or (800) 270–3991; www.bellemeadeplantation.com.

Description: The Belle Meade Plantation was founded in 1807 by John Harding and eventually grew to 5,400 acres. When Tennessee entered the Civil War, Gov. Isham G. Harris appointed John Harding's son, William J. Harding, to the Military and Financial Board. During the Battle of Nashville in December 1864, Confederate Gen. James R. Chalmers made his headquarters at Belle Meade. Bullet scars from a cavalry skirmish on the front lawn are visible on the limestone columns of the front porch. After the war Belle Meade became one of the nation's finest stables for thoroughbred horses.

Admission Fees: Adults $11.00, children $5.00, seniors $10.00; group rates available.

Open to Public: Mon.–Sat. 9:00 A.M.–5:00 P.M., Sun. 11:00 A.M.–5:00 P.M.; last tour at 4:00 P.M.

Visitor Services: Public restrooms, information, handicapped access on first floor, gift shop, museum, tours.

Regularly Scheduled Events: Third weekend in September, Fall Fest (antiques, music, crafts, food, children's activities).

Directions: From I–440 take U.S. 70S exit; proceed approximately 4 miles on U.S. 70S; Belle Meade is on the left.

 BELMONT MANSION

1900 Belmont Boulevard, Nashville, TN 37212; (615) 460–5459; www.belmont mansion.com; info@belmontmansion .com.

Description: Belmont Mansion was built by Joseph and Adelicia Acklen in 1853 and enlarged in 1859–60. During the Civil War the house served as headquarters for Union Gen. David Stanley and for Gen. Thomas J. Wood, commander of the Fourth Army Corps. At Belmont, Wood gave orders to all division commanders for the first day of the Battle of Nashville.

Admission Fees: Adults $10.00, children $3.00, under six free, seniors $9.00, groups $8.00/person.

Open to Public: Mon.–Sat. 10:00 A.M.–4:00 P.M., Sun. 1:00 P.M.–4:00 P.M.; last tour at 3:15 P.M.

Visitor Services: Public restrooms, handicapped access, gift shop, tours.

Regularly Scheduled Events: Mid.-March, celebration of Adelicia Acklen's birthday;

Day after Thanksgiving–December, Christmas at Belmont.

Directions: From I–65 take Wedgewood exit. Travel west on Wedgewood Avenue. Turn left on Magnolia; turn left onto 18th Avenue; turn left onto Acklen Avenue.

 MOUNT OLIVET CEMETERY

1101 Lebanon Road, Nashville, TN 37210; (615) 255–4193; www.mountolivet .com.

Description: This cemetery is the final resting place of nearly 1,500 Confederate soldiers. The Confederate Circle Monument marks the remains of individuals of all ranks. Mount Olivet is also the burial place for seven generals.

Admission Fees: Free.

Open to Public: Grounds, daily 7:00 A.M.–dusk; office, Mon.–Fri. 8:30 A.M.–5:00 P.M., Sat.–Sun. 10:00 A.M.–4:00 P.M.

Visitor Services: Information.

Regularly Scheduled Events: Annual tour of cemetery with living history; call for schedule.

Directions: From I–40 exit at Fesslers Lane; proceed north on Fesslers Lane until it dead-ends into Hermitage Avenue/Levanon Road. Turn right onto this road and continue to Mount Olivet Cemetery, which is on the right, past Calvary Cemetery.

 TENNESSEE STATE MUSEUM AND STATE CAPITOL

505 Deaderick Street, Nashville, TN 37243; (615) 741–2692 or (800) 407–4324; www.tnmuseum. org; info@tnmuseum .org.

Description: The capitol was completed in 1859. The fortifications around the capitol consisted of four earthworks connected by a stockade with loopholes. The Tennessee State Museum traces the history of the state from prehistory until the early 1900s, including a large section on the Civil War. This section includes descriptions and artifacts from each major battle in Tennessee, audio-visual presentations, firearms, uniforms, paintings of notable soldiers, and a large collection of battle flags.

Admission Fees: Free.

Open to Public: State museum, Tues.–Sat. 10:00 A.M.–5:00 P.M., Sun. 1:00 P.M.–5:00 P.M.; state capitol, Mon.–Fri. 9:00 A.M.–4:00 P.M.

Visitor Services: State museum, public restrooms, information, handicapped access, gift shop; state capitol, information, guided tours.

Regularly Scheduled Events: None.

Directions: From I–40 take Broadway exit and travel toward downtown. From Broadway turn left onto Fifth Avenue; after third intersection, museum is on left at Fifth Avenue and Deaderick Street. State capitol is located 1 block away at Sixth and Charlotte Avenues.

 TRAVELLERS REST PLANTATION AND MUSEUM

636 Farrell Parkway, Nashville, TN 37220; (615) 832–8197 or (866) 832–8197; www.travellersrestplantation.org; travellersrest@earthlink.net.

Description: Travellers Rest Plantation was built in 1799 by Judge John Overton. His descendants occupied the home continuously until 1946. Union troops camped on the grounds during the Federal occupation of Nashville. For two weeks before the Battle of Nashville, Travellers Rest was the headquarters of Confederate commander Gen. John Bell Hood. Riding from Murfreesboro to confer with Hood, Gen. Nathan Bedford Forrest spent the night on December 11, 1864. During the second day of the Battle of Nashville, December 16, 1864, Federal forces charged the Confederate right flank on Peach Orchard Hill, located on the Overton property and within sight of the house. It was the scene of several charges by the U.S. Colored Infantry.

Admission Fees: Adults $10.00, children six–twelve $3.00, seniors $9.00; group rates available.

Open to Public: Mon.–Sat. 10:00 A.M.–4:00 P.M., Sun. 1:00 P.M.–4:00 P.M.

Visitor Services: Public restrooms, information, gift shop.

Regularly Scheduled Events: March, annual Civil War symposium.

Directions: Take I–65 south from downtown Nasvhille to exit 78 west. Go south on

Travellers Rest, Nashville, Tennessee. Courtesy of Travellers Rest.

Franklin Road to Lambert Drive and turn left onto Farrell Parkway. The entrance is on the left.

New Johnsonville

 156 JOHNSONVILLE STATE HISTORIC AREA

Route 1, P.O. Box 374, New Johnsonville, TN 37134; (931) 535–2789; www .state.tn.us/environment/parks/ johnsonville.

Description: On November 4, 1864, at Johnsonville, Gen. N. B. Forrest's cavalry took up artillery positions on the west bank of the Tennessee River. The Confederates destroyed the Federal depot at Johnsonville. Union losses in the raid were 4 gunboats, 14 steamboats, 17 barges, 33 cannons, and more than 75,000 tons of supplies valued at $6.7 million. Two large Civil War field fortifications are interpreted at the park.

Admission Fees: Free.

Open to Public: Daily 8:00 A.M.–sunset.

Visitor Services: Public restrooms, information, handicapped access, museum, picnic area, trails.

Regularly Scheduled Events: Every other year, reenactment, living history; call for schedule.

Directions: From I–40 at Memphis travel to Highway 13; go north to Waverly, to Highway 70 west; follow signs.

Parker's Crossroads

 157 PARKER'S CROSSROADS BATTLEFIELD SELF-GUIDED TOUR CWPT

c/o PCBA, P.O. Box 265, Parker's Crossroads, TN 38388; (731) 989–7944; www .parkerscrossroads.com.

Description: The Battle of Parker's Crossroads was fought on December 31, 1862. Union forces sought to capture Confederate troops on their return from their "First West Tennessee Raid." When Confederate Gen. Nathan Bedford Forrest found himself caught between two Union forces at Parker's Crossroads, each roughly the size of his own, he ordered his troops to "charge both ways" and made a successful escape.

Admission Fees: Free.

Open to Public: Daily from dawn to dusk.

Visitor Services: Restrooms; free brochure available at Log Cabin Welcome Center or by request through the mail or Web site.

Regularly Scheduled Events: Every even-numbered year in June, reenactment of the Battle of Parker's Crossroads.

Directions: The site is traversed by I–40; starts at I–40 and Highway 22 at exit 108.

Pocahontas

 158 DAVIS BRIDGE BATTLEFIELD CWPT

Essary Springs Road, Pocahontas, TN 38061; (731) 658–6554.

Description: After the Battle of Corinth on October 5, 1862, the retreating Confederate army under Gens. Sterling Price and Earl Van Dorn met Gen. Edward Ord and 8,000 Union troops at Davis Bridge over the Hatchie River. An all-day battle for the bridge ensued. The Confederates managed to hold off the attacking Union forces and cross the Hatchie farther south at Crum's Mill.

Admission Fees: Free.

Open to Public: Daily from dawn to dusk.

Visitor Services: Interpretive signs, monument and flag memorial.

Regularly Scheduled Events: Call for schedule of reenactments and living history.

Directions: From I–40 at Jackson take Highway 45 south to Highway 18; take Highway 18 south to Bolivar. At Bolivar continue south on Highway 125 to Middleton. Turn left on Highway 57 east to Pocahontas Road. Turn right on Pocahontas Road, bear left on Essary Springs Road, and travel approximately 1.5 miles. Look for signs.

SOUTHERN HEARTLAND

SAVANNAH

TENNESSEE RIVER MUSEUM

495 Main Street, Savannah, TN 38372; (901) 925–2363 or (800) 552–3866; www.tourhardincounty.org; teamhardin@charterinternet.com.

Description: The Tennessee River was the invasion route for the Union armies in the West. Exhibits at the museum include *The War on the River*, which begins with a one-half-scale model of the bow of the USS *Cairo*. The exhibit contains many artifacts from this ill-fated ironclad and other gunboats. The *Army* exhibit features a collection of Shiloh field artillery, firearms, and personal items. The *Johnsonville* exhibit features Gen. Nathan Bedford Forrest's cavalrymen.

Admission Fees: Adults $2.00, children under eighteen free.

Open to Public: Mon.–Sat. 9:00 A.M.–5:00 P.M., Sun. 1:00 P.M.–5:00 P.M.

Visitor Services: Public restrooms, information, handicapped access, gift shop.

Regularly Scheduled Events: None.

Directions: From I–40 take Highway 22 to Crump; stay on Highway 22/64; cross Tennessee River; stay on Highway 64 into Savannah (becomes Main Street). Tennessee River Museum is at 495 Main Street.

SHILOH

SHILOH NATIONAL MILITARY PARK CWPT

1055 Pittsburgh Landing Road, Shiloh, TN 38376; (731) 689–5275; www.nps .gov/shil.

Description: Gen. Albert Sidney Johnston's Army of the Mississippi, marching north from its base at Corinth, attacked and partially overran Ulysses S. Grant's Federal Army of the Tennessee. The April 6–7, 1862, Battle of Shiloh was the first large-scale conflict of the Civil War, and the magnitude of casualties shocked the nation. There were 65,000 Federal troops at Shiloh and 13,000 casualties. Confederate troop strength was 44,700, with 10,700 casualties.

Admission Fees: Adults $3.00, families $5.00.

Open to Public: Daily 8:00 A.M.–5:00 P.M.

Visitor Services: Public restrooms, infor-

Shiloh National Military Park, Shiloh, Tennessee. Chris E. Heisey–CWPT files.

mation, handicapped access, gift shop, museum, trails.

Regularly Scheduled Events: First weekend in April, Living History Weekend.

Directions: From I–40 at Parker's Crossroads, travel south on Highway 22, 57 miles south to Shiloh Park entrance; follow signs.

Smyrna

161 SAM DAVIS HOME

1399 Sam Davis Road, Smyrna, TN 37167; (615) 459–2341; www.samdavis home.org.

Description: The Sam Davis Home is the family home and farm of Tennessee's "Boy Hero of the Confederacy," Sam Davis. The land consists of 168 acres of the original 800-acre plantation. Sam Davis was serving as a member of the Coleman Scouts when he was captured by the Union army and accused of being a spy. He was executed at age twenty-one.

Admission Fees: Adults $8.50 (CWPT members receive a discount), children $3.00, seniors $6.50; group rates available.

Open to Public: June–Aug., Mon.–Sat. 9:00 A.M.–5:00 P.M., Sun. 1:00 P.M.–5:00 P.M.; Sept.–May, Mon.–Sat. 10:00 A.M.–4:00 P.M., Sun: 1:00 P.M.–4:00 P.M.; last tour one hour before closing.

Visitor Services: Public restrooms, information, limited handicapped access, gift shop, museum.

Regularly Scheduled Events: May, Days on the Farm; June, Civil War Show; September, Heritage Days; December, Civil War Christmas.

Directions: From I–24 east take exit 66B; go approximately 5.5 miles to Sam Davis Road. From I–24 west take exit 70; proceed approximately 5 miles to Sam Davis Road.

Spring Hill

162 RIPPAVILLA PLANTATION

5700 Main Street, Spring Hill, TN 37174; (931) 486–9037; www.rippavilla .org; info@rippavilla.org.

Description: Rippavilla Plantation was completed in 1853. Early in the Civil War its owner, Confederate Maj. Nathaniel Cheairs, had carried the white flag of surrender to Gen. Ulysses S. Grant at Fort Donelson. On November 30, 1864, Major Cheairs welcomed Confederate Gen. John Bell Hood and his ranking officers to breakfast. It was here that Hood angrily accused his staff of letting the entire Federal army escape to Franklin. Five Confederate generals at that breakfast were dead by evening in the bloody Battle of Franklin.

Admission Fees: Adults $8.00, children six–twelve $4.00, seniors $6.00.

Open to Public: Mon.–Sat. 9:00 A.M.–5:00 P.M.; Sun. 1:00 P.M.–5:00 P.M.

Visitor Services: Public restrooms, information, limited handicapped access, gift shop, museum.

Regularly Scheduled Events: Call or check Web site for events.

Directions: From I–65, 35 miles south of Nashville, take Saturn Parkway; travel west on Saturn Parkway 5 miles and take exit 31 south. Rippavilla is the first drive off the exit.

163 SPRING HILL BATTLEFIELD <u>CWPT</u>

c/o Civil War Preservation Trust, 1331 H Street NW, Suite 1001, Washington, DC 20005; (202) 367–1861; www.civilwar.org.

Description: A prelude to the Battle of Franklin, the Battle of Spring Hill was fought on November 29, 1864. The main fight was preceded by cavalry skirmishes between troops under the command of Confederate Maj. Gen. Nathan Bedford Forrest and Union Brig. Gen. James H. Wilson. Confederates under Gen. John Bell Hood crossed

SOUTHERN HEARTLAND

the Duck River to assault a reinforced Federal position at the crossroads in Spring Hill. By late afternoon, the piecemeal Southern attack had been repulsed. The victorious Northern troops now had an open road to Franklin, where the entire army was congregating in preparation for the next day's massive battle.

Admission Fees: Free.

Open to Public: Daily from dawn to dusk.

Visitor Services: Interpretive signage.

Regularly Scheduled Events: None.

Directions: From Spring Hill take Highway 31 south to Kedron Parkway. Turn left and proceed about 0.75 mile. CWPT property stretches along the western side of the road, almost to the entrance to Saturn Parkway.

 TENNESSEE ANTEBELLUM TRAIL

5700 Main Street, Spring Hill, TN 37174; (800) 381–1865.

Description: A 90-mile self-driving loop tour featuring more than fifty-five Civil War sites, battlefields, antebellum homes, and plantations. The route traces Gen. John Bell Hood's Nashville campaign from Spring Hill through Franklin, and north to Nashville. Historic homes are open to the public along the trail, each playing an important role in the campaign. The homes include the following:

- Belle Meade Plantation
- Belmont Mansion
- Travellers Rest
- Carnton Plantation
- Rippavilla Plantation
- The Athenaeum
- Polk Home

  Other significant sites include the following:

- McGavock Confederate Cemetery
- Winstead Hill
- Spring Hill Battlefield

Admission Fees: Range from $6.00 to $11.00 at each of the sites.

Open to Public: The trail is open daily. The seven historic homes have varying hours but are generally open Mon.–Sat. 10:00 A.M.–5:00 P.M., Sun. 1:00 P.M.–5:00 P.M.

Visitor Services: The free map guide to the trail is available from the address and phone listed earlier. The seven historic homes have tours, gift shops, and restrooms. The map guide includes bed-and-breakfasts, dining establishments, and antiques shops along the trail.

Regularly Scheduled Events: December, Majestic Middle Tennessee home tour; the map guide includes an extensive calendar of events.

Directions: The tour can be started at any point along the trail. The map guide provides detailed directions.

TULLAHOMA

 TULLAHOMA CAMPAIGN CIVIL WAR TRAIL

Tennessee's Backroads, P.O. Box 52, Tullahoma, TN 37388; (615) 454–9446 or (800) 799–6131; www.tennesseeback roads.org; info@tennesseebackroads .org.

Description: The Tullahoma Campaign Civil War Trail is a 130-mile trail that links historic sites, cemeteries, museums, and battlefield sites together in what one brochure describes as the story of the "cat and mouse" maneuvers of the Union and Confederate forces before the Confederate retreat to Chattanooga, January–July 4, 1863.

Admission Fees: Free.

Open to Public: Daily from dawn to dusk.

Visitor Services: The "Tennessee Backroads Tullahoma Campaign Civil War Trail" brochure is free and available from the Tennessee Backroads office at (800) 799–6131. All sites are free and open to the public unless noted as private property.

Regularly Scheduled Events: None.

Directions: From I–24 exit 111, travel 12 miles to Tullahoma, take a right on Highway

41A north and travel 2 blocks. The building is on the left-hand side at 300 South Street.

WARTRACE

 HISTORIC CHOCKLEY TAVERN

111 Spring Street, Wartrace, TN 37183; (615) 389–0545; www.chockleytavern .com; mschockley@charter.net.

Description: Standing at a strategic junction in the Duck River Line established by the Army of Tennessee in 1863, Chockley Tavern, circa 1852, served as headquarters for Gen. Patrick Cleburne's division, Gen. William Hardee's corps, from March 1863 until June when the Army retreated under attack toward Chattanooga.

Admission Fees: Free.
Open to Public: Sat. 11:00 A.M.–5:00 P.M.; other times and services by appointment.
Visitor Services: Public restrooms, information, handicapped access, gift shop, educational seminars and interpretive tours available for all ages.
Regularly Scheduled Events: Call or check Web site for events.
Directions: From I–24 take exit 97 at Hoover Gap Battlefield/Beechgrove Confederate Cemetery. Take Scenic Route 64 (Walking Horse Parkway) west 10 miles toward Wartrace/Shelbyville and turn onto Route 269 in Wartrace. The tavern faces the mainline railroad tracks.

SOUTHERN HEARTLAND

MIDWEST

❖ ILLINOIS ❖

ALTON

ALTON MILITARY PRISON SITE

**212 William Street, Alton, IL 62002;
(618) 465–6676; www.visitalton.com.**

Description: Erected as the first Illinois State Penitentiary, it served as the Alton Federal Military Prison from February 1862 to July 1865, housing more than 15,000 prisoners during the Civil War. Confederate prisoners of war, Federal soldiers, guerrillas, and civilians were held as prisoners. More than 2,000 died of disease. A portion of the prison wall remains. A monument to 1,543 Confederate soldiers who died at the prison is located 2 miles north of the site.

Admission Fees: Free.

Open to Public: Daily from dawn to dusk.

Visitor Services: Interpretive signage.

Regularly Scheduled Events: None.

Directions: From I–270 take Route 367 north. Cross Clark Bridge and turn left at the Alton end of the bridge. Follow U.S. 67 to Broadway and turn left. Proceed 2 blocks to Williams Street and turn right. Proceed ½ block; the prison site is on the left.

CAIRO

CAIRO PUBLIC LIBRARY

1609 Washington Avenue, P.O. Box 151, Cairo, IL 62914; (618) 734–1840.

Description: Cairo played a critical role in the Civil War. Projecting deeply into the South, controlling major waterways and railroads, Cairo was a bastion for the Union. Gen. Ulysses S. Grant's Army of the Tennessee, the siege of Vicksburg, and the naval battle for the Mississippi were all launched from Cairo's riverbanks. The library contains an extensive collection of primary and secondary research documents relating to the city's role in the Union army's control of the western theater in the Civil War.

Admission Fees: Free.

Open to Public: Mon.–Fri. 10:00 A.M.–5:00 P.M.

Visitor Services: Information.

Regularly Scheduled Events: None.

Directions: From I–57 take exit 1 and proceed south on U.S. 51 to downtown Cairo. The library is located on the west side of Washington Avenue.

CUSTOMS HOUSE

1400 Washington Avenue, Cairo, IL 62914-0724; (618) 734–9632.

Description: This local history museum offers exhibits on Cairo's pivotal role in the Civil War. These include artifacts from the USS *Cairo,* a gunboat built in the local shipyards which was sunk by a Confederate torpedo in 1862 and raised in 1964.

Admission Fees: $2.00.

Open to Public: Mon.–Fri. 10:00 A.M.–noon and 1:00 P.M.–3:00 P.M.

Visitor Services: Information, museum.

Regularly Scheduled Events: None.

Directions: From I–57 take exit 1 and proceed south on U.S. 51 to downtown Cairo. The Customs House is located on the east side of Washington Avenue.

CHICAGO

ROSEHILL CEMETERY AND CIVIL WAR MUSEUM

5800 North Ravenswood Avenue, Chicago, IL 60660; (773) 561–5940.

Description: Rosehill Cemetery contains the graves of fourteen Union generals, six drummer boys, and hundreds of Civil War soldiers. Members of the Eighth Illinois Cavalry, the unit that fired the first shots at Gettysburg, are buried here. Also buried

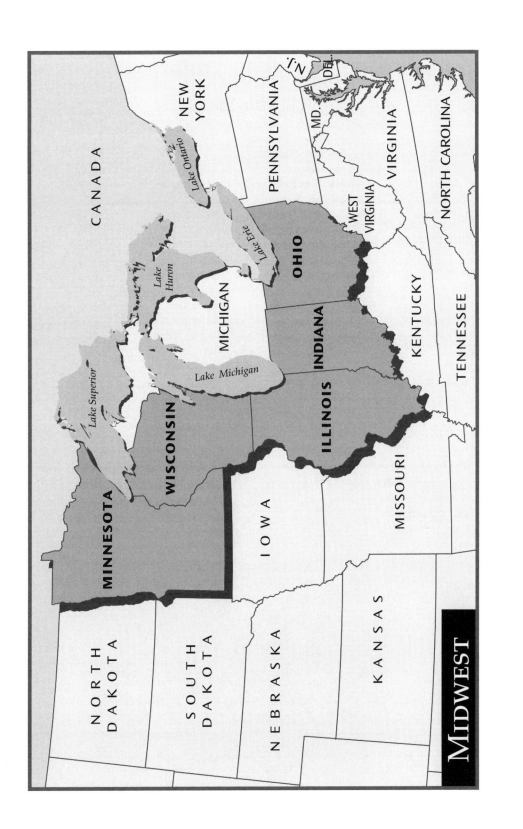

CANADA

NEW YORK

Lake Ontario

PENNSYLVANIA

N.J.

DEL.

MD.

WEST VIRGINIA

VIRGINIA

NORTH CAROLINA

Lake Erie

OHIO

KENTUCKY

TENNESSEE

Lake Huron

MICHIGAN

INDIANA

Lake Superior

Lake Michigan

WISCONSIN

ILLINOIS

MINNESOTA

MISSOURI

IOWA

NORTH DAKOTA

SOUTH DAKOTA

NEBRASKA

KANSAS

MIDWEST

Illinois Sites

1   Alton Military Prison Site
2   Cairo Public Library
3   Customs House
4   Rosehill Cemetery and Civil War Museum
5   Illinois Iron Furnace
6   U. S. Grant Home State Historic Site
7   Thomas Lincoln Cemetery
8   Mound City National Cemetery
9   General John A. Logan Museum
10   Bureau County Historical Society Museum
11   Rock Island Arsenal Museum and Rock Island Arsenal
12   St. Charles Heritage Center and Camp Kane
13   Abraham Lincoln Presidential Library and Museum
14   Camp Butler National Cemetery
15   Daughters of Union Veterans of the Civil War
16   Grand Army of the Republic Memorial Museum
17   Lincoln Home National Historic Site
18   Lincoln Tomb, Oak Ridge Cemetery
19   Museum of Funeral Customs
20   Old State Capitol

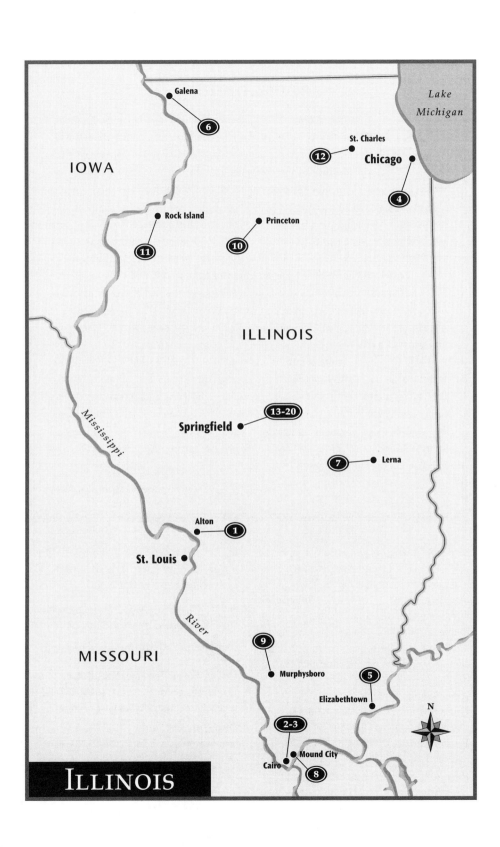

ROSEHILL CEMETERY

Rosehill Cemetery is nothing less than 350 sprawling acres of American history. Every walk through the cemetery reveals different gravestones, and every new marker reveals a different story. The stories may be old, but they are not simply relics of a bygone people facing bygone challenges. To me, one of the most fascinating stories of those resting in the cemetery is that of Thomas Ransom.

Ransom was a Union general nicknamed the "Phantom Ghost," who was thought to be dead several times after sustaining serious wounds, yet somehow he survived and remained in the army. He eventually passed away while marching with Gen. William T. Sherman on Sherman's famous March to the Sea. In these trying times we look for inspiration and resilience like that shown by Thomas Ransom. And as we look to our elders, ancestors, and other great Americans for examples, we need look no further than Rosehill Cemetery. Rosehill is the resting place of more than 1,500 Chicago notables, but among their memorials, none are as poignant as the graves of the Union soldiers.

Today, we compare the great courage and sacrifice of the Union soldiers with that of the firefighters and police officers who rose to a tremendous challenge on September 11, 2001. Both the Union soldiers and the rescue workers responding to the terrorist attacks saw their country facing great adversity. These brave patriots did not shrink from the fire, rather, they charged ahead. As we move forward in our fight for freedom, we draw strength from such historical sights as Rosehill Cemetery. Rosehill Cemetery is not only a marker of the past, but also a reminder of the present and future.

—U.S. Congressman Mark Steven Kirk, Illinois

here is a Chicago mayor who was charged with, and later acquitted of, assisting Confederate prisoners in escaping from Camp Douglas. A portion of the administration building is devoted to a Civil War museum that features exhibits on the war, emphasizing the roles of those who are buried in the cemetery and the city of Chicago's part in the conflict.

Admission Fees: Free.

Open to Public: Mon.–Sat. 8:00 A.M.–4:00 P.M., Sun. 10:00 A.M.–5:00 P.M.

Visitor Services: Public restrooms, information, handicapped access, tours.

Regularly Scheduled Events: None.

Directions: From I–94 (Edens Expressway) travel east on Foster Avenue and then north on Ravenswood. From Lake Shore Drive travel north on Lake Shore (U.S. 41), then west on Foster to Ravenswood.

ELIZABETHTOWN

 ILLINOIS IRON FURNACE

USDA Forest Service, RR2 Box 4, Elizabethtown, IL 62931; (618) 287–2201; www.fs.fed.us/r9/forests/shawnee.

Description: During the Civil War this structure was a principal furnace used for smelting iron ore. The restored structure features interpretive information; fishing, hiking, and picnicking facilities are available.

Admission Fees: Free.

Open to Public: Daily 6:00 A.M.–10:00 P.M.
Visitor Services: Information, fishing, hiking, picnicking.
Regularly Scheduled Events: None.
Directions: Located about 5 miles from Rosiclare near the intersection of Routes 146 and 34. Follow signs.

GALENA

 U. S. GRANT HOME STATE HISTORIC SITE

500 Bouthillier Street, Galena, IL 61036; (815) 777–3310; www.granthome.com; granthome@granthome.com.

Description: On August 18, 1865, citizens of Galena celebrated the return of Civil War hero Gen. Ulysses S. Grant by presenting him with this handsome furnished home. The house is typical of the Italianate style and is furnished with many original items from the Grant family.
Admission Fees: Suggested donations, adults $3.00, children seventeen and under $1.00.
Open to Public: Daily 9:00 A.M.–4:45 P.M.; winter hours, Wed.–Sun. 9:00 A.M.–4:00 P.M.;

closed most state and federal holidays.
Visitor Services: Public restrooms, information, museum, tours.
Regularly Scheduled Events: Call or check Web site for events.
Directions: Galena is located off of U.S. 20; follow signs to the Grant home. Galena is 160 miles from Chicago; 85 miles from Moline; and 95 miles from Madison, Wisconsin.

LERNA

 THOMAS LINCOLN CEMETERY

12988 Lincoln Highway, Lerna, IL 62440; (217) 345–1845.

Description: This cemetery is the final resting place for many Civil War veterans and for Thomas and Sarah Lincoln, Abraham Lincoln's father and stepmother.
Admission Fees: Free.
Open to Public: Daily from dawn to dusk.
Visitor Services: None.
Regularly Scheduled Events: None.
Directions: From I–59 exit at Route 16 east and proceed toward Charleston. At the first

MIDWEST

Ulysses S. Grant's Home, Galena, Illinois. Jim Quick–CWPT files.

traffic light, turn south; follow markers to Lincoln Memorial Highway to Thomas Lincoln Cemetery (approximately 10 miles).

MOUND CITY

 MOUND CITY NATIONAL CEMETERY

Highway Junction 37 and 51, Mound City, IL 62963; (314) 260–8691 or (800) 535–1117; www.cem.va.gov.

Description: During the Civil War the large naval shipyards around Mound City provided the eighty-vessel Union Mississippi Squadron with warships, including the USS *Cairo,* USS *Cincinnati,* and USS *Mound City.* The hotel and foundry in Mound City were converted to a large Civil War hospital complex that served both Union and Confederate casualties at Shiloh and Vicksburg. In 1864 the federal government designated a plot of land near the general hospital to serve as a national cemetery. Today approximately 2,300 known and 2,400 unknown Civil War soldiers are buried in the cemetery.

Admission Fees: Free.

Open to Public: Daily from dawn to dusk

Visitor Services: Contact Jefferson Barracks National Cemetery at (800) 535–1117 for grave location information.

Regularly Scheduled Events: None.

Directions: From I–57 take the Mounds exit and follow signs to U.S. 51. Turn left and travel 4 miles to the cemetery.

MURPHYSBORO

 GENERAL JOHN A. LOGAN MUSEUM

1613 Edith Street, Murphysboro, IL 62966; (618) 684–3455; www.logan museum.org; johnaloganmuseum @globaleyes.net.

Description: The museum, located on the site of Maj. Gen. John A. Logan's birth, focuses on the lives and times of Logan and the volunteer soldiers of the Civil War before, during, and after the war. Logan, considered by some historians to be the best of the political generals to serve in the war, wrote the book *The Volunteer Soldier;* was three times commander in chief of the Grand Army of the Republic; established Memorial Day as a national holiday; and, as a major political force at the end of the nineteenth century, fought for pensions for Union veterans. The site also includes the 1887 home of Samuel B. Dalton, former slave and Civil War veteran.

Admission Fees: Free.

Open to Public: Tues.–Sun. 1:00 P.M.–4:00 P.M.; Sept.–May, closed Sun.

Visitor Services: Public restrooms, information, handicapped access, gift shop (10 percent discount for CWPT members), tours.

Regularly Scheduled Events: None.

Directions: From I–57 take the Carbondale exit at Marion, Illinois; follow Illinois Highway 13 through Carbondale to Murphysboro; take Illinois 149 (Walnut Street) through Murphysboro and at 17th Street turn left; drive 2 blocks and turn left on Edith Street.

PRINCETON

 BUREAU COUNTY HISTORICAL SOCIETY MUSEUM

109 Park Avenue West, Princeton, IL 61356-1927; (815) 875–2184; www .bureaucountymuseum.com; bchs museum@yahoo.com.

Description: The Ninety-third Illinois Infantry was mustered from Bureau County for service in the Union army. The Bureau County Historical Museum contains an outstanding and extensive collection of artifacts and documents associated with the regiment. The collection is well researched and documented.

Admission Fees: Adults $3.00, children $1.00.

Open to Public: Tues.–Wed., Sun. 1:00 P.M.– 5:00 P.M.; closed Mon.; closed Dec.–Feb.

Visitor Services: Gift shop, tours, genealogy research.

Regularly Scheduled Events: September, cemetery tour.

Directions: From I–80 take Princeton exit; proceed into Princeton (this road becomes Main Street). Continue on Main through two business districts to the four-way stop, just before the courthouse. Turn right onto Park Avenue, which curves around. The museum is located at the end of the curve, across from the courthouse.

ROCK ISLAND

ROCK ISLAND ARSENAL MUSEUM AND ROCK ISLAND ARSENAL

Building 60, Rock Island Arsenal, Rock Island, IL 61299-5000; (309) 782–5021; www.ria.army.mil.

Description: This was the site of the Rock Island Prison barracks, a Confederate prison camp. The cemetery contains the graves of nearly 2,000 Confederate prisoners. The adjoining national cemetery is the burial place of Union prison guards and military veterans. The museum displays the history of Rock Island Arsenal and features an extensive collection of small arms. Rock Island Arsenal is currently an active U.S. Army installation.

Admission Fees: Free.

Open to Public: Tues.–Sun. 10:00 A.M.–4:00 P.M.; closed major holidays. Valid photo ID required for entrance to military base.

Visitor Services: Public restrooms, information, handicapped access, gift shop, food available Monday through Friday.

Regularly Scheduled Events: None.

Directions: From I–74 in Moline take Seventh Avenue exit west to 14th Street. Turn right and follow to the island. Follow signs to museum.

ST. CHARLES

ST. CHARLES HERITAGE CENTER AND CAMP KANE

215 East Main Street, St. Charles, IL 60174; (630) 584–6967; www.stcmuseum .org; info@stcmuseum.org.

Description: St. Charles played an important role in the Civil War. It served as a training ground for the Eighth and Seventeenth Illinois Cavalry, as a recruiting center, and as home to Gen. John Farnsworth. The museum exhibits artifacts, pictures, and written information about the community's association with the Underground Railroad and the Civil War. Camp Kane trained more than 1,000 men for the Union army. General Farnsworth donated the land for Camp Kane, which today is a community park. The museum interprets the Civil War history of St. Charles and Camp Kane.

Admission Fees: Suggested donation, adults $2.00, seniors and students $1.00.

Open to Public: Tues.–Sat. 10:00 A.M.–4:00 P.M., Sun. noon–4:00 P.M.; Langum Park (former site of Camp Kane) is open daily from dawn to dusk.

Visitor Services: Public restrooms, information, handicapped access, gift shop, museum.

Regularly Scheduled Events: Call or check Web site for events.

Directions: From I–88 exit at North Farnsworth; follow north to Route 64 (Main Street), turn left (west) on Main Street, and proceed into downtown. Museum is at the northeast corner of Third Avenue and Main Street.

MIDWEST

ABRAHAM LINCOLN PRESIDENTIAL LIBRARY AND MUSEUM

212 North Sixth Street, Springfield, IL 62701; (217) 782–5764 or (800) 610–2094; www.alplm.org.

Description: The Abraham Lincoln Presidential Library and Museum collects the political, social, business, and military history of Illinois. The collections include many Civil War letters, manuscripts, photographs, maps, Illinois regimental histories, and other memorabilia. The collections also include the largest single collection devoted to the pre-presidential career of Abraham Lincoln. At the museum, visitors can experience the life and legacy of the sixteenth president from his birth in Kentucky to his assassination and return to Springfield, Illinois.

Admission Fees: Free.

Open to Public: Library, Mon.–Tues. and Thurs.–Fri. 9:00 A.M.–4:30 P.M., Wed. 9:00 A.M.–8:30 P.M., Sun. 8:30 A.M.–3:30 P.M.; museum, daily 9:00 A.M.–5:00 P.M., Wed. 9:00 A.M.–8:30 P.M.

Visitor Services: Public restrooms, information, handicapped access, gift shop, food, museum, research library.

Regularly Scheduled Events: None.

Directions: From I–55 take the West Clear Lake Avenue exit. Proceed west on Clear Lake, which turns into Jefferson Street. Turn right onto Sixth Street. The parking ramp is off Sixth Street between Madison and Mason streets.

 CAMP BUTLER NATIONAL CEMETERY

5063 Camp Butler Road, Springfield, IL 62707; (217) 492–4070; www.cem.va.gov.

Description: This was once the site of a Union Civil War training camp and prison for approximately 2,000 Confederate soldiers. It is now a cemetery for veterans and their dependents.

Admission Fees: Free.

Open to Public: Office, Mon.–Fri. 8:00 A.M.–4:30 P.M.; grounds, daily from dawn to dusk.

Visitor Services: Public restrooms, information.

Regularly Scheduled Events: Memorial Day, program and Avenue of Flags displayed; November, Veterans Day program.

Directions: From I–55 south take exit 100. From I–55 north take exit 100A. From I–72 exit at Camp Butler Road; continue north on Camp Butler Road to the cemetery entrance.

 DAUGHTERS OF UNION VETERANS OF THE CIVIL WAR

503 South Walnut Street, Springfield, IL 62704-1932; (217) 544–0616.

Description: Collections of this museum include Civil War medals, photographs, currency, drums, uniforms, and a complete set of the official records.

Admission Fees: Free; donations welcome.

Open to Public: Apr.–Sept., Mon.–Sat. 9:00 A.M.–4:00 P.M.; Oct.–Mar., Mon.–Sat. 10:00 A.M.–3:00 P.M.

Visitor Services: Gift shop, museum.

Regularly Scheduled Events: None.

Directions: From I–55 take the South Grand Avenue west exit to Walnut Street.

 GRAND ARMY OF THE REPUBLIC MEMORIAL MUSEUM

629 South Seventh Street, Springfield, IL 62703; (217) 522–4373; www.gar-museum.com; beardhd@yahoo.com.

Description: This museum includes a large assortment of Civil War memorabilia, including tintypes by Civil War photographer Matthew Brady.

Admission Fees: Free; donations welcomed.

Open to Public: Tues.–Sat. 10:00 A.M.–4:00 P.M.; closed Dec. 15–first Tuesday in Mar.

Visitor Services: None.

Regularly Scheduled Events: April 15, Anniversary of Lincoln's Death Open House.

Lincoln Home, Springfield, Illinois. David Wachtreitl–CWPT files.

Directions: From I–55 take the South Grand Avenue west exit to Ninth Street; turn north on Ninth Street to Cook Street; turn west on Cook Street to Seventh Street.

 LINCOLN HOME NATIONAL HISTORIC SITE
17
426 South Seventh Street, Springfield, IL 62701; (217) 492–4241; www.nps.gov/ liho; liho_information@nps.gov.

Description: The Lincoln Home National Historic Site preserves 4 city blocks surrounding the only home Abraham Lincoln ever owned. Erected in 1839, the house was purchased by Lincoln in 1844 and served as the Lincolns' home for seventeen years until their departure for Washington, D.C., in 1861.

Admission Fees: Free.

Open to Public: Daily 8:30 A.M.–5:00 P.M.

Visitor Services: Public restrooms, gift shop, museum, tours.

Regularly Scheduled Events: None.

Directions: From I–55 take the South Grand

Avenue west exit to Ninth Street; turn north on Ninth Street and proceed to Capitol Avenue; turn west on Capitol Avenue to Seventh Street; turn south to the Lincoln Home Visitors Center.

 LINCOLN TOMB, OAK RIDGE CEMETERY
18
1500 Monument Avenue, Springfield, IL 62702; (217) 782–2717; www.state.il .us.hpa.

Description: The 117-foot-tall tomb is constructed of granite and is the final resting place of President Abraham Lincoln; his wife, Mary; and three of their four children: Edward, William, and Thomas. Near the entrance is a bronze bust of Lincoln. The tomb designer, Larkin Mead, created the monumental bronze military statues and the statue of Lincoln on the terrace. Mead's design has been popularly interpreted as symbolizing Lincoln's role in the preservation of the Union.

Admission Fees: Free.

Open to Public: Daily 9:00 A.M.–5:00 P.M.; site closes at 4:00 P.M. Nov.–Feb.; closed NewYear's Day, Martin Luther King Jr. Day, Presidents Day, Election Day,Veterans Day, Thanksgiving, and Christmas.

Visitor Services: Public restrooms, information, handicapped access.

Regularly Scheduled Events: None.

Directions: From I–55 take Sangamon Avenue exit to Fifth Street. Turn left on Fifth Street to North Grand; turn right on North Grand Avenue to Monument Avenue; turn right on Monument to the cemetery.

 MUSEUM OF FUNERAL CUSTOMS

1440 Monument Avenue, Springfield, IL 62702; (217) 544–3480; www.funeral museum.org; funeralmuseum@ifda.org.

Description: Embalming came to America in 1840, but it was not widely used until the need arose during the Civil War to prepare bodies for shipment to their homes for interment. This use of embalming on soldiers and, after his assassination, on President Lincoln is credited with popularizing the technique as well as demonstrating to the public the positive effect of embalming and funeral services. Civil War embalmers were private contractors who contributed to the development of a profession. At the museum a home parlor, circa 1865, re-creates a home funeral service. You can also see a full-size reproduction of Abraham Lincoln's coffin and a scale model of Lincoln's railroad coach and Chicago funeral arch.

Admission Fees: Adults $4.00; children six–seventeen $2.00, under five free, seniors $3.00.

Open to Public: Tues.–Sat. 10:00 A.M.–4:00 P.M., Sun. 1:00 P.M.–4:00 P.M.; closed major holidays.

Visitor Services: Public restrooms, information, handicapped access, gift shop.

Regularly Scheduled Events: None.

Directions: From I–55 take exit 100A/B west on Sangamon Avenue to Peoria Road; turn southwest and go to North Grand Avenue; turn right, drive to Monument Avenue, and turn right again. Museum is at the end of the street, just outside the gate to Oak Ridge Cemetery.

 OLD STATE CAPITOL

1 Old State Capitol Plaza, Springfield, IL 62701; (217) 785–7960; www.oldstate capitol.org.

Description: The Old State Capitol is a magnificently restored Greek Revival building that served as the center of the Illinois government from 1839 to 1876. U.S. senator Stephen Douglas and a young legislator, Abraham Lincoln, were powerful figures who frequented the halls of the capitol. Abraham Lincoln delivered his famous "House Divided"speech in the Representatives Hall and, in 1865, lay in state at the capitol building before his interment in Oak Ridge Cemetery.

Admission Fees: Free.

Open to Public: Daily 9:00 A.M.–5:00 P.M.; Sept.–Apr. 15, closed Sun. and Mon.; closed state and national holidays.

Visitor Services: Public restrooms, handicapped access from elevator in kiosk south of the main entrance, Braille guide available, gift shop, museum, tours.

Regularly Scheduled Events: None.

Directions: From I–55 take Clear Lake exit to Ninth Street; turn south on Ninth Street to Adams Street; turn west on Adams Street to the Old State Capitol.

❖ INDIANA ❖

CORYDON

 CORYDON BATTLEFIELD

c/o 310 North Elm Street, Corydon, IN 47112; (888) 738–2137; www.thisis indiana.org.

Description: The Battle of Corydon was the only official Civil War battle in Indiana, and the battle site is the only one north of the Ohio River. The site commemorates the effort of Confederate Gen. John Hunt Morgan to spread the war to the north. The Corydon Battlefield is a five-acre park located on the east side of Route 135, just south of Corydon. The park is a heavily wooded area covered with hardwood trees, some of which date from 1863. Although the park area looks much as it did in 1863, a drive to a parking lot on the property, several historic markers, and a log cabin moved to the site in the 1930s represent changes to the historic landscape.

Admission Fees: Free.

Open to Public: Daily from dawn to dusk.

Visitor Services: Information.

Regularly Scheduled Events: None.

Directions: From I–64 take Route 135 (exit 105) south through Corydon. The battle site is approximately 1 mile south of the city.

CRAWFORDSVILLE

 GENERAL LEW WALLACE STUDY AND MUSEUM

200 Wallace Avenue, Crawfordsville, IN 47933; (765) 362–5769; www.ben-hur .com; study@wico.net.

Description: The site encompasses the personal study of Lew Wallace, who was commissioned colonel of the Eleventh Indiana Volunteer Infantry in 1861. Wallace was pro-

General Lew Wallace Study and Museum, Crawfordsville, Indiana. CWPT files.

Indiana and Ohio Sites

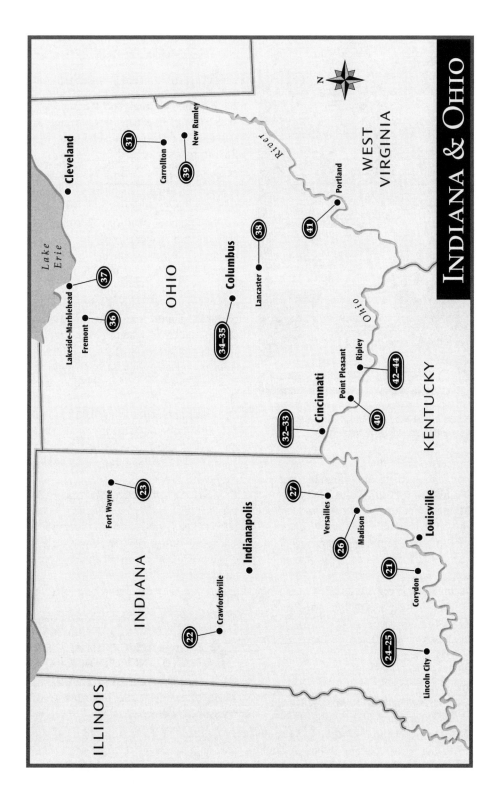

INDIANA & OHIO

Statue of Lew Wallace, Crawfordsville, Indiana.
General Lew Wallace Study and Museum.

moted to major general within the year and led troops at Fort Donelson, Shiloh, and Monocacy, among other battles. He served on courts-martial for the Lincoln conspirators and for Henry Wirz, Commander of Andersonville prison camp. He is best known as the author of *Ben-Hur.*

Admission Fees: Adults $3.00, students $1.00, no charge for children under six.

Open to Public: Feb.–mid. Dec., Wed.–Sat. 10:00 A.M.–5:00 P.M., Sun. 1:00 P.M.–5:00 P.M. extended summer hours.

Visitor Services: Public restrooms, information, gift shop.

Regularly Scheduled Events: Call or check Web site for schedule of events.

Directions: From I–74 exit U.S. 231 south to downtown, turn left on Wabash Avenue, go 4 blocks to Elston Avenue, turn left, and go 1 block.

FORT WAYNE

 THE LINCOLN MUSEUM

200 East Berry Street, Fort Wayne, IN 46802; (260) 455–3864; www.thelincoln museum.org; lincoln.museum@the lincolnmuseum.org.

Description: The museum's award-winning permanent exhibit, *Abraham Lincoln and the American Experiment,* includes eleven exhibit galleries featuring hundreds of artifacts and artwork from Lincoln's era. Eighteen interactive exhibits allow visitors to read Lincoln's mail, decorate the White House, fight a Civil War battle, or take a history quiz. Also on public display are a copy of the Thirteenth Amendment and a rare copy of the Emancipation Proclamation of 1864 signed by Lincoln.

Admission Fees: Adults $4.99, children and seniors $3.99; group rates and tours available by reservation.

Open to Public: Tues.–Sat. 10:00 A.M.–5:00 P.M., Sun. 1:00 P.M.–5:00 P.M.; closed major holidays.

Visitor Services: Handicapped access, gift shop.

Regularly Scheduled Events: October, Civil War Ball.

Directions: From I–69 north take U.S. 24 exit east to downtown Fort Wayne, turn left on Lafayette Street, turn left on Berry Street, enter museum parking lot on the southeast corner of Berry and Clinton Streets.

LINCOLN CITY

 LINCOLN AMPHITHEATER AND LINCOLN STATE PARK

Highway 162, Box 216, Lincoln City, IN 47552; (812) 937–4710 or (800) 264–4ABE; www.in.gov/dnr/parklake.

Description: Within walking distance of the Lincoln homestead, the 1,747-acre Lincoln State Park features 10 miles of hiking trails through the region where Abraham Lincoln spent his youth. Among the Lincoln-era sites is the home of Col. Williams Jones, the merchant employer of young Abraham Lincoln. The outdoor amphitheater is expected to recommence the annual *Young Abe Lincoln* summer production for the 2008 season.

Admission Fees: Park, $5.00/vehicle. *NOTE:* There's an additional charge for camping and boat rental.

Open to Public: Park, daily 8:30 A.M.–4:00 P.M.

Visitor Services: Public restrooms, information, handicapped access, food, gift shop,camping, picnicking, hiking, swimming, boating, fishing.

Regularly Scheduled Events: Call or check Web site for schedule of events.

Directions: From I–64 take exit 63; take Route 162 to Lincoln State Park. Amphitheater is located in state park.

 LINCOLN BOYHOOD HOME NATIONAL MEMORIAL

P.O. Box 1816, Lincoln City, IN 47552; (812) 937–4541; www.nps.gov/libo.

Description: This was the boyhood home of Abraham Lincoln, where he lived from ages seven to twenty-one. The park includes the Memorial Visitor Center; the grave site of Nancy Hanks Lincoln, Abraham Lincoln's mother; and the Lincoln Living Historical Farm, a typical nineteenth-century farm on the Indiana frontier.

Admission Fees: Adults $3.00, maximum of $5.00/family.

Open to Public: Daily 8:00 A.M.–5:00 P.M.; Dec.–Feb., park closes at 4:30 P.M.; closed Thanksgiving, Christmas, and New Year's Day.

Visitor Services: Public restrooms, handicapped access to Memorial Visitor Center, museum, tours.

Regularly Scheduled Events: February, Sunday closest to Lincoln's birthday, Lincoln Day.

Directions: From I–64 exit at U.S. 231 and travel south for 8 miles. Travel east on Indiana Highway 162 at Gentryville. Proceed 2 miles to site.

MADISON

HISTORIC ELEUTHERIAN COLLEGE

6927 West Route 250, Madison, IN 47250; (812) 273–9434; www.eleutherian.us.

Description: Eleutherian College was established as an abolitionist school in 1848. The college offered education to all students, regardless of sex or race, and was the first of its kind in the state of Indiana. The college was located along the Underground Railroad and served as a stop. Many of the students enlisted in the Civil War, and the grounds were used as a training center during the Civil War for the Sixth Indiana Regiment. The Lyman Hoyt House, the original 1850 home of an Underground Railroad conductor, will open for tours in 2007.

Admission Fees: Adults $3.00, seniors $2.00, children free; groups $2.00.

Open to Public: Mon.–Sat. 10:00 A.M.–4:00 P.M.; closed Nov.–Mar.; available for tours by appointment year-round.

Visitor Services: Public restrooms, information, gift shop, museum, tours.

Regularly Scheduled Events: None.

Directions: From I–65 exit at the Seymour/North Vernon exit; proceed 16 miles on U.S. 50 to Indiana Highway 7; proceed south on Highway 7 toward Madison. Turn left on State Road 250 to site.

VERSAILLES

 JOHN HUNT MORGAN HERITAGE TRAIL

c/o Historic Hoosier Hills, P.O. Box 407, Versailles, IN 47042; (812) 689–6410, ext. 5; www.hhhills.org; jhmht@seidata.com.

Description: The John Hunt Morgan Trail is a 185-mile driving tour that passes through seven southern Indiana counties. The trail allows motorists to retrace the route taken

MIDWEST

by Confederate Gen. John Hunt Morgan in his famous raid of 1863.

Admission Fees: Free.

Open to Public: Daily from dawn to dusk.

Visitor Services: Brochure available by calling (812) 689–6410, ext. 5.

Regularly Scheduled Events: None.

Directions: The first stop on the John Hunt Morgan Heritage Trail is near Mauckport, Indiana, at the junction of Routes 135 and 11. The driving tour continues northeast.

❖ MINNESOTA ❖

FAIRFAX

 FORT RIDGELY STATE HISTORIC SITE

72404 County Road 30, Fairfax, MN 55332; (507) 426–7888 or (507) 934–2160; www.mnhs.org; ftridgely@mnhs.org.

Description: A federal military fort, Fort Ridgely was established in 1853 to provide a military presence along the upper Minnesota River, between the line of settlement and the Dakota (Sioux) reservation system farther upriver. A training facility for state forces during the Civil War, the fort came under direct attack twice during the U.S.–Dakota War in August 1862. The fort held, and it became a staging ground for punitive expeditions against the Dakota over the next three years.

Admission Fees: Park, vehicle permits re-

quired, fee charged; museum, adults $2.00.

Open to Public: Memorial Day–Labor Day weekend, Fri.–Sun. 10:00 A.M.–5:00 P.M.; after Labor Day–mid. Oct., Sat.–Sun. 10:00 A.M.–5:00 P.M.

Visitor Services: Public restrooms, handicapped access, gift shop (10 percent discount for CWPT members), museum, camping, trails.

Regularly Scheduled Events: None.

Directions: From I–90 across southern Minnesota, take Highway 15 north to New Ulm (50 miles) on the Minnesota River and continue to County Road 5 (just north of the Minnesota River). Take County Road 5 northwest, following the Minnesota River all the way to Fort Ridgely State Park, approximately 15 miles. The historic fort is located within the state park.

Fort Ridgely State Park, Minnesota. CWPT files.

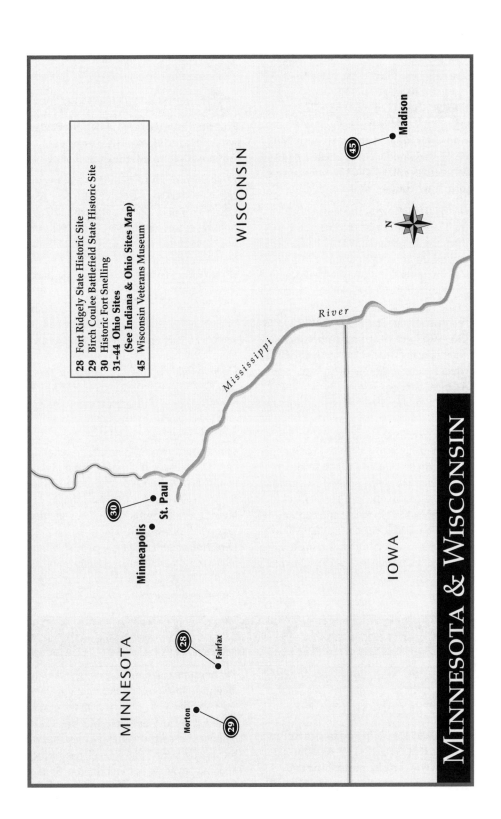

28 Fort Ridgely State Historic Site
29 Birch Coulee Battlefield State Historic Site
30 Historic Fort Snelling
31-44 Ohio Sites
    (See Indiana & Ohio Sites Map)
45 Wisconsin Veterans Museum

MINNESOTA

WISCONSIN

IOWA

Mississippi *River*

Madison

45

N

30
St. Paul
Minneapolis

28
Fairfax

Morton
29

MINNESOTA & WISCONSIN

MORTON

 BIRCH COULEE BATTLEFIELD STATE HISTORIC SITE

c/o Lower Sioux Agency Historic Site, 32469 Redwood County Road 2, Morton, MN 56270; (507) 697–6321; www.mnhs .org; birchcoulee@mnhs.org.

Description: One of the fiercest battles of the U.S.–Dakota War of 1862, the fight at Birch Coulee erupted when Dakota forces ambushed an encampment of Minnesota state troops and civilians on the morning of September 2, 1862. Dakota forces laid siege to the camp for thirty-six hours before relief arrived from Fort Ridgley. Although the camp was not overrun, twenty men and ninety horses were killed on the U.S. side, while Dakota losses are unknown.

Admission Fees: Free.

Open to Public: May–Oct., daily from dawn to dusk.

Visitor Services: Handicapped access, information, trails, picnic tables, small shelter.

Regularly Scheduled Events: None.

Directions: From I–90 across southern Minnesota, go north on U.S. 71 at Jackson. Proceed to Morton (90 miles) and continue up the Minnesota River bluffs. Watch for the brown signs directing you to make a left turn and taking you east of U.S. 71 to reach the battlefield.

ST. PAUL

 HISTORIC FORT SNELLING

Fort Snelling History Center, St. Paul, MN 55111; (612) 726–1171; mnhs.org/ fortsnelling; fortsnelling@mnhs.org.

Description: Fort Snelling is a restored/ reconstructed massive stone fortress. Between 1861 and 1865 the fort was used as a training center for thousands of volunteers who joined the Union army. Fort Snelling features extensive displays and living history programs, plus numerous special events.

Admission Fees: Fort Snelling, adults $8.00 (CWPT members get two admissions for the price of one), children six–seventeen $4.00, seniors $6.00; Fort Snelling History Center, free.

Open to Public: May, Sat. 10:00 A.M.–5:00 P.M.; Memorial Day–Labor Day weekend, Mon.– Sat. 10:00 A.M.–5:00 P.M., Sun. noon–5:00 P.M.; after Labor Day–Oct., Sat. 10:00 A.M.–5:00 P.M., Sun. noon–5:00 P.M.; closed Nov.–Apr.

Visitor Services: Public restrooms, handicapped access, gift shop, museum, living history programs.

Regularly Scheduled Events: Summer, living history programs; second weekend in June, Civil War weekend.

Directions: From the junction of I–35W and I–494, travel east 6 miles on Highway 5 past the Mall of America and the international airport to the Historic Fort Snelling exit.

❖ OHIO ❖

CARROLLTON

 McCOOK HOUSE

P.O. Box 174, Public Square, Carrollton, OH 44615; (330) 627–3345 or (800) 600– 7172; www.carrollcountyohio.com/ history; www.ohiohistory.org/places/ mcookhse.

Description: This house is a memorial to the "Fighting McCooks," a nickname given to the family because of their military service. During the Civil War, Daniel McCook's family contributed three major generals, two brigadier generals, one colonel, two majors, and one private to the Union cause. Brother John's side of the McCook family produced one major general, one brigadier general, two lieutenants, and a lieutenant in the navy. Four of Daniel's family, including Daniel himself, lost their lives in the conflict.

Admission Fees: Adults $3.00, children $1.00, Ohio Historical Society members free.

Open to Public: Memorial Day weekend–Labor Day weekend, Fri.–Sat. 10:00 A.M.–5:00 P.M., Sun. 1:00 P.M.–5:00 P.M.; after Labor Day–mid-Oct., Sat. 10:00 A.M.–5:00 P.M., Sun. 1:00 P.M.–5:00 P.M.; tours other times by appointment.

Visitor Services: Restrooms, information, museum.

Regularly Scheduled Events: None.

Directions: From I–77 south take Route 39 east to Carrollton. From I–77 north take Route 43 from Canton. Located on the west side of the public square in Carrollton, Carroll County.

CINCINNATI

 32 THE HARRIET BEECHER STOWE HOUSE

2950 Gilbert Avenue, Cincinnati, OH 45206; (513) 751–0651; www.ohiohistory .org/places/stowe; saratoga@choice.net.

Description: The Harriet Beecher Stowe House was built by Lane Seminary in 1833 to serve as the residence of that institution's president. Harriet Beecher Stowe moved to Cincinnati from Connecticut in 1832 with her father, Dr. Lyman Beecher, who had been appointed president of the seminary. During her stay in Cincinnati, she learned of the evil of slavery and later expressed it through her book *Uncle Tom's Cabin.* The Cincinnati Citizens Committee on Youth has restored the Stowe House. The Ohio Historical Society and the city of Cincinnati funded recent renovations.

Admission Fees: Free; donations accepted.

Open to Public: May–Labor Day weekend, Tues.–Thurs. and Sat. 10:00 A.M.–3:00 P.M.; after Labor Day–Nov., Tues.–Wed. and first Sat. of the month, 11:00 A.M.–3:00 P.M.; Dec.–Apr., Sat. 11:00 A.M.–3:00 P.M.

Visitor Services: Restrooms, gift shop, tours.

Regularly Scheduled Events: Fourth Sunday evening of the month, open house and programs.

Directions: From I–71 south take William Howard Taft exit; turn right onto Reading Road; travel north to Martin Luther King Jr. Drive; turn right onto Gilbert Avenue; house is located on the corner of Gilbert and King Drive.

 33 SPRING GROVE CEMETERY AND ARBORETUM

4521 Spring Grove Avenue, Cincinnati, OH 45232; (513) 681–6680; www.spring grove.org.

Description: Spring Grove Cemetery and Arboretum, serving the community for more than 150 years, encompasses 733 acres. It is known worldwide for its beautiful landscaping and unique "lawn plan." Preserved within this "museum without walls" are exquisite illustrations of art, statuary, and architecture. Among its notable burials are 999 Civil War soldiers, 40 of whom are generals, including Gen. Robert McCook of the "Fighting McCooks" and Gen. Joseph Hooker.

Admission Fees: Free.

Open to Public: Daily 8:00 A.M.–6:00 P.M.

Visitor Services: Public restrooms, information, self-guided tour; guided tours available for groups of twenty or more.

Regularly Scheduled Events: September, lantern memorial service.

Directions: From I–75 take Mitchell Avenue exit; go south on Spring Grove Avenue to entrance.

COLUMBUS

 34 CAMP CHASE CONFEDERATE CEMETERY

2900 Sullivant Avenue, Columbus, OH 43204; (614) 276–0060.

Description: Camp Chase, the largest camp in the area, was used for training Union soldiers. Later, it served as a prison for captured

Confederates. Camp Chase is one of the largest Confederate cemeteries in the north, with 2,260 prisoners buried there.

Admission Fees: Free.

Open to Public: Daily.

Visitor Services: None.

Regularly Scheduled Events: First Sunday in June, annual Confederate memorial services.

Directions: From I–70 exit at Broad Street; proceed west on Broad Street to Hague Avenue; turn left on Hague, turn right on Sullivant Avenue, and proceed 1 block to cemetery.

 OHIO STATEHOUSE

Corner of Broad and High Streets, Columbus, OH 43215; (614) 752–9777 or (888) OHIO–123; www.statehouse .state.oh.us.

Description: The Ohio Statehouse is the finest example of Greek Revival architecture in the United States. Built between 1839 and 1861, it is a National Historic Landmark and has been restored to its 1861 appearance. President Abraham Lincoln visited the statehouse three times: in 1859, shortly after his involvement with the Lincoln-Douglas debates; in 1861, when he spoke to a joint session of the Ohio legislature in the house chamber; and in 1865, when he was laid in state in the rotunda. A monument, *These Are My Jewels*, pays tribute to seven Ohioans who played key roles in the Civil War, honoring Ulysses S. Grant, Philip Sheridan, Edwin M. Stanton, James A. Garfield, Rutherford B. Hayes, Salmon P. Chase, and William Tecumseh Sherman.

Admission Fees: Free.

Open to Public: Mon.–Fri. 7:00 A.M.–7:00 P.M., Sat.–Sun. 11:00 A.M.–3:00 P.M.; tours can be scheduled by calling (614) 728–3726.

Visitor Services: Public restrooms, information, handicapped access, museum.

Regularly Scheduled Events: Call or check Web site for a schedule of other events.

Directions: From I–71 take Broad Street exit; go west on Broad, turn south onto Third Street. Parking is available underground.

FREMONT

 RUTHERFORD B. HAYES PRESIDENTIAL CENTER

Spiegel Grove, Fremont, OH 43420; (419) 332–2081; www.rbhayes.org.

Description: This site features a museum, the first presidential library, and the thirty-one-room Victorian mansion of Rutherford B. Hayes, nineteenth president of the United States. The tomb of the president and his wife, Lucy Webb Hayes, are located on the twenty-five-acre Spiegel Grove estate. During the Civil War, Hayes was wounded five times and achieved the rank of brevet major general. Hayes served three terms as Ohio governor and one term as president. The two-story museum has Civil War artifacts and one of the nation's finest antique weapons collections. The library contains works of American history from the Civil War to the twentieth century.

Admission Fees: House and museum, adults $10.50, children $4.00, seniors $9.50; per site, adults $6.00, children $2.00, seniors $5.00.

Open to Public: Mon.–Sat. 9:00 A.M.–5:00 P.M., Sun. noon–5:00 P.M.

Visitor Services: Public restrooms, information, handicapped access, gift shop, museum; trails.

Regularly Scheduled Events: July Concert; October, Civil War reenactment; December, Christmas dinners at Spiegel Grove.

Directions: From I–75 take U.S. 6 25 miles east to intersection of Route 53. Continue east on U.S. 6 (Hayes Avenue) about 2 miles. Entrance to site is at the corner of Hayes and Buckland Avenues.

LAKESIDE-MARBLEHEAD

 JOHNSON'S ISLAND CEMETERY

c/o Johnson's Island Preservation Society, 414 West Main Street, P.O. Box 1865, Marblehead, OH 43400; Ottoway County Visitors Bureau, (800) 441–1271; www.johnsonsisland.org; jipres@johnsonsisland.org.

Description: The Union army established a prisoner-of-war depot on Johnson's Island from April 1862 to September 1865. This cemetery holds the graves of 206 Confederates who died while imprisoned here. Individual home owners privately own the remainder of the island. The nearby museum exhibits images, artifacts, letters, and other materials covering the island's history, including the forty months that the POW depot existed.

Admission Fees: Free; $2.00 toll to cross causeway.

Open to Public: Cemetery, daily from dawn to dusk; museum, Memorial Day–Labor Day, weekends and holidays noon–5:00 P.M.; other times by appointment.

Visitor Services: None.

Regularly Scheduled Events: None.

Directions: From I–80/90 take exit 6A north on Route 4 to Route 2 west; take Route 269 north to Danbury and Bay Shore Road; travel east on Bay Shore Road to Johnson's Island entrance. Cross the causeway to Johnson's Island.

LANCASTER

 SHERMAN HOUSE

137 East Main Street, Lancaster, OH 43130; (740) 687–5891; www.shermanhouse.org; fairheritage@greenapple.com.

Description: Sherman House is the birthplace of William Tecumseh Sherman. The site

includes a museum with war memorabilia and artifacts from the general's collection.

Admission Fees: Adults $6.00, seniors $3.50, children six–eighteen $1.00.

Open to Public: Apr.–mid.-Dec., Tues.–Sun. 1:00 P.M.–4:00 P.M. or by appointment.

Visitor Services: Museum, gift shop, tours.

Regularly Scheduled Events: Early February, Sherman's birthday celebration.

Directions: From I–270 travel south on Route 33 to downtown Lancaster; turn left on Route 22 and proceed 2 blocks to house.

NEW RUMLEY

 CUSTER MONUMENT STATE MEMORIAL

Route 646, New Rumley, OH 43984; (740) 945–6415; www.ohiohistory.org/places/custer.

Description: This 8½-foot bronze statue stands on the site of George Armstrong Custer's birthplace. Custer, born in 1839, became famous as a daring young cavalryman in the Civil War, fighting in the battles of Bull Run, Shenandoah, Waynesboro, Appomattox, and many others.

Admission Fees: Free.

Open to Public: Daily from dawn to dusk.

Visitor Services: None.

Regularly Scheduled Events: None.

Directions: Located on the north side of Route 646, at the west edge of New Rumley, north of Cadiz, in Harrison County.

POINT PLEASANT

 ULYSSES S. GRANT BIRTHPLACE STATE MEMORIAL

1551 Route 232, Point Pleasant, OH 45157; (513) 553–4911; www.ohiohistory.org/places/grantbir.

Description: Ulysses S. Grant, eighteenth president of the United States, was born in this small frame cottage in Point Pleasant.

MIDWEST

Today, Grant's birthplace is restored and open to the public.

Admission Fees: Adults $2.00, children six–twelve $1.00, seniors $1.50; call for group rates.

Open to Public: Apr.–Oct., Wed.–Sat. 9:30 A.M.–noon and 1:00 P.M.–5:00 P.M., Sun. noon–5:00 P.M.; Nov.–Mar. by group reservation only.

Visitor Services: Tours.

Regularly Scheduled Events: April, Grant's Birthday Celebration.

Directions: Located in the Clermont County Village of Point Pleasant, off Route 52 about 5 miles east of New Richmond (near the intersection of Route 132).

PORTLAND

 BUFFINGTON ISLAND STATE MEMORIAL CWPT

Route 124, Portland, OH 45770; (614) 297–2630 or (800) 686–1535; www.ohio history.org/places/buffingt.

Description: Commemorates the only significant Civil War battle that took place on Ohio soil. Here, the Union army routed a column of Confederate cavalry commanded by Gen. John Hunt Morgan in 1863.

Admission Fees: Free.

Open to Public: Daily from dawn to dusk.

Visitor Services: Handicapped access, picnicking.

Regularly Scheduled Events: None.

Directions: The memorial is approximately 20 miles east from Pomeroy, in Meigs County, on Route 124 in Portland.

RIPLEY

 **JOHN P. PARKER HISTORIC SITE**

300 Front Street, Ripley, OH 45167; (937) 392–4188; www.johnparkerhouse .org; webmaster@johnparkerhouse.org.

Description: John P. Parker was a slave in Alabama prior to 1845; however, he was ap-

prenticed as an iron molder and raised $1,800 to purchase his freedom. He left Alabama and settled in Ripley, Ohio, in 1845, where he lived until his death in 1900. Parker is credited with aiding 400 slaves escaping through Ripley on the Underground Railroad. He made forays at night across the Ohio River into Kentucky to bring slaves to Ohio. Parker was also influential in recruiting African-American troops for the Twenty-seventh Volunteer Infantry Regiment in Ripley.

Admission Fees: Free.

Open to Public: Memorial Day weekend–Labor Day weekend, Wed.–Sat. 10:00 A.M.–5:00 P.M., Sun. noon–5:00 P.M.; after Labor Day–Oct. 31, Sat. 10:00 A.M.–5:00 P.M., Sun. noon–5:00 P.M.; or by appointment.

Visitor Services: Public restrooms, information, handicapped access, gift shop, museum.

Regularly Scheduled Events: None.

Directions: From I–275 take Route 32 (Appalachian Highway) to U.S. 62/68 exit, 62/68 dead-ends into U.S. 52 at Ripley. Turn right onto U.S. 52, turn left at first stoplight (Main and Second), and turn right on Front Street. The Parker House will be located 3 blocks down on Front Street.

 RANKIN HOUSE

6152 Rankin Hill Road, Ripley, OH 45167; (937) 392–1627 or (800) 752–2705; www.ohiohistory. org/places/rankin.

Description: Rankin House was the home of Presbyterian minister and ardent abolitionist Rev. John Rankin. The brick house was his home from 1828 until the early 1860s. He and his family are credited with aiding 2,000 slaves and boasted they "never lost a passenger." Harriet Beecher Stowe was a guest in his home on several occasions, and her character "Eliza" in *Uncle Tom's Cabin* was based on stories of assisting slaves she heard from the Rankin family. The house is now a National Historic

PASTIMES

To fill the long hours between marches and battles, soldiers on both sides of the conflict found ways to amuse themselves. Reading was a popular way to pass the time. Soldiers read letters, newspapers, novels, the Bible, and whatever printed material they could find. In fact, when stationed not far from enemy lines, they would occasionally trade newspapers with their opponents. Milton Barrett, a soldier in the Eighteenth Georgia Volunteers, wrote in 1863:

> Our regiment had just come off the picket. We stood close together and could talk to each other, then when the officers were not present we exchanged papers and barter tobacco for coffee. The way we managed this is with a small boat. With sail set it will go over by itself then they send it back in return the same way.

Union soldiers who had not brought their own Bible could obtain a free copy from the U.S. Christian Commission. When soldiers on either side had not brought reading matter, they wrote it themselves, sometimes even publishing their own camp or hospital newspapers. These newspapers often contained accounts of battles, poetry and essays, or propagandistic messages for the enemy. Some enterprising soldiers established literary or debating societies. Music was a popular diversion, as well—from informal singing around the fire to staged balls.

Gambling prevailed in every conceivable form, from horse races to louse races. Games like cards, chess, checkers, and dominoes, which could be played for money or simply for fun, were quiet and could be carried in a knapsack. Card games, such as poker, twenty-one, keno, and euchre, were played on both sides of the line, but by the last years of battle, decks of cards were hard to come by in Southern ranks. Confederate soldiers obtained additional decks from Union prisoners, fallen soldiers, or by trading with their Federal counterparts.

More athletic activities included wrestling, boxing, leapfrog, racing on foot or horseback, cricket, and—in at least one instance—bowling, using cannon balls to knock down rough wooden pins. Baseball, played differently than it is today, was another popular sport. (The ball was soft and the field could contain either two or four bases. Runners were only considered "out" when the pitcher hit them with the ball.)

Semipermanent winter quarters meant that soldiers had time to develop more ambitious ways to pass the time. Occasionally, they would establish their own theater companies, such as the "Essayons" of the Union's Fiftieth New York Engineers or the drama club of the Confederacy's Ninth Kentucky Infantry. Winter, with its attendant cold weather, also brought a new range of activities, such as ice skating, sledding, and building "snow effigies." One of the more violent winter games was the snowball battle. Whole brigades would form up in lines, develop plans of attack, and set out to pummel the other side with hard missiles of snow and ice. Even officers joined in the battles, which often resulted in black eyes, bruises, and an occasional broken limb.

—CWPT *CIVIL WAR EXPLORER*

NOTE: Sources include *The Life of Billy Yank* and *The Life of Johnny Reb* by Bell Irvin Wiley (Louisiana State University Press, 1979 and 1989, reissue editions), *The Fighting Men of the Civil War* by William C. Davis (Smithmark Publishers, 1991), and *The Confederacy Is on Her Way Up the Spout: Letter to South Carolina, 1861–1864* by J. Roderick Heller III and Carolynn Ayres Heller (The University of Georgia Press, 1992).

Landmark and sits on a bluff overlooking the village of Ripley, the Ohio River, and the Kentucky hills.

Admission Fees: Adults $3.00, students $1.00, children five and under free.

Open to Public: Tues.–Sat. 10:00 A.M.–5:00 P.M., Sun. noon–5:00 P.M.; mid-Dec.–Apr. closed Tues. Tours in the off-season may be arranged by appointment.

Visitor Services: Restrooms, information, handicapped access, gift shop, museum.

Regularly Scheduled Events: None.

Directions: Take I–275 to Route 32 (Appalachian Highway) to U.S. 62/68 turnoff, which dead-ends in Ripley. Turn right on U.S. 52. Go 2 blocks on U.S. 52 and look for signs to the right to Rankin Hill Road.

 44 RIPLEY MUSEUM

219 North Second Street, Ripley, OH 45167; (937) 362–4660; www.ripley museum.org; curator1224@yahoo.com.

Description: Housed in a ten-room 1850s Federal-style home, the Ripley Museum is filled with more than 600 unique and rare items relating Ripley's rich historical past. The Civil War collection includes locally found weapons, photographs, and letters home from the men of Ripley and the surrounding region. The museum can provide information about the marker at the nearby site of Camp Ripley, which served as a training and mustering camp during 1861–64.

Admission Fees: Adults $3.00, students $1.00.

Open to Public: Apr.–mid. Dec., Sat. 10:00 A.M.–4:00 P.M.; Sun. noon–4:00 P.M.; or by appointment.

Visitor Service: Genealogical library, information about other Civil War attractions and events in Ripley.

Regularly Scheduled Events: December, historic homes tour.

Directions: From Cincinnati take I–275 to U.S. 52 east toward New Richmond. Continue on U.S. 52 east for approximately 37.5 miles to Ripley.

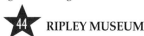

❖ WISCONSIN ❖

MADISON

 45 WISCONSIN VETERANS MUSEUM

30 West Mifflin Street, Suite 200, Madison, WI 53703; (608) 267–1799; www.museum.dva.state.wi.us; veterans.museum@dva.state.wi.us.

Description: The main attraction of the nineteenth-century gallery is the Civil War diorama dramatizing the Sixth Wisconsin Infantry in the Miller cornfield during the Battle of Antietam. Visitors can also find information about their Civil War ancestors on computer displays listing details of all 95,000 Wisconsin Civil War soldiers.

Admission Fees: Free.

Open to Public: Mon.–Sat. 9:00 A.M.–4:30 P.M., Sun. noon–4:00 P.M.; Oct.–Mar., closed Sun.

Visitor Services: Public restrooms, information, handicapped access, gift shop.

Regularly Scheduled Events: Summer, Camp Randall Civil War Encampment; October, Forest Hill Cemetery Tour.

Directions: From I–90 west exit onto U.S. 12/18 west, take exit 263 (John Nolan Drive) to U.S. 151 (East Johnson Avenue). Turn left on Fairchild Street and continue around the square to parking ramp.

TRANS-MISSISSIPPI

Shadows-on-the-Teche, Louisiana. Shadows-on-the-Teche National Historic Site.

❖ ARKANSAS ❖

BLUFF CITY

 POISON SPRING STATE PARK

Highway 76, Bluff City, AR 71722; (870) 685–2748; wwwarkansasstateparks .com; whiteoaklake@arkansas.com.

Description: Poison Spring State Park is a day-use park complete with picnic furnishings, a trail, and a diorama summarizing the Battle of Poison Spring. This site is dedicated to the battle fought on April 18, 1864, during the Camden expedition of the Red River campaign. Confederate troops attacked Union soldiers returning from taking supplies from the city of Camden.

Admission Fees: Free.

Open to Public: Daily, one hour after sunrise–10:00 P.M.

Visitor Services: Information, trails.

Regularly Scheduled Events: April, living history.

Directions: From I–30 take exit 44 for Prescott. Proceed east on Highway 24 through Prescott for the next 33 miles. Turn right on Highway 76, go approximately 6 miles to the park, located on the right-hand side.

 WHITE OAK LAKE STATE PARK

563 Highway 387, Bluff City, AR 71722; (870) 685–2748; www.arkansasstateparks .com; whiteoaklake@arkansas.com.

Description: The evening before the Battle of Poison Spring, fought on April 18, 1864, Union forces camped on White Oak Creek, near where the state park is located today. The park is the "gateway" to Poison Spring and is the nearest campground to the southern arm of the Red River Campaign National Historic Landmark. It provides a convenient and comfortable site from which to tour the area from Old Washington State Park to Camden. The park visitor center includes

displays of battle artifacts and images, and information on the Red River campaign.

Admission Fees: Free; fee for camping.

Open to Public: Visitor center, daily 8:00 A.M.–5:00 P.M.; park, daily twenty-four hours.

Visitor Services: Public restrooms, information, handicapped access, food, gift shop, camping, trails.

Regularly Scheduled Events: Call or check Web site for events.

Directions: From I–30 exit 44 at Prescott, proceed east for 20 miles on Highway 24; turn right at Bluff City onto Highway 229. Turn left on Highway 387 and proceed for 2 miles to the park's entrance.

CABOT

 CAMP NELSON CONFEDERATE CEMETERY

Cabot, AR 72023; (501) 843–5754.

Description: While camped near Old Austin, Arkansas, a large group of Texas Confederate soldiers were overcome by a measles epidemic, which caused the deaths of several hundred. The soldiers were buried near the encampment. In 1907 the general assembly appropriated funds to remove the remains into the area that became the cemetery. The remains were not identified on the stone markers; a monument at the cemetery tells this story.

Admission Fees: Free.

Open to Public: Daily from dawn to dusk.

Visitor Services: Handicapped access.

Regularly Scheduled Events: June, Flag Day celebration.

Directions: From I–40 take Remington exit (7 miles west of Lonoke). Take Highway 15 north for 2.5 miles to where it crosses and becomes Highway 89. Continue on Highway 89 to its junction with Highway 321. Turn right on Highway 321 and continue

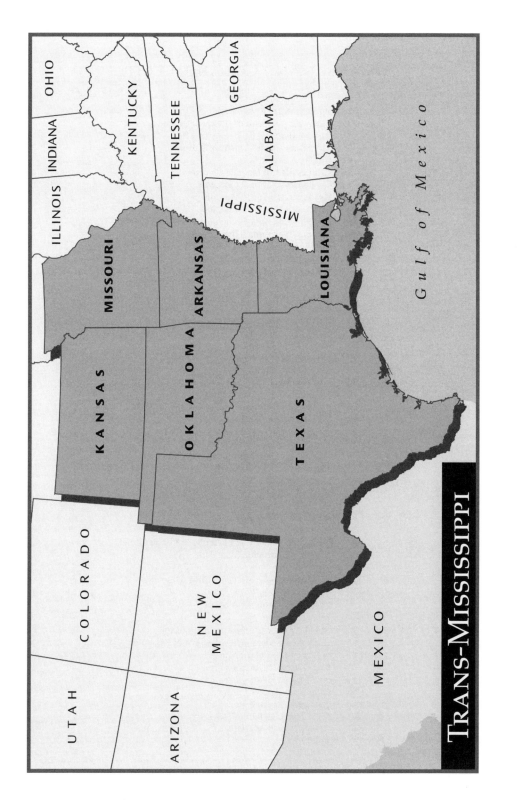

Arkansas and Oklahoma Sites

1   Poison Spring State Park
2   White Oak Lake State Park
3   Camp Nelson Confederate Cemetery
4   Fort Southerland Park
5   McCollum-Chidester House Museum
6   City of Clarendon
7   Fayetteville Confederate Cemetery
8   Fayetteville National Cemetery
9   Headquarters House Museum
10   Fort Smith Museum of History
11   Fort Smith National Cemetery
12   Fort Smith National Historic Site
13   Massard Prairie Battlefield Park
14   Pea Ridge National Military Park
15   Arkansas Post National Memorial
16   Battery C Park
17   Delta Cultural Center
18   Helena, Arkansas, Civil War Sites Driving Tour
19   Helena Confederate Cemetery
20   Jacksonport State Park
21   Reed's Bridge Battlefield
22   Ditch Bayou Battlefield
23   Lake Chicot State Park
24   Little Rock Campaign Driving Tour
25   Little Rock National Cemetery
26   MacArthur Museum of Arkansas Military History
27   Mount Holly Cemetery
28   Old State House Museum
29   Marks' Mills Battlefield State Park
30   Camp White Sulphur Springs Confederate Cemetery
31   Marks' Mill Cemetery State Park
32   Prairie Grove Battlefield State Park
33   Jenkins' Ferry State Park
34   Mount Elba Battlefield
35   St. Charles Museum
36   Chalk Bluff Park
37   Buffalo National River, Tyler Bend Visitor Center
38   Historic Washington State Park
39-43   **Kansas Sites**
      (See Kansas & Missouri Sites Map)
44-71   **Louisiana Sites**
      (See Louisiana Sites Map)
72-94   **Missouri Sites**
      (See Kansas & Missouri Sites Map)
95   Confederate Memorial Museum and Cemetery
96   Fort Washita Historic Site
97   Fort Gibson Historic Site
98   Fort Towson Historic Site
99   Oklahoma History Center
100   George M. Murrell Home
101   Honey Springs Battlefield
102   Cabin Creek Battlefield

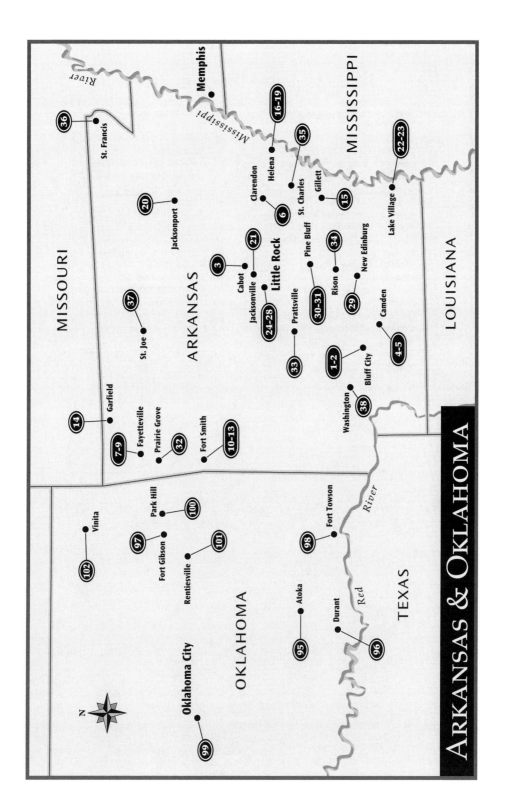

ARKANSAS & OKLAHOMA

Kansas and Missouri Sites

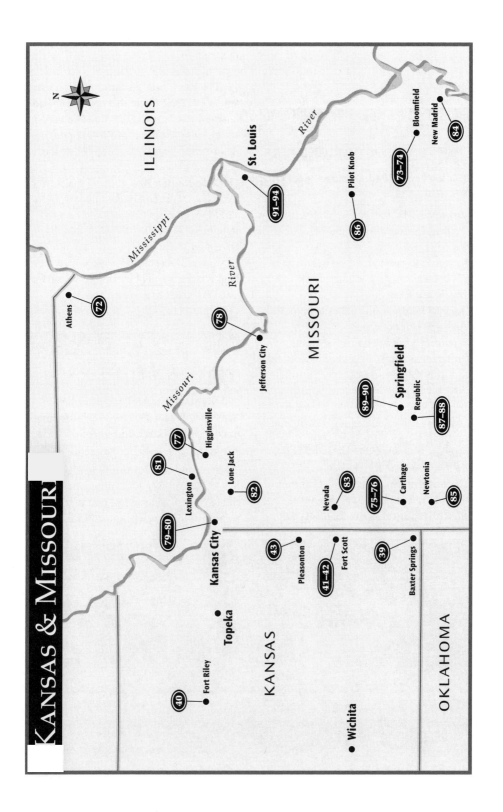

approximately 2 miles to Cherry Road. Turn left on Cherry Road. Site is about 0.5 mile on the right.

CAMDEN

 FORT SOUTHERLAND PARK

Bradley Ferry Road, Camden, AR 71701; (870) 836–6436.

Description: Fort Southerland represents an excellently preserved example of urban Civil War defensive earthworks, erected along the periphery of Camden in 1864 in anticipation of a Federal attack from Little Rock.
Admission Fees: Free.
Open to Public: Daily from dawn to dusk.
Visitor Services: None.
Regularly Scheduled Events: None.
Directions: From I–30 at Prescott take Highway 24 east to Camden; turn from Highway 24 onto Highway 4 Spur and follow 4 Spur and U.S. 79 to Bradley Ferry Road. Site is located 2 blocks down on left.

 McCOLLUM-CHIDESTER HOUSE MUSEUM

926 Washington Street NW, Camden, AR 71701; (870) 836–9243; www .ouachitacountyhistoricalsociety.org.

Description: This house, built in 1847, retains its furnishings brought here by steamboat in 1863 by the Chidester family. Union Gen. Frederick Steele made this house his headquarters and occupied the city of Camden in 1864, during the Battle of Poison Spring.
Admission Fees: Adults $5.00, students $2.00.
Open to Public: Wed.–Sat. 9:00 A.M.–4:00 P.M.; closed Feb. and major holidays.
Visitor Services: Public restrooms, tours.
Regularly Scheduled Events: None.
Directions: From I–30 at Prescott take Highway 24 east to Camden, turn from Highway 24 onto Highway 4 Spur, and follow Washington Street to museum at 926 Washington Street.

CLARENDON

 CITY OF CLARENDON

270 Madison Street, Clarendon, AR 72029; (870) 747–3802; www.clarendon-ar.com; info@clarendon-ar.com.

Description: Under the cover of darkness, 1,000 cavalrymen of Confederate Gen. J. Shelby's "Iron Brigade," along with an artillery battery of four ten-pounder Parrott guns, formed a battle line 200 yards from

McCollum-Chidester House Museum, Camden, Arkansas. Hubert Boddie–CWPT files.

the anchored *Queen City*. At 4:00 A.M. Shelby attacked and after twenty minutes of intense fire, captured the vessel and the crew.

Admission Fees: Free.

Open to Public: Daily from dawn to dusk.

Visitor Services: None. (You can get information at city hall, open Mon.–Fri. 8:00 A.M.–5:00 P.M.)

Regularly Scheduled Events: November, Civil War reenactment.

Directions: From I–40 take the Brinkley exit. Travel south through Brinkley on Highway 49. Two miles into Brinkley, Highways 49 and 70 merge; continue south/southwest on Highway 70 for 5 miles; turn south on Highway 17 and travel for 10 miles. Turn west at the intersection of Highway 17 and Highway 79 and follow Highway 79 for 3 miles into Clarendon.

FAYETTEVILLE

 ### FAYETTEVILLE CONFEDERATE CEMETERY
514 East Rock Street, Fayetteville, AR 72701; www.rootsweb.com/~arsma.

Description: The Confederate Cemetery was started in 1872 by the Southern Memorial Association of Washington County to provide a fitting resting place for Confederate soldiers killed at Prairie Grove, Pea Ridge, and in other battles and skirmishes in northwest Arkansas.

Admission Fees: Free.

Open to Public: Daily from dawn to dusk.

Visitor Services: None.

Regularly Scheduled Events: None.

Directions: From I–40 take U.S. 71 to Fayetteville; U.S. 71 becomes College Avenue. Turn east on Rock Street to Confederate Cemetery.

FAYETTEVILLE NATIONAL CEMETERY
700 Government Avenue, Fayetteville, AR 72701; (501) 444–5051; www.cem.va .gov.

Description: Fayetteville National Cemetery was constructed to bury the Civil War Union soldiers killed during the Battles of Pea Ridge, Prairie Grove, and Fayetteville. Nineteen hundred seventy-five Union soldiers, including more than 800 unknown soldiers, were disinterred from battlefield graves and local family grave sites and brought to the cemetery.

Admission Fees: Free.

Open to Public: Daily from dawn to dusk; office, Mon.–Fri. 8:00 A.M.–4:30 P.M.

Visitor Services: Public restrooms, information available during office hours.

Regularly Scheduled Events: May, Memorial Day program.

Directions: From I–540 take exit 62 and go east on Highway 62 approximately 1.5 miles to Government Avenue. Turn right directly into entrance of cemetery.

 ### HEADQUARTERS HOUSE MUSEUM
118 East Dickson Street, Fayetteville, AR 72701; (501) 521–2970; www.washco historicalsociety.org.

Description: Judge Jonas Tebbetts, a Northern sympathizer, built Headquarters House in 1853. Tebbetts was jailed by Gen. Ben McCulloch and then released to go to St. Louis for the duration of the Civil War. The house was used at various times as headquarters for both the Federal and Confederate armies. The Battle of Fayetteville was fought on the house grounds and across the street on April 18, 1863. One of the doors still carries the hole made by a minié ball.

Admission Fees: Adults $5.00, children $1.00.

Open to Public: Mon.–Fri. 1:00 P.M.–4:00 P.M., Sat. 10:00 A.M.–2:00 P.M.

Visitor Services: Living history tours by appointment, bookstore, public restrooms.

Regularly Scheduled Events: April, Battle of Fayetteville commemoration; third Saturday in August, ice-cream social.

Directions: From I–40 take the Farming-

ton/Fayetteville exit; travel north on U.S. 71 to Fayetteville. U.S. 71 turns into College Avenue. House is at corner of College Avenue and Dickson.

FORT SMITH

10 FORT SMITH MUSEUM OF HISTORY

320 Rogers Avenue, Fort Smith, AR 72901; (479) 783–7841; www.fortsmith museum.com.

Description: The Fort Smith Museum of History is a museum dealing with the history of Fort Smith, including the periods of occupation by both Confederate and Federal forces during the Civil War.

Admission Fees: Adults $5.00 ($1.00 off admission for CWPT members), children $2.00.

Open to Public: Tues.–Sat. 10:00 A.M.–5:00 P.M.; June–Aug., also open Sun. noon–5:00 P.M.

Visitor Services: Information, handicapped access, food, gift shop, museum.

Regularly Scheduled Events: October, Murder and Mayhem Trolley Tour.

Directions: From I–540 take Rogers Avenue exit west to historic downtown, following signs for the Fort Smith National Historic Site. Fort Smith Museum of History is a four-story warehouse at the corner of Fourth Street and Rogers Avenue.

11 FORT SMITH NATIONAL CEMETERY

522 Garland Avenue and South Sixth Street, Fort Smith, AR 72901; (479) 783–5345; www.cem.va.gov.

Description: Burial place for Union and Confederate soldiers, including 3 generals and 1,500 unknown soldiers. Site offers brochure, minimuseum of local military history, and tours if arranged ahead.

Admission Fees: Free.

Open to Public: Grounds open daily twenty-four hours; office, Mon.–Fri. 8:00

A.M.–4:30 P.M.

Visitor Services: Public restrooms, information, handicapped access.

Regularly Scheduled Events: Sunday closest to Memorial Day, Memorial Day ceremony; November, Veterans Day ceremony; December 7, Pearl Harbor Day of Remembrance.

Directions: From I–540 take exit 8A (Rogers Avenue) west and proceed toward downtown area. At the Y go to the right and take Garrison Road to Sixth Street. Turn left on Sixth Street. Cemetery is at the end of Sixth Street where it intersects Garland.

12 FORT SMITH NATIONAL HISTORIC SITE

301 Parker Avenue, Fort Smith, AR 72901; (501) 783–3961; www.nps.gov/ fosm.

Description: Fort Smith National Historic Site preserves the site of two military posts and the historic Federal Court for the Western District of Arkansas. Fort Smith changed hands twice during the war. The U.S. Army, under the command of Capt. Samuel Sturgis, abandoned the fort to the state militia on April 23, 1861. The Confederate occupancy lasted until September 1863. The Union remained in control throughout the rest of the war, despite Confederate attacks led by Gen. Stand Watie. During the Union occupation the fort served as a refuge from guerrilla activity.

Admission Fees: Adults $4.00, children under sixteen free; group guided tours by reservation.

Open to Public: Daily 9:00 A.M.–5:00 P.M.

Visitor Services: Public restrooms, information, handicapped access, gift shop, museum.

Regularly Scheduled Events: April, Confederate encampment; September, Union Commemoration Weekend; programs and demonstrations throughout the year.

Directions: From I–40 west take Rogers Avenue. Go west on Rogers Avenue downtown. Go south on Fourth Street and turn west on Garland Avenue to reach the parking lot. From I–40 east exit at Roland and go 6 miles east on Highway 64 to downtown. After crossing the bridge over the Arkansas River, follow the directions from Fourth Street.

 MASSARD PRAIRIE BATTLEFIELD PARK
Corner of Morgan's Way and Red Pine Drive, Fort Smith, AR 72901; (479) 784–1006; www.fortsmithparks.com.

Description: On July 27, 1864, 800 Confederate cavalry troops attacked a corps of 200 Federal troops of the Sixth Kansas Cavalry. The battle lasted fifteen minutes, and 140 prisoners were taken. The Confederate forces included a number of Native American troops from the Choctaw, Cherokee, Seminole, Creek, and Chickasaw nations.
Admission Fees: Free.
Open to Public: Daily from dawn to dusk.
Visitor Services: Information.
Regularly Scheduled Events: July, battle reenactment.
Directions: From I–540 take Zero Street

east to Highway 45. Take Highway 45 to Geren Road, then to Morgan's Way. Turn right on Morgan's Way to Red Pine Drive; the park is on the right-hand side.

GARFIELD

 PEA RIDGE NATIONAL MILITARY PARK
15930 Highway 62 East, Garfield, AR 72732; (479) 451–8122; www.nps.gov/ peri; peri_interpretation@nps.gov.

Description: On March 7 and 8, 1862, the 10,500-man Union Army of the Southwest and the 16,200-man Confederate Army of the West met in combat at two separate battlefields, Leetown and Elkhorn Tavern, on the gently rolling plain called Pea Ridge. The battle at Leetown ended after the death of two Confederate generals on March 7; the battle at Elkhorn Tavern continued until the Confederates ran out of ammunition on March 8. The decisive Union victory ensured that Missouri would remain in Federal control and paved the way for Grant's Vicksburg campaign.
Admission Fees: Adults $3.00, cars $5.00.

Elkhorn Tavern, Pea Ridge National Military Park, Garfield, Arkansas. CWPT files.

Open to Public: Daily 8:00 A.M.–5:00 P.M.

Visitor Services: Public restrooms, information, handicapped access, orientation film, gift shops, museum, trails.

Regularly Scheduled Events: March, weekend nearest the anniversary of the battle, living history exhibit.

Directions: Take I–540 to exit 86 (Highway 62). Stay on Highway 62 east and follow signs to the park.

GILLETT

 ARKANSAS POST NATIONAL MEMORIAL

1741 Old Post Road, Gillett, AR 72055; (870) 548–2207; www.nps.gov/arpo.

Description: By mid-1862 Union gunboats commanded most of the Mississippi River. When the gunboats went up the White River into the heart of Arkansas, the Confederates began to prepare defenses on the Arkansas River, an important water route to the capital at Little Rock. Before the end of 1862, Confederate Gen. Thomas J. Churchill completed an earthen fortification at Arkansas Post called Fort Hindman or Post of Arkansas. In January 1863 the Battle of Arkansas Post saw nearly 25,000 Union soldiers tangle with almost 6,000 Confederate troops. Union ironclad gunboats showered the greatly outnumbered defenders of Fort Hindman. The resulting Union victory opened the way for the capture of Little Rock and later the siege and capture of Vicksburg, Mississippi.

Admission Fees: Free.

Open to Public: Park, daily 8:00 A.M.–dusk; visitor center, daily 8:00 A.M.–5:00 P.M.

Visitor Services: Public restrooms, information, gift shop, museum, trails.

Regularly Scheduled Events: None.

Directions: From Pine Bluff take U.S. 65 south to Gould and take Highway 212 east at Gould to Highway 165; take 165 north to Highway 169 and follow to park. From Brinkley take Highway 49 south to Marvell

and take Highway 1 to 165 to 169. From Forrest City take Highway 1 to Dewitt and take 165 to 169.

HELENA

 BATTERY C PARK

P.O. Box 248, Helena, AR 72342; (870) 338–9831.

Description: The Battery C Park is a hilltop site of Helena's four Civil War batteries. The site offers interpretation of the July 4, 1863, Battle of Helena.

Admission Fees: Free.

Open to Public: Daily 8:00 A.M.–5:00 P.M.

Visitor Services: Information.

Regularly Scheduled Events: None.

Directions: From I–40 take Highway 61 south to Highway 49 east. Follow Highway 49 into West Helena. Take Highway 49 bypass, and follow into downtown Helena. At second stoplight, Perry Street, turn left. Follow Perry Street until street veers to the left and follow sign to the park.

 DELTA CULTURAL CENTER

141 Cherry Street, Helena, AR 72342; (870) 338–4350; www.deltacultural center.com; info@deltaculturalcenter .com.

Description: The Delta Cultural Center presents and interprets the history of the Arkansas Delta. Included in the exhibits are areas dedicated to the Civil War, including the seven generals from Phillips County; Fort Curtis; and the Battle of Helena.

Admission Fees: Free.

Open to Public: Tues.–Sat. 9:00 A.M.–5:00 P.M.

Visitor Services: Public restrooms, information, handicapped access, gift shop, museum.

Regularly Scheduled Events: Call or check Web site for events.

Directions: From I–40 take Highway 61

HELENA, ARKANSAS

The legacy of the Civil War surrounds you when you are raised in a town like Helena, Arkansas. This legacy has become part of many Southern towns' identities because this was a war that was fought not halfway around the world but in fields that are now our own backyards. I am fortunate to have grown up in a place where you not only learned about history, you were surrounded by it.

When I was growing up in Helena, I saw the artillery batteries more as my own playground than military monuments. The Confederate Cemetery, which overlooks the Mississippi River, provided a great spot for family picnics. Minié balls were prizes my brother and I collected and stored away in cigar boxes. During campouts, we would scare each other with ghost stories about Civil War soldiers haunting the town. Even my elementary school was connected to the Civil War. Helena Elementary stood on the site where Confederate Maj. Gen. Thomas Hindman once lived, and the front of the building was designed to resemble his house.

That is what is great about growing up in Helena, now Helena–West Helena. History isn't some distant concept from a dusty book. It is alive at your school, at your playground, and even in campfire stories.

As I grew up, I learned that Helena's historical monuments are important for reasons other than childhood fun. I realized how fortunate I was that those before me had preserved these landmarks for future generations to experience. These sites are vital to our national heritage and will continue to tell the story of a pivotal moment in our nation's history.

—Senator Blanche Lincoln, Arkansas

south approximately 35 miles to Highway 49 east. Follow Highway 49 into West Helena. At the first stoplight turn right onto Highway 49 bypass. Take bypass approximately 3 miles and follow signs.

 HELENA, ARKANSAS, CIVIL WAR SITES DRIVING TOUR
P.O. Box 248, Helena, AR 72342; (870) 338–9831.

Description: See Batteries A, B, C, and D and the Helena Confederate Cemetery.

Admission Fees: Free.

Open to Public: Daily from dawn to dusk; tourist information center, daily 8:30 A.M.–5:00 P.M.

Visitor Services: None.

Regularly Scheduled Events: October, Columbus Day weekend, King Biscuit Blues Festival.

Directions: From 1–40 east take Highway 49 southeast to Helena. From I–40 at Memphis, Tennessee, take Highway 61 south to Highway 49. Take Highway 49 west to Helena. Pick up driving tour brochure at the tourist information center on Highway 49.

 HELENA CONFEDERATE CEMETERY
1801 Holly Street, Helena, AR 72342; (870) 338–8221.

Description: The cemetery contains grave sites of Confederate soldiers who died during the 1863 Battle of Helena, as well as the graves of soldiers who died in other engagements in eastern Arkansas. The cemetery is also the final resting place of Confederate Gen. Patrick Cleburne, who was killed at the Battle of Franklin, Tennessee.

Admission Fees: Free.

NORTHWEST ARKANSAS
CIVIL WAR HERITAGE TRAIL

Points of interest include the following:

Arkansas—Pea Ridge National Military Park, Prairie Grove Battlefield State Park, Fort Smith National Historic Site, Buffalo National River, Headquarters House Museum, Old Fort Museum, Fayetteville National Cemetery, Fayette Confederate Cemetery, Fort Smith National Cemetery, Fort Smith Oak Cemetery

Missouri—Wilson's Creek National Battlefield, Carthage Museum, Springfield National Cemetery

Oklahoma—Fort Gibson Historic Site, Cabin Creek Battlefield, Honey Springs Battlefield Site

Kansas—Fort Scott National Historic Site, Mine Creek State Historic Site, Baxter Springs Museum

The Union armies of Samuel Curtis and James Blunt and the Confederate armies of Earl Van Dorn, Sterling Price, and Stand Watie, along with hordes of (pro-Union, antislavery) "Jayhawkers" and (proslavery) "Bushwhackers" roamed and fought throughout this frontier region. The Northwest Arkansas Civil War Heritage Trail includes national, state, and local historic sites associated with Union and Confederate activities in northwest Arkansas, northeast Oklahoma, southwest Missouri, and southeast Kansas.

Directions are available in the "Northwest Arkansas Civil War Heritage Trail" brochure, a general guide to Civil War sites in this much-fought-over region of the Trans-Mississippi theater of operations. To receive a copy, call Pea Ridge National Military Park (501–451–8122), Fort Smith National Historic Site (501–783–3961), Prairie Grove Battlefield State Park (501–846–2990), or Buffalo National River (501–741–5443). Copies are also available at most Arkansas Tourist Information Centers.

Open to Public: Daily 8:00 A.M.–5:00 P.M.
Visitor Services: None.
Regularly Scheduled Events: None.
Directions: From I–40 take Highway 61 south to Highway 49 east. Follow Highway 49 into West Helena. Take Highway 49 bypass, and follow into downtown Helena. Follow historic route signs.

JACKSONPORT

 JACKSONPORT STATE PARK

205 Avenue Street, Jacksonport, AR 72075; (870) 523–2143; www.arkansas stateparks.com; jacksonport@arkansas. com.

Description: During the Civil War, Jacksonport was occupied by both Confederate and Union armies due to its strategic position accessible to the Mississippi and Arkansas Rivers. Five generals used the town as their headquarters. On June 5, 1865, Confederate Gen. Jeff Thompson, "Swampfox of the Confederacy," surrendered 6,000 troops to Lt. Col. C. W. Davis at the Jacksonport Landing. Tour the Jacksonport Courthouse and its War Memorial Room, and the *Mary Woods No. 2* steamboat, restored to the 1890s period.

Admission Fees: Park, free; museum, adults $3.00, children $1.50; riverboat, adults $3.00, children $1.50. Combination ticket to museum and riverboat, adults $5.00, children $2.75.

Open to Public: Park, open daily all year; visitor center, Mar.–Oct., Sat.–Sun. 8:00 A.M.–5:00 P.M.; Nov.–Feb., Mon.–Sat. 8:00 A.M.–5:00 P.M., Sun. 1:00 P.M.–5:00 P.M.; museum, open all year Tues.–Sat. 8:00 A.M.–5:00 P.M., Sun. 1:00 P.M.–5:00 P.M.; closed Mon.; riverboat, Apr.–Oct., Sun. 1:00 P.M.–5:00 P.M., Tues.–Thurs. 10:00 A.M.–5:00 P.M., Fri.–Sat. 9:00 A.M.–5:00 P.M.; closed Mon.

Visitor Services: Public restrooms, information, handicapped access, gift shop, museum, camping, trails.

Regularly Scheduled Events: First weekend in June, Portfest; December, Christmas open house.

Directions: From Highway 67 at Newport, take exit 83 and follow the Jacksonport State Park signs.

JACKSONVILLE

21 REED'S BRIDGE BATTLEFIELD

Highway 161 at Bridge over Bayou Meto, Jacksonville, AR 72076; (501) 833–0265.

Description: On this site, which includes seven acres on the banks of the Bayou Meto, Confederates stopped Union troops in August 1863 by burning the bridge. The escalated tensions from the battle led to a duel a week later between two Confederate commanders, Gen. Lucius M. Walker and Gen. John Sappington Marmaduke.

Admission Fees: Free.

Open to Public: Daily from dawn to dusk.

Visitor Services: Information, handicapped access, trails.

Regularly Scheduled Events: None.

Directions: Take I-40 to I-440 north. Exit onto Highway 161 and travel approximately 2 miles to the bridge at Bayou Meto.

LAKE VILLAGE

22 DITCH BAYOU BATTLEFIELD

Lake Chicot State Park, 2542 Highway 257, Lake Village, AR 71653; (870) 265–5480; www.arkansasstateparks.com.

Description: Roadside exhibits interpret the 1864 Battle of Ditch Bayou, in which a small Confederate force under Col. Colton Greene inflicted heavy casualties on a much larger Union formation commanded by Gen. A. J. Smith. This was the largest battle in Chicot County and the last significant battle on Arkansas soil. It is part of a driving tour of Civil War sites along Lake Chicot. Brochures are available at Lake Chicot State Park.

Admission Fees: Free.

Open to Public: Daily from dawn to dusk.

Visitor Services: Wayside exhibits.

Regularly Scheduled Events: None.

Directions: From I-20 at Tallulah, Louisiana, take Highway 65 north 85 miles to the intersection with Highway 82 in Chicot County, Arkansas. Turn right and proceed east for 2 miles. The exhibits are on the left.

23 LAKE CHICOT STATE PARK

2542 Highway 257, Lake Village, AR 71653; (870) 265–5480; www.arkansas stateparks.com.

Description: Lake Chicot State Park interprets the impact of the Civil War on Chicot County through exhibits, programs, living history, and an annual reenactment. Research materials are located on-site, available through the interpreter's office. A brochure and driving tour are available of local Civil War sites.

Admission Fees: Free.

Open to Public: Visitor center, daily 8:00 A.M.–5:00 P.M.; park, daily twenty-four hours.

Visitor Services: Lodging, public restrooms, information, gas, handicapped access, food, gift shop, museum, camping, trails.

Regularly Scheduled Events: October, Civil War Weekend.

Directions: From I-20 at Tallulah, Louisiana, take Highway 65 north 85 miles to the intersection with Highway 82. Turn left and proceed north to Lake Village. Take Highway 144 for 8 miles to park.

LITTLE ROCK

 LITTLE ROCK CAMPAIGN DRIVING TOUR

Central Arkansas Civil War Heritage Trail Committee, P.O. Box 2125, Little Rock, AR 72203; (501) 699–1403 or (501) 376–3800.

Description: The Little Rock campaign of 1863 began with the Union advance from Helena, culminating forty days later in seizure of the state capitol from Confederate forces after numerous actions and skirmishes. Driving tour includes detailed exhibit panels at Brownsville, near Lonoke; Reed's Bridge at Jacksonville; Ashley's Mills and Willow Beach Lake near Scott; and Fourche Bayou and Riverfront Park in Little Rock.

Admission Fees: Free.

Open to Public: Daily from dawn to dusk.

Visitor Services: Roadside pull-offs with wayside exhibits.

Regularly Scheduled Events: None.

Directions: All sites are accessible from I–40 between Lonoke and Little Rock. Contact Central Arkansas Civil War Heritage Trail for driving tour brochure with detailed directions.

 LITTLE ROCK NATIONAL CEMETERY

2523 Confederate Boulevard, Little Rock, AR 72206; (501) 324–6401; www .cem.va.gov.

Description: Grounds were used as a Union campground by U.S. troops. When the troops left, the Confederates buried their dead on the west side. It was then bought in 1868 by the U.S. government for use as a military burial ground for occupation troops. A wall was erected between Union and Confederate sections but was taken down in 1913. The cemetery is one of the few national cemeteries where Confederate soldiers are buried.

Admission Fees: Free.

Open to Public: Grounds, daily from dawn to dusk; office, Mon.–Fri. 8:00 A.M.–4:30 P.M.

Visitor Services: Public restrooms, information.

Regularly Scheduled Events: April, Confederate Memorial Day; May, Memorial Day; November, Veterans Day.

Directions: From I–30 take the Roosevelt Road exit; go east 3 blocks to Confederate Boulevard. From I–440 take the Confederate Boulevard exit; go north about 1 mile.

 MacARTHUR MUSEUM OF ARKANSAS MILITARY HISTORY

503 East Ninth Street, Little Rock, AR 72202, (501) 376–4602; www.arkmilitary heritage.com.

Description: In February 1861 Arkansas citizens marched on Little Rock and took the arsenal, even though Arkansas had not yet seceded from the Union. For the next two years, the arsenal was under the control of the Confederacy. It was reclaimed when Federal troops took Little Rock in 1863. Located in the historic Tower Building—the birthplace of Gen. Douglas MacArthur and sole remaining building of the Little Rock Arsenal—the museum interprets the military heritage of the state and its citizens.

Admission Fees: Free.

Open to Public: Tues.–Sat. 10:00 A.M.–4:00 P.M., Sun. 1:00 P.M.–4:00 P.M.; guided tours by appointment.

Visitor Services: Public restrooms, information, handicapped access, gift shop.

Regularly Scheduled Events: Call or check Web site for events.

Directions: From I–30 take the Ninth Street exit, turning west onto Ninth Street. Museum is located within 1 block of I–30 in MacArthur Park.

MOUNT HOLLY CEMETERY

1200 Broadway, Little Rock, AR 72202; (501) 376–1843.

Description: Mount Holly, started in 1843, was the only cemetery in Little Rock until 1863 when Oakland Cemetery opened. In 1884, 640 bodies of unnamed Civil War soldiers were removed from Mount Holly to a mass grave in Oakland, marked by one monument. Several CSA veterans remain at Mount Holly, including Gens. James Fleming Fagan and Thomas Churchill; the latter also served as governor of Arkansas.

Admission Fees: Free.

Open to Public: Daily 8:00 A.M.–5:00 P.M.

Visitor Services: Public restrooms.

Regularly Scheduled Events: None.

Directions: From I–630 take the Route 67/Broadway Street exit south.

 OLD STATE HOUSE MUSEUM

300 West Markham Street, Little Rock, AR 72201; (501) 324–9685; www.oldstate house.com.

Description: Constructed from 1836 to 1842, the Old State House was the state's original capitol. It was the site of many significant events, including the 1861 secession convention. In 1863 the Confederate government fled the area, and the town fell to Union troops. Gen. Frederick Steele quartered his army in the State House during this occupation. It is now a museum of Arkansas history.

Admission Fees: Free.

Open to Public: Mon.–Sat. 9:00 A.M.–5:00 P.M., Sun. 1:00 P.M.–5:00 P.M.; office, Mon.–Fri. 8:00 A.M.–5:00 P.M.

Visitor Services: Information, tours, gift shop.

Regularly Scheduled Events: None.

Directions: From I–30 take the Markham Street/Cantrell Road exit and follow the signs.

NEW EDINBURG

 MARKS' MILLS BATTLEFIELD STATE PARK

c/o Arkansas State Parks, One Capitol Mall, Little Rock, AR 72201; (888) 287–2757; www.arkansasstateparks.com.

Description: Marks' Mills was one of four battles that defined the limits of Union Gen. Frederick Steele's foray into south Arkansas during the Red River campaign of 1864. Following the crushing Federal defeat, Steele abandoned Camden and retreated to Little Rock.

Admission Fees: Free.

Open to Public: Daily from dawn to dusk.

Visitor Services: Wayside exhibit panels.

Regularly Scheduled Events: None.

Directions: From I–30 at Malvern turn south on U.S. 270. In Malvern take Highway 9 south; 2 miles south of Princeton, take Highway 8 and continue through Fordyce to the site, near New Edinburg. This route traces a significant portion of Steele's retreat from Camden, going through Tulip and Princeton and passing just 13 miles southwest of the final battle of the campaign at Jenkins' Ferry.

PINE BLUFF

 CAMP WHITE SULPHUR SPRINGS CONFEDERATE CEMETERY

Mailing Address: 2620 West 28th Avenue, Pine Bluff, AR 71603; (870) 534–1909 or (870) 879–1150; www.wss cemetery.com.

Description: Sulphur Springs was used as a campground by a number of Arkansas, Texas, and Louisiana units between late 1861 and early 1863. Many of them died of disease and were buried in this cemetery. Units known to have camped at the site include the 19th, 24th, 33rd, and 38th Arkansas Infantry and Hart's Arkansas Battery; Nutt's and Denson's Louisiana Cavalry companies; the 6th and 17th Texas Infantry;

THE RED RIVER CAMPAIGN

There are several significant sites associated with the Arkansas leg of the Union Red River campaign of 1864, in which a Union army under Maj. Gen. Frederick Steele sought to link up with an army under Gen. Nathaniel Banks in Louisiana and capture a cotton-rich section of Texas. Both Banks and Steele suffered a series of defeats. Steele's starving army managed to escape pursuing Confederates and returned to Little Rock a little more than a month after advancing into southern Arkansas. It was the last major Union military campaign in Arkansas.

The Arkansas Department of Parks and Tourism offers a brochure, "The Red River Campaign," that guides visitors to many of the sites included in the Arkansas portion of the campaign. To receive a copy, write Arkansas State Parks, One Capitol Mall, Little Rock, AR 72201, or call (888) 287–2757. The brochure is also available at many of the tourist information centers in Arkansas.

---

and the 24th and 25th Texas Cavalry, dismounted. The site is currently maintained as a cemetery and features interpretive signs.

Admission Fees: Free.

Open to Public: Daily from dawn to dusk.

Visitor Services: Information, tours by appointment, trails.

Regularly Scheduled Events: Second weekend in October, memorial service and living history.

Directions: From I–530 take exit 39 south to U.S. 79; turn right onto Sulphur Spring Road; turn right onto Luckwood Road.

 MARKS' MILL CEMETERY STATE PARK

8501 Woodhaven Drive, Pine Bluff, AR 71603; (870) 879–3712.

Description: Marks' Mills Cemetery State Park features an intact section of the Camden–Pine Bluff Road, where one of Union Gen. Frederick Steele's foraging parties was ambushed and decimated by Confederates under Gen. James Fagan on April 25, 1864. The Federal forces suffered some 1,500 casualties, mostly captured. The Marks' Mills Cemetery Park features wayside exhibits interpreting the battle.

Admission Fees: Free.

Open to Public: Daily from dawn to dusk.

Visitor Services: Wayside exhibits; trails.

Regularly Scheduled Events: April, reenactment; third Sunday in July, Marks Family Reunion.

Directions: From U.S. 65 at Pine Bluff, take U.S. 65 south to Kingsland; take Highway 97 south for 5 miles. Road entrance is approximately 0.25 mile north of intersection of Highways 8 and 97 on the east side of the road.

PRAIRIE GROVE

 PRAIRIE GROVE BATTLEFIELD STATE PARK CWPT

506 East Douglas, Prairie Grove, AR 72753; (479) 846–2990; www.arkansas stateparks.com.

Description: The Battle of Prairie Grove was fought on December 7, 1862, between the Confederate Army of the Trans-Mississippi and the Federal Army of the Frontier, and resulted in more than 2,700 casualties. It was the last major Civil War battle in northwest Arkansas and paved the way for control of the region by the Federal army.

Admission Fees: Park, free; museum, adults $5.00, children six–twelve $3.00.

Open to Public: Park, daily 8:00 A.M.–dusk; museum, daily 8:00 A.M.–5:00 P.M.

Prairie Grove Battlefield, Arkansas. CWPT files.

Visitor Services: Public restrooms, information, handicapped access, gift shop, museum, Civil War Explorer, trails.

Regularly Scheduled Events: May, Memorial Day Tribute; Labor Day weekend, Clothesline Fair; first full weekend in December in even-numbered years, battle reenactment.

Directions: From I–540 at Alma, turn north on U.S. 71 for 40 miles to Fayetteville; then turn west on U.S. 62 for 10 miles to Prairie Grove Battlefield.

PRATTSVILLE

 JENKINS' FERRY STATE PARK

1200 Catherine Park Road, Hot Springs, AR 71913; (501) 844–4205; www .arkansasstateparks.com.

Description: This site is connected with the Battle of Jenkins' Ferry, the last major Arkansas battle in the Camden expedition of the Red River campaign. The April 30, 1864, battle was fought in flooded, foggy conditions as Gen. Frederick Steele's Union army desperately and successfully withstood Confederate attacks and crossed the Saline River to escape to Little Rock. The park only encompasses the Ferry Crossing site and not the battleground, which is about a mile from the park on private land.

Admission Fees: Free.

Open to Public: Daily from dawn to dusk.

Visitor Services: Picnicking, information, boat ramp.

Regularly Scheduled Events: None.

Directions: From I–30 take exit 98, Highway 270 to Prattsville; turn right on Highway 291; turn right on Highway 46 to the ferryboat site.

RISON

 MOUNT ELBA BATTLEFIELD

Mount Elba Road, Rison, AR 71655; (870) 325–7243.

Description: This site marks the location of the March 30, 1864, skirmish at the town of

Mount Elba between Confederate and Union forces involved in operations connected to Gen. Frederick Steele's Camden expedition.

Admission Fees: Free.

Open to Public: Daily from dawn to dusk.

Visitor Services: Boat ramp.

Regularly Scheduled Events: None.

Directions: From I–530 at Pine Bluff, take U.S. 79 south at exit 39 to Rison. Turn left at the intersection of Highway 35 south; go 2 miles on Highway 35 to Mount Elba Road, turn right, and travel 9 miles to the end of the road.

ST. CHARLES

 ST. CHARLES MUSEUM

608 Broadway Street, St. Charles, AR 72140; (870) 282–3704.

Description: This town was the site of the single shot that disabled the ironclad USS *Mound City.* The shot caused the steam drum to explode, killing 125 men. A monument stands in the center of Broadway Street and commemorates fallen Union and Confederate soldiers. The museum interprets the events.

Admission Fees: Free.

Open to Public: Mon.–Fri. 10:00 A.M.–3:00 P.M.

Visitor Services: Public restrooms, information, handicapped access, gift shop.

Regularly Scheduled Events: None.

Directions: From Brinkley Highway turn right onto Sixth Street. Take Sixth Street 2 blocks, then turn right on Broadway.

ST. FRANCIS

 CHALK BLUFF PARK

70 County Road 368, Piggott, AR 72454; (870) 598–2667.

Description: Chalk Bluff was a strategic crossing into Missouri used by both sides during the Civil War. Gen. John Marmaduke's 1863 raid into Mississippi ended here as he fought off pursuing Union troops.

Admission Fees: Free.

Open to Public: Daily from dawn to dusk.

Visitor Services: Public restrooms, handicapped access; camping, trails.

Regularly Scheduled Events: May, Civil War encampment.

Directions: Take U.S. 62 to St. Francis; turn west from town for 1.5 miles; then turn north for 1.25 miles to Chalk Bluff site. There are signs from St. Francis.

ST. JOE

 BUFFALO NATIONAL RIVER, TYLER BEND VISITOR CENTER

Route 1, Box 46, St. Joe, AR 72675; (870) 741–5443 (headquarters), (870) 439–2502 (visitor center); www.nps.gov/buff; buff_information@nps.gov.

Description: Buffalo National River's 95,000-acres preserve the unique natural and cultural features of the Arkansas Ozarks. During the Civil War the rugged terrain became a battleground between aggressive independent Confederate units and the Union forces holding northwest Arkansas. The residents caught in the middle of the constant skirmishing lost farms, possessions, and lives. Skirmish sites, saltpeter caves, and Civil War–era farms are interpreted. For Civil War orientation the park staff recommends visiting the Tyler Bend Visitor Center, near Marshall, Arkansas.

Admission Fees: Free.

Open to Public: Park, daily from dawn to dusk; Tyler Bend Visitor Center, daily 8:30 A.M.–4:30 P.M.

Visitor Services: Lodging, public restrooms, information, gift shop, museum, camping, trails.

Regularly Scheduled Events: Summer tours and interpretive talks; call for schedule.

Directions: From I–40 at Conway exit onto

U.S. 65 and proceed north. The Tyler Bend Visitor Center is about 10 miles north of Marshall. Follow the signs. Tyler Bend Visitor Center is about 100 miles from Little Rock and from Springfield, Missouri.

WASHINGTON

 ### HISTORIC WASHINGTON STATE PARK

Corner of Highway 195 and Highway 278, Washington, AR 71862; (870) 983–2684; www.historicwashingtonstate park.com; owashington@arkansas .com.

Description: Historic Washington State Park offers insight into a nineteenth-century community and builds understanding of the people, times, and events of the Territorial, Antebellum, Civil War, and Reconstruction eras in Arkansas history. This was the state capital from 1863 to 1865 and a cultural, economic, and political center, especially after Little Rock was taken by the Union army in 1863. The site is on the Southwest Trail. Interpreted by guides in period attire, a collection of the park's thirty historical structures and homes are open for tours according to the theme of the day.

Admission Fees: Historic Parks Tour (ten–twelve sites), adults $8.00, children six–twelve $4.00, family pass $30.00; single-site tours, two-site tours, and group rates available.

Open to Public: Daily 8:00 A.M.–5:00 P.M.

Regularly Scheduled Events: February, Frontier Days (nineteenth-century crafts), Valentine's Day dinner in tavern; March, Jonquil Festival with tours, special events, arts and crafts; November, Civil War Reenactments Weekend; December, Christmas and Candlelight.

Directions: From I–30 take exit 30. Go north on Highway 278 for 9 miles. Historic Washington State Park is located east and west of Highway 278. Information desk is located in the 1874 Court House, which is just off Highway 278.

❖ KANSAS ❖

BAXTER SPRINGS

 ### BAXTER SPRINGS HERITAGE CENTER AND MUSEUM

740 East Avenue, Baxter Springs, KS 66713; (620) 856–2385.

Description: On October 6, 1863, Fort Blair was attacked by William Quantrill and more than 300 guerrilla troops. Though greatly outnumbered, two companies of the Third Wisconsin Cavalry and a company of Second Kansas Colored Infantry at the fort repulsed the attack. Quantrill turned north and attacked a military supply train under Gen. James Blunt, killing nearly all of Blunt's command, many who were trying to surrender. The victims are buried in the national cemetery plot west of the present town of Baxter Springs. The Baxter Springs Heritage Center features an extensive collection of Civil War artifacts and gives a detailed account of the events in Baxter Springs and at Fort Blair. The Fort Blair Historic Site features a replication of the log breastworks at Fort Blair as well as interpretive signage. A twenty-three-minute video at the heritage center describes and interprets the October 6, 1863, events. The self-guided Civil War driving tour has been developed with roadside signage and an accompanying map and brochure.

Admission Fees: Free.

Open to Public: Fort site, daily from dawn to dusk; museum, Tues.–Sat. 10:30 A.M.–4:30 P.M., Sun. 1:00 P.M.–4:30 P.M. Museum is closed during the week in the winter.

Visitor Services: Information, handicapped access, gift shop (10 percent discount for CWPT members), trails.

Regularly Scheduled Events: October, observance of Baxter Springs anniversary.

Directions: Take exit 8B off I–44 west of Joplin, Missouri. Follow Baxter Springs turnoff approximately 9 miles.

FORT RILEY

 U.S. CAVALRY MUSEUM

Building 500, Huedner Road, Ft. Riley, KS 66442-0160; (785) 239–2737; www .riley.army.mil.

Description: Fort Riley was established in 1853 near where the Smoky Hill and Republican Rivers join to form the Kansas River. During the 1850s officers such as Philip St. George Cooke, "Jeb" Stuart, and John Buford were stationed here and participated in events that came to be known as "Bleeding Kansas." The first territorial legislature met at the fort in the summer of 1855. During the Civil War, as regular troops returned East, the fort was garrisoned by state militia units who continued to protect the frontier.

Admission Fees: Free.

Open to Public: Mon.–Sat. 9:00 A.M.–4:30 P.M., Sun. noon–4:30 P.M.; closed major holidays. Visitors must present photo ID, vehicle registration, and proof of insurance to enter military base.

Visitor Services: Public restrooms, information, handicapped access, gift shop.

Regularly Scheduled Events: None.

Directions: Located approximately 120 miles west of Kansas City on I–70. From I–70 take exit 301 (Marshal Army Airfield); follow signs after crossing the Kansas River bridge.

FORT SCOTT

 FORT SCOTT NATIONAL CEMETERY

900 East National Avenue, Fort Scott, KS 66701; (316) 223–2840; www.cem.va.gov.

Description: Established in 1862 as one of the twelve original national cemeteries, this cemetery is the final resting place of Union, Native American, African-American, and Confederate soldiers who died during the Civil War.

Admission Fees: None.

Open to Public: Daily from dawn to dusk; office, Mon.–Fri. 8:00 A.M.–4:30 P.M.

Visitor Services: Public restrooms, brochure available.

Regularly Scheduled Events: May, Memorial Day ceremony; November 11, Veterans Day ceremony.

Directions: From U.S. 54 at Fort Scott, turn south on National Avenue for 20 blocks, to East National Avenue; proceed 5 blocks to cemetery.

 FORT SCOTT NATIONAL HISTORIC SITE

Old Fort Boulevard, Fort Scott, KS 66701; (620) 223–0310; www.nps.gov/ fosc.

Description: Fort Scott mirrored the course of western settlement along the middle border. From 1842 to 1853, troops helped keep peace on this Indian frontier. Between 1854 and 1861, the years of "Bleeding Kansas," the town was caught up in the violent struggle between "Free-Soilers" and pro-slavery advocates. During the Civil War the fort served as the headquarters of the Army of the Frontier, a supply depot, a refugee center for displaced Indians, and a base for one of the first African-American regiments raised during the war, the First Kansas Colored Infantry.

Admission Fees: Ages sixteen and over $3.00.

Open to Public: Daily, Apr.–Oct. 8:00 A.M.–5:00 P.M.; Nov.–Mar. 9:00 A.M.–5:00 P.M.; closed Thanksgiving, Christmas, and New Year's Day.

Visitor Services: Public restrooms, information, limited handicapped access, gift shop, museum.

Regularly Scheduled Events: April, Civil War Encampment; May, Memorial Day weekend, Frontier Garrison Life; June, Good Ol' Days; July, military holiday; summer, daily guided tours; Labor Day weekend, Frontier Garrison Life; September, Frontier Days; December, candlelight tour.

Directions: Located about 90 miles south of Kansas City and 60 miles north of Joplin, Missouri. Go 1 mile west of the intersection of U.S. 69 and U.S. 54 east. Take Wall Street west to Old Fort Boulevard.

PLEASANTON

 43 MINE CREEK BATTLEFIELD STATE HISTORIC SITE CWPT

20485 Highway 52, Pleasanton, KS 66075; (913) 352–8890; www.kshs.org; minecreek@kshs.org.

Description: On October 25, 1864, some 10,000 Union and Confederate troops clashed at Mine Creek. They had been fighting off and on for several days as Gen. Sterling Price's Confederates marched through Missouri and then were turned back at the Battle of Westport. The Union cavalry caught up with the rear guard of Price's wagon train at Mine Creek and crushed them in the second-largest cavalry charge of the Civil War. A portion of the battlefield is being preserved by the state of Kansas. A 1.5-mile interpretive trail along Mine Creek is now in place.

Admission Fees: Free; donations are accepted.

Open to Public: Mar.–Nov., Wed.–Sat. 9:00 A.M.–5:00 P.M., Sun. 1:00 P.M.–5:00 P.M.; Dec.–Feb., open for special events and by appointment only.

Visitor Services: Public restrooms, gift shop, museum, visitors center, trails. Special tours and programs can be arranged by calling the site office.

Regularly Scheduled Events: None.

Directions: Take U.S. 69 to Pleasanton. Turn west on Highway 52 for 0.5 mile. Visitors center is on the south side of the road.

❖ LOUISIANA ❖

ALEXANDRIA

 44 KENT PLANTATION

3601 Bayou Rapides Road, Alexandria, LA 71303; (318) 487–5998; www.kent house.org; admin@kenthouse.org.

Description: Kent House, a raised French-Creole cottage built in 1796, is the oldest remaining structure in central Louisiana. The courageous owner, Robert Hynson, refused to leave his home, thus preventing Union troops retreating from the Battle of Mansfield from setting it on fire. Unfortu-nately, Hynson could not save his stock or outbuildings from the ravaging army. Many of Kent House's destroyed structures have been replicated using antebellum buildings from other plantations. The complex includes a kitchen, slave cabins, carriage house, milk house, blacksmith shop, and sugar mill. The site features living history events throughout the year.

Admission Fees: Adults $6.00, children six–twelve $2.00, under six free, seniors $5.00.

Open to Public: Mon.–Sat. 9:00 A.M.–5:00 P.M.; tours at 9:00, 10:00, and 11:00 A.M.; 1:00, 2:00, and 3:00 P.M.

TRANS-MISSISSIPPI

Louisiana Sites

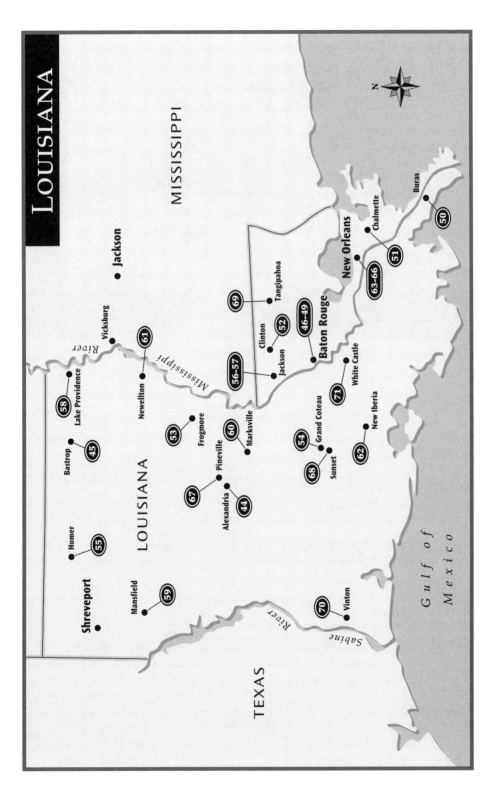

Kent House, Alexandria, Louisiana. Kent Plantation House.

Visitor Services: Public restrooms, information, gift shop, museum, tours.

Regularly Scheduled Events: May, Alexandria Afire! living history event.

Directions: From I–49 exit onto MacArthur Drive. Remain on MacArthur until it intersects Bayou Rapides Road. Turn right on Bayou Rapides Road and continue 0.5 mile; turn left to Kent House.

BASTROP

 SNYDER MUSEUM

1620 East Madison Street (U.S. 165N), Bastrop, LA 71220; (318) 281–8760.

Description: This museum highlights local history, including a special display dedicated to the Civil War. It also houses a genealogical section.

Admission Fees: Free.

Open to Public: Tues.–Fri. 9:00 A.M.–4:00 P.M.; call to confirm hours.

Visitor Services: Public restrooms.

Regularly Scheduled Events: None.

Directions: From I–20 take U.S. 165 through Monroe to Bastrop. U.S. 165 becomes East Madison Street.

BATON ROUGE

 MAGNOLIA CEMETERY

North Dufrocq and Main Streets, Baton Rouge, LA 70821; (225) 387–2464; www .fhl.org.

Description: Much of the heaviest fighting of the Battle of Baton Rouge took place in this cemetery on August 5, 1862. The battle pitted Union forces under the overall command of Brig. Gen. Thomas Williams against the Confederate forces of Maj. Gen. John C. Breckinridge. Though Union forces were pushed back to the river, guns from the Federal fleet forced Confederate withdrawal after expected support from the Rebel ironclad gunboat *Arkansas* did not materialize. The ferocity of the attack, however, convinced the Federal command to withdraw their forces to protect New Orleans, allowing Gen. John Breckinridge to fortify Port Hudson. This delayed Federal domination of the Mississippi River until July 1863. Confederate soldiers who died at Magnolia Cemetery are buried in a mass grave. A brochure is available.

Admission Fees: Donations welcome.

Open to Public: Daily from dawn to dusk.

Visitor Services: None.

Regularly Scheduled Events: Saturday closest to August 5, Battle of Baton Rouge commemoration.

Directions: From I–10 exit onto Florida Street. Circle around; the cemetery is bounded by Florida and Laurel Streets and 19th and 22nd Streets, near downtown Baton Rouge.

 OLD ARSENAL POWDER MAGAZINE MUSEUM

P.O. Box 94125, Baton Rouge, LA 70804-9125; (225) 342–0401; www.sec.state.la.us.

Description: Before Louisiana seceded from the Union on January 26, 1861, the governor ordered the state militia to seize the arsenal. Shortly thereafter, Louisiana joined the Confederate States of America, and the weapons, ammunition, and powder stored in the Baton Rouge compound was rushed to the embattled Southern armies. In May 1862 Union forces captured Louisiana's capital city. Federal troops occupied the arsenal and the fortifications.

Admission Fees: Adults $1.00.

Open to Public: Tues.–Sat. 9:00 A.M.–4:00 P.M.

Regularly Scheduled Events: None.

Visitor Services: Interpretive center, tours.

Directions: From I–10 take Capitol Access/Governor's Mansion exit. Keep straight toward the State Capitol. Arsenal is located on the State Capitol grounds, between the capitol and the governor's mansion.

 OLD STATE CAPITOL

100 North Boulevard, Baton Rouge, LA 70801; (225) 342–0500; www.sec.state.la .us/osc; osc@sos.louisiana.gov.

Description: Completed in 1850, this building served as the State House of Louisiana until the state capital was moved to Opelousas to avoid capture by Federal troops. The Gothic structure was burned in 1862 when it was a Federal prison. On the grounds is the grave of Henry Watkins Allen, Confederate governor of Louisiana and brigadier general.

Admission Fees: Adults $4.00, children eighteen and under free.

Open to Public: Tues.–Sat. 10:00 A.M.–4:00 P.M., noon–4:00 P.M.; closed most major holidays and periodically for maintenance.

Visitor Services: Public restrooms, information, handicapped access, gift shop, museum, tours.

Old State Capitol, Baton Rouge, Louisiana. CWPT files.

Regularly Scheduled Events: None.
Directions: From I–110 take the Government Street exit and head west toward the river. Stay straight on Government Street; it will turn sharply to the right and become River Road. Turn right on the first street, North Boulevard. The Old State Capitol can be seen on the right.

 **PENTAGON BARRACKS**

959 North Third Street, Baton Rouge, LA 70802; (225) 387–2464; www.fhl.org.
Description: The Pentagon Barracks were constructed in 1819–29 to house U.S. troops and were used as a garrison until 1877. From 1861 to 1862, the barracks was held by the Confederates. It served as quarters for many famous soldiers, including Gens. Wade Hampton, Robert E. Lee, and Stonewall Jackson. *NOTE:* The Pentagon Barracks currently houses private apartments for state legislators and the offices of the lieutenant governor; it is not open for public tours.
Admission Fees: Call for information.
Open to Public: Call for information.
Visitor Services: None.
Regularly Scheduled Events: None.
Directions: From I–10 take Capitol Access/Governor's Mansion exit. Keep straight around capitol until you see a flashing light; turn left. The Pentagon Barracks is the two-story brick building on the right. Parking lot in front.

 BURAS

 FORT JACKSON

P.O. Box 7043, Buras, LA 70041; (985) 657–7083; Plaquemines Parish, (504) 392–6690; www.plaqueminesparish .com/tourism.

Description: This restored fort (1822–32) was built to defend New Orleans and the mouth of the Mississippi River. In April 1862 Flag Officer David Farragut's mortar boats bombarded Fort Jackson in order to move upriver. Thirteen ships succeeded in passing the fort and continued on to capture the city of New Orleans. *NOTE:* Fort Jackson suffered severe damage due to Hurricanes Katrina and Rita and is closed to the public until further notice.
Admission Fees: Free.
Open to Public: Call for information.
Visitor Services: Call for information.
Regularly Scheduled Events: Call or check Web site for events.
Directions: From I–10 through New Orleans, cross the New Orleans Bridge going west to Gretna. Get onto Westbank Expressway; proceed 1.5 miles to Louisiana Highway 23. The fort is 60 miles south.

CHALMETTE

RENE BEAUREGARD HOUSE/ JEAN LAFITTE NATIONAL HISTORICAL PARK AND PRESERVE

8686 West St. Bernard Highway, Chalmette, LA 70043; house (504) 589–4430, park (504) 589–4428; www.nps.gov/jela.

Description: Located on the Battle of New Orleans (War of 1812) site, this two-story, cement-covered house was the home of Judge Rene Beauregard, son of Confederate Gen. P. G. T. Beauregard.
Admission Fees: Free.
Open to Public: Daily 9:00 A.M.–5:00 P.M.
Visitor Services: Public restrooms, information, interpretive center, tours.
Regularly Scheduled Events: None.
Directions: From I–10 through the city of New Orleans, take I–610 east. Take Chalmette/Littlewood exit south to I–510 to Highway 47; turn right onto St. Bernard Highway. After 2 miles the Chalmette National Park sign will be visible.

CIVIL WAR SITES EXPERIENCE KATRINA'S WRATH

On August 29, 2005, Hurricane Katrina made landfall along the Gulf Coast, devastating historic sites throughout the region. Many sites along the Civil War Discovery Trail suffered severe or catastrophic damage from the storm; some were completely and regrettably destroyed.

During the war, Fort Jackson in Plaquemines Parish, Louisiana, was the most formidable obstacle to the Union navy's capture of New Orleans. Situated between two levees, the fort sat in 8 feet of water for 6 weeks after Katrina before it could be properly drained. The lengthy submersion weakened the fort's brick walls, leaving its structural integrity uncertain. The submersion also ruined the site's museum. Cleanup efforts have emptied the area of the storm's debris, but returning Fort Jackson to its pre-Katrina status will be a challenge.

Farther north in New Orleans, the storm caused an estimated $17 million in damages at Fort Pike. The storm turned minor preexisting structural and cosmetic problems into a perilous situation. Massive cracks developed at the fort's corner bastions, and water damage in the casements made the site unstable and unsafe. Large signs from Fort Pike washed up as far away as Ship Island, Mississippi. Restoration efforts are underway through the Louisiana Office of State Parks and the Federal Emergency Management Agency.

Other important Civil War sites in Biloxi, Mississippi, also suffered catastrophic damage from the tidal surge. Situated only 12 feet above sea level, Beauvoir, site of the Jefferson Davis Home and Presidential Library, was devastated by the storm. Prior to Katrina, seven structures stood on the property; today, only portions of two remain. The core of the Jefferson Davis Mansion survived, though much of the roof and all of the porches were destroyed. Sixty-five percent of the Presidential Library was destroyed, including the first-floor museum. Among the priceless artifacts lost were Jefferson Davis's authorization of the Confederate navy, the Davis family Bible, Davis's desks, and numerous portraits and manuscripts. Thanks to generous contributions, restoration and reconstruction efforts began in February 2007.

Elsewhere in Biloxi, two Discovery Trail sites were so damaged that they have closed their doors permanently. The Episcopal Church of the Redeemer, where Jefferson Davis worshipped, and the Father Ryan House, home of the poet laureate of the Confederacy, were not able to recover from the devastation caused by the storm.

The damage also reached far inland. One hundred and fifty miles north of the coast, the Old Capitol Museum of Mississippi History had a portion of its copper roof ripped off by storm winds. Although the artifacts were removed and saved from damage, the building will require a $14.2 million restoration.

Other Discovery Trail sites to suffer at the hands of Katrina include: Forts Gaines and Morgan off Mobile Bay in Alabama; Fort Pickens in Gulf Shore, Florida; Fort Jefferson in Key West, Florida; Port Hudson State Historic Site in Jackson, Louisiana; Tupelo National Battlefield in Tupelo, Mississippi; Brice's Crossroads National Battlefield in Baldwyn, Mississippi; and Sabine Pass State Historical Park in Sabine Pass, Texas.

CLINTON

 CLINTON CONFEDERATE STATE CEMETERY

East Feliciana Parish, Marston Street, Clinton, LA 70722; (225) 634–7155.

Description: This four-acre cemetery contains the remains of hundreds of Civil War troops from both sides. Because Clinton was connected to the Mississippi River by railroad, the town received many sick and wounded soldiers from nearby Port Hudson.
Admission Fees: Free.
Open to Public: Daily from dawn to dusk.
Visitor Services: Tours by appointment.
Regularly Scheduled Events: None.
Directions: Located north of Baton Rouge on Louisiana 67 in Clinton; go straight to the caution light on Louisiana 67; turn left on St. Helen Street, turn left on Bank Street, and go 2 blocks and turn right. Continue 1½ blocks. Cemetery is on the right.

FROGMORE

 FROGMORE COTTON PLANTATION AND GINS

11054 Highway 84, Frogmore, LA 71334; (318) 757–3333; www.frogmore plantation.com; frogmore@bayou.com.

Description: Frogmore is an antebellum cotton plantation, with twenty historic buildings. The plantation tour gives a comprehensive understanding of pre– and post–Civil War plantation life. Details regarding the effects of the war on both slaves and women are included.
Admission Fees: Adults $10.00, children $5.00.
Open to Public: Mar.–mid-Nov. Mon.–Fri. 9:00 A.M.–3:00 P.M., Sat. 10:00 A.M.–2:00 P.M.; June–Aug. Mon.–Fri. 9:00 A.M.–1:00 P.M.; winter, by reservation only.
Visitor Services: Public restrooms, information, handicapped access, gift shop.
Regularly Scheduled Events: Saturdays in

September and October, cotton harvest.
Directions: From I–20 at Tallulah travel south on U.S. 65 to Ferriday. Turn right onto U.S. 84 west and go 7 miles to Frogmore Plantation.

GRAND COTEAU

 ACADEMY OF THE SACRED HEART

1821 Academy Road, Grand Coteau, LA 70541; (337) 662–5275; www.ashcoteau .org; info@ashcoteau.org.

Description: This Catholic girls' school was established in 1821 and is known for its beautiful formal gardens and oak alley. The academy has remained in continuous operation through fire, epidemics, and the Civil War. In 1863 Gen. Nathan Banks commanded Federal troops pouring into the Teche country, and he made his headquarters at Grand Coteau for a brief time. His daughter attended a Sacred Heart school in New York, and the superior of the convent there requested that the general look after the nuns at Grand Coteau. The general protected the students and the nuns and even provided food and supplies to the convent, allowing the school to remain open during the war.
Admission Fees: Adults $5.00.
Open to Public: Only open for visitation by appointment; please call ahead to make arrangements.
Visitor Services: Public restrooms, information, gift shop, museum, tours.
Regularly Scheduled Events: None.
Directions: From I–10 take I–49 exit. Follow I–49 toward Opelousas to the Grand Coteau/Sunset exit. Exit on Highway 93 toward Grand Coteau. Highway 93 becomes Main Street. Turn left at the traffic light onto Church Street. Follow Church Street to the academy.

HOMER

 HERBERT S. FORD MEMORIAL MUSEUM

519 South Main Street, Homer, LA 71040; (318) 927–9190; www.claiborne one.org; fordmu@shreve.net.

Description: Homer was a departure point for Confederate soldiers during the Civil War and also served as a regional refugee center for persons fleeing Union-occupied territory. The museum houses a fascinating collection of memorabilia and artifacts from the north Louisiana hill country, including Civil War items.

Admission Fees: Adults $3.00, children $1.00, families $5.00.

Open to Public: Mon., Wed., Fri. 9:00 A.M.– noon, 1:00 P.M.–4:00 P.M.; or by appointment.

Visitor Services: Public restrooms, information.

Regularly Scheduled Events: None.

Directions: From I–20 west exit at Minden; follow U.S. 79 for approximately 20 miles. The museum is on the right at the first light in Homer.

JACKSON

 CENTENARY STATE HISTORIC SITE AND JACKSON CONFEDERATE CEMETERY

3522 College Street, Jackson, LA 70748; (225) 634–7925 or (888) 677–2364; www .lastateparks.com.

Description: Centenary State Historic Site is a former college that interprets the history of education in Louisiana. The college buildings were used as hospitals for Confederate soldiers from 1862 to 1863. A small skirmish was fought on the grounds on August 3, 1863. The Jackson Confederate Cemetery is located on the grounds and contains more than one hundred unmarked graves of soldiers who died during the war.

Admission Fees: Centenary State Historic Site, adults $2.00, children under twelve and adults sixty-one and over free, school groups free; Jackson Confederate Cemetery, free.

Open to Public: Daily 9:00 A.M.–5:00 P.M.; closed on Thanksgiving, Christmas, and New Year's Day.

Visitor Services: Public restrooms, handicapped access, museum, tours, visitor center; Jackson Confederate Cemetery, none.

Regularly Scheduled Events: June, Confederate Memorial Day service; July, Old Fashioned Fourth of July; October, Ghosts of Centenary.

Directions: Take I–10 north through Baton Rouge. Exit at U.S. 61; turn right. Turn right at Louisiana 10 and follow signs to Centenary State Historic Site, which is located at East College and Pine Streets in the town of Jackson in East Feliciana Parish. Jackson Confederate Cemetery is located adjacent to Centenary State Historic Site. Information on the cemetery can be obtained at Centenary State Historic Site.

 PORT HUDSON STATE HISTORIC SITE CWPT

236 U.S. Highway 61, Jackson, LA 70748; (225) 654–3775 or (888) 677–3400; www.lastateparks.com.

Description: Port Hudson was the site of the longest siege in U.S. military history and the last Confederate stronghold on the Mississippi River. The Union force of 30,000 to 40,000 was held off by 6,800 Confederate soldiers from May 23 to July 9, 1863. This conflict was also one of the first in which free black soldiers fought on the side of the Union.

Admission Fees: Adults and groups $2.00, seniors and children under twelve free.

Open to Public: Daily 9:00 A.M.–5:00 P.M.; closed on Thanksgiving, Christmas, and New Year's Day.

Visitor Services: Public restrooms, information, research library, handicapped access, trails, picnicking.

FOR MORE INFORMATION

"The Louisiana Civil War Heritage Guide," available through the Louisiana Office of Tourism, outlines significant military actions in Louisiana during the Civil War (such as the role it played in the capture of the Mississippi River). The guide also highlights some of the economic and social issues in the state at the time and lists cultural attractions of the era that are of interest to visitors.

A copy of the guide can be obtained from any of the state's welcome centers or by calling (504) 342–8119 or (800) 695–1638.

Regularly Scheduled Events: Last weekend in March, battle reenactment; first Sunday of every month, Civil War weapons demonstration; Fall and Spring School Day. *Directions:* Take I–10 to U.S. 61 (Natchez exit). Turn right and go north on U.S. 61 for 14 miles; park entrance is on the left.

LAKE PROVIDENCE

 GRANT'S CANAL, BYERLEY HOUSE

600 Lake Street, Lake Providence, LA 71254; (318) 559–5125; byerley@bayou.com.

Description: Grant's Canal and Park and Lake Overlook are located on U.S. 65. The canal is all that remains of Gen. Ulysses Grant's 1863 attempt to circumvent the fortifications at Vicksburg through the backwater of Louisiana. It is approximately 1,000 feet long. The western end of the canal can be viewed from the 600-foot pier and nature walk, which also offers a view of Lake Providence. Byerley House, adjacent to the park, serves as a visitor information center. *Admission Fees:* Free. *Open to Public:* Park, daily from dawn to dusk; Byerley House, Mon.–Fri. 9:00 A.M.– 5:00 P.M. *Visitor Services:* Information at visitor center. *Regularly Scheduled Events:* None. *Directions:* From Vicksburg take I–20 west to Tallulah. In Tallulah take the U.S. 65 north exit to Lake Providence. Grant's Canal and Byerley House are located on U.S. 65 at the eastern end of Lake Providence.

MANSFIELD

 MANSFIELD STATE HISTORIC SITE CWPT

15149 Highway 175, Mansfield, LA 71052; (318) 872–1474; www.lastateparks.com; mansfield_int@crt.state.la.us.

Description: The Battle of Mansfield took place on April 8, 1864. Under the leadership of Gen. Richard Taylor, an army of fewer than 9,000 Confederate soldiers from Texas and Louisiana defeated 13,000 Union troops under Gen. Nathaniel Banks. The day after the Battle of Mansfield, on April 9, the fierce Battle of Pleasant Hill was fought, with both sides taking heavy losses and withdrawing from the field after dark. *Admission Fees:* Adults $2.00, seniors and children under twelve free. *Open to Public:* Daily 9:00 A.M.–5:00 P.M. *Visitor Services:* Public restrooms, museum, maps, interpretive programs. *Regularly Scheduled Events:* April, reenactments and living history program. *Directions:* From I–20 go through Shreveport to Highway 171 south; go approximately 35 miles to Mansfield and turn onto U.S. 84 west. Turn south on Highway 175 and travel 3 miles to the site. From I–49, exit at U.S. 84 west and proceed as above.

Mansfield State Historic Site, Louisiana. CWPT files.

MARKSVILLE

 FORT DeRUSSY STATE HISTORIC SITE CWPT

Fort DeRussy Road, Marksville, LA 71351; (888) 253–8954; marksville_mgr @crt.state.la.us.

Description: The Fort DeRussy site consists of an earthen fort and a water battery. Union forces captured the fort as part of the Red River campaign in 1864.
Admission Fees: Free.
Open to Public: By appointment.
Visitor Services: Information.
Regularly Scheduled Events: None.
Directions: From I–49 take Louisiana Highway 115 through Bunkie to Marksville. In Marksville take Acton Street to Preston Street. Turn off Preston Street to Martin Luther King Drive.

NEWELLTON

 WINTER QUARTERS STATE COMMEMORATIVE AREA

Highway 608, Newellton, LA 71357; (888) 677–9468; winterquarters@crt .state.la.us.

Description: Winter Quarters, a home listed on the National Register of Historic Places, stands today as a rare survivor of the ravages of the Civil War and as a tribute to the courage of one woman. During the Vicksburg campaign, Gen. Ulysses S. Grant's soldiers marched through northeast Louisiana, destroying everything not needed by the Union army. Julia Nutt was able to save the home designed by her husband, Dr. Haller Nutt, a talented planter and inventor.
Admission Fees: Adults $2.00, children twelve and under and seniors free.
Open to Public: Daily 9:00 A.M.–5:00 P.M.;

closed on Thanksgiving, Christmas, and New Year's Day.

Visitor Services: Public restrooms, information, museum, plantation home, tours.

Regularly scheduled events: December, Christmas open house.

Directions: From 1–20 take the U.S. 65 south (Tallulah exit) approximately 30 miles to Newellton. Turn left on Highway 4. Go approximately 5 miles to Highway 605 and turn right. Turn left onto Highway 608. Winter Quarters is located approximately 3 miles down Highway 608.

New Iberia

 SHADOWS-ON-THE-TECHE

317 East Main Street, New Iberia, LA 70560; (337) 369–6446; www.shadowsontheteche.org; shadows@shadowsontheteche.org.

Description: This 1834 plantation home and gardens on the banks of Bayou Teche was home to the Weeks family for four generations before becoming a National Trust site in 1958. Letters found in trunks in the attic provide documentation for tours, which give an authentic picture of life on a Louisiana sugar plantation, particularly during the Civil War years and the 1863 occupation of the site.

Admission Fees: Adults $7.00, children six–eleven $4.00.

Open to Public: Daily 9:30 A.M.–4:30 P.M.

Visitor Services: Public restrooms, information, handicapped access, gift shop, tours, museum.

Regularly Scheduled Events: November, Civil War encampment.

Directions: From I-10 take exit 103A. Take Evangeline Thruway (U.S. 90); take Louisiana 14 exit off U.S. 90; take left offramp on Center Street and go to end. In New Iberia, turn left at East Main Street. Located at 317 East Main Street.

Shadows-on-the-Teche, New Iberia, Louisiana. Shadows-on-the-Teche National Historic Site.

"DIXIE"

The term *Dixie* is often used to refer to the Deep South, but do you know where the term came from? Just before the Civil War, New Orleans was a booming port city. There were steamships lined up for miles, and there was no room to unload their cargo. Money was flowing like water, but there was one small problem: The city at this time was still divided between the Americans and the Creoles, with Canal Street serving as the dividing line. The boatmen who wished to spend their money were inconvenienced because they had to use American money on the upriver side of Canal Street and French money on the downriver side. Citizens Bank on Toulouse Street solved the boatmen's problem. The most common bill in use was the $10 bill, and they printed the bill both in English and French. The French word for ten is *dix*, so the bill read both "ten" and "dix" on each side. Eventually, the boatmen began to call the bills "dixies" and the Deep South has been known as "Dixie" ever since.

—CWPT *CIVIL WAR EXPLORER*

NEW ORLEANS

 CABILDO

On Jackson Square, 701 Chartres Street, New Orleans, LA 70116; (540) 568–6968 or (800) 568–6968; www.lsm.crt.state.la .us/cabex.htm.

Description: Built in 1795 to house the municipal government of the Spanish colony, the Cabildo was also the setting for transfer of the Louisiana Purchase. Part of the state museum, the landmark houses exhibits that chronicle Louisiana's past from European settlement through Reconstruction. Of particular interest are sections on the antebellum era and the Civil War. Artifacts of slavery, weaponry, uniforms, documents, and photographs are included. A rare prototype of the Confederate battle flag and the quill used to sign documents emancipating Louisiana slaves are also on view.

Admission Fees: Adults $6.00; students, seniors, and active military $5.00; children twelve and under free.

Open to Public: Tues.–Sat. 9:00 A.M.–5:00 P.M., Sun. noon–5:00 P.M.

Visitor Services: Public restrooms, information, handicapped access.

Regularly Scheduled Events: None.

Directions: From I–10 take French Quarter exit (Orleans). Follow Basin to signs for French Quarter via Toulouse. Take Toulouse several blocks to Chartres. Turn right on Chartres to St. Peter. The Cabildo is at the corner of St. Peter and Chartres.

 CONFEDERATE MUSEUM

929 Camp Street, New Orleans, LA 70130; (504) 523–4522; www.confederate museum.com.

Description: This is the oldest museum in Louisiana. Civil War memorabilia include flags, uniforms, weapons, medical instruments, currency, and personal effects of Confederate president Jefferson Davis, Gen. Robert E. Lee, and other Southern leaders.

Admission Fees: Adults $7.00, students and seniors $5.00, children $2.00.

Open to Public: Mon.–Sat. 10:00 A.M.–4:00 P.M.

Visitor Services: Tours.

Regularly Scheduled Events: None.

Directions: From Baton Rouge take I–10 to New Orleans. Take Business District/ Tchoupitoulas Street exit; turn left at Calliope Street. Continue to Camp Street and

TRANS-MISSISSIPPI

turn right. Get in left-hand lane. The Confederate Museum is located on the corner of Camp and Howard Streets.

FORT PIKE STATE HISTORIC SITE

U.S. 90 at the Rigolets, New Orleans, LA 70129; (504) 662–5703 or (888) 662–5703; www.crt.state.la.us/ifort pike.aspx; fortpike@crt.state.la.us.

Description: Originally built in 1818 to prevent British reinvasion of the United States, Fort Pike was turned over to the Louisiana Continental Guard in January 1861. Within several weeks the state of Louisiana joined the Confederacy. For the next year Confederate troops trained under the command of Maj. Henry A. Clinch. The troops departed for Vicksburg in April 1862. In May 1862 Lt. Joseph DeHaven and his Union ship *Calhoun* retook the fort without incident. It was later used to train new African-American soldiers in the use of artillery. *NOTE:* This site is closed due to damage from Hurricane Katrina and is expected to reopen in late 2007.

Admission Fees: Call for information.
Open to Public: Call for information.
Visitor Services: Call for information.
Regularly Scheduled Events: Call or check Web site for events.
Directions: Fort Pike is located on U.S. 90, 23 miles east of downtown New Orleans. It is also accessible from I–10 via Louisiana 11 south, which connects to U.S. 90.

OLD U.S. MINT

400 Block of Esplanade Avenue, New Orleans, LA 70116; (504) 568–6968 or (800) 568–6968; www.lsm.crt.state.la.us/ mintex.htm.

Description: Operational from 1838 to 1909, the Old U.S. Mint at peak produced $5 million in coins monthly. For a short time during the Civil War, it was the only mint of the Confederate states. Now part of the

Louisiana State Museum, the building has been restored and houses popular exhibits on jazz, plus a collection of historical documents. *NOTE:* This site is closed due to damage from Hurricane Katrina and is projected to reopen in 2008.

Admission Fees: Call for information.
Open to Public: Call for information.
Visitor Services: Call for information.
Regularly Scheduled Events: None.
Directions: Take I–10 to Elysian Fields; go south toward the river; turn right to Esplanade Avenue.

PINEVILLE

ALEXANDRIA NATIONAL CEMETERY

209 East Shamrock Street, Pineville, LA; (318) 449–1793; www.cem.va.gov.

Description: Alexandria National Cemetery was established in 1867 as a burial site for Civil War soldiers. The cemetery also contains graves of soldiers from every American war since the Spanish-American War.

Admission Fees: Free.
Open to Public: Grounds, daily 8:00 A.M.–dusk; office, Mon.–Fri. 8:00 A.M.–4:30 P.M.
Visitor Services: None.
Regularly Scheduled Events: None.
Directions: Located on U.S. 165, north of Alexandria (across Red River Bridge).

SUNSET

CHRETIEN POINT PLANTATION

665 Chretien Point Road, Sunset, LA 70584; (337) 662–7050; www.chretien point.com; reservations@chretienpoint .com.

Description: Chretien Point Plantation was at the center of the Battle of Buzzard's Prairie, October 15, 1863. The home was surrounded by Union troops but is said to have been spared when owner Hypolite Chretien gave the Masonic sign. Today, there

is a memorial in the front of the property. The mansion is open for historic tours that include information about the Civil War, the battlefield, and plantation life.
Admission Fees: Adults $10.00, children $5.00, seniors $8.00.
Open to Public: Mon.–Fri. 1:00 P.M.–4:00 P.M., Sat.–Sun. 10:00 A.M.–4:00 P.M.; call in advance as it is sometimes closed for special events.
Visitor Services: Public restrooms, limited handicapped access, tours, gift shop.
Regularly Scheduled Events: Monthly, tea parties; October, Annual Civil War Living History Weekend. Call or check Web site for other events.
Directions: From Lafayette take I–49 north to exit 11 (Sunset). At the T-intersection turn right on Highway 93 and drive through the town of Sunset. At the flashing caution light, turn left and continue on Highway 93 for 5 miles. Turn right on Parish Road 356 (Bristol-Bosco exit). Go 1 block and turn right on Chretien Point Road. The site is 1 mile down on left.

TANGIPAHOA

CAMP MOORE/ CONFEDERATE MUSEUM AND CEMETERY
U.S. 51, Tangipahoa, LA 70465; (985) 229–2438; www.campmoore.com.

Description: Established in the summer of 1861, Camp Moore, named after Civil War Gov. Thomas Moore, served as one of the largest Confederate training bases in the Southern states. The Confederate cemetery, adjacent to Camp Moore, contains the remains of more than 400 Confederate soldiers.
Admission Fees: Adults $2.00, children $1.00, under six free.
Open to Public: Tues.–Sat. 10:00 A.M.–4:00 P.M. The last tour begins at 3:00 P.M.
Visitor Services: Information, trails.
Regularly Scheduled Events: Saturday and Sunday before Thanksgiving, annual reen-

actment and living history weekend.
Directions: From I–55 take the Tangipahoa exit. Go east to U.S. Highway 51. Camp Moore is located on U.S. 51, 0.5 mile north of the village of Tangipahoa.

VINTON

NIBLETT'S BLUFF PARK
Route 1, P.O. Box 358, Vinton, LA 70668; (337) 589–7117.

Description: Overlooking the Old Sabine River, Niblett's Bluff is the site of an old Civil War encampment. Confederate breastworks may still be seen.
Admission Fees: Free; call for camping and cabin rates.
Open to Public: Daily 7:00 A.M.–10:00 P.M.
Visitor Services: Lodging, public restrooms, camping, trails.
Regularly Scheduled Events: None.
Directions: From I–10 take exit at Tommey Starks; follow Highway 109 and go north for 2.9 miles. At yellow light look for directional sign on left.

WHITE CASTLE

NOTTOWAY PLANTATION RESTAURANT AND INN
30970 Highway 405, White Castle, LA 70788; (866) 4–A–VISIT; www.nottoway .com; innkeeper@nottoway.com.

Description: This is the largest plantation home in the South, an outstanding example of the opulent lifestyle enjoyed by the wealthy sugar planter before the Civil War. The three-story mansion has sixty-four rooms and was considered immense even by the standards of the antebellum "Golden Age."
Admission Fees: Call for current rates.
Open to Public: Daily 9:00 A.M.–5:00 P.M.; closed on Christmas Day.
Visitor Services: Lodging, public restrooms, food, museum, tours.

TRANS-MISSISSIPPI

Nottoway Plantation, White Castle, Louisiana. CWPT files.

Regularly Scheduled Events: December, candlelight Christmas tours.

Directions: From I–10 go over Mississippi River Bridge at Baton Rouge; take Plaque- mine exit south to Louisiana 1. Continue south on Louisiana 1 for 18 miles. Nottoway Plantation is on the left.

❖ MISSOURI ❖

ATHENS

 BATTLE OF ATHENS STATE HISTORIC SITE

Located off Highway 81 on Highway CC in Clark County, Athens, MO 63465; (660) 877–3871 or (800) 334–6946; www .mostateparks.com.

Description: This is the site of the northernmost Civil War battle west of the Mississippi: Union home guardsmen defeated southern Missouri state guard forces here on August 5, 1861. Thome-Benning House (open to the public) was struck by Southern artillery fire during the battle and has since been known as the "Cannonball House."

Admission Fees: Free.

Open to Public: Grounds, daily from dawn to dusk; Thome-Benning House, daily 9:00 A.M.–5:00 P.M.

Visitor Services: Public restrooms, information, museum, tours, camping, trails, picnicking, hiking, fishing, boating.

Regularly Scheduled Events: Every three years in August, major Civil War reenactment of the battle; spring and Christmas, open house; November, Veterans Day observance and open house.

Directions: From I-70: take U.S. 61 Wentzville exit (exit 210); proceed north on U.S. 61 approximately 135 miles to Highway 81 at Canton; proceed north on Highway 81 for approximately 40 miles to Highway CC. Follow Highway CC east 4 miles to Athens.

Bloomfield

 THE STARS AND STRIPES MUSEUM AND LIBRARY

17377 Stars and Stripes Way, Bloomfield, MO 63825; (573) 568–2055; www.starsandstripesmuseumlibrary.org; stripes@newwavecomm.net.

Description: This 7,500-square-foot museum is dedicated to commemorating military journalism, photography, cartoons, and poetry of our country's military newspaper, *Stars and Stripes.* It was here on November 9, 1861, that ten Illinois Union soldiers, using the vacated press of the *Bloomfield Herald,* published the first issue of *Stars and Stripes,* which they named after the American flag.

Admission Fees: Free.

Open to Public: Mon., Wed.–Fri. 10:00 A.M.–4:00 P.M., Sat. 10:00 A.M.–2:00 P.M., Sun. 1:00 P.M.–4:00 P.M.

Visitor Services: Public restrooms, information, gas, handicapped access, food, gift shop.

Regularly Scheduled Events: Call or check Web site for events.

Directions: From the intersection of I–55 and I–57 at Sikeston, travel west on U.S. 60 for approximately 20 miles; turn north on Highway 25, and travel 4 miles; museum will be on the left-hand side.

 STODDARD COUNTY CIVIL WAR CEMETERY

Bloomfield Cemetery at Missouri State Route E, Bloomfield, MO 63825; (573) 624–6168.

Description: More than 150 military markers memorialize soldiers and citizens who died in Stoddard County, Missouri, during the Civil War. Each monument carries a cause of death inscription, making this site unique and informative.

Admission Fees: Free.

Open to Public: Daily from dawn to dusk.

Visitor Services: None.

Regularly Scheduled Events: April, Confederate Memorial Day.

Directions: From the red stoplight on Highway 25 in Bloomfield, turn east on Highway E; go to the top of the hill and turn south on Stoddard County Road 517. Go 0.125 mile to end of blacktop.

Carthage

 BATTLE OF CARTHAGE CIVIL WAR MUSEUM

205 Grant Street, Carthage, MO 64836; (417) 237–7060; www.carthage-mo.gov.

Description: The Battle of Carthage was the first full-scale land battle of the Civil War. The museum features a wall-sized mural of the battle, as well as a video explaining the Civil War in the Ozark Mountains and numerous artifacts and displays.

Admission Fees: Free.

Open to Public: Mon.–Sat. 8:30 A.M.–5:00 P.M., Sun. 1:00 P.M.–5:00 P.M.

Visitor Services: Public restrooms, information, handicapped access, museum.

Regularly Scheduled Events: None.

Directions: Take Highway 71 to Central Avenue. Turn right on Grant Street to Second Street.

 BATTLE OF CARTHAGE STATE HISTORIC SITE

East Chestnut Street, next to Carter Park, Carthage, MO 64836; (417) 682–2279 or (800) 334–6946; www.mostateparks.com.

Description: This 7.4-acre tract was the site of the final confrontation of the Battle of Carthage, a day-long running skirmish that began on July 5, 1861, some 9 miles northeast of Carthage. An interpretative shelter with displays explains the history of this early armed confrontation (it preceded the first Battle of Bull Run by seventeen days).

Admission Fees: Free.

Open to Public: Daily from dawn to dusk.

Visitor Services: Information.

Regularly Scheduled Events: July, Vesper's

Service to honor the battle and the fallen soldiers.

Directions: From I–44 take Highway 71 (Carthage exit), exit 18; proceed north on 71 for 6 miles to Highway 571 at Carthage; travel east on Chestnut Street 10 blocks to site.

HIGGINSVILLE

 CONFEDERATE MEMORIAL STATE HISTORIC SITE

211 West First Street, Higginsville, MO 64037; (660) 584–2853 or (800) 334–6946; www.mostateparks.com.

Description: Opened in 1891, the Confederate home provided refuge to more than 1,600 veterans and their families for nearly sixty years. These veterans hailed from points throughout the South and served in every major battle of the Civil War. The very last of the former Rebel soldiers, John T. Graves, died at the home in 1950 at the age of 108. Visitors to the site can venture to the locations of the former house buildings and stroll through the restored chapel, which dates back more than 100 years, and historic cemetery.

Admission Fees: Free.

Open to Public: Grounds, daily from dawn to dusk; chapel and museum, Mon.–Sat. 9:00 A.M.–4:00 P.M.; Sun. noon–5:00 P.M.; Nov.–Mar., closed Mon.–Wed.

Visitor Services: Public restrooms, information, fishing, picnicking.

Regularly Scheduled Events: Call or check Web site for events.

Directions: From I–70 take Lexington-Higginsville exit (exit 49); proceed north on Highway 13 for approximately 7 miles to Business Highway 13. Proceed on Business Highway 13 1.5 miles to junction of Highways 20, 213, and Business 13. Entrance is on the left.

JEFFERSON CITY

 MISSOURI STATE CAPITOL AND STATE MUSEUM

Room B-2, State Capitol, Jefferson City, MO 65101; (573) 751–2854 or (800) 334–6946.

Description: The capitol, built between 1913 and 1918, contains the legislative chambers and state offices. Flanking either side of the magnificent rotunda is the Missouri State Museum. The museum features several exhibits on the Civil War and a collection of battle flags as well as other displays pertaining to the state's history and natural resources.

Admission Fees: Free.

Open to Public: Daily, except New Year's Day, Easter, Thanksgiving, and Christmas. Tours run every half hour 8:00 A.M.–11:00 A.M. and 1:00 P.M.–4:00 P.M. For group reservations, call (573) 751–4127.

Visitor Services: Public restrooms, information, handicapped access, food, gift shop, tours.

Regularly Scheduled Events: None.

Directions: From I–70 take Highway 63 exit (Jefferson City exit/exit 128a); proceed south on Highway 63 to Jefferson City; take first exit after crossing Missouri River; turn east on West Main Street to the capitol.

KANSAS CITY

 BATTLE OF WESTPORT

c/o Monnett Battle of Westport Fund, Inc., of the Civil War Round Table of Kansas City, 23414 West 54th Street, Shawnee, KS; (816) 356–1113; www.mocivilwar.org.

Description: The Battle of Westport, fought October 21–23, was the largest battle west of the Mississippi River and the decisive battle of Confederate Gen. Sterling Price's 1864 Missouri campaign. Directions guide the visitor to the first of twenty-five narrative

markers on a 32-mile, self-guided automobile tour and a self-guided walking tour of Byram's Ford and the Big Blue Battlefield. Each marker provides directions to the next stop on the tour. A written brochure is available from the address above. Tour brochures are also available at Wornall House Museum, 146 West Terrace; and Harris Kearney House, 4000 Baltimore Avenue, Kansas City.
Admission Fees: Free.
Open to Public: Daily from dawn to dusk.
Visitor Services: Information, tours.
Regularly Scheduled Events: None.
Directions: From I–70 take I–435 south, then west; or take I–470 west to I–435. Exit State Line Road north. Proceed north to 43rd Avenue. Travel east on 43rd Avenue to Westport Road and Tour Stop 1, at the northeast corner of Westport Road and Broadway.

 FOREST HILL CEMETERY

6901 Troost Avenue, Kansas City, MO 64131; (816) 523–2114.
Description: This cemetery is on the site of the celebrated Confederate cavalryman

Gen. J. O. Shelby's heroic stand that saved Price's army. A large Confederate monument in the cemetery is surrounded by graves of the Confederate dead, including Shelby's.
Admission Fees: Free.
Open to Public: Daily from dawn to dusk.
Visitor Services: None.
Regularly Scheduled Events: None.
Directions: From I–70 take I–435 from the west or I–470 from the east to Highway 71; proceed north on Highway 71 to 75th Street; proceed west on 75th Street to Troost Avenue; proceed north on Troost Avenue to cemetery.

LEXINGTON

 BATTLE OF LEXINGTON STATE HISTORIC SITE

Highway 13 North, John Shea Drive, Lexington, MO 64067; (816) 259–4654 or (800) 334–6946; www.mostateparks.com.

Description: This is the site of the famous "Battle of the Hemp Bales," fought on September 18–20, 1861. Victorious Southerners under Gen. Sterling Price besieged and cap-

Anderson House, Lexington, Missouri. Ken Mitchell–CWPT files.

TRANS-MISSISSIPPI

tured a Union garrison. A 106-acre section of the battlefield is preserved, as is the Anderson House, a brick mansion that served as a field hospital and was occupied by both sides during the battle.

Admission Fees: Tour, Adults $2.50, children six–twelve $1.50.

Open to Public: Battlefield grounds daily from dawn to dusk; visitor center and Anderson House, Mon.–Sat. 10:00 A.M.–5:00 P.M., Sun. 10:00 A.M.–6:00 P.M.

Visitor Services: Public restrooms, information, handicapped access, gift shop, museum, tours, visitor center.

Regularly Scheduled Events: Call or check Web site for living history events throughout the year.

Directions: From I-70 take Lexington-Higginsville exit (Highway 13 north); proceed north on Highway 13 for 20 miles to Lexington; take 13th Street to site.

LONE JACK

 LONE JACK CIVIL WAR BATTLEFIELD MUSEUM AND CEMETERY

301 South Bynum Road, Lone Jack, MO 64070; (816) 697–8833; www.historiclonejack.org; president@historiclonejack.org.

Description: Fought on August 16, 1862, the battle at Lone Jack was, by all accounts, the bloodiest battle fought on Missouri soil. The battle, a Confederate victory, left 270 dead, most of whom were buried on the battlefield in two 80-foot-long trenches. Also on-site is the only Civil War museum in Jackson County, Missouri.

Admission Fees: Adults $3.00, children twelve and under $1.00, seniors $2.00.

Open to Public: Wed.–Sat. 10:00 A.M.–4:00 P.M., Sun. 1:00 P.M.–4:00 P.M.; Nov.–Mar., open weekends only.

Visitor Services: Public restrooms, information, handicapped access, gift shop (of-

fers a 10 percent discount to CWPT members), research center, museum.

Regularly Scheduled Events: August, Battle commemoration; October, Walk with the Civil War Spirits.

Directions: Located 12 miles east of Lee's Summit and 25 miles west of Warrensburg on U.S. 50; at the Lone Jack exit, the battlefield is 100 feet north of the eastbound lane of U.S. 50.

NEVADA

 BUSHWHACKER MUSEUM

212 West Walnut Street, Nevada, MO 64772; (417) 667–9602; www.bushwhacker.org; bushwhacker-jail@sbcglobal.net.

Description: In May 1863 Confederate Bushwhackers, or guerrilla fighters, ambushed a Federal militia party on the Nevada square and fought a running battle through the streets and around the buildings. During the Civil War, Nevada became known as the "Bushwhacker Capitol" and was burned to the ground by Federal troops on May 26, 1863. The museum commemorates the important role the partisan rangers played in the war along the Western border. The nearby Bushwhacker Jail, located at 231 North Main Street, is restored as a nineteenth-century jail and jailer's home.

Admission Fees: Adults $3.00, students $2.00, children $1.00.

Open to Public: Mon.–Sat. 10:00 A.M.–4:00 P.M.; call ahead for winter hours.

Visitor Services: Public restrooms, handicapped access, research archives, information, gift shop.

Regularly Scheduled Events: June, Bushwhacker Days.

Directions: From Highway 71 turn west on Highway 54; travel 1.5 miles west to Ash Street. Turn north on Ash Street and travel 2 blocks to the parking lot.

NEW MADRID

 HUNTER-DAWSON STATE HISTORIC SITE

312 Dawson Road, New Madrid, MO 63869; (573) 748–5340 or (800) 334–6946; www.mostateparks.com; moparks@dnr.mo.gov.

Description: Antebellum house containing about 80 percent of the original furnishings. Finished in the spring of 1860 and standing during the siege of New Madrid and Island No. 10 in the spring of 1862.

Admission Fees: Adults $2.50, children $1.50.

Open to Public: Mon.–Sat. 10:00 A.M.–4:00 P.M., Sun. noon–4:00 P.M.; Dec.–Feb., closed Sun.–Mon.

Visitor Services: Public restrooms, information, gift shop, museum.

Regularly Scheduled Events: December, Christmas candlelight tours

Directions: From I-55 take New Madrid exit; follow U.S. 61 for 3 miles. Turn right on Dawson Road and follow signs.

NEWTONIA

 NEWTONIA BATTLEFIELD CWPT

930 Mill General Delivery, Newtonia, MO 64853; (417) 472–3842.

Description: Two major Civil War battles were fought at Newtonia: one on September 30, 1862, and the other on October 28, 1864. The first battle pitted Brig. Gen. James Blunt against Col. J. O. Shelby. Confederate forces numbered 4,000; Union forces numbered about 6,500. The 1862 battle was one of the very few Civil War encounters in which Native Americans fought on both sides. Southern forces had Choctaw, Cherokee, and Chickasaw soldiers, while other Cherokee soldiers fought with the North. The 1864 battle was a delaying action by Shelby to protect Gen. Sterling Price's re-treat to Arkansas. It was the last battle of the Civil War fought in Missouri. The site includes twenty acres of the battlefield and the Ritchey Mansion, which served as headquarters for both Union and Confederate troops at different points.

Admission Fees: Free.

Open to Public: Daily during daylight hours; Ritchey Mansion, by appointment only.

Visitor Services: Information, tours by appointment; trails.

Regularly Scheduled Events: April and September, open house.

Directions: From Missouri I–44 turn south on Highway 59. Near Neosho, turn east on Highway 86, travel approximately 25 miles to Newtonia.

PILOT KNOB

 FORT DAVIDSON STATE HISTORIC SITE CWPT

Highway 21 and Route V, P.O. Box 509, Pilot Knob, MO 63663; (573) 546–3454 or (800) 334–6946; www.mostateparks.com.

Description: Site of earthwork remnants of Fort Davidson, which was assaulted by the forces of Maj. Gen. Sterling Price on September 27, 1864, during the two-day Battle of Pilot Knob. Some 1,200 Confederates fell within an hour in an unsuccessful effort to capture the fort held by Gen. Thomas Ewing Jr. and 1,450 men.

Admission Fees: Free.

Open to Public: Fort and surrounding grounds, daily from dawn to dusk; visitor center, Mon.–Sat. 10:00 A.M.–4:00 P.M., Sun. 11:00 A.M.–5:00 P.M.; Dec.–Feb., closed Mon.

Visitor Services: Public restrooms, information, handicapped access, gift shop, museum, tours, visitor center.

Regularly Scheduled Events: September, every three years, major Civil War reenactment of the battle; periodic living history events, call for information.

Directions: From I–55 at Cape Girardeau,

Pilot Knob, Fort Davidson, Missouri. Eileen Sutis–CWPT files.

take Highway 72 (exit 99); proceed west approximately 70 miles to Ironton. Turn north on Highway 21; proceed 2 miles to Highway V and turn right to site.

REPUBLIC

 WILSON'S CREEK CIVIL WAR MUSEUM

5228 South Highway ZZ, Republic, MO 65738; (417) 732–2662; ww.nps.gov/wicr.

Description: Formerly the General Sweeny's Museum, this museum displays more than five thousand artifacts. The focus is the trans-Mississippi theater. The exhibits are arranged chronologically, from John Brown and the 1850s to the last battle between Missourians at Fort Blakely, Alabama, in April 1865. Highlights include a rare Confederate Indian flag of the "Cherokee Braves," the sash and sword belt of Gen. Pat Cleburne, Civil War medical displays, and the presentation sword and binoculars of Gen. Thomas W. Sweeny.

Admission Fees: Adults $5.00, family $10.00

per vehicle; admission to Wilson's Creek National Battlefield includes museum.

Open to Public: Daily 9:00 A.M.–5:00 P.M.; Nov.–Feb., closed Mon.–Tues.

Visitor Services: Handicapped access, guided tours for groups.

Regularly Scheduled Events: None.

Directions: From I–44 exit onto Highway MM and travel south for 8 miles to a traffic signal at the intersection with U.S. 60, where Highway MM becomes Highway M. Continue south through the intersection on Highway M to Highway ZZ; turn right on Highway ZZ and proceed south 1 mile to the museum. Located next to Wilson's Creek National Battlefield.

 WILSON'S CREEK NATIONAL BATTLEFIELD CWPT

6424 West Farm Road 182, Republic, MO 65738; (417) 732–2662; www.nps .gov/wicr.

Description: Wilson's Creek National Battlefield preserves 1,750 acres of the land where a battle was fought on August 10,

1861. Called "Oak Hills" by the Confederates, the bloody six-hour battle pitted 5,400 Union troops under Gen. Nathaniel Lyon against more than 10,000 Confederates under the combined commands of Gens. Sterling Price and Ben McCulloch in the first major battle in the trans-Mississippi region. Following the death of Lyon, Federal forces withdrew to Springfield. The failure of Confederate forces to consolidate the gains of this hard-earned victory resulted in their losing control of Missouri in the early spring of 1862.

Admission Fees: Adults $5.00, family $10.00 per vehicle.

Open to Public: Daily 8:00 A.M.–5:00 P.M.; call for extended spring and summer hours; closed Christmas and New Year's Day.

Visitor Services: Public restrooms, information, handicapped access, gift shop, museum, tours, research library, visitor center, trails.

Regularly Scheduled Events: Weekends Memorial Day–Labor Day, Historic Ray House; selected weekends Memorial Day–Labor Day, artillery demonstrations and living history programs; August 10, anniversary celebration; weekend in August after the anniversary, Moonlight Bloody Hill tour.

Directions: From I–44 take exit 70 (Missouri Highway MM, becomes Missouri Highway M) south to U.S. 60; cross U.S. 60 and drive 0.75 mile to Missouri Highway ZZ and turn south. The battlefield is located 2 miles south on Missouri Highway ZZ. From U.S. 60 and U.S. 65, take the James River Expressway to Missouri Highway FF; turn left (south) on FF; proceed to Missouri Highway M and turn right (west). Proceed to Missouri Highway ZZ and turn south; travel 2 miles to the park.

SPRINGFIELD

 BATTLE OF SPRINGFIELD

P.O. Box 8163, Springfield, MO 65801; (417) 864–3041.

Description: Brig. Gen. John Marmaduke's expedition into Missouri approached Springfield on the morning of January 8, 1863. Around 10:00 A.M. the Confederates advanced in battle line to the attack. The day included desperate fighting, with attacks

Wilson's Creek, Missouri. Melissa Meisner–CWPT.

and counterattacks until after dark, but the Federal troops held and the Rebels withdrew during the night. The Confederates appeared in force the next morning but retired without attacking. The Federal depot was successfully defended, and Union strength in the area continued.

Admission Fees: Free.

Open to Public: Daily from dawn to dusk.

Visitor Services: Walking tour brochures also available at Wilson's Creek National Battlefield, (417) 732–2662, and the Springfield Convention and Visitor's Bureau, (417) 881–5300.

Regularly Scheduled Events: None.

Directions: Take I–44 to downtown Springfield. The first site on the walking tour is on Jefferson Street, just north of Park Central Square.

 SPRINGFIELD NATIONAL CEMETERY

1702 East Seminole, Springfield, MO 65804; (417) 881–9499; www.cem.va.gov.

Description: The cemetery was established in 1876 because of the critical need for suit-able burial space for the remains of the men who fell at the Battle of Wilson's Creek. Other remains removed from original burial sites at Forsyth, Newtonia, Carthage, Pea Ridge, and Springfield were among the early interments. There are 1,514 Union burials in the cemetery, of which 719 are unknown. There are 566 Confederate grave sites in the Confederate section, most of which are unknown. Adjoining the original site was the only Confederate cemetery in Missouri; the two sites are now united. There are monuments to Confederate Gen. Sterling Price; the Federal troops who fought in the Battle of Springfield; Union Gen. Nathaniel Lyon, who died in the Battle of Wilson's Creek; and a memorial stone in memory of Confederate soldiers, placed where many unknown soldiers are buried.

Admission Fees: Free.

Open to Public: Grounds, daily from dawn to dusk; office, Mon.–Fri. 8:00 A.M.–4:30 P.M.

Visitor Services: Grave site locator available.

Regularly Scheduled Events: None.

Directions: From I–44 take U.S. 65 south

Calvary Cemetery, Saint Louis, Missouri. CWPT files.

(Branson exit) and proceed to the Sunshine exit. Travel west on Sunshine into Springfield. Proceed to Glenstone Avenue and travel south to Seminole Street; proceed on Seminole Street to cemetery.

St. Louis

 91 BELLEFONTAINE CEMETERY

4947 West Florissant Avenue, St. Louis, MO 63115; (314) 381–0750.

Description: Many Civil War notables are buried in this beautiful cemetery, including Edward Bates, Lincoln's attorney general; Union Maj. Gens. Frank P. Blair Jr. and John Pope; Confederate Maj. Gen. Sterling Price; Confederate senator and later U.S. senator George Graham Vest; Unionist provisional governor Hamilton Gamble; and ironclad boat builder James B. Eads.
Admission Fees: Free.
Open to Public: Grounds, daily 8:00 A.M.–5:00 P.M.; office, Mon.–Fri. 8:00 A.M.–4:00 P.M.
Visitor Services: Information on burial locations available in office, public restrooms, handicapped access.
Regularly Scheduled Events: None.
Directions: From I–70 take West Florissant exit (exit 245B) and proceed north approximately 0.7 mile to cemetery (next to Calvary Cemetery).

 92 CALVARY CEMETERY

5239 West Florissant Avenue, St. Louis, MO 63115; (314) 381–1313; www.stlcath cem.org.

Description: This Catholic cemetery contains the grave of Gen. William T. Sherman. Several other prominent Civil War personages are interred here, including Thomas Reynolds, Confederate governor in exile.
Admission Fees: Free.
Open to Public: Grounds, daily 8:00 A.M.–5:00 P.M.; office, Mon.–Fri. 8:30 A.M.–4:30 P.M., Sat. 8:30 A.M.–12:30 P.M.

Visitor Services: Information on burial locations available in the office; restrooms.
Regularly Scheduled Events: None.
Directions: From I–70 take West Florissant exit (exit 245B) and proceed north approximately 1.1 miles to cemetery (next to Bellefontaine Cemetery).

 93 JEFFERSON BARRACKS STATE HISTORIC SITE

345 North Road, St. Louis, MO 63125; (314) 544–5714 or (314) 638–2100; www .stlouisco.com/parks.

Description: In 1861 troops from Jefferson Barracks, led by Gen. Nathaniel Lyon, participated in the "Camp Jackson Affair," which saved the St. Louis Arsenal from prosecessionist state forces. In 1862 Jefferson Barracks was turned over to the Medical Department of the U.S. Army and became one of the largest and most important Federal hospitals in the country. Sick and wounded soldiers were brought to Jefferson Barracks by riverboat and railroad car. In 1864 it became a concentration point for the defense of St. Louis during "Price's Raid," the last major Confederate invasion of Missouri. In 1866 a national cemetery was established.
Admission Fees: Free; there may be a small charge for special events and exhibits.
Open to Public: Wed.–Sun. noon–4:00 P.M.; closed Thanksgiving, Christmas, and New Year's Day.
Visitor Services: Public restrooms, information, handicapped access, gift shop, museum, visitor center; camping, trails.
Regularly Scheduled Events: None.
Directions: From I–255 exit at Telegraph Road and proceed north approximately 3 miles. Stay in right-hand lane and turn right at Grant Road.

 94 ULYSSES S. GRANT NATIONAL HISTORIC SITE

7400 Grant Road, St. Louis, MO 63123; (314) 842–3298; www.nps.goc/ulsg.

Description: The Ulysses S. Grant National

Historic Site encompasses five historic structures (with exhibits) from the core of a 1,000-acre plantation owned by General Grant. The personal life and the partnership with his wife, Julia Dent Grant, provide the context for understanding his military leadership as Union general during the Civil War and his subsequent presidency. The historic barn houses a new 4,000-square-foot interpretive museum.

Admission Fees: Free.

Open to Public: Daily 9:00 A.M.–5:00 P.M.; closed January, Thanksgiving, Christmas, and New Year's Day.

Visitor Services: Information, handicapped access, gift shop (10 percent discount for CWPT members), tours, visitor center, museum.

Regularly Scheduled Events: Call or check Web site for events.

Directions: Located in suburban St. Louis County, immediately across from the Anheuser-Busch "Grant's Farm" attraction. From I–270 exit at Gravois Road and go northeast approximately 2.5 miles. Turn left onto Grant Road. The site is approximately 0.5 mile down on the right.

❖ OKLAHOMA ❖

ATOKA

 CONFEDERATE MEMORIAL MUSEUM AND CEMETERY
258 North U.S. Highway 69, Atoka, OK 74525; (580) 889–7192; www.civilwaralbum.com/atoka; atokamuseum@yahoo.com.

Description: Confederates maintained camps nearby along the Middle Boggy River in the Choctaw Nation of Indian Territory. Some died of disease and were buried on the grounds where the museum now exists. The Battle of Middle Boggy was fought on February 13, 1864, when Col. William Phillips and 350 Union troops surprised about 90 Confederates where the Texas Road crossed the Middle Boggy River. Forty-seven Confederates were killed in the Union victory. The museum includes memorabilia from that Civil War battle. The grounds include a cemetery and a section of the Butterfield Mail Route. The Battle of Middle Boggy is reenacted every third year at a nearby site by the Oklahoma Historical Society and Atoka County Historical Society.

Admission Fees: Free; admission fee charged for the reenactment.

Open to Public: Mon.–Fri. 9:00 A.M.– 4:00 P.M.; closed national holidays.

Visitor Services: Public restrooms, information, limited handicapped access, gift shop, visitor center.

Regularly Scheduled Events: Last weekend of September, every third year (2009, 2012), Battle of Middle Boggy reenactment.

Directions: From I–40 (exit 264A) travel south on U.S. 69 to Atoka; museum is located with the Oklahoma Travel Information Center 1 mile north of downtown Atoka.

DURANT

 FORT WASHITA HISTORIC SITE
Star Route 213, Durant, OK 74701-9443; (580) 924–6502; www.okhistory.org; ftwashita@okhistory.org.

Description: Fort Washita was established in 1842 in the Choctaw Nation of Indian Territory and was used as a staging ground for the Mexican War. In the 1850s it was a United States Army Artillery School. Famous Civil War leaders who served earlier at Fort Washita included Randolph B. Marcy, George McClellan, William G. Belknap,

Theophylus H. Holmes, and numerous others. Federal troops abandoned Fort Washita in 1861, and it was occupied by Confederate troops during the Civil War as the headquarters of Brig. Gen. Douglas Cooper. Fort Washita Historic Site today includes ruins, restored barracks, and the parade ground.

Admission Fees: Free.

Open to Public: Mon.–Sat. 9:00 A.M.–5:00 P.M., Sun. 1:00 P.M.–5:00 P.M.

Visitor Services: Public restrooms, information, handicapped access, gift shop, visitor center.

Regularly Scheduled Events: February, Mexican War living history; March, Civil War living history; April, 1840s Fur Trade Rendezvous (admission charge); November, candlelight tours (admission charge), instruction camp for male reenactors (admission charge); December, Mexican and Civil War Christmas living history.

Directions: From I–35, exit 15, travel east on U.S. 70 to Madill; continue 11 miles east on Oklahoma 199 to Fort Washita Historic Site. From I–40, exit 264A, travel south on U.S. 69 to Caddo, take Oklahoma 22 west to Oklahoma 78 at Nida, then take Oklahoma 78 south 3 miles to Oklahoma 199. Then go west on Oklahoma 199 3 miles to site.

FORT GIBSON

 FORT GIBSON HISTORIC SITE

907 North Garrison, Fort Gibson, OK 74434; (918) 478–4088; www.okhistory .org; fortgibson@okhistory.org.

Description: Fort Gibson was constructed in 1824 to keep peace between warring Indian tribes in the area and was a base of operations for many expeditions. The fort was abandoned in 1857 but reactivated during the Civil War and used as a base for postwar Reconstruction activities. From this point Federal Maj. Gen. James Blunt marched

25 miles south to combat the Confederate buildup at Honey Springs depot. The army permanently abandoned the fort in 1890. This National Historic Landmark includes seven original structures and a reconstructed 1830s log garrison. A new museum and gift shop are housed in the 1840s commissary. A hiking trail connects the early fort with the post–Civil War buildings.

Admission Fees: Adults $3.00, students six–eighteen $1.00, children five and under free, seniors $2.50. Call for group rates.

Open to Public: Apr. 15–Sept. 15, Tues.–Sun. 10:00 A.M.–5:00 P.M.; Sept. 16–Apr. 14, Thurs.–Sun. 10:00 A.M.–5:00 P.M.

Visitor Services: Public restrooms, information, handicapped access, gift shop, museum, tours, visitor center.

Regularly Scheduled Events: April, Heritage Day; October, Mexican War encampment; December, Mexican War candlelight tour; educational tours by reservation.

Directions: From I–40 take exit 264B; travel north on U.S. 69 to Muskogee, go east on U.S. 62 to Oklahoma 80, then north on Oklahoma 80 to site. From I–44 travel south on U.S. 69 to Muskogee, then east on U.S. 62, following directions given above.

FORT TOWSON

 FORT TOWSON HISTORIC SITE

HC 63, Box 1580, Fort Towson, OK 74735; (580) 873–2634; www.okhistory .org; fttowson@okhistory.org.

Description: Fort Towson was established in 1824 by Col. Matthew Arbuckle near the Red River in Indian Territory. The town of Doaksville was founded 1 mile away in 1831 and became the capital of the Choctaw Nation during the Civil War. The fort was expanded for the Mexican War but closed by the army in 1854. Confederate Maj. Gen. Sam Bell Maxey established his command post at Fort Towson during the Civil War.

Brig. Gen. Stand Watie, a Cherokee who commanded the Indian Brigade for the Confederates, completed the last surrender of the Civil War by a general officer near Doaksville on June 23, 1865. Today Fort Towson consists of extensive masonry ruins of barracks, officers' quarters, a bakery, a powder magazine, and other buildings. A sutler's store has been replicated at Fort Towson.

Admission Fees: Free; donation suggested.

Open to Public: Mon.–Fri. 9:00 A.M.–5:00 P.M., Sat.–Sun. 1:00 P.M.–5:00 P.M.

Visitor Services: Public restrooms, information, gift shop, visitor center, tours, trails.

Regularly Scheduled Events: Call or visit Web site for schedule of events.

Directions: From I–35, exit 29, go east on U.S. 70 through Hugo to town of Fort Towson; continue east of town for 0.5 mile, then proceed north for 1 mile, following signs. From I–40, exit 264A, go south on U.S. 69 to McAlester, south on Indian Nations Turnpike to Hugo, then east on U.S. 70 to town of Fort Towson; continue east of town following directions as above.

OKLAHOMA CITY

 OKLAHOMA HISTORY
99 CENTER

2401 North Laird Avenue, Oklahoma City, OK 73105; (405) 533–5248; www.ok history.org; okhc@okhistory.org.

Description: The Oklahoma History Center, a division of the Oklahoma Historical Society, tells the comprehensive story of Oklahoma from the beginning. Commemorating the Civil War and its impact on Oklahoma, the Union and Confederate Memorial Research Room includes artifacts, relics, paintings, exhibits, and interpretations of the Civil War in Indian Territory. The same building houses the Oklahoma Historical Society Research Division—with extensive holdings of Indian units that fought in the

Civil War, interviews with other veterans of the war, and "Ex-Slave Interviews" conducted in the 1930s—and the Oklahoma Historical Society Research Library.

Admission Fees: Adults $5.00, students $3.00, seniors $4.00; group rates available.

Open to Public: Mon.–Sat. 9:00 A.M.–5:00 P.M., Sun. noon–5:00 P.M.

Visitor Services: Public restrooms, information, handicapped access, gift shop, research library, visitor center.

Regularly Scheduled Events: None.

Directions: From I–40 travel north on I–235 near downtown Oklahoma City; exit at Lincoln Boulevard and take Northeast 23rd Street. Turn left on Laird Avenue and follow the signs to the History Center.

PARK HILL

 GEORGE M. MURRELL
100 HOME

19479 East Murrell Home Road, Park Hill, OK 74451-9601; (918) 456–2751; www.okhistory.org; murrellhome @intellex.com.

Description: George M. Murrell, of Lynchburg, Virginia, married Minerva Ross, niece of principal chief John Ross of the Cherokee nation. The Murrells built their home in Park Hill starting in 1844. It became known as Hunter's Home, a social center for Cherokee nation leaders and Fort Gibson officers. After Minerva died, George married her younger sister, Amanda. During the Civil War the Cherokee nation split. Murrell, a slave owner with strong family ties in Virginia and Louisiana, was married into the Ross family, which was led by strong Unionists. The Murrell home was one of the few in Indian Territory not burned by one side or the other. The homes of John Ross, leader of the pro-Union faction, and Gen. Stand Watie of the Confederates were both burned. Restoration of the Murrell Mansion is ongoing.

Admission Fees: Free; donation suggested. *Open to Public:* Mar.–Oct., Wed.–Sat. 10:00 A.M.–5:00 P.M., Sun. 1:00 P.M.–5:00 P.M.; Nov.– Feb., Sat. 10:00 A.M.–5:00 P.M., Sun. 1:00 P.M.– 5:00 P.M. Open to groups of more than twenty by appointment. *Visitor Services:* Public restrooms, tours, information, handicapped access, trails. *Regularly Scheduled Events:* June, mid-nineteenth century Lawn Social living history; October, Halloween Week Ghost Stories; December, Christmas open house. *Directions:* From I–40, exit 264B, go north on U.S. 69 to south side of Muskogee, east on U.S. 62 to Oklahoma 82 at west edge of Tahlequah, then approximately 2 blocks south on Oklahoma 82 to Park Hill. Then go east 1 mile to site. From I–44 travel south on U.S. 69 to Muskogee, then east on U.S. 62 following directions above.

RENTIESVILLE

 HONEY SPRINGS BATTLEFIELD CWPT

1863 Honey Springs Battlefield Road, Checotah, OK 74426-6301; (918) 473–5572; www.honeysprings.org; honeysprings@okhistory.org.

Description: On July 17, 1863, 3,000 Union troops under Maj. Gen. James Blunt defeated Confederates under Brig. Gen. Douglas Cooper in the Battle of Honey Springs. The largest battle in Indian Territory, it was among the first Civil War battles in which African Americans fought as a unit—in this case, the First Kansas Volunteer Infantry (Colored). They carried the day, defeating three veteran Texas cavalry units (fighting dismounted). It was also the largest battle in which Native Americans fought on both sides and was a turning point of the war in Indian Territory. The Union controlled the Cherokee nation, the upper Arkansas River, and most of Indian Territory for the rest of the war. The site includes a battlefield access road, with six

walking trails and interpretive wayside exhibits. A temporary visitor center is in use until the permanent facility is completed. *Admission Fees:* Free; donation suggested. *Open to Public:* Battlefield and access road, Tues.–Sat. 8:00 A.M.–5:00 P.M., Sun. 1:00 P.M.–5:00 P.M.; interpretive center closes at 4:30 P.M.; closed Mon. and major holidays. *Visitor Services:* Handicapped-accessible temporary interpretive center, orientation video, information, free booklet with text of fifty-five interpretive signs for those who cannot walk the trails ($3.00 for others). *Regularly Scheduled Events:* March, candlelight tour; periodic Civil War Life programs, call for more information. *Directions:* From I–40, exit 264B; go north/northeast on U.S. 69 for 2.5 miles to the exit for Business U.S. 69. Follow the signs 4 miles to site. (*NOTE:* The gate is locked at 5:00 P.M. each day.)

VINITA

 CABIN CREEK BATTLEFIELD

442370 East 367 Road, Big Cabin, OK 74332; (918) 256–4406.

Description: Two Civil War battles were fought at Cabin Creek; both were Confederate raids on Union supply wagon trains moving from Fort Scott toward Fort Gibson. On July 1–2, 1863, Gen. Stand Watie and the Confederates failed to stop the wagon train as it crossed Cabin Creek about 10 miles south of what is today Vinita. It was one of the first battles in which African Americans fought as a unit west of the Mississippi River. On September 18, 1864, Watie and the Confederates won the Second Battle of Cabin Creek, capturing 740 mules, 130 wagons, and more than $1.5 million in supplies, for which they received commendations from Confederate president Jefferson Davis and the Confederate Congress. Monuments to the leaders and soldiers of both sides

Cabin Creek Battlefield, Big Cabin, Oklahoma.
CWPT files.

were erected by the United Daughters of the Confederacy and are maintained by the Oklahoma Historical Society and the Friends of Cabin Creek at the battle site.

Admission Fees: Free.

Open to Public: Daily during daylight hours.

Visitor Services: Information, handicapped access.

Regularly Scheduled Events: September, last weekend every third year, battle reenactment (admission fee).

Directions: From I–44 exit at Vinita onto U.S. 60/Oklahoma 82. Proceed east for 3 miles until these roads split; turn right, continuing to follow Oklahoma 82 for another 10 miles south to Oklahoma 28. Turn right, following Oklahoma 28 for 5 miles to Pensacola; turn right onto county road and proceed about 2.5 miles to the monument site. From I–40, exit 264B, take U.S. 69 north to Oklahoma 28 in town of Adair; turn right (east) and travel 8 miles to Pensacola; turn left (at sign) on county road and travel 2.5 miles to monument site.

❖ TEXAS ❖

ALAMO

 PALMITO RANCH BATTLEFIELD CWPT

c/o Refuge Manager, USFWS, Lower Rio Grande Valley National Wildlife Refuge, Route 2, Box 202A, Alamo, TX 78516; (956) 784–7500; www.fws.gov/ southwest/refuges/texas/lrgv.html.

Description: More than one month after Lee's surrender to Grant at Appomattox, the battle at Palmito Ranch represented the last known land engagement fought as part of the Civil War and the ongoing conflict between the Confederacy's Trans-Mississippi Department and the Union army. Fought May 12–13, 1865, the Confederates were protecting the center of their clandestine cotton shipping operation with Mexico and European mills. The battle was the Union's last unsuccessful attempt to seize control of the Lower Rio Grande region.

Admission Fees: Free.

Open to Public: Daily from dawn to dusk. Visitors can drive or bicycle along Highway 4, Boca Chica Highway, and view the battlefield and related historical markers. However, most of the property is an undeveloped, remote area within the National Wildlife Refuge.

Visitor Services: None.

Regularly Scheduled Events: None.

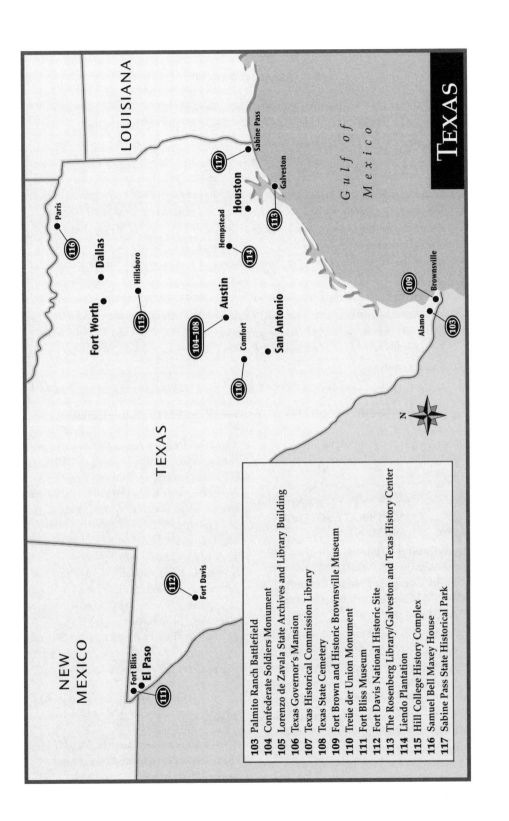

TEXAS

NEW MEXICO

LOUISIANA

TEXAS

Gulf of Mexico

Fort Bliss
El Paso — 111

Fort Davis — 112

Paris — 116

Dallas

Fort Worth

Hillsboro — 115

104–108

Austin

Comfort — 110

San Antonio

Hempstead — 114

Houston

Galveston — 113

Sabine Pass — 117

Brownsville — 109

Alamo — 103

N

103 Palmito Ranch Battlefield
104 Confederate Soldiers Monument
105 Lorenzo de Zavala State Archives and Library Building
106 Texas Governor's Mansion
107 Texas Historical Commission Library
108 Texas State Cemetery
109 Fort Brown and Historic Brownsville Museum
110 Treüe der Union Monument
111 Fort Bliss Museum
112 Fort Davis National Historic Site
113 The Rosenberg Library/Galveston and Texas History Center
114 Liendo Plantation
115 Hill College History Complex
116 Samuel Bell Maxey House
117 Sabine Pass State Historical Park

PALMITO RANCH

As a fifth-generation Texan, I have had a lifelong interest in preserving the rich and diverse history of our state. Like many Texans, I have a number of ancestors who fought in the Civil War. My great-great-grandfather, Charles S. Taylor, who signed the Texas Declaration of Independence, had four sons who served in the Confederate army.

You may be surprised to learn that that last land battle of the Civil War was fought on Texas soil on May 13, 1865. The Battle of Palmito Ranch occurred more than one month after General Lee's surrender in Virginia. Hispanic and Anglo Texans fought for Union and Confederate forces, and 250 men from the Sixty-second U.S. Colored Infantry Regiment fought for the North. Even though Confederate forces prevailed this day, the fate of the Confederacy had already been sealed.

Palmito Ranch Battlefield is one of only five documented Civil War battlefields in Texas. It has already been designated as a National Historic Landmark. Historic sites are constantly being lost to urban sprawl, neglect, and the impact of natural forces. That is why it is important to protect the Palmito Ranch Battlefield site and its undisturbed archaeological evidence for future generations.

—*U.S. Senator Kay Bailey Hutchison, Texas*

Directions: From Brownsville follow Highway 4 to the Gulf of Mexico.

AUSTIN

 CONFEDERATE SOLDIERS MONUMENT

Texas Capitol Grounds, 11th and Congress, Austin, TX 78701; (512) 305–8400 (Capitol Complex Visitors Center); (512) 463–0063 (Capitol Information and Guide Service).

Description: The Confederate Soldiers Monument, located on the historic south grounds of the Texas State Capitol near the Congress Avenue entrance gates, was begun in 1900 and completed in 1903. It consists of bronze figures representing the infantry, cavalry, Confederate states, and battles fought between 1861 and 1865. Pompeo Coppini executed the bronze figures, and Frank Teich erected the monument.

Admission Fees: Free.

Open to Public: Accessible twenty-four hours; visitor center, Mon.–Sat. 9:00 A.M.–5:00 P.M., Sun. noon–5:00 P.M.

Visitor Services: The Capitol Complex Visitors Center, located ½ block east of the monument at 112 East 11th Street, offers an exhibitions program, an educational video presentation, and a gift shop. The facility is accessible to people with disabilities; public restrooms, a drinking fountain, and pay telephones are located in the basement.

Regularly Scheduled Events: None.

Directions: From I–35 take 11th Street exit to downtown Austin. Proceed west on 11th Street about 0.5 mile to the capitol.

 LORENZO DE ZAVALA STATE ARCHIVES AND LIBRARY BUILDING

1201 Brazos Street, Austin, TX 78701; (512) 463–5480; www.tsl.state.tx.us/ agency/visit.html.

Description: The Texas State Archives con-

tain Civil War records related to the state of Texas. These records consist primarily of Confederate pension applications and records of Texas state troops and militias.
Admission Fees: Free.
Open to Public: Mon.–Fri. 8:00 A.M.–5:00 P.M.
Visitor Services: Public restrooms, information, handicapped access.
Regularly Scheduled Events: None.
Directions: From I–35 take 12th Street exit in downtown Austin. Proceed west on 12th Street for about 0.25 mile. The State Archives Building is located directly east of the Texas State Capitol.

TEXAS GOVERNOR'S MANSION
1010 Colorado Street, Austin, TX 78701; (512) 463–5518, (512) 463–5516 (for twenty-four-hour tour information); www.governor.state.tx.us/mansion.

Description: The Greek Revival house was built in 1856, and every Texas governor since has lived in the mansion. Abraham Lincoln reputedly offered Gov. Sam Houston Federal military assistance during the secession crisis to keep Texas in the Union. Houston may have burned Lincoln's letter in a mansion fireplace. He left office in March 1861 after refusing to sign an oath of allegiance to the Confederacy and was replaced by Lt. Gov. Edward Clark. Clark was succeeded by Gov. Francis R. Lubbock, who later resigned his office to join the Confederate army, becoming an aide-de-camp to Jefferson Davis.
Admission Fees: Free.
Open to Public: Mon.–Thurs. 10:00 A.M.–11:40 A.M.; tours every twenty minutes. For security reasons, all visitors must make reservations at least one day in advance and must present a photo ID.
Visitor Services: Handicapped access, tours.
Regularly Scheduled Events: None.
Directions: From I–35 take State Capitol exit, 11th Street west to Colorado Street.

TEXAS HISTORICAL COMMISSION LIBRARY
1510 North Congress Avenue, P.O. Box 12276, Austin, TX 78701; (512) 463–8817 or (512) 463–6100; www.thc.state.tx.us; history@thc.state.tx.us.

Description: Many of Texas's 11,500 historical markers are Civil War–related. A high percentage of the historical marker files, which are located in the Texas Historical Commission Library, contain documented narratives supporting the historical significance of the subject matter of each marker.
Admission Fees: Free.
Open to Public: Mon.–Fri. 1:00 P.M.–4:00 P.M.
Visitor Services: Public restrooms, information, main floor and library handicapped accessible; files are hand delivered to the public.
Regularly Scheduled Events: None.
Directions: From I–35 take the 15th Street exit in downtown Austin. Proceed west on 15th Street for approximately 0.5 mile and turn right onto Congress Avenue. Turn left onto 16th Street to look for parking meters.

TEXAS STATE CEMETERY
909 Navasota Street, Austin, TX 78702; (512) 463–0605; www.cemetery.state.tx .us.

Description: The Texas State Cemetery was established in 1851 with the burial of Edward Burleson. The southeast section of the cemetery has historically been referred to as the Confederate Fields. More than 2,200 Confederate veterans and their wives are buried here, including Gen. Albert Sydney Johnston. The general's metal Gothic-style tomb and white marble recumbent statue were designed and carved by noted sculptor Elisabet Ney in 1902. Along with Johnston, other Civil War notables buried in the cemetery are Brig. Gens. William Polk Hardeman, Adam Rankin "Stovepipe" Johnson, Ben

McCulloch, William Read Scurry, and Maj. Gen. John Austin Wharton.

Admission Fees: Free.

Open to Public: Grounds, daily 8:00 A.M.–5:00 P.M.; visitor center, Mon.–Fri. 8:00 A.M.–5:00 P.M.

Visitor Services: Public restrooms, handicapped access; Internet access to biographies, photos, and Confederate records; visitor center; library.

Regularly Scheduled Events: None.

Directions: From I–35 south use exit 234B or from the north, use exit 234C, turn onto Seventh Street, and proceed east for 5 blocks. (Brown directional signs are posted on Seventh Street.) Turn left on Navasota Street and drive ⅔ of a block to the Texas State Cemetery Visitors Center at 909 Navasota Street.

BROWNSVILLE

 FORT BROWN AND HISTORIC BROWNSVILLE MUSEUM

c/o Historic Brownsville Museum, 641 East Madison Street, Brownsville, TX 78520; (956) 548–1313; www.brownsville museum.org.

Description: Fort Brown, established in 1846, housed Federal troops during the Mexican War. In 1861 Texas state troops occupied the fort. With the southern Atlantic coast blockaded, Brownsville became an important Confederate port, with cotton and war material flowing back and forth. To eliminate the trade a Union army landed near the mouth of the Rio Grande in November 1863, occupying Fort Brown and Brownsville. Eight months later a strong Confederate army drove out the Federal forces and held the fort until the end of the war. The original hospital building is now the administration building for Texas Southmost College. Other extant buildings include a medical laboratory, guardhouse, and morgue. The Historic Brownsville Mu-

seum houses materials related to Brownsville's long military history.

Admission Fees: Grounds, free; museum, adults $2.00, children 50 cents.

Open to Public: Tues.–Fri. 10:00 A.M.–4:00 P.M., Sat. 10:00 A.M.–2:00 P.M.; closed Sun.–Mon. and major holidays.

Visitor Services: Public restrooms, information, tours.

Regularly Scheduled Events: None.

Directions: Fort Brown/Texas Southmost College adjoins International Boulevard at Jefferson Street in Brownsville. Historic Brownsville Museum is in the restored Southern Pacific Depot at 641 East Madison Street.

COMFORT

 TREÜE DER UNION MONUMENT

(German for "True to the Union")

c/o Comfort Heritage Foundation, Box 433, Comfort, TX 78013; (830) 995–3131 (chamber of commerce), (830) 995–2398 (public library).

Description: The oldest Civil War monument in Texas (dedicated August 10, 1866), this limestone obelisk is inscribed with the names of the thirty-six men captured and killed in the Battle of the Nueces, in Kinney County, on August 10, 1862. The battle and ensuing pursuit were initiated when Confederate forces attacked a group of Hill Country Union sympathizers, mostly German immigrants, who were trying to make their way to Mexico rather than fight against their adopted homeland. The Treüe der Union monument is the only memorial to the Union (outside national cemeteries) in Confederate territory, and one of only six places in the nation permitted by Congress to fly the flag at half-staff in perpetuity (and the only one of these to fly a flag with thirty-six stars). The memorial is listed on the National Register of Historic Places, is a Texas State

Historical Landmark, and a Texas State Archaeological Landmark.

Admission Fees: Free.

Open to Public: Daily twenty-four hours.

Visitor Services: Information.

Regularly Scheduled Events: Ceremonies on major anniversaries.

Directions: The town of Comfort is approximately 40 miles northwest of San Antonio, just off I–10. Proceed through Comfort on Highway 27 west, toward the towns of Center Point and Kerrville. The monument is on the right (west) side of the road, just past the intersection of High Street and Highway 27.

FORT BLISS

 FORT BLISS MUSEUM

Building 1735 Marshall Road, Fort Bliss, TX 79916; Old Fort Bliss Replica, (915) 568–4518; Fort Bliss Museum, (915) 568–5412; www.blissarmy.mil/museum/fort_bliss_museum.htm.

Description: Fort Bliss, a U.S. Army post established in 1848 to assert authority over lands acquired after the Mexican War, served as headquarters for Confederate forces in the Southwest during the Civil War. The Old Fort Bliss Replica is an exact replica of the original adobe fort that was part of the frontier military era, 1854–68. Exhibits include living history period rooms. A separate museum facility features exhibits and artifacts of Fort Bliss history, including the Civil War period.

Admission Fees: Free.

Open to Public: Daily 9:00 A.M.–4:30 P.M.; closed major holidays. Reservations recommended; photo ID required.

Visitor Services: Public restrooms, information, handicapped access, gift shop.

Regularly Scheduled Events: May, Armed Forces Day: "Playtimes and Pastimes," a living history event featuring games circa 1857, including vintage baseball; Decem-

ber, "Star-Spangled Holiday at Old Fort Bliss," a living history event circa 1857.

Directions: To the living history site, from I–10 take U.S. 54 north to Cassady Road; turn right on Pershing Road. Follow Pershing Road to Pleasanton Road, where the site is located. To the museum, from I–10 take U.S. 54 north to Cassady, turn left on Marshall Road, continue past Haan Road, and turn right at the sign for the museum.

FORT DAVIS

 FORT DAVIS NATIONAL HISTORIC SITE

Highway 118, Fort Davis, TX 79734; (432) 426–3224; www.nps.gov/foda.

Description: Fort Davis, established in 1854, was the first military post to guard the route westward and offer haven by the precious waters of Limpia Creek. Col. John R. Baylor's Confederate cavalry brigade reached Fort Davis on April 13, 1861, and Union troops withdrew in compliance with orders already received from Brig. Gen. David E. Twiggs, commanding the Eighth United States Military District. The Confederates remained a few months, then vacated the post. Federal troops returned in June 1867, but little of value remained and construction ensued.

Admission Fees: Adults $3.00, children fifteen and under free; free admission with Golden Age, Eagle, or Access Passports.

Open to Public: Daily 8:00 A.M.–5:00 P.M.; closed major holidays.

Visitor Services: Public restrooms, information, limited handicapped access, gift shop, museum, visitor center, trails.

Regularly Scheduled Events: June–mid-August, third-person living history.

Directions: From I–10 take Highway 17 south; this joins Highway 118. The site is located just before the town of Fort Davis. Fort Davis is approximately 39 miles from I–10.

GALVESTON

 THE ROSENBERG LIBRARY/ GALVESTON AND TEXAS HISTORY CENTER

2310 Sealy, Galveston, TX 77550; (409) 763–8854; www.rosenberg-library.org.

Description: The Rosenberg Library contains Civil War artifacts in a museumlike setting. The Galveston and Texas History Center contains Civil War muster rolls, Civil War–era Galveston newspapers, Civil War maps, and a manuscript collection, which includes letters and diaries written by Civil War participants from Galveston.

Admission Fees: Free.

Open to Public: Rosenberg Library, Mon.–Thurs. 9:00 A.M.–9:00 P.M., Fri.–Sat. 9:00 A.M.–6:00 P.M.; Galveston and Texas History Center, Tues.–Sat. 10:00 A.M.–5:00 P.M.

Visitor Services: Public restrooms, information, handicapped access, museum.

Regularly Scheduled Events: None.

Directions: From I–45, southeast from Houston, merge into Broadway Avenue in Galveston. Continue east on Broadway to 24th Street; turn left (north) on 24th and proceed 1 block. The Rosenberg Library and the History Center are located just past Ashton-Villa Historic House Museum.

HEMPSTEAD

 LIENDO PLANTATION

P.O. Box 454, Hempstead, TX 77445; (979) 826–3040; www.liendo.org; info @liendoplantation.com.

Description: This Greek Revival–style home was built by Leonard Waller Groce and is among the most famous and historic plantations in Texas. Liendo was built by slave labor and completed in 1853. During the Civil War, Camp Groce was established at Liendo, where cavalry, artillery, and infantry were recruited. Converted to a prisoner-of-war camp, it housed troops captured at the Battle of Galveston. From September 1 to December 1, 1865, the plantation was the camp for Gen. G. A. Custer and his command.

Admission Fees: Adults $7.00, seniors and children $5.00.

Open to Public: First Sat. of each month; tours given at 10:00 A.M., 11:30 A.M., and 1:00 P.M.; open to group tours with advance reservations.

Visitor Services: Information, tours.

Regularly Scheduled Events: November, Civil War weekend.

Directions: From Highway 290 take the FM 1488 exit; travel 1 mile northeast and turn right on Wyatt Chapel Road. The plantation is 0.5 mile on the right on Wyatt Chapel Road.

HILLSBORO

 HILL COLLEGE HISTORY COMPLEX

112 Lamar Drive, Hillsboro, TX 76645; (254) 582–2555; www.hillcollege.edu/ museum/museum.html.

Description: The mission of the Hill College History Complex is to explore the experiences of Texans during wartime. The research center houses an extensive collection of archival materials and books, microfilm, and vertical files on the Civil War, with emphasis on Confederate military history. The museum displays a collection of military art, guns, photographs, original battle flags, and artifacts.

Admission Fees: Free.

Open to Public: Mon.–Thurs. 8:30 A.M.–4:30 P.M., Fri. 8:30 A.M.–4:00 P.M.; closed college holidays.

Visitor Services: Public restrooms, information, handicapped access, museum.

Regularly Scheduled Events: First Saturday in April (except on Easter weekend), Confederate History Symposium. *NOTE:*

Reservations should be made before March 1 because space is limited.

Directions: Located 0.5 mile east of I–35 at Hillsboro on the Hill College campus, south of Dallas.

PARIS

 ### SAMUEL BELL MAXEY HOUSE

812 South Church Street, Paris, TX 75460; (903) 785–5716; www.maxey house.org.

Description: The Samuel Bell Maxey House, a two-story residence, was constructed in 1866–67 by General Maxey on his return to Paris, Texas, after the Civil War. General Maxey, born in Kentucky on March 30, 1825, graduated from West Point Military Academy and went on to fight in the Mexican War with Gen. Zachary Taylor. At the start of the Civil War, Maxey headed to the field to fight for the Confederacy. In the spring of 1865, he was promoted to major general; but the war was coming to a close, and his army disbanded in May 1865. Some of General Maxey's Civil War items are on temporary and permanent display at his home.

Admission Fees: Adults $4.00, seniors and children $2.00.

Open to Public: Tours Fri. and Sun. 1:30 P.M., 2:30 P.M., and 3:30 P.M., Sat: at 9:30 A.M. and 10:30 A.M.; open by appointment on Wed. and Thurs. for large groups.

Visitor Services: Public restrooms, information, limited handicapped access, gift shop, museum, tours.

Regularly Scheduled Events: Call or check Web site for events.

Directions: From I–30 exit on Highway 24 north; proceed to Paris. In Paris Highway 24 becomes Church Street; proceed approximately 1 mile past the railroad tracks. The Samuel Bell Maxey House is on the left.

SABINE PASS

 ### SABINE PASS STATE HISTORICAL PARK

c/o Sea Rim State Park, P.O. Box 1066, Sabine Pass, TX 77655; (409) 971–2559; www.tpwd.state.tx.us.

Description: Two naval engagements of the Civil War occurred at Sabine Pass. The first took place September 24–25, 1862, and the second on September 8, 1863. Sabine Pass was a major Confederate center for the shipment and trade of cotton in exchange for supplies and arms. To protect Sabine Pass from Union incursions, the Confederates first constructed Fort Sabine, and then constructed Fort Griffin, both earthworks along the pass. Twice the Union army attempted to overrun these Confederate fortifications, briefly but successfully in 1862 in preparation for the invasion of Galveston and Houston, and then unsuccessfully in 1863. The 1863 engagement that ended in the repulse of the Union forces (twenty-two ships and troops) is commemorated by a monument to Confederate Lt. Richard W. ("Dick") Dowling and his men.

Admission Fees: Age thirteen and up $2.00.

Open to Public: Daily dawn to dusk.

Visitor Services: Interpretive exhibits, public restrooms; camping, trails, historical markers.

Regularly Scheduled Events: September, Dick Dowling commemoration.

Directions: From Houston take I–10 east, exit onto Highway 73 at Winnie (Port Arthur exit). In Port Arthur take Highway 82 east and turn right at stoplight onto Highway 87 south. At Sabine Pass continue straight after four-way stop 1.5 miles to park. From the east take I–10 west; take Highway 87 west out of Orange through Bridge City; take the Highway 82 east exit; turn right at stoplight onto Highway 87 south. At Sabine Pass continue straight after four-way stop 1.5 miles to park.

FAR WEST

❖ CALIFORNIA ❖

SAN FRANCISCO

 PRESIDIO OF SAN FRANCISCO

Mailing Address: Building 201, Fort Mason, San Francisco, CA 94123; (415) 561–4323; www.nps.gov/prsf.

Description: The Presidio was the oldest operating U.S. Army post until it became part of the Golden Gate National Recreation Area in 1994. Fort Point National Historic site was built between 1853 and 1861 on the Golden Gate. Because of the military importance of the San Francisco Bay, the Union stationed soldiers at the Presidio during the Civil War.

Admission Fees: Free.

Open to Public: Visitor center, daily 9:00 A.M.–5:00 P.M.; Fort Point, Fri.–Sun. 10:00 A.M.–5:00 P.M.

Visitor Services: Public restrooms, information, handicapped access, gift shop, trails.

Regularly Scheduled Events: National Park Service ranger-led talks; call ahead for schedule.

Directions: Highway 101/Lombard Street leads to the Lombard Street gate of the Presidio.

❖ NEW MEXICO ❖

FORT STANTON

 FORT STANTON

Mailing Address: P.O. Box 1, Fort Stanton, NM 88323; (505) 937–1897; www.fortstanton.com; photoman @windstream.net.

Description: Fort Stanton was established in May 1855 as a staging area for sending troops to control the Apache Indians. It grew as a garrison and was manned by Union soldiers at the start of the Civil War. The fort was suddenly abandoned and set on fire by the Union in August 1861; however, the fire was extinguished by torrential rain, and much of the fort was salvaged. Fort Stanton was subsequently occupied by Confederate troops until October 1862, when Kit Carson and five companies of New Mexico volunteers reoccupied the fort.

Admission Fees: Free.

Open to Public: Apr.–Nov., Thurs.–Mon 10:00 A.M.–4:00 P.M., closed Tues. and Wed.; Dec.–Mar., closed.

Regularly Scheduled Events: August,"Fort Stanton Live"reenactment, festival, and entertainment.

Visitor Services: Public restrooms, gift shop, museum; trails.

Directions: From El Paso, go north on U.S. 54 to U.S. 70 east toward Ruidoso. Take Highway 48 through Ruidoso to Route 220 (Airport Road). After passing the airport, turn left at the stop sign and continue to Fort Stanton.

PECOS

 GLORIETA BATTLEFIELD CWPT

Pecos National Historical Park, 2 miles south of Pecos on Highway 63, Pecos, NM 87552; (505) 757–6414; www.nps .gov/peco/.

Description: Pecos National Historical Park preserves two sites associated with the Civil War: the sites of the Battles of Glorieta Pass. These are Apache Canyon (also called Canoncito) and Pigeon's Ranch. Texan and Coloradan volunteers skirmished at Apache Canyon on March 26, 1862. The

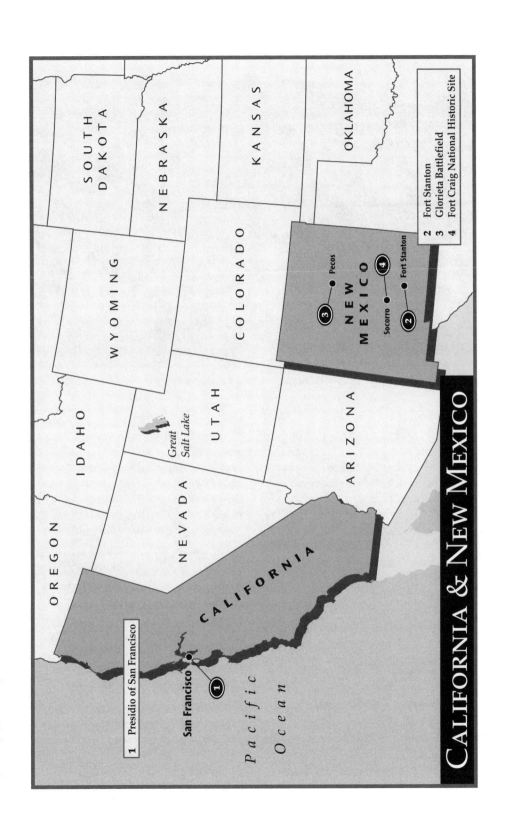

CALIFORNIA & NEW MEXICO

1 Presidio of San Francisco

2 Fort Stanton
3 Glorieta Battlefield
4 Fort Craig National Historic Site

Glorieta Battlefield, Pecos National Historical Park, New Mexico. CWPT files.

final encounter took place at Pigeon's Ranch on March 28, 1862. Texan troops withdrew after their supplies were destroyed at Apache Canyon on March 28. The battle ended the Confederate attempt to gain Federal supplies at Fort Union and the plans to invade Colorado and California. The park also preserves Kozlowski's Ranch, the site of the Union field headquarters during the battle. Much of the Glorieta Battlefield is still in private ownership. The sites are currently closed to public visitation. The visitor center at Pecos National Historical Park contains exhibits and information relating to the battle. Battlefield tours must be ranger guided, and tours are booked in advance. The size of tour groups is limited; call (505) 757–6414 for further information.

Admission Fees: Adults $3.00/person, children under sixteen free.

Open to Public: Visitor center, daily 8:00 A.M.–4:30 P.M.; Memorial Day–Labor Day, open daily until 6:00 P.M.; closed Christmas. Battlefield closed at all times unless on ranger-guided tour.

Visitor Services: Restrooms, museum, tours, visitor center, ruins trail (80 percent wheelchair accessible).

Regularly Scheduled Events: March, Civil War Weekend.

Directions: From I–25, southeast of Santa Fe, take exit 307. Turn left on Highway 63 north; travel 4 miles to visitor center.

SOCORRO

 FORT CRAIG NATIONAL HISTORIC SITE

USDI Bureau of Land Management, Socorro Field Office, 901 South Highway 85, Socorro, NM 87801; (505) 835–0412; www.nm.blm.gov/sfo/fort_craig/fort_craig_home.htm.

Description: One of the largest forts constructed in the West, Fort Craig was strategically situated on the primary road between New Mexico and Mexico. In February 1862 the fort supplied U.S. troops to thwart the invasion of Texas Confederates under the command of Gen. Henry H. Sibley. Troops from the fort, under the command of Col. E. R. S. Canby, bolstered by a contingent of New Mexico volunteers commanded by Kit Carson, engaged Sibley's invasion force at a nearby crossing of the Rio Grande. The day-long Battle of Valverde on February 21, 1862, was a decisive Confederate victory. However, the U.S. troops retreated into the fort, which was never attacked. Sibley's Confederates pressed northward to attack Albuquerque and Santa Fe. Their goal was the capture of Fort Union and the Colorado gold fields. Sibley's troops were defeated one month later, southeast of Santa Fe. Today Fort Craig is in ruins.

Admission Fees: Free.

Open to Public: Daily from dawn to dusk.

Visitor Services: Information, interpretive center, handicapped accessible restrooms, shelters with picnic tables, tours, trails.

Regularly Scheduled Events: Civil War reenactments and living history events; call for information.

Directions: From I–25 take San Marcial exit; take Highway 1 and follow the signs. Fort Craig is approximately 10 miles from I–25 and located 32 miles from Socorro and 121 miles from Las Cruces.

FOREIGN SITES

Grave of Seaman George Appleby, CSN, Cherbourg, France. Henry Simpson—CWPT files.

BERMUDA, FRANCE, AND UNITED KINGDOM SITES

1 The Globe Hotel and Bermuda
  National Trust Museum
2 La Cité de la Mer

3 Wirral Maritime Heritage Trail/
  Borough of Wirral

BERMUDA

 THE GLOBE HOTEL AND BERMUDA NATIONAL TRUST MUSEUM

32 Duke of York Street, St. George's, Bermuda GE 05; 1–441–297–1423; www.bnt.bm/places_to_visit/bnt_museum.htm.

Description: During the American Civil War, Bermuda was central to Confederate blockade-running efforts due to its excellent harbors and proximity to Southern ports. The Globe Hotel served as the headquarters of Confederate purchasing agent Maj. Norman S. Walker throughout the war. Now the Bermuda National Trust Museum, it features a permanent exhibit called *Rogues and Runners: Bermuda and the American Civil War*. Among the items on display is a rare copy of the Great Seal of the Confederacy, which was smuggled through the island.

Admission Fees: Adults $5.00, children six–eighteen $3.00; combination tickets to all three Bermuda National Trust Museums $10.00.

Open to Public: Mon.–Sat. 10:00 A.M.–4:00 P.M.

Visitor Services: Museum, video presentation, gift shop, public restrooms.

Regularly Scheduled Events: None.

Directions: The museum is located on the corner of Duke of York Street, just north of King's Square. It is easily accessible from the cruise ship terminal, bus routes 1, 3, 10, and 11, as well as the Yellow Line of the St. George's Ferry (April–November).

FRANCE

 LA CITÉ DE LA MER

50100 Cherbourg-Octeville, France; 011 (33) 2 33 20 26 26; www.citedelamer.com/uk.

Description: La Cité de la Mer is a vast scientific, historic, and recreational complex, created on the initiative of the Cherbourg Urban Community to chronicle the nautical history of the Cotentin region. Visitors interested in the American Civil War will be most interested in the display of the pivoting Blakely cannon and other artifacts from the wreck of the CSS *Alabama*, the Confederate navy's most successful commerce raider. *Alabama* was sunk 12 miles offshore from Cherbourg on June 19, 1864, by the USS *Kearsarge*.

Admission Fees: Adults EUR 14, children six–seventeen EUR 10, children under six free.

Open to Public: Call or check Web site for current hours.

Visitor Services: Museum, Welcome Hall, gift shop, food, multimedia library.

Regularly Scheduled Events: Call or check Web site for events.

Directions: Located in the old Transatlantic Terminal of Cherbourg, at the tip of the Cotentin Peninsula.

THE CIVIL WAR OVERSEAS

Although the American Civil War was largely fought in America, the conflict's scope was global. Great Britain and France both played important roles in the four-year struggle, as did numerous other nations.

Even before the war began, there existed among the ruling class in the South the popular misconception that France and England would side with the cotton-producing states. The textile industry in those two countries would collapse without Southern cotton, or so the argument ran. Unfortunately for Confederate hopes, there was a surplus of cotton in the years immediately preceding the war, and it took some time before Europe's textile mills suffered from war-imposed shortfalls.

However, an early misstep by President Abraham Lincoln gave the fledgling Confederacy early hope of international recognition. When Lincoln announced a blockade of the Southern states, he unintentionally raised the status of the new nation—although a government can close its own ports, it can only blockade a separate country. Great Britain and France were quick to exploit this mistake, and both countries granted the Confederate States "belligerent" status.

Belligerent status also allowed the South to purchase weapons and other materials in Europe, and the Confederacy was able to build "blockade runners" to evade the Union blockade and unload foreign goods in Southern ports. Much of this clandestine trade was run through Bermuda, bringing tremendous wealth to that small English colony. Mexico was also a popular spot to unload goods destined for the Confederacy.

As helpful as belligerent status was to the South, Confederate leaders continued to seek recognition of their status as a full and independent nation. French recognition of the United States during the Revolutionary War brought aid that was absolutely vital to Gen. George Washington's army. The South was determined to get similar assistance for their "second Revolution."

In the fall of 1862, hopes for foreign recognition of the Confederacy seemed bright. In both the eastern and western theaters, Confederate armies were on the offensive. However, expectations for foreign recognition of the South all but died with the issuance of the preliminary Emancipation Proclamation on September 22, 1862. Lincoln's proclamation to free the slaves in areas currently in rebellion transformed the war into a conflict against slavery—a cause England and France were reluctant to fight against.

Despite this setback for the South, England and France remained an arsenal for the Confederacy, as well as the primary source of oceangoing vessels for the Rebel navy. The shipyards of both nations busied themselves building warships and commerce raiders for the South, including CSS *Alabama* and CSS *Florida*. They even built ironclads for the Confederacy, although only one, CSS *Stonewall*, was commissioned into the Confederate navy.

CSS *Alabama* and the other commerce raiders played havoc on the U.S. merchant fleet, destroying or capturing hundreds of Union vessels. Almost no ocean on the planet was safe from the Rebel flag, as Southern raiders set fire to Union merchant vessels in the East Indies, the northern Pacific, the Mediterranean, and elsewhere. Eventually, *Alabama* succumbed to the guns of the

(continued)

USS *Kearsarge* off Cherbourg, France. The last Confederate commerce raider, CSS *Shenandoah*, lowered its colors in Liverpool, England, on November 6, 1865.

After the war, the Federal government did not quickly forget the damage caused by the Confederate commerce raiders. The United States pursued its *Alabama* claims until 1871, when an international tribunal awarded it $15.5 million for damages caused by the commerce raiders built in England.

UNITED KINGDOM

WIRRAL MARITIME HERITAGE TRAIL/ BOROUGH OF WIRRAL

Hamilton Square, Birkenhead, Wirral, U.K., CH41 5BR; Wirral Museum, 011 (44) 151 666 4010; Tourist Information Centre, 011 (44) 0151 647 6780; www .visitwirral.com; www.wirral.gov.uk/ ed/wirral_museum.htm; juggylanday @wirral.gov.uk.

Description: With its large shipbuilding tradition, the Wirral Peninsula in southwestern England played an important role in the American Civil War when the Confederate navy contracted for two of its most successful commerce raiders, CSS *Alabama* and CSS *Shenandoah*, from the Laird Brothers' shipyard at Birkenhead. The Wirral Museum, formerly the Birkenhead Town Hall, marks the beginning of the Wirral Maritime Heritage Trail. The museum features a major American Civil War exhibition complete with an original model of the *Alabama*, which raided Union naval and merchant ships for two years before being sunk in combat off the coast of Cherbourg, France, in 1864. Other highlights along the Heritage

Trail include the Argyle Rooms, an important meeting place for England's antislavery campaign; the townhouse and statue of John Laird, whose company built *Alabama*; and No. 4 Dock, where the keel of *Alabama* was fitted out.

Admission Fees: Free; individual site admission fees may vary.

Open to Public: Wirral Museum, Tues.–Sun. 10:00 A.M.–5:00 P.M.; Heritage Trail, open daily twenty-four hours. Some sites on the trail are industrial and business premises and may not be open to the public.

Visitor Services: Information.

Regularly Scheduled Events: Call or check Web site for information

Directions: To reach the Wirral Museum from M53, follow ALL DOCKS signs and go straight ahead at first roundabout. Continue along Dock Road (A5139) to second roundabout and take second exit across the bridges. After the bridges turn left at the roundabout, and at second set of traffic lights, turn right. Follow road to the end and arrive at Hamilton Square. From Liverpool go through Wallasey Tunnel and, on exiting, take the first slip road on left and continue as above.

INDEX

The following sites are all battlefields included in the Civil War Discovery Trail guidebook.